IN SEARCH OF WILL CARLING

An epic journey through Africa
to the Rugby World Cup

Charles Jacoby

SIMON & SCHUSTER

LONDON · SYDNEY · NEW YORK · TOKYO · SINGAPORE · TORONTO

First published in Great Britain by Simon & Schuster Ltd, 1996
A Viacom Company

The right of Charles Jacoby to be identified as author of this work has
been asserted in accordance with sections 77 and 78 of the Copyright,
Designs and Patents Act 1988

Simon & Schuster Ltd
West Garden Place
Kendal Street
London W2 2AQ

Simon & Schuster of Australia Pty Ltd
Sydney

A CIP catalogue record for this book is available
from the British Library

ISBN 0-684-81673-3

Typeset in New Caledonia 11/14pt by
Palimpsest Book Production Limited, Polmont, Stirlingshire
Printed and bound in Great Britain by
Butler & Tanner, Frome & London

To my grandmothers – the best of all possible natives – Helen Jacoby and in memory of Venetia Hesketh-Prichard.

CONTENTS

PART I

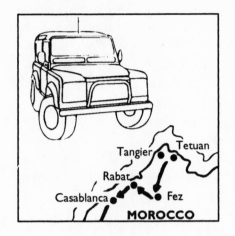

Chapter 1

THE ARRIVAL

Spain. George, Red, Emma and me in the Land Rover. 240 days to the World
Cup opening ceremony.

L et me introduce you to the others. The tallest one –
six feet four inches, no less, same as me – is George
Wilson-Fitzgerald. He has just left the army. He was on
a short service commission with the Blues & Royals. It was at his
leaving party at Combermere Barracks in Windsor that Bunbury fell
off the banisters, taking the chandelier and an octagonal table with
him – you may have heard about it.

George is from Somerset, like I am. He has been farming there
for most of the last six months, spending the rest of it and his army
resettlement grant on learning to be a mechanic. George does not
talk a great deal – sometimes he pauses mid-sentence for half a day
– but he knows a lot about Land Rovers, which is useful.

The one next to him with the curly hair is Red Walsh. He played
rugby at Exeter University with George and has recently been living
and working at this and that in London. Red and George now belong
to a London rugby team with the proud Latin title Date Caput et
Bibite. It is not worth translating, save to say that in this context *bibite*
means 'swallow' or 'gargle'. The Give Heads, as they are known, are a

Sunday side and the teams they were playing in those days may have thanked England's punitive licensing laws that they turned up at all. They are far more unreliable nowadays. Once on the pitch, they are prone . . . actually, prone is probably about right, but what I was going to say was that once on the pitch they are prone to stopping play and bursting into song. A vicious-looking oncoming scrum may be met with a sudden rendering of Simon and Garfunkel's hit, 'The 59th Street Bridge Song' (Feelin' Groovy): 'Do-do-do-da, 'Slow down, you move too fast. You got to make the mornin' last . . .'

The team is drawn mainly from men who went to Exeter. You know the type: you are too thick for Oxbridge so you try for Durex – Durham or Exeter. Amazingly, the Give Heads win most of their matches. They usually lose only when more than half the forwards or the threequarters fail to turn up from lunch, or worse still, from the night before.

Red comes from Ireland, from Achill Head in County Mayo, but he was brought up in Abu Dhabi and is well travelled in East Africa. He has been up and down several mountains there, including Mount Kenya and the Rawanziris. We are rather looking to him for direction since he seems to have the keenest idea about where we are going and how we will get there. I met him a year ago through Jane Charley. I met George through Jane two years ago. George and Red have been planning this trip since then at least. Jane knows everybody – you may have met her yourself. She was thinking of coming on this trip, in my place in fact, but she is really too busy knowing people to travel much. It's lucky she couldn't come as there would have been no room for me. I came on board two weeks before we left when Martin, my editor at Simon & Schuster, said I could write this book. I only just had time to fix the jabs and buy a sleeping bag.

Red is really the most organised, though George is the one who has sorted out the technical side, building and equipping the Land Rover, doing all the checking and balancing. Red is always patient, despite being Irish and naturally noisy. He is always the one I ask questions of.

'What's the name of those Swiss soldiers who guard the Vatican, Red?'

'The Swiss Guard, Charlie.'

'What do you call the rail that goes round a room, the one you hang pictures from, Red?'

'A picture rail, Charlie.'

The third member of the party is Emma Tindal. She is Irish as well, from Donegal, and all three of them are Catholics (God preserve me, for I am a Prot). There is a book to be written about Emma alone. In her five years since university – she read photography at Reading – she has established herself as a gifted travel photographer and a brilliant sponsorship-snatcher, having got Fuji Films on her side. She has spent a year working in orphanages in Romania and another year travelling through South America.

Emma is also a charming person. Behind her accent, or lilt, or brogue, you can hear the sounds of Irish pipes and smell the heather, even in the desert. Her laughter trickles out like the water in a Donegal brook. It is a clear and lovely sound which, carried on the heather-scented breeze, may eventually find its way into Donegal Bay. But we are still rude about her to her face. The Team Mascot, we call her, or leprechaun, towering as she does at least a foot shorter than the rest of us. Her plan is to go as far as Nairobi in Kenya with us, two-thirds of the trip, and then decide whether or not to carry on.

I have only just met Emma. She turned up at my flat in London and three hours later we were on the aeroplane together, bound for Madrid to join the boys, who had driven there in the Land Rover. We were leaving behind the rain, the gossip, girlfriends and a boyfriend – even Britain's imminent economic recovery – for nine months' drive to the 1995 Rugby World Cup in South Africa. I brought a rugby ball with me because I hoped that George and Red would play some local sides along the way. I never quite got the hang of the game myself, even though I went to Sherborne School, which is better (it goes without saying) than Downside, where George was, and Douai School, the dark satanic mill through which Red trod, a scholarship boy.

Emma and I met the Land Rover in Madrid, despite its best efforts to the contrary. George and Red had tried to leave London several times before they succeeded, but the vehicle kept going wrong. Series 3, 1978, an ex-military long-wheelbase, she had so many new bits on her that she was like an old broom which lasted well owing to its two new heads and three new handles. On the way to our first campsite we decided we needed a name for her. In her Q-reg glory we thought of 'Quick' or 'Quiet', because she was neither. Or 'Quasimodo, The Roof-Rack of Rusty Charm'. In the end we settled on 'Mistress Quickly', to show that our educations had not been completely wasted. Emma continued to call her 'The Jeep', which George felt was something of a slight on British engineering.

George had already learned to hate Mistress Quickly. He would mutter about the engine being the Devil. Emma sprinkled it with holy water, which she thought might help. Red had suggested driving the whole beast into the holy spring at Lourdes, but Emma reflected that that might have got them all excommunicated.

Mistress Quickly could do fifty miles per hour on tarmac with the elements on her side and a good run-up. But she had learned little party tricks, like overheating every two hours or suddenly shedding a piece of her person. As Red's book of top tips, *Desert Driving* (Abu Dhabi Petroleum Company Limited, 1969) proclaims in its classic BBC style: 'Remember that the Land Rover is a workhorse, not a racehorse.'

What she was really good at was consuming gallons and gallons of diesel, which we bought, all the way through Africa, from gleaming petrol stations in the most undeveloped countries, and from roadside barrels in the countries which claimed to be civilised, This was an African paradox – rather like Mistress Quickly. George would drive her, arms folded and bent over the top of the steering wheel, hoping the gears stayed in place and remarking: 'I think . . . um. Satan.' George could, on occasions, be surprisingly eloquent: sometimes every week. He would launch forth on subjects like Tactics Used During the Raid on Entebbe, or the Strange Power of Mediums to Contact the Dead. Finding George's topics of conversation required a scattergun approach and the best part of a nine-month trip through Africa.

Conversation was not, however, a problem for Red and Emma, who each came in at a little over the nineteen-to-the-dozen mark on chat. Not much crossed Emma's mind before she opened her mouth, though she made up for it afterwards. Red had a firecracker mind.

He often looked as if he was thinking before he started talking, but we knew he never really did. George, by comparison, made Rodin's *Thinker* look like a gadabout jazzgirl.

When the Land Rover broke down, George would lose his temper. He made so little noise normally that this always took us all by surprise. Marching round to the back of the vehicle, he would cry, 'Pee-sosh-it,' probably a native expression, and kick the rear door with enough force to make him stagger backwards into the crowd of passersby which invariably gathered to watch.

That first campsite in Madrid set the daily routine for our trip through Africa. George had built a canvas awning on one side of Mistress Quickly. It rolled out to form a waterproof roof, held up by aluminium poles and guy ropes. Around the awning each evening we velcroed a mosquito net curtain. This mainly had the effect of trapping the mosquitoes in with us rather than keeping them out. We had canvas chairs to sit on while we cooked up supper on a gas stove and later cleared them away in order to fall asleep in a row of sleeping bags on four army-issue campbeds. This outdoor dormitory was a dramatic change from the warmth and comfort of beds at home.

Despite our straitened living conditions, the four of us got on well – a good sign at this stage at the journey. We formed low-tension rivalries to keep us stable, between Ireland and Somerset, and between Exeter University and the Rest of the World. There was a continual spat between Emma and Red about which had the highest sea cliffs, Mayo or Donegal, but the only real point of friction between us was the Irish Question, so no change there, I suppose. Our opinions varied so widely we might have been talking about different subjects. Emma sympathised with the republicans, Red was broadly a nationalist, I quite liked it as it was, and George fell in with the army tradition of unionism. Usually the appearance of Irish politics in the conversation was simply a signal that one of us was hungry.

'You don't know what you're talking about,' says Emma to George.

'Look, I was in the army,' says George to Emma.

'Well, what kind of an angle do you think that gives you?' says Red to George.

'Bunch of murderers,' says Emma to Red, half under her breath. George stomps off.

'Now, Emma,' says Charlie to Emma.

'Shall I cook supper, or er . . .' calls out George.

Food was a shock. Our diets dived from a healthy mix of home cooking and junk to an endless round of mashed greens and potatoes. If, as the saying goes, we are what we eat, we were quickly to become vegetables. Dire parental warnings about not trusting the meat or the water left us with rather uniform grub to start with, but by the end we would be sucking biltong with the best of them. We would have more antibodies than red blood cells coursing through our capillaries. At least Emma spoke Spanish, so for the first week, when we were in Spain, we did not have to live off the dogfood and J-cloths that I suspected Red and George had been eating through France and Andorra. Red and George were not linguists, and their lack of skill in this area had had a dire effect on their diet in the first weeks of their journey. It was Red who, tired of using *absolument* and *actuellement* to stress a point, first brought *infactement* to the French language.

It was a pity that Emma and I had not been able to do the whole trip from London, but Africa, I think, starts in Madrid. To save petrol, the taxi-drivers at Madrid Airport push their cabs forward in the queue rather than starting their engines. And they do it in that stiff Hispano-Moorish way – shoulders locked upright, strutting like farmyard geese. There is a lot of the Moor in the Spaniard, and a lot of the Arab in the Moor. As we learned from our friend Nancy (you will meet Nancy later), 'The Arabs really think they are the cat's pyjamas and everyone else is dirt. Even other Muslims are second-class citizens. You have to show a little humility in front of them, a little modesty – but not too much – and then their world is the right way up.'

In any case, we had to go to Madrid to pick up visas for Mauritania, a recently opened country with few embassies in Europe. The fat and bustling lady at the Mauritanian Embassy started to speak French as soon as she established that Emma could speak Spanish. Luckily my French is so bad that it gave her no excuse to switch to Hassini Arabic. She took our passports and told us to come back tomorrow, *mañana*. She understood that concept well.

We could be bolshie, too. We would like a photocopy of our passports as a receipt, we said. This threw her. She did not like tourists with attitude. She wobbled off with the documents, leaving us in her comfortable waiting room with French-language official newspapers.

After half an hour I went in search of the photocopies. The man I found was the same podgy shape as his colleague, but with Tony Blair eyebrows and beetle-black eyes. He would have made a good chief of secret police. Perhaps he was. He spoke a slow and definite kind of English. I need have no fear that even if what he announced was wrong, he knew that it would happen all the same. 'The information you require is coming,' he assured me.

'I don't want information, I want photocopies,' I said.

'The information *and* the photocopies,' he replied.

I might have asked for a racing camel. It would have been supplied, in the fullness of time, along with all the information and photocopies I would ever need. Within ten minutes our passports were returned with the required visa stamps.

Apart from that, Spain was but a swirl of dust and olive groves until we reached my father's house in the south of the country. Oh, the joy of being back in a proper bed again.

Father is a naturalist. He left Britain six years ago with a thin story about there being better bugs and slugs to bother in Andalucia, the lazy region of Spain that consists mostly of cork oaks and mountains with a strip flash of Costa del Sol at the bottom. He had lived in a Spanish farmhouse in ten acres ever since, and took keen twitchers to punish the birds and butterflies through binoculars as far afield as Morocco and Mauritania in North Africa, up to the Pyrenees, and even to Switzerland. He was confined, he complained, to the western Palearctic and was jealous of our trip to the sub-Sahara. The first part of our journey would be through his own stamping ground. He furnished the Land Rover with books entitled *The Larger Mammals of This and That*, and *Birds of the Other*, in the event that we should ever come face to face with a masked shrike, say, a black drongo or a fulvous whistling duck.

He also put us up as we made the final preparations for our assault. That week's grace allowed George to curse Mistress Quickly ever more violently. She required parts from Estepona on the coast, which necessitated borrowing Father's car for the drive to get them.

Emma, like Tigger, can do anything. Great blasts of enthusiasm see her through where lack of skill beats lesser men. 'I drove trucks in Bolivia,' she announced as she took the wheel of the car on the way back from Estepona. Do they have cars in Donegal? Forty miles later, at revs so low that George was weeping, she swerved, mounted the kerb, blew the nearside tyre in two places and, narrowly missing a group of people and two cars, came clattering to a halt.

Father's Peugeot 205 was equipped with a nut wrench that was no match for the machismo of a Spanish nut-screwing machine, the one that goes *zzjjweejj* in garages. To make amends, Emma went off to the garage up the road to borrow another one in her best Spanish. Terms of engineering defeated her. 'My pneumatico is schwish,' she told them.

'You English?' asked a lad in a greasy monkey overall. 'I'm English, too.' And the spanner was secured.

I went with Emma for a day out to Ronda, where she was going to take pictures. This famous little town straddles a magnificent gorge with a tall arched bridge. The citizens of Ronda were able to resist the invading armies that swept backwards and forwards across Andalucia for centuries by running to the opposite side of the gorge and burning the bridge. In these peaceful times they have been able to build a more permanent structure.

The town was a snapshot of the tourism we sought to avoid, set in a scene we hoped to find. Mobs of Spanish sightseers from the cities – you could tell they were from the cities because they did not wear black – trotted around the streets led always by a sour-looking lady holding a clipboard high in the air. The natives of Ronda either ignored them, or ignored them until they had something to sell them. An old woman on the bridge in the midday heat, wrapped in black shawls like a nineteenth-century Covent Garden flower-seller, mourning a long dead husband or brother, called out her wares reedily. Tourist coaches parked in a line away from the centre, their drivers in pairs talking in low tones as if planning a revolution, or standing singly, smoking, perhaps keeping a lookout for their comrades.

Yet this was a world of pastel shades to make the ghost of Laura Ashley shed a tear. Against the white of the houses and the black of their window bars casting silver shadows were the faded green shutters, butterscotch stone doorframes and a pearly blue sky to lift the whole picture heavenwards. The tourists abused this picture with their Dulux-fresh clothes, cars and attendant Coca-Cola signs.

A bright red T-shirt and totally tropical baseball cap went by and, behind them, who should walk past, led by two women with fierce hairstyles, but that former philandering MP Cecil Parkinson, dressed in casual blue trousers with a leisure-green collar on his golf-white shirt. In what low regard we British hold our politicians, and still we had an empire. We learned later that he had just bought a house in Andalucia. 'Hasn't been made a lord?'

'Don't know. Expect so.'

'Lord Parkinson of Disease, probably.'

It was time to leave Spain. We were off to Africa to see empire in all its forms but one. We would pass through Gibraltar, which is a colony; through Cameroon, which is a stable ex-colony; through Kenya, a destabilising ex-stable ex-colony; and many other variations besides. The only one we would not see was a country with potential to be a British colony (possibly excepting Spain). There has been no need for an empire since television became so effective at selling British products, and since the British army was renamed the American-led UN Peace-Keeping Force.

We could always tell how stable or established a country was by the quality of the rugby we found there. A century before the World Cup took place in South Africa, Great Britain made her formal declaration of rule over the East African Protectorate, later Kenya. This was the end of the road for years of fighting between Europeans in Africa which largely ignored the native black Africans. They must have watched the struggle with something like relief, being more used to Europeans simply coming in and fighting them in order to capture slaves. Of course, European nations were to fight bigger and bloodier wars in Africa during the next century.

It was the discovery of diamonds in South Africa in 1869 that prompted the first big land-grab by Europe. The Suez Canal opened in the same year. Britain moved in on Cairo and raced south as near to Kenya as possible. Rhodes came up north from South Africa on Britain's behalf to take Rhodesia, now Zimbabwe. Savorgnan de Brazza claimed all land north of the Congo River for France, adding to a collection which already included the Saharan Maghreb. Leopold II of Belgium took over the Congo Basin. Otto von Bismarck fashionably snatched South-West Africa, now Namibia, and German East Africa, now Tanzania. And Portugal was delighted to find that despite all this activity it still seemed to own Mozambique in the south.

By the start of the First World War, only Liberia in the west and Ethiopia in the east remained truly independent. Morocco was still a kingdom, but under French management, and Libya was under Italian administration. In our capacity as Children of Empire – Red, George, Emma and me – this was the Africa we were out to find.

We were off, too, to find Will Carling, the man who encapsulates so much that is English, ball in hand, in charge; the sort of chap who can run things, like empires, for example. Any sportsman who can be loved all the more by team and public for calling the most senior establishment in world rugby fifty-seven old farts must be a good bloke. Carling even made Old Fart into a term of respect, like Sea Lord or Grand Vizier.

Nigel Molesworth, the philosopher and famous prep-school boy in Ronald Searle's and Geoffrey Willans' book *Down With Skool*, observed as long ago as 1953 that:

(a) the russians are rotters.
(b) americans are swankpots.
(c) the french are slack.
(d) the germans are unspeakable.
(e) the rest are as bad if not worse than the above.
(f) the british are brave super and noble cheers cheers cheers.

That was the Will Carling we wanted to see: George and I did, anyway. The Irish needed convincing. The Irish always do.

To the cerebral, rugby is an outdated celebration of empire.

The game is a channel for the same qualities that maintained our empire: controlled aggression, competitiveness and nationalism. Public schoolboys in the late nineteenth century learned hacking after a game of rugby. This was where you paired off with your opposite number from the other team and took turns to kick each other in the shins. It was considered bad form to flinch. The cerebral were appalled, and hacking was eventually discontinued, much to the chagrin of many die-hards. As well as this element, rugby provides a healthy sense of sacrifice and amateur spirit: winning despite and losing because of the odds.

To people who like rugby, it is a jolly good team game with room for heroes. It is part of Britain's tally-ho culture, I admit, and rather like running an empire, since you ask, but who cares? Come on Lions! Drive forward! (Damage him, Deano!) Drive!

And drive we did, Emma, Red, George and I, with the rising sun on our left and the setting sun on our right, to a land of which Pliny once said: 'There is always something new out of Africa.' He said it in Latin, of course, to give it more gravitas. But he was right in any language. The continent was constantly to take us by surprise.

Travel is like young love: a foolish cross between passion and vanity. Embarking on a trip is like your wedding. You expect nothing and everything thereafter. You may make your promises to your God, but you cannot say where you will be – dead, mad, repatriated – in six months. All you have is hope.

Ever since I was small and first went to the southern part of Spain, the word Africa has conjured up the image I saw across the Straits of Gibraltar: mountains hung from a picture rail, as Red confirmed, of huge puffy clouds – the kind of clouds that do not rain much, but herald what Africa is always known for: big, big skies. One day I would go there. Now, in the straits themselves, it was disappointing to see similar clouds hanging over the sierras of Spain. But the stamp of Europe was there in Spain as well, and that made it different from Africa. The continent behind us was shrouded in heat-haze smog from the cars and lorries that serve the Costa and from the belching refineries of Algeciras that they say were General Franco's bid to dissolve Gibraltar off the map. The continent in front was too massive, too unnavigated, to have that pall.

I could sympathise with Franco about Gibraltar. The place is a pit. It was with a glad heart that I said napoo and cheerio to the ever-awful rock that crouches facing up the Med. The whole town is on the rock. To build the airport runway, the British annexed Spanish land on the isthmus that connects Gib's sleazy dives and speakeasies to the continent.

As I started to make my last walk across the tarmac runway that every car has to cross to reach the town, the lights went red. First a GB Airways passenger jet took off. GB Airways was called Gib Air until, according to legend, some bright prankster painted 'Yo' in front of the logo, making it YoGibAir. Then a Hercules lumbered, as only Hercs can lumber, down the runway to turn, rev, and trundle along like an armoured knight on a warhorse until it took off. It carved left over the indigo sea across the sweep of Algeciras Bay, colouring the haze over the town blacker towards Africa. When a Hercules takes off it is empire on the move.

It took a complaining American lady in a piercing orange T-shirt, Barbara Cartland sunglasses and Daz-white shorts and sandals to break the moment. 'Why'd they build the airport across the only road into Gibraltar? They stupid?'

'Why'd they build Windsor Castle so close to Heathrow?' the rest of the crowd thought. It is a European plot, madam, to confuse Americans.

We loaded Mistress Quickly on to the ferry to cross to Ceuta, a Spanish city in North Africa, before driving on to Morocco. We sailed the straits which science has said were once a land bar separating the dry Mediterranean basin from the Atlantic Ocean. Then, it is said, the sea cut through, and as the Med filled up there was a waterfall there for a hundred years. Even if it is not true, it is a wonderful story.

Unaware of their geological heritage, a shoal of fish gave us a goodbye swimpast. Grey mullet – or, as Red called them, 'finest Algeciran sewer fish'. Further out, two porpoises hooped the hoop beside our wash. 'They's shaggin',' observed Red, Irishly.

Ceuta itself was but a glimpse of faded Spanish colonialism. A peeling costa-style harbour frontage, peopled by men in half-football-style helmets riding mopeds, and women, always women, shuffling under the great bundles of belongings on their backs.

A Moroccan gent is one who does not ride his mule home while his wife staggers behind him carrying his goods from the market.

The border was with us quickly. Here humanity bottlenecked and passed, stopped at times by uniformed officers of every law in the land. And such uniforms: blue, khaki, white-belted, all ill fitting with colours ill matched. Morocco is a policeman's country. To their credit, however, we never saw outright corruption. We never paid a bribe there. They were always helpful and sometimes charming, if less literate and trained than their brother officers in England. We often saw them at major road junctions, performing a kind of t'ai chi which we supposed they imagined helped to direct the traffic. Tiny inflections of the smallest wrist muscles, waving us on, or left against approaching lorries, as if wafted by a light wind.

'Please,' said the man behind the passport window, as if declaring war. And then: 'People of the Car,' indicating us all to draw near. This was terrific. People of the Desert I knew: wild-haired Tuareg, proud Bedu and Fulani. And People of the Plain, of the Hills, of the Forest. We were People of the Car. What kind of race is that? Is this how we should introduce ourselves to village chiefs? 'Hail,' we would say mysteriously, 'pale-faced and great-nosed we come, the People of the Car.' Welcome to North Africa.

We were travelling, like all travellers do, in search of local tribal colour, piles of old stones and, above all, wilderness and challenge. In addition, Africa offered two more bits: its wildlife and a sense of nostalgia for when the British ran things. But it also inflicted on us its politics and its spiritual values, two aspects of the place that really dragged it down.

We had to keep up a fair pace for the first half of the trip. We reached Morocco in October. It was vital to cross central Africa, especially Zaïre, during the annual January pause in the rains, or we could face being bogged down there through most of February. After that we knew there would be time to rest up and repair in East Africa. Others we were to meet felt this same urgency.

Unlike others doing this trip, we had rugby in mind as well. And still the rugby ball sat, receiving an occasional boot from the boys. Most of our talk on the trip was to be of bowel movements and border crossings rather than ballplay. But the end, always keeping the wheels in motion, was that World Cup.

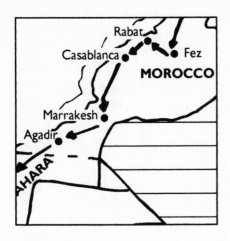

Chapter 2

CHEESE AND HONEY

Morocco. George, Red, Emma and me in Mistress Quickly. 235 days to the World Cup opening ceremony.

P overty, and skippity-jump to a better life if they can. The people of the north Moroccan biblical landscape are a shooting gallery for European products, except they are not loaded with money to return. They make up for it by aspiring like mad. The thin ivory trail the tourists tread shows little more than ranks of cadgers and salesmen tarred by money. And so it was with us. We were easy-target tourists heading south in search of rugby. But now and then we might catch a glimpse of a Morocco steeped in the desert traditions of generosity, harsh pride and struggle to survive – a land of cheese and honey.

I sat on the roof of the Land Rover outside the medina, the old walled part of the town, in Chefchouaen. One of us always guarded the vehicle outside campsites. Above me the western scarp of the very dangerous Riff Mountains rose straight upwards for 2,000 feet. Behind me was the bustle and pong of the souk. What, I wondered, is the secret of Chefchouaen's souk's-cess? Those very dangerous Riff Mountains are where Moroccans grow hashish, called *kif* locally, where they mug tourists who do not buy it and where they report those who do to the police: not brilliant long-term marketing, they admit.

There was a raggedy Riff man below me, the first of many hundreds of hawkers we would meet in Africa. He was convinced I would buy *kif*, postcards and whisky if asked enough. Then he said he would kill me. Marvellous. My first death threat. Multicoloured trucks with flashing lights hooted their way down the road from the Riff into the hot and dusty valleys, carrying fresh supplies of *kif*, whisky and postcards.

Great-grandfather Hesketh-Prichard, known as HP, was a travel writer, naturalist and sportsman. He visited Morocco in 1896, ninety-nine years before me. He wrote to his mother of his arrival there:

> I was attacked by numberless hordes who demanded presents, the honour of carrying my bag. I'd heard it was impossible to stop them, so I thought I'd see, and I told them to *allez-vous-en* – 'go away' and 'make tracks' – and then, as that made no impression, I picked them out of my way, cursed them, and triumphantly arrived with my own bag at the Customs. There I went up to a stout man sitting on a praying carpet, black-bearded, turbaned and white-robed, and he bowed, and I gave the bag to a tall man and told him to take it to the Hotel Bristol, which he did. There I got an interpreter, breakfasted and informed the proprietor that I was going to ride to the international signal station at Spartel. And incidentally, by the way, to pass through the Riffian village that took an Italian steamer and a Portuguese steamer – you remember it in the papers? Rank pirates, these fellows with long yellow guns, bare legs, ragged quilts, and shaven heads with one knot of crumpled hair three feet long growing out of the middle and about as thick as a chair leg. The road is unsafe for passengers, the Riffs being an independent tribe who let no one come alive out of their big village further down the coast.

Nothing changes.

Our next proper salesman was one hundred miles further south. On our way into Fez we took a wrong turning. As luck would have it, a dumpy Moroccan on a moped appeared who spoke good English. His name, it turned out, was Mohammed. Where were we going? Camping? Allah be praised, it was fortunate that he was going that way too. Was this our first time in Fez? He would be happy if we would follow him there. Money? No, no. It would be his pleasure. His gold-rimmed sunglasses twinkled in the sun.

He did not, after all, lead us down a back street where an armed gang left us in our underclothes. As good as his word, and his pleasure, he took us to within a mile of a campsite.

Did we need a guide for tomorrow? Ah, that was it. 'You must not trust the guides at the campsite. They rip you off. They are bad men. I alone am a good guide. See, I work for many overland companies already.' He named some buzzword examples – Guerba, Truck Africa. 'What time I meet you?'

Always establish what you want before they think you want it. We did not commit to him, although a guide seemed an attractive idea. The medina in Fez is a maze. We said we might meet him at ten o'clock, or we might not.

'You must tell me now. I must know. Do not trust others.' It was a sophisticated chat-up, pulling every trick in the Tupper book of emotional blackmail. He bobbed at our window; his glasses sparkled with renewed sales pitch; he talked in staccato bursts.

We might.

At the campsite, who should we meet but another guide called, you may be surprised, Mohammed. He loitered by the gate with his friends and rivals Mohammed and Mohammed, but not with our first Mohammed on the bike. This was not his pitch. We guessed that Mohammed 1 was not offering enough *baksheesh* to the campsite gatemen. A mile was his limit.

Mohammed 2 launched his product before we had stretched our legs out of Mistress Quickly. He did not use the overland companies ploy, but he threw in words like 'official' and 'government'. We mentioned Mohammed 1. A cloud crossed Mohammed 2's face. 'Mohammed is evil, wicked. Do not trust him. I do not know him. He is just some hustler.'

Mohammed 3 joined in: 'I never heard of Mohammed. I know he has many problems in the old city.'

Mohammed 4 nodded and shook his head in agreement. This was a cut-throat business. The end of the tourist season brought out the desperado in each Mohammed.

On Fez day 2 we chose Mohammed 2, simply because the engine of his Fiat was running as we walked out of the gate. He had dressed up specially for us in jellaba and famous Fez hat. All the grandest Moroccans wore jellabas, a kind of ethnic cotton duffel coat worn with the hood up that makes you think you are at a convention of Rasputins.

Mohammed's initial delight at our choice was interrupted only by a torrent of What Tourists Want to Hear. 'Fez souk? It is the largest in the world of Arabs.' What about the grand bazaar in Istanbul? 'That is not the same. Fez souk is the best in the world of Arabs. You can buy many things in Fez souk that you can't buy in the world of Arabs.' What about the market in Marrakesh? 'That is not the same.'

Along the way we stopped at a set of lights to find Mohammed 1 on his moped. He showed no initial delight at seeing us, nor secondary happiness, nor pleasure of any kind. He stared at us through infinitely regretful sunglasses. The gold rims no longer shone; they burned with chagrin and a soupçon of diseased jealousy. He would never forgive the guilt he was confident we felt. We were meant to know, in the words of the old curse, that the fleas of a thousand camels were already route-marching to infest our armpits. Mohammed 2 opened the door and dismissed him in short Arab commands.

The ill wishes of Mohammed 1 may have had some influence, however, as the rest of Mohammed 2's day was beset by the army. He was stopped directly by a soldier for jumping a red light and another man in uniform hung around the stalls we visited in the medina. Whatever curse Mohammed 1 cast came to rest firmly in the armpits of Mohammed 2. He took us at speed through the medina before ending up at the expensive Arab carpet shop owned by his friend, where, doubtless, he took a cut. We whizzed through the medina to get there with hardly a chance to whistle, let alone stop, and all the time he invoked the Arabic saying: 'We are not in hurry. People in hurry have left this world already. They are in cemetery.' So that is the meaning of the quick and the dead.

Bad luck on Mohammed 2: we were not in the market for carpets.

He was forced to shrug off this insult. He took us, a little grumpy in his manner, to a cheaper Berber rug and blanket shop.

Mohammed's gaucheness embarrassed the carpet-, rug- and blanket-sellers. They had set up in cool mosaic-pillared houses, out of the heat and noise of the medina's slim passages. Their walls were hung with wares and their floors scuffed by the shoes of many tourists. Mint tea to soften us up; always a calculator and terms of payment at the end of each sentence. Practised one-liners: 'Berber credit – half now, half immediately!' 'You must be students – champagne taste and a beer budget.' 'Pay by credit card over several months – each month we cash a different slip.'

Again, no dice. Some exasperation overtook Mohammed's grump now – and he had started the day so well. Here were four European tourists, overflowing with spending money, as all Europeans are – Mohammed would be able to settle many debts from his commission – yet they were not biting. And in Fez, the largest – no, the greatest – souk in the world of Arabs. What about brass? Leather? He lost his rag a bit.

Silly man. He should have asked. We would have paid money for a saucepan because we needed one. We would have commissioned a forge to make a ground anchor in case we ever wanted to winch the Land Rover out of soft sand in the desert. We might even have purchased a groundsheet and table for camping. Our lives revolved around the mechanics of travelling, not knicknacks. As it was, he grudgingly stopped at a vegetable stall, where we bought supper. No commission there.

Seeing the souk itself, a factory for the human condition, was our interest. It was like sticking your nose into a Magimix full of several ounces of indigo, cobalt, turpentine, donkey dung, finest yoghurt, smoking charcoal, musty-flavoured goat's cheese and burning dark honey. Alleys were barraged by high buildings of flat sandy bricks mashed together with mortar. Windows were small holes, iron-barred. These alleys could be as narrow as five feet and as wide as ten, opening on to tiny piazzas with mosaic drinking fountains. Through them, anxious men drove donkeys carrying cotton-wrapped bundles, shouting 'urr, urr'. Doors opened into mosques tiled in earthenware, in blue, dark green and yellow mosaic patterns with Koranic texts inlaid around them. Trestles sold hand-moulded candles, and sticks with tinsel and net on them to offer to Allah opposite ornate brass coin slots where you could make a wish. Whole streets sold nothing but garish nylon goods with spangly buttons or lovingly repaired cassette recorders. Knife-grinders bent over millstones, working with their feet, and open ironwork forges roared, never more than six feet square. For hundreds of yards, best camel-skin shoes were sold for hundreds of prices. Wheelbarrows? Never leave home without one. Rooms full of children could be heard chanting the Koran from behind closed wooden windows, along with the high-pitched voices of old men teaching them. Gaudy gilt-framed photographs of lakeland scenes, one with a moose in it. Dyers' row, with steaming pots of indigo, bright orange, saffron and poppy, and a rich Irish green. Stalls took on European advertising techniques: a Nescafé Instant Coffee box filled with beans; a faded photograph of George Michael at his bouffant best outside a barber. And so many people: Arabs, short, tall, black Senegalese, from the Gambia, devout, hunched, toothless, toothy, happy, mock-fighting, chattering, staring, begging, selling, yelling.

Mohammed interrupted with his own comments. Most were related to health. He bought garlic, which he recommended as a cure for many ills. I asked if it kept vampires away. He said yes, it was well known as a cure for all people with vampires.

'Pomegranates,' he said, outside the shop of his friend who sold pomegranates. 'If you eat thirty, no sixty, pomegranates every year, you will never be ill.'

'Carpets,' he even informed us in the carpet shop. 'You never have allergies from Moroccan carpets because only natural dyes and fibres are used.'

'Moroccan honey is best honey because the beans put their noses in spices.' We washed it down with a light goat's cheese on dry husk bread. But still we bought no carpets.

Mohammed's temper was spitting angry as he drove us home. And he drove us home badly. He had driven in the morning with studied carelessness. He must have worked out from American films that it is widely known all Arabs drive badly and he had a part to play today. His driving on the way home, bereft of commission, was dangerous. He was looking for an argument. He swerved hard around a lipsticked lady with an angry shout of 'La vache!' 'You cow!', which is a fundamentalist reaction to any woman wearing make-up. Mohammed, as we knew by then, was not a Muslim. He implied, without actually saying so, that religion was codswallop. It may have been as close to the real Mohammed as we were allowed to come. But it could just have been another example of him telling us What We Wanted to Hear.

We were careering out of the city when suddenly I spotted rugby goalposts on a dusty patch. 'Rugby?' I ventured.

'Rugby, of course. Of course, rugby,' replied Mohammed angrily. 'You don't believe? First you don't believe we have Jews, so I show you a synagogue. Now rugby. Yes.' He was in no mood to take us there.

We abandoned Fez and headed for the capital, Rabat, in search of a game and a jar or two of their finest, which naturally comes after it. But Morocco is, as we could not have failed to notice, a dry country: desert-dry, and Muslim-dry – no alcohol. The British Embassy might be a good place to start. It was a whole world removed from Mohammed's, and it was bound to have booze. Oh, wheels within wheels, what should we find but that George's father had been platoon commander of the British ambassador to Morocco, Sir Alan Ramsay, at Sandhurst in the late 1950s. And that the defence attaché, Lt-Col Christopher Anderson, was in the Household Cavalry, George's own regiment, and that Anderson had once met George, nay, inspected his kit, even.

Anderson met George at the British Embassy. George had a great thirst for a real live gin and tonic, but it was eleven o'clock in the morning and they never got further than mirth over the tale of George swapping his smart job in the army for life as a mechanic.

We all met Anderson on the embassy steps. He was in an immaculate dark suit, with a silk tie and a handkerchief perched on his breast pocket, his regimented dark hair combed precisely. We had done our best to look smart, but travel-soiled was the reality. He offered us his good wishes (no gin yet), information on Mauritania (still no gin) and even an embassy driver to help us find the Mali Embassy for our visas (damn, definitely no gin).

So we remained the same ginless wonders as before. As for rugby, he suggested we tried Casablanca, Morocco's largest city, which was on our route south.

A driver's first view of Casablanca from the north is the yellow flames of the Mohammedia Oil Refinery, which our sickening imaginations instantly converted into 'Tuareg campfires'. Quoting Rowan Atkinson, even in a Barclaycard advertisement, reminded us of home. The adjective Tuareg, taken from the desert tribe of the same name, would be an ever-present one on the rest of the Sahara part of the trip.

Casablanca itself is as far short of the film as could be possible. Everyone had warned us off the place. There is a Rick's Bar in the Hyatt Regency Hotel, but Sam has swapped his piano for a piped-muzak cassette. The city has approach roads even the burghers of Birmingham might blanch at and a Turin-type shroud of smog.

Our other reason for going there was due to Land Rover comedy engineering. Mistress Quickly had the ability to shatter only her most irreplaceable parts. One of them was an archaic device called a voltage stabiliser. This piece of electronic wizardry threw up many fascinating questions. These are not necessarily interesting to the uninitiated, but they grabbed us like anything. Fixing it was truly a rite of passage – I had always wondered exactly what that phrase meant. It was a rite we performed virtually everywhere we went.

In Spain the Land Rover garage at Estepona had sold us a flasher unit, the electronic box that makes the blinker blink. The essential problem with our voltage stabiliser was that it was already behaving like a flasher unit, and not stabilising the voltage. The next main Land Rover agent was in Casablanca. The factory workshop of SMEIA, the Casablanca dealer, is on the main road in from the north and we saw it as we arrived, a stroke of luck. They gave us a driver to find the SMEIA shop in the town centre. This was in an unhealthy area, where various Moroccans hung around in stoned groups next to piles of rubbish. It is just round the corner from the abattoir, and the popular Café et Rotisserie de l'Abattoir, which did a nice line in offal sandwiches and skinburgers.

The SMEIA shop did not have the part. 'Truly this is an ancien

Land Rover. South Africa, you say? Puf, pah,' commented a mechanic. They gave us a diagram and the part number of what we wanted and sent us to Standard Auto Accessories, which was rather tricky to find by car.

There are two ways to get through the one-way system in Casablanca. Either you fix the building you want in your rear-view mirror and reverse towards it, or you go faster and faster around the roads and roundabouts until you achieve a kind of escape velocity, spin off and correct. Unfortunately, our Land Rover was equipped with neither a rear-view mirror nor velocity, though I believe they come as standard on more modern models. We parked and George and I walked.

After diverse directions from the Volvo dealership we found it, as well as finding that Casablancans are incapable of giving directions. From SAA back to Volvo we went, armed with the knowledge that we wanted a *bilarme de securité*, now only made for Chevrolets, and that Volvo had a subsidiary called Voitures Americains. Not Volvo? Who, then? Ah, Volkswagen. To VW. Not here either. Try Bosch. No? Try Autos Mourins. No? Right.

Plan B was to telephone our GHQ, the Drovercare Garage in Winchester, and ask our friend Ben, the owner, to send us the part poste restante to Agadir, where we planned to be in a week's time. We could use George's American Express poste restante facility. No? No packets or parcels. How about sending it to the British consul in Agadir? I mean, after all, what do consuls actually do?

The honorary British consul in Agadir delights in the name Ouakrim Ben Lahcen. He runs the Agadir Beach Club Hotel, among other enterprises, and is far too busy to answer Her Majesty's telephone so, enterprisingly, has left it off the hook. That leaves DHL. DHL does have an office in Agadir but it is not in the telephone book. Does DHL in Casablanca (which, amazingly, is in the book) know where it is? No. No, wait a moment . . . no. No – yes! And so Ben is instructed to DHL the part to Agadir and at sunset we all bow our heads towards Mecca in thanks. We were not surprised to learn one week later that DHL was too expensive for so puny a part, so in the end we drove on to South Africa with our voltage thoroughly unstabilised.

It really was sunset in Casablanca by the time Mistress Quickly was done with us. We celebrated it in a McDonald's (how awful) overlooking the beach, just down the road from the tallest mosque in the world. 'Colonel Gadaffi's Kentucky Fried Chicken,' said Red, referring to the food. We had Big Macs, hamburgers, cheeseburgers, chips, Cokes, then more cheeseburgers as chasers – unlikely as it may seem, a great improvement on perpetual veg – and set off to find a campsite.

This was where Casablancan directions really came into their own. Everyone we asked had their own ideas about time, space and the difference between left and right. I found a simpleton in a deserted beach bar who held my hand a lot in his excitement. He offered to come with us as he was Going That Way Anyway. He took us to a campsite – fully manned, lights blazing, good throughput of traffic. They were closed, they assured us. We gave our fool some money to go away and left the campsite staff arguing among themselves about which way was right and right again. We tried right and right again, throwing in a few lefts and U-turns for good measure. Some twenty minutes further on we found a boy in a group of boys who said he lived at a place called Tamaris, which was a campsite, but he was hazy about where it was. Since he was on foot, we hoped we were getting warm. A mere hour later we found it: a Tuareg trailer park called Tamaris, 500 caravans with 500 families and their dogs who chanted and howled into the night. There was, of course, a man wanking in the loo when Emma went, which became a traditional feature of our stays at campsites. And to cap it all, a dog, pausing between howls, or possibly chants, peed on me in the night.

Emma had a constant battle with personal hygiene – not in the sense that she had any problem with it in itself, not like me and my dog, but in that every trip to the loo or shower proved a harrowing experience of male depravity at its worst. The shower in the gleaming campsite in Fez, for example, had a woman whose only job was to clean it. It also had a scowling old man perched on a stone outside and this man had a cat. When Emma took a shower, the man would toss in the cat and then follow it, explaining that his job was to make sure that cats did not enter the women's shower. He would then launch into a discourse, in Arabic and French, about how difficult it was to catch soapy cats. Emma would lash him with shrift in Gaelic, English and sewer Spanish. He would leave.

Each evening we watched the cats fighting among the eucalyptus trees. We mused on whether they were arguing about whose job it would be to go into the shower the next day.

From Tamaris we moved back to a site in the centre of Casablanca and swapped chanting and howling for the murmuration of mosques and the muezzin reminding us that God was great, that there was only one God but God. In Arabic, at five in the morning, it goes a bit like this: 'Hadjiaaaaar! Aish shachmaaaaaa! Haiid Allaaaaaah!'

So Casablanca had traffic problems, social depravation and a McDonald's restaurant. It stood to reason there would be rugby too. Following Anderson's advice, I made the British consulate my first stop. Nick McDuff, consul, commercial section, was most obliging. I was shown into his office through a waiting room filled with back copies of *Tunnels and Tunnelling* magazine. He was the opposite of Anderson. Bearded and balding, grey suit, grey tie, brown shoes, he might once have been an East India clerk in a book by Kipling. His job is the real reason we keep ambassadors like Ramsay and defence attachés like Anderson to the style they enjoy. Yet he had Middle Management writ large over his office door while they had Grandee. McDuff was the teamiest team player of the three and knew all about rugby in Casablanca. He pointed me towards the international ground, which was only two blocks from where we were staying.

That evening, seeing a lad sitting on the kerb outside the rugby ground, I asked him where the door to the club was. He introduced himself as Youssef, fly-half for the Moroccan team. Players crave recognition in Morocco and he was in full photo-call kit when I came back two hours later with Emma, George and Red. At that moment Bougja bounded into view and bought a round of beers in the club bar, and Youssef, eclipsed, faded sadly into the background. Perhaps his time will come.

Abderrahim Bougja is president of the Moroccan rugby federation. He is a stocky ex-international centre, scrum-half and full-back – quite a variety of experience – with a rich and high-pitched laugh that interrupts his sentences. Elsewhere on the West Coast they call him Boo-Boo, but in Morocco his team respect him. 'I am ... er, polyvalent – ha!' he told us. When not laughing he griped, and the grumble was always the same: money. He had just come back with the team from the International Sevens Tournament in Taiwan, and he had a few days before jetting off to a conference of international rugby federations in Vancouver. 'Taiwan was expensive, whooo,' he exclaimed. 'It was the first experience for our team so we lose, but good experience. We lost 10–19 to Tonga. No difference, huh?'

He bounced off for another beer and bounced back. George and Red beamed. 'The International Rugby Board must put more money into the sport in smaller countries to develop it worldwide.' Bougja was furious about the way the rugby league board was helping to set up the game in Morocco, in direct competition to rugby union, while still he remained woefully underfunded. Rugby league had pinched thirty players from rugby union to form a team.

Moroccan rugby union, we learned, has a proud heritage. It started during the French occupation, and the French army built the Casablancan ground in the early 1920s – 'Thus the high walls,' noted Bougja. We looked. It was a beautiful, spongy field, and well watered, unlike the grass-and-dust area we had seen in Fez. This was where Africa's final world cup qualifying matches had taken place, the scene of the Ivory Coast's unprophesied victories over Namibia and Zimbabwe which enabled them to join South Africa as the other African nation in the World Cup.

The Moroccan national team was born with the country's independence in 1956, and their federation in 1979. Bougja was made its president in 1980. 'The ground is full when we play internationals here in Casablanca, and sometimes we have television. We have all the Five Nations here on TV, ha!' he said. 'The interest in rugby is growing, but we need much money.'

Schoolboys start playing the game at the age of thirteen in the dozen rugby-playing cities, which include Marrakesh, Rabat and Fez. In addition Casablanca has a rugby school which trains junior cadets from the age of eight and rugby coaches for schools all over the country. 'This place is a mission where we send out teachers,' said Bougja.

Though the French team holds workshops in Casablanca, France has largely abandoned her former colony. France's most notable contribution to Moroccan rugby in recent years was to steal the top international Abdélatif Benazzi for her own team, Bougja told us. 'It was a sad moment for Morocco when Benazzi went,' he said. 'But he comes back – ha, ha. He is a natural successor to me.'

'Moroccan rugby culture is the same as the French,' pointed out the team's technical adviser, Ouasfi Latif, who had brought up his own Fanta to join our ranks of beers. He was a taller, rather lugubrious man, an ex-Moroccan international hooker. As he said 'hooker' he looked at Bougja, and both of them looked at Emma, the only woman in the room, and smirked.

'Glad to see the same jokes are current worldwide,' murmured Red.

'Rugby in Morocco only exists thanks to the French military. But the French do not help Morocco now. I don't know why,' said Latif.

'I think it's a question of money,' put in Bougja, his favourite refrain.

Bougja and Latif would have liked some support from the Moroccan army, but it was not forthcoming. 'The army doesn't have a rugby team,' said Bougja ruefully, 'but the president of the army promised me they will have one. There is a giant new sports complex being built in Rabat. Ha!'

Like Mohammed 2, Bougja was a salesman. But like McDuff he thought like a European and was a team player. Rugby in Morocco is similar to rugby in England. There is the same amateur spirit, put up with in the same way, though more noisily by Bougja and his friends. Players, when not in kit, wear smartish clothes and drink in a well-appointed bar. And, praise Allah, they drink beer. So we abandoned our embassy brown-nosing on the spot.

It is a moot point whether rugby is really a civilising influence. Morocco stands at the T-junction that leads one in one direction to the European and in the other to the Arab way of life. The Confédération Africaine de Rugby Amateur may be based in the Magreb, in the Sahara, in Tunis, but rugby is a European acolyte which has no place among Arabs.

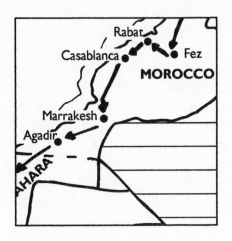

Chapter 3

HIGH ATLAS
INTERLUDE

Morocco. Me in Mistress Quickly. Emma, George and Red up a mountain.
225 days to the World Cup opening ceremony.

The Berber village of Imlil is splashed over the head of a
hidden valley in the High Atlas Mountains like a giant brown
bird-dropping. We slithered the Land Rover over a loose
stone road for ten miles to find it. Whoever designed the roads in
the Atlas was a Scalextric freak, we discovered, as the twists and curves
became ever more flamboyantly cambered. It took unnatural speed
from Mistress Quickly to cope with the mad mapster's inventions.
We arrived in daylight at the Café Soleil, a tea, carpet and boot-hire
shop which commanded a view across Imlil village square, a small
patch of rough dirt.

It was the aim of the others to climb Jebel Toukbal, the highest
peak north of the Sahara. It was my aim to catch some R&R in
the village's dives and fleshpots. So on the light and happy morrow
I watched them leave, laden with their backpacks. That was the
morning of the Wedding. Apart from my sadistic joy at the sight of
the others taking their masochistic pleasure, the day dawned badly.
Emma, Red and George were looking forward to gorging themselves
on the views from the mountainside, but I was left with the discovery

that the French, who had arrived cackling in their truck during the night, had already blocked the loo. The Café Soleil had only one loo, but many cackling French.

I had no idea at this stage that today was a wedding day, nor that the previous four days had also been wedding days, nor that the next two were as well. After a marriage Berbers enjoy seven days of high living. While the others headed off into the sunrise above Imlil to catch the first rays of the day at 4,167 metres, my exercise was less ambitious. A half-hour scramble left me gasping on the top of a shaly hillock which also overlooks Imlil. As I sat recovering and scanning the distant peaks through my binoculars, from nowhere nine snot-nosed boys appeared.

Conversations with children in tourist areas like Imlil follow much the same routine: 'Bonjour.'

'Bonjour.'

'Dirham?'

'Non.'

'Stylo?'

'Non.' 'Cigarette pour Papa?'

'Non.' 'Non, non, non!'

Shrieks of laughter.

This lot tried a few variations on the theme. They offered me a puppy in exchange for dirham. Non. They endearingly tried throwing sheep shit at me. Non, not a good begging ploy.

A shepherd appeared and called the boys to heel. He spoke no French, which made little difference to me. I gave him a cigarette, which provoked an extra shower of sheep shit, and we talked to each other in sign language.

I waved my hands in the air to ask if it might rain. He pursed his lips and pondered this and at last agreed that these were mountains all around us. I counted to four on my fingers, and showed three fingers walking up a rock while one stayed at the bottom. He looked at me curiously, then concurred that the mountains I had so cleverly spotted were, on the whole, very tranquil. When I tried to ask him the best way down from the hill he gazed sadly at me before admitting that mountains, the same mountains I had seen, were an excellent habitat for sheep. Baa, baa. Or perhaps it was an observation that all tourists are without doubt mad. I walked away like a pied piper with the children, who still offered me puppies and shit in great quantities. And still I did not know about the Wedding.

I came back to the centre of Imlil at last to spend the rest of the day pottering around the Land Rover, drinking sickly milk coffee and writing letters. Many people came to visit. The elderly Husain Amaradu arrived, as he learned to do every day, to smoke my cigarettes and offer me as much couscous in his home as I could pay for. His house was over the wall, over the river and over the small hill, in one of Imlil's unfashionable suburbs. His main route in and out of the village square was via the yard behind the Café Soleil, where we had parked, so each morning I was treated to the sight of him hobbling down the hill on frail and skinny legs, hopping heron-like across the brook, and hitching his jellaba around his waist to scale the wall.

Aitclahsen Abudlahadi came by. Would I like to eat couscous with him? No. Not at any price? He smoked my cigarettes in silence until he spotted some old friends among the new Dutch who had just arrived in a lorry, and bounded up to them with a grin of welcome and a keen price for couscous.

The young Mostapha Aitifraden arrived at the time of day when the mountain afternoon crisped into evening and I had my six o'clock coffee in front of me, and my quarter-past-six and ten-to-seven cigarettes. He smoked the former with one eye on the latter as we discussed the merits of his father's couscous. This boy sparkled with unsummed paradoxes. His father, he told me, kept an astonishing table but he was, it turned out, still very poor. Could Mostapha have some money for his father anyway? Father was very energetic in the kitchen and bought only the best ingredients, yet he was also very ill, spent much time lying down and Mostapha must find a packet of cigarettes to sustain him. What illness does he have? Oh, he is dying of cigarettes in the lungs. Mostapha blithely went on with a further catalogue of his father's skills, needs and apparent death wish.

Wheedling was apparently not working, so Mostapha had an idea. He was now going to the wedding of his cousin Mostapha, and would I like to come? I said yes, perhaps in some minutes, and extracted my eight o'clock cigarette from him before he left.

Mostapha the bridegroom, as opposed to Mostapha the wheedler, was the twenty-year-old brother of Brahim the wearer of hearing aids, aged sixty, who owned the Café Soleil. Brahim had many sons and brothers and this brother worked at the café. Brahim also had other kinsmen in Imlil, such as Mostapha the wheedler and his fast-decaying father. In fact, all of Imlil was related to Brahim in one way or another.

One of Brahim's smallest relations was a boy clearly employed to ride his new bicycle around the yard at the Café Soleil as close to the Land Rover as possible. It may have been part of an obscure youth training scheme so I did not stop him. Just after the eight o'clock cigarette, the smallest relation came out to see me with an urgent warning. Do not trust Mostapha (the wheedler). He is zigzag, bad man. Luckily I had worked that out. 'You want to come to wedding? You come with me, not Mostapha.' Not quite sure where zig stopped and zag began, I said yes.

There followed an hour of bluff and counter-bluff as Mostapha the wheedler hung around the Café Soleil, waiting to see whether I was going to the wedding and whether I was going with the smallest relation. I knew he knew I would, and he knew I knew he knew I would, and the smallest relation knew too, but I quickly learned that despite his warnings to me he did not really mind because secretly he admired his elder cousin's blarney and blather. Both wheedler Mostapha and the smallest relation owned crackly new leather jackets from Marrakesh, and you could see who had had the idea first, despite the imminent death of his father.

Shortly after my ten-past-nine cigarette, the three of us set off up the road. The full moon burned blue light across the mountains and on to the valley floor. The smallest relation shadowboxed like the Karate Kid and shot at shut windows with imaginary machine-guns. Mostapha playfully kickboxed the smallest relation in the backside.

We climbed the hill to Brahim's house. It was perched above the village in the grand manner that only a senior dignitary of Imlil could afford. It was still unfinished and would need several more weeks of slapping wattle and daub on to exposed breezeblocks to match the ruddy brown of Imlil's other grand houses, but it was already laid out as a home of substance. A gatehouse and two four-storey buildings nestled into the hill, surrounded by a walled courtyard. Roofed outside staircases led to rooms whose tiny windows peeked out on to the moonlit valley. A large roof area on the gatehouse gave a view of the courtyard.

By now I was in. Mostapha and the smallest relation went to join other relations in decreasing sizes downstairs. Above them there was a roomful of women dressed in glittering gold-etched dresses, but kept firmly out of sight. One or two of the more matronly marched up and down the first balcony in an organisational way, but the nearest most of them came to the action was to jam the doorway and shout an ululating yip, 'Yalabalabalabalaoueee,' as high and as fast as they could.

The action was the Berber dance in the courtyard. Two dozen young men in white jellabas stood in a small circle and wailed a Berber chant. I stood on the roof of the gatehouse and watched with some of the older men in blue, grey and brown newly pressed jellabas. We were the audience, but as in any celebration, the audience are actors too and this was not, I observed, like an English wedding. I had no clue how to behave. Did I chat with the chief or just *salaam al'leikum* him solemnly? Did I congratulate the bridegroom or dance with him? It was that awful nightmare where you find yourself onstage and you do not know your lines, nor even which play you are in. I kept thinking, never use your left hand (it is unclean), never use your left hand (it is unclean).

The chant turned into a laughing, cheering procession which wound up the stairs beside me. Should I join them? Was I welcome here? Who was Mostapha the groom, anyway? One of the old men beckoned me so I went up. I did not, it seemed, have to take my shoes off to go into the room, but Brahim who stood at the door to greet his guests thought it was a nice touch.

'You are welcome,' he said in English. 'This is Mostapha, my brother.' Thank goodness.

Shake hands all round. Sit down. Smile and nod to the man on my left. He is called Lahcen, he tells me in English. And the other men in my group? Brahim, Brahim and Lahcen. That's easy – I have a half-chance of getting their names right. What happens next? Am I still welcome? 'You are welcome,' said Lahcen, or was it Brahim? 'Next we eat. But first we talk and sing.'

The atmosphere of the evening had changed. The room at the top was the main entertaining hall, about twenty yards square, with tables and cushioned benches around the walls. Some sixty men were sitting there in chatting groups. The gang next to mine were the younger men, in white jellabas. They now held drums, non-jangling tambourines. The appearance from nowhere of these *tambos*, the foetid pot of smoking incense that was passed around and the food which followed later gave the occasion even more of a dreamlike feel.

The boys started to beat the drums. They made a booming noise to the rhythm, clattery-clat, clattery-clat, and four-time variations on that. And they sang – a caller and a chorus – as we handclapped a beat Keith Moon would have got off on. The tempo grew faster and faster, and the veins stood out on the boys' faces, which went redder and redder. And still they sang, to an energetic climax: boom boom-boom.

Other groups tried it, but the first was the best of the evening. And then they asked me, the only white face in the room, to sing. Oh, gosh.

Foolhardy, I had brought my banjo ukulele. Brahim was not completely impressed by this westernisation of his brother's wedding, but, 'Inshallah,' his guests reminded him, a phrase which ranges in meaning from 'It is Allah's will' to 'Who cares?' My uke has been used in anger at a couple of weddings in England, but not at anything quite like this. A hush thundered up and down the room. I stood up and tried a chord. The boys who had been admiring the instrument earlier had also retuned it. Oh, golly. There was a very long hush indeed as I went plink-plonk trying furiously to find some notes I recognised. More hush. Done it, and now some confidence.

I instructed the drummers to start booming and, as Walt Disney swivelled in his grave, I belted out a speedy 'I'm the King of the Swingers', King Louis's number from *The Jungle Book*, which I reckoned would leap the language barrier nicely. Crikey, but they loved it. The handclapping turned into the roar of a cheer. I sat down, dry-throated, as hands forced mint tea upon me. Phew. For the next two days I would be welcomed all over Imlil by men, young and old, strumming imaginary banjos. Red, George and Emma, who were to return the following day, were bemused by this.

Mint tea was the only liquid served that wedding evening apart from water. 'Boyzuran,' said the water-carrier frequently, and laughed. 'Boyz-uran,' I returned with a guffaw. Boyz-uran? Who knows, best play along with it. But getting the water-carrier on my side was a good move. Food is coming, will I wash my hands? No, thank you (I washed them ages ago). Huge joke. Yes you will! Everyone wants to wash their hands! Silly me.

Food came: first *tajine*, which is a Moroccan goat hotpot, then couscous. We ate with our fingers, making squishy balls of the couscous and popping them into our mouths. That, at least, is the theory. I scalded my fingers on the juice in the *tajine* and scattered couscous in a wide arc over my own and my neighbours' laps. I did not spill my mint tea, though by now lumps of goat and almonds were floating dismally on its surface. No, I drank my mint tea. Explosion of laughter. You must save your mint tea for a toast! Everyone does that! Stupid me.

But a toast? That means speeches, thanking the caterers and that sort of thing. I knew about listening to speeches. Anyone could do that. But there were no speeches. After the fruit, everyone finished their mint tea. So no toast, either. This must be a dream. Could I smoke now? Never do anything first. I could smoke if I handed round cigarettes.

I was drunk on the dream, despite the lack of stimulants, on the flashes of gold from their clothes and teeth, the booming and the incense. The night became a blur of singing, wailing, ululating, guests peeing on the gatehouse roof and a series of interminable boys-only Berber dances, which married a minuet with the hokey-cokey. The action moved to the courtyard, beneath the stately moonlit mountains and a banner of stars.

The dancing part was where I stopped keeping the pace. It was time for bed. My last sight of the party was Mostapha, wheedling, being beaten out of the door by the senior Brahim for some crime or other. That boy is too zigzag for his own good.

Chapter 4

HEAT AND DUST

Morocco and Mauritania. George, Emma, Red and me in Mistress Quickly. Mike and Suggs in the red Land Cruiser. Clive, Jeremy and Jesper in the white 109 Land Rover. Urs and Lara in the red 109 Land Rover. Neil, Hazel and Michelle in the white 130 Land Rover. 211 days to the World Cup opening ceremony.

The rugby ball sailed high in the air over the desert peninsula of Dakhla. 'I don't know anyone who can throw a ball like Suggs,' said Clive, the Australian.

It arched for a moment over the sandflats, over the rippled turquoise spit of sea and over the grey cliffs on the other shore. It landed in George's arms. The man who had thrown it, Suggs, was Derek Pringle, the former England cricketer, who was travelling south with an old Essex team-mate of his, Mike Garnham, Mike's brother Clive, and their cousin Jeremy.

We were killing time, waiting for other members of our convoy of vehicles to turn up. We did a lot of waiting in the desert. George pointed out that, like that of a professional sportsman, most of a traveller's time involves the dull and mundane, like waiting. We had swapped sightseeing for the challenge of crossing the Sahara and had teamed up with several other trans-African travellers. We made our own small convoy within a larger one and we all had call signs. Suggs and his group were the Lads. They were in two vehicles, an old and disintegrating Land Rover and a large, blustering Toyota. Both had stickers on their doors advertising an Essex brewery. Another group of three people had come from Bury St Edmunds in a Land Rover so clean and so well-equipped with modern conveniences that they at once became the Dust Busters. They were Neil, who used to fly Hercules in the RAF, his sister Hazel, and girlfriend Michelle, also ex-RAF. Neil's Land Rover was so weighed down with luxuries that it kept sinking in the sand. He drove it slowly and ponderously, much as if it were a Hercules. The Swiss Family Robinson consisted of a serious young man with dreadlocks from Zurich called Urs and his bubbling German friend Lara from Hanover. Urs pronounced his Vs as Ws, but otherwise spoke excellent English. We were delighted when he said he was 'wery worried about getting my Mauritanian wisa' and when he saw his first 'wulture'. Lara spoke English, too, though with a tendency to make her S into a Sch. We were to hire a guide called Achmed, whom she described as schlimy, which had him spot-on. But more of Achmed later.

Everybody called us the Hoorays, which we considered unflattering.

We were to meet these people again and again, and others like them, on the way to Johannesburg. We felt the bond of all pioneers, especially since we had already eased away from the last tourist honeypots of North Africa. Soon we would turn off the Paris–Dakar route altogether.

A week before, we had left the cool of Imlil to corkscrew down the little mountain roads. At once it hit us, the heat, the torrid plains and the lacquered air that led to the north-western edge of the Sahara. Something else hit us too – a donkey cart. Asleep in the back of the Land Rover, parked in a small street in a tiny town near Agadir, I woke up to a crash and the wrench of metal. A donkey pulling a cartful of rubble was hopping up and down outside the front passenger door. We were not long out of Casablanca so it was easy to say, in Bogey's voice, 'Of all the cars in all the world you had to walk into mine.'

George exploded spectacularly, breaking his vow of silence. He marched round to look at the damage. 'Pee-sosh-it,' he cried. The donkey had embedded its cart in our rear passenger door and our exhaust pipe. This was serious, not to say quite a few quid down the tube; not to say, even, a new tube altogether. It took some seconds to extricate the donkey, which had started to panic in the bloodyminded way donkeys do, putting yet greater rents into our coachwork, flesh wounds for Mistress Quickly.

The small boy in charge of the donkey was alarmed. He knew he was in trouble. His father might have to sell the donkey to pay for the damage, and he would be reduced to wheeling a barrow. He blamed his friend, also leading a donkey cart and rubble, who had recklessly tried to overtake him, thus forcing him into our side.

The Fuzz arrived, two of them, on a farty moped. From that moment it was obvious what would happen. Tourists are rich, donkey boys are poor. The boys would be made to disappear, the tourists would be made to pay for their own repairs. Certainly there would be forms to fill out, but what can you do? If it meant, officially speaking, of course, that the famous Sûreté Marocaine would have to be economical with the truth to accomplish this, these tourists might have to learn once again the ubiquitons shrug phrase 'Inshallah' – it is, as ever, the will of Allah; it is beyond our control.

Always work out what is going to happen before the natives do. We did, and to the policemen's credit, they had a word with a mate, who spoke to another mate, who happened to know a Berber with a laugh like a laryngitic hyena who owned a welding shop, who bodged the job nicely for a small, small sum. And that is how things are done in Morocco.

Agadir, in the cool of the coast, was the last place we saw Europeans in their natural habitat. On the beach, a vast naked European woman of unknown background and uncertain backside waddled out of the sea like a sumo bull seal and flumped down on her front beside her husband, who lay on his back in the sand. I assume he was her husband. Surely he was not hanging around with her for fun. He, too, was bare all over, apart from a white baseball cap perched over his privates. He was quite right, of course. Imagine the agony of a sunburned willy.

Agadir had a truly European flavour, ranging from fat and furry German middle management in panzer convoys of campervans to small chattering Spaniards who always travelled in pairs. It was a low-rise, low-level holiday resort, and unashamedly infidel.

We fell in with five hairy leatherclad Transylvanians riding large Teutonic motorbikes. They had names like Arnold and Freia, and possibly Siegfried and Brunhilda as well; I don't know, my German is not so good. They did not have sharp pointed canines, luckily, or a penchant for black and crimson Gothic capes, but they did mention that they had come to Agadir to buy sharks' teeth. My hand went automatically to my neck. But Transylvanians, I knew, generally fall into one of two groups, the vampires and the hapless victims. The latter are normally harmless as, I think, were this lot. They did not, I observed, mind garlic in their food, and their motorbikes had wing mirrors.

Two of the Spaniards organised a night on the bare mountain, a picnic on a flat-topped col they had found up one of the rivers. We arrived in darkness, having borrowed a cassette-player from a local fossil salesman. Four nationalities were there, spanning Europe from Romania to Ireland, so I was pleased that the prevailing language was English. We ate blackening bananas and drank filthy Moroccan wine while listening to the fossil man's failing batteries slow a tape of filthier music from Marrakesh to . . . a . . . stand . . . still. But the col, which sat at the bottom of steep cliffs with a pretty river snaking round it, was close to perfect. The same bright moon we had seen in Imlil picked out every detail of the palm and banana trees around us and we burned the embers of our Tuareg campfire into the morning.

One of the Spaniards was called Mañuel. He came from Barcelona. He even announced, 'I speak English very good,' but sadly he did not add: 'I learn it from a book.' At one stage he confided: 'I don't like the food in Morocco because it has many species.' He could have been right, but I think he meant many spices.

The Spaniards' conversation with the Transylvanians was limited. Each side could muster a 300-word vocabulary in English, but unfortunately they were not the same words. To make up for it they all laughed raucously during the many intervening silences.

'These place iss . . . paradise,' said Manu. 'Ha, ha, ha, ha, ha.'

'Ho, ho, ho,' replied Arnold. 'Ho, ho. Good.'

'Theess iss paradise reever. Ha, ha, ha.'

'Ho, ho. Good fish here. Ho, ho, ho. Ja.'

There were plenty of charming mixtures and mix-ups in language in Morocco. We saw shops advertising sand witch, first cousin to dust devil, no doubt, and the entertaining House of Pain, where we bought bread. Maybe it is unfair to mock. Having English as your mother tongue is a great stroke of luck abroad. Thank goodness for American films, which have taught it to the rest of the world. Its most important advantage was that it infuriated the French, who always resented the noise of English chatter.

We left the Transylvanians, the Spaniards and the fossil salesman, and started the journey south through the Western Sahara. The first half of it was tarmac road, the second half sand. After Agadir came desert. Miles and miles of it. Really miles of it. It varied from flat dry bits to gently rising dry bits, which tended to be drier on top. The dips, which were marked as *oueds*, or rivers, on our maps, came with exciting signs promising flash floods, but they were dry when we went through them. After a while in the desert, they stopped being marked at all. They just felt bumpier.

I do not know, dear reader, what you do in the daytime. You wake up, I guess, in the morning. Imagine then, before breakfast, shaking the sand off yourself and getting into a Land Rover. You mooch around a bit through elevenses until lunch. Count all that time as Land Rover time, rumbling along the road through the sands, sometimes hypnotised, sometimes bored, sometimes lost in a dream which could last, you hope, but only does so for a few minutes. How long do you take over lunch? An hour? Still the same scenery goes by, without relief.

At times the sand enveloped the road, and round breasts of dunes lined the horizon in varying sizes. At other times it was flat and brown in all directions, rather like parts of Norfolk and Lincolnshire, except without the features. We crept, we felt, through it at a petty pace from day to day to the last syllable of recorded time. When not like breasts, the dunes reminded me of sleek flying saucers, fresh from the showroom, either parked near the road, or far away, floating on distant mirages, shaped by the wicked desert wind.

If you are looking forward to the evening, there are times in normal life when the afternoon can drag. In the desert it tugs in the other direction. Heat clots you. Sand sticks. The sun stings. You start to think about the most curious things: what average speed must we maintain to make it to the World Cup? Why did John in *Swallows and Amazons* never get off with Peggy? How exactly do you whistle fulvously? Where, or what, is the Akond of Swat? Thoughts like 'I am actually crossing the Sahara' were only brief interruptions to the searing monotony.

It is teatime and the long two hours since lunch are over. The end is in sight. Still, in the desert, you move at a steady forty miles per hour. You watch, entranced for a full minute as one of the big Berliet lorries comes swimming out of the mirage on the metalled Moroccan road in a wash of heat haze. These lorries feed the towns that work the phosphate mines further into the Sahara. Moments like that can make your hour, if not your day.

There was excitement when on our right we saw a Lloyd's nightmare. Along the coast was a litter of rusting husks – not even hulks – of boats, everything from trawlers to container ships. On the beaches one wreck, two wrecks, three wrecks, four wrecks – Castlemaine! Bad puns sustained me and exasperated Red and Emma, while they drove George further towards the pure silence he was seeking.

Sand to the left of me, sand to the right of me. Into the thingummy-bob rode the 600. Or was it only 400? Perhaps at school we were not allowed to know the full horrifying truth.

Africa addles. When we talked to each other we spoke of where we should camp, what we should eat, and less and less of what we remembered of home. This last subject started to become difficult. We had only been away a few weeks, but we all started to forget little things – friends' names, film stars' names. It was infuriating. We spent a fortnight trying to remember the name of one actor. We could recall his film parts – Dick Tracy, Bugsy Siegel – and we could sing the Carly Simon song 'You're So Vain' right up to the bit where she mispronounces 'Saratoga', but his name was beyond our grasp. For a while, Red believed that the name we wanted had the initials B.W., but that only made us think of Bruce Willis. In the end, it came to me in a dream. It was Warren Beatty. I woke up. It was dawn. I woke the others to tell them. They were not, I noticed, that impressed.

Mistress Quickly was our escape pod from the gigantic expanse of nothing that imprisoned us. We clattered through the desert in a diesel roar, the cab filled with cigarette smoke which curled and jiggled over the bumps, and Def Leppard, Led Zeppelin, Goats Don't Shave, a little London flat in Morocco's empty quarter. We arrived at a small desert town where there was a parked car. 'This,' exaggerated Red, 'is the Dagenham of the Western Sahara. Let's cruise the main drag'. A minute later we were out of it.

We collected pets and trophies to fill Mistress Quickly to provide interest. Emma had Grace, a pot plant given to her by a local admirer in Agadir. Grace's job was to sit on the dashboard and fall off from time to time to spread soil on Red's feet. Sometimes Red spotted the bumps coming up in the road and would catch Grace. Sometimes George, who was driving, spotted them before Red, reached across to catch Grace, and we swerved across the road. Then there would be the pun, along the lines of 'fallen from grace'.

I had Sharon, a spider who had spun a web across one of Mistress Quickly's less trendy nooks. It was not a good web, so I took it upon myself to flick and swat flies to feed her with on the end of my finger. She was delighted, for she knew her spinning abilities were limited. She would dash out and grab her fly, flash me a smile and sometimes a provocative wiggle of her abdomen, before dragging the corpse back to her lair. One day, perhaps, Sharon and I would raise a family of little Kevins. No, we were not going strange in the heat – the Dust Busters owned a spider called Harry of whom we had high hopes. But it was not to be. Sharon and I were too far apart, both in character and reproductive organs. One day I forgot to feed her. She sulked for two days afterwards, refusing even bluebottles, her favourite. Then came a gesture of despair: she walked across the ceiling of the Land Rover towards the cabin light and cast herself off, to drown or be crushed in the sea of belongings we kept at our feet.

It is now past teatime. It is six o'clock, and that is when we stop. It has been a long day. In the desert it went on like that for many long days.

The town of Dakhla marked the end of Morocco. It was a haze among the images that filled the time between our departure from Agadir and arrival in Mauritania. This was where we were to join the military convoy which would escort us to the Mauritanian border. Dakhla was an odd little town, 200 miles from anywhere, where forty per cent of the Moroccan army were stationed. It was a little like an airport terminal. People only came there to leave as quickly as possible, especially us.

It was filled with officials of varying sorts, many of whom looked like the actor Tom Conti, and most of whom we had to visit. There was *Sûreté*, Customs, gendarmerie, army – and the same again on the other side in Mauritania. The Lads had trouble explaining the profession 'cricketer' to the form-fillers. They did much arm-waving, smiling and shadow bowling to illustrate the game but the officials reacted with mournful incomprehension. In the end, they persuaded the officials to put the job down on paper as something between PE teacher and table-tennis player.

The Dakhla campsite was an international settlement, sealed hermetically from south Moroccan civilisation. We had joined a convoy of two dozen vehicles, ranging from motorbikes through Land Rovers to the gigantic Dutch truck from Imlil which had twenty people on board. Half of them were going to South Africa. We waited at this campsite for two days, working out which among the other vehicles would make it and who would fall by the wayside, or give up and fly.

We started to take more notice of other people's camping arrangements. The Swiss Family Robinson, being only two, slept in the back of their Land Rover. The Dust Busters had an immaculate roof tent. The Lads had a roof tent too, designed carefully by Mike from models he had built. Though impressive in its intricacy, we felt Mike's tent was a little over-complicated. And he had a bad habit of telling us how well it compared to ours whenever he could.

We had every reason to feel graceless, of course. Our tent really was meagre by comparison. Everyone took every opportunity to remind us of the deadly desert scorpions that lurked under every rock, ready to run up a bed's legs and inflict agonising death on the happy camper above. Scorpion nightmares kept Red awake, especially. He was always careful to check his shoes – even his washbag – in the morning.

Days in Dakhlar dawned happier, all fears banished of being topped by unbalanced arachnids. There was a white baby camel there to keep us amused. He only came up to my chest. When not being fussed over by the other happy campers he staggered around extremely cutely, making a noise halfway between a sheep bleating and someone being sick. We had seen camels in herds, strolling across the roads. They have a beautiful, careful stride. Their gait is so perfect they should be imported by headmistresses of great girls' schools as examples of How to Walk Properly. 'Now, girls, arch your back and take a step on to the ball of your foot. Stop chewing the cud, Camilla.' Perhaps not. If the baby was anything to go by, their diction is terrible, despite their good posture.

Coincidentally, like great headmistresses, camels have profoundly solemn faces, as if they had just caught you smoking behind the bike sheds and they felt it their duty, painful though it might be, to report you to your housemaster at your own school. 'What is his name, please?'

'Mr Beatty, ma'am, Warren House, Harrow.' We saw one – a camel, of course, not a headmistress – trussed up and thrust into the back of a Land Rover, looking out over the tailgate. There was no fear on its face, just an expression of 'Oh, the ignominy, and one a beast of such breeding.'

A Dane rolled up in Dakhla on the back of a German's motorbike. This was Jesper. We would see a lot more of him. Jesper, pronounced Yesper, was hitch-hiking, bussing, biking and taxi-ing to Cape Town, and at one time or another he would join all of us for part of the journey. The Dust Busters had said they could take him to Mauritania and he was anxiously asking for them. In the end the Lads took him on board for that leg of the journey, and for a fortnight afterwards as well.

Jesper was a tall, fair-haired and rather gawky Viking. He had an earnest expression, not unlike that of a tortoise, and when later he bought a small round tent, the picture was complete. He had left Copenhagen armed only with a sleeping bag, a change of clothes and a backpacker's guide to South America. In Spain he had changed his mind and crossed to Africa instead. He had been working in a Bang & Olufsen hi-fi shop to raise money to send his parents on a holiday to Canada. Jesper's father, a Copenhagen plumber, had once been a gold prospector there, he told us. Jesper's parents were so pleased with this present that they gave him some money for his own trip.

Jesper had a small but candid English vocabulary, heavily layered with a Scandiwegian accent. His Is sounded like Es, his Os like Øs, and he put extra Js into words, which he pronounced as Ys, as in 'fjord'. 'E had a prøblem with the pjølice,' he declared. 'When E leave Mørøccø E'm gjøing to gjive them the fjinger.'

Jesper learned new idioms from the Lads. 'Spewin',' he announced in Australiwegian when he did not like his food. 'Laughin' geezer,' he said in Cockneywegian when happy. And whenever possible, 'E'm gjøing to tek a shjit now.'

Jesper had an instant rapport with Suggs. Only Suggs really understood Jesper. They had the same charm: both were oafish and yet also intelligent and warm people. With Jesper it was a dry warmth. He would make a comment and then stare at you intently. You were not quite sure whether he had made a joke, or thought he had said something wrong or even more profound than he hoped, or had realised he had said something stupid. Suggs always knew, and giggled, and Jesper would giggle at him. Jesper would say, 'Spewin' mate,' and they would giggle in turn for minutes.

Jesper did not know that Suggs was a sporting hero in the way the British among us did. Jesper saw the man, we saw the legend. It was Suggs' deeds that determined him, just as he had determined his deeds, and yet it was his character I could not help examining. I could not avoid looking for the best and the worst in him. I wanted to judge him both greatest and least. His ability to bat and bowl had little part in summing him up, only in condemning him. He did throw the ball prettily over Dakhla, but it was not enough to show skill and flair: I wanted hubris as well, to see a chance that he could be cut down. Odd, really, because he was just an ordinary bloke who had done spectacularly well at sport. By becoming one of the mighties he had given away his soul to an admiring public. So to know, to find that he was only a bloke, with the qualities and shortcomings of all blokes, was to kick away the pedestal. He was what Youssef in Casablanca wanted to be. Thus is it ever for those in competition.

Both Suggs and Mike Garnham were used to this attitude from others. They felt beleaguered, and I felt sorry for that. They batted defensively, apologists for their sport. 'I'm not really a cricket supporter; it's just my job,' said Mike. He went through the usual patter of excuses that crop up in radio and television interviews after a bad Test. 'It's a professional game, run by amateurs', 'It's the journalists' fault', 'It's always Botham, Botham, Botham, never the game'. They spoke with broken spirit. The celebration and the nationalism were gone, and only a long drudging innings was left for them. They lacked Bougja's boundless optimism. But perhaps Poms only win by whingeing.

To their credit, Red and George refused to judge Suggs and Mike, publicly at least. And Emma said cricket bored her, though she was fairly sure her father watched it. Red and George just enjoyed booting the ball around with people who had seen one before. And they were always happy to go out for a beer with other good sports. On the sandflats, while waiting in the convoy, the Dutch from the truck set up a rival game of rather limp-wristed football alongside the rugby practice.

'Eurotrash,' commented Red.

At last it was back to the vehicles to start the engines. There were many more fits than starts on this part of the trip, as the French kept breaking down. Most of the convoy was French, in dreadful old Renault 4s and Peugeot 404s, en route to Dakar in Senegal where they hoped to sell them. Do they have MOTs in France?

We did a lot of waiting during the fits. Waiting was like driving the road from Agadir to Dakhla, except without the movement. We quickly became bored with the scenery. We became bored with each other. Then we became bored, one by one, with everyone in the convoy. I even saw Emma talking about cricket with Suggs. So we went back to the Land Rover and played cards with each other. Backgammon scores started running into hundreds.

'God, it's dull.'

Pause.

'You can say that again.'

Short pause.

'Say what again?'

'God, it's dull.'

Silence.

'You can say that again.'

After Dakhla the road became more and more ropy and our momentum ever more fitful. When the Moroccan military abandoned us to make our own way over the last few miles to Mauritania, it was just sand. We spent hours digging the French out of dunes, changing their tyres for them, roping the rusting exhausts to their roof-racks and using the Dust Busters' smart front-winch. Whenever the French dug themselves in, the British among us mounted a British-led expedition in Land Rovers with a few places allotted for observers from European nations.

'She's really earning her spurs,' remarked George of Mistress Quickly. He started to warm to her in the desert. She would glide over the soft sand, and when she sank in he would slam into low ratio and she would grind out again.

At all times we had to stick to the designated track, for we were now crossing a minefield. We knew of the mines mainly from the Moroccan soldiers' worry about the expense incurred when they exploded – mines are not cheap. But I was disappointed not to see a rotting wooden sign with a stencilled skull and crossbones bearing the words 'Achtung Minen', and perhaps a Jerry helmet hanging off it. No style, your modern sapper. Jesper threw stones from the marked track at likely-looking spots, but even Suggs pointed out that he would not be universally popular if he set one off. A Frenchman died in the following week's convoy when he tried to overtake off the track and he ran over one.

The Dutch truck annoyed the rest of Europe by ploughing through the sand, churning the surface crust and rutting it to make it impossible for the smaller cars to negotiate. Neither did they help to push the cars out, but sat in their vehicle listening to techno-pulp music instead. 'A plague and a curse on the Dutch,' we cried. And later it came true. When they reached the border, the Dutch loaded their truck on to a train to skip the worst of the desert drive to the Mauritanian capital, Nouakchott. Once the lorry was on the train, they were not able to leave it. A stomach bug struck, and their assorted alimentary canals evacuated in both directions. Twelve hours down the track, the truck was swimming in the stuff.

'Spewin'?' asked Jesper.

'Yes,' we said.

We made it unscathed to the Mauritanian border town of Nouadhibou, and there a sea change came over the character of the Arab people. Up until then they had often been charming as individuals but, as a mass, conniving and untrustworthy. In Mauritania, however, they lost their desire to aspire. They were even generous in a vague kind of way.

We had no local currency. The man in the bread shop thought of taking a proffered pen in exchange for a loaf. Then he thought, oh, well, no, you have as much bread as you like. Butter with it? Jam? A child came up with the usual: 'Tourist, give me a . . .' but his voice trailed off, as if to say, '. . . biro. No. Actually, forget it, I've got one.' This was the nature of Mauritania.

Araby's last insult was the man named Achmed, the schlimy one. We needed a guide for the 300-mile drive from Nouadhibou to Nouakchott. Although half of the drive was along the beach, the rest was across quicksand flats and towering dunes. People had been lost for days there – some of whom we met later. You can get into a situation in the desert where you simply drive around in circles.

Achmed, in flowing white *boubou*, the local version of the jellaba, and cool-guy mirrored sunglasses, was recommended as a guide by the police. He was a short man with broken raptor nose, classic jawline and shifty manner. He failed to endear himself to us immediately. He was aggressive, expensive and hopelessly lazy. He lied and exaggerated.

'You must drive in the desert. The train is broken. Last week fifty people died on it in a crash,' he fibbed.

He annoyed the Dust Busters at once by announcing that he did not like women and by attempting to smoke in their car. He got on everyone's nerves by cadging all he could, from cigarettes to food, shoes and a pair of binoculars. He even rocked Urs's normal calmness by getting caught stealing one of Lara's silver bangles. He tried to tell George how to drive. Our collective mastery of the French language went as far as 'teaching your grandmother', but could not cope with 'to suck eggs'. So we let it pass and sat with him in brooding silence. Perhaps he thought we were being rude about his grandmother.

There was also officialdom, but that is the same in every country. I was surprised how painless a brush we had with it in Nouadhibou, but I was more surprised at the manner in which we escaped its wrath.

There is not much for a policeman to do on desert duty. If his solitary wooden shack attracts flies it is an excitement. If he kills one, doubly so. And that is why he finds fun in form-filling. If a car comes, it makes his day; his week, even. When a convoy passes, he may go delirious with bureaucracy.

We had slipped through the Nouadhibou check on the way in without the gurgling guard noticing that our Mauritanian visas did not start for three days. Unfortunately, on the way out with Achmed, the guard did notice, and for him, this was bliss. Better still, Emma, who never held authority in any great regard, whiled away the empty minutes by taking pictures. A camera confiscation – what more could there be to life? The guard's official badge and epaulettes shone and bristled with officious pride. His reactolite sunglasses darkened and lightened gleefully as he dodged in and out of his shack, and he milked it as only an official can.

Did we not realise the seriousness of our position? Our visas showed we did not exist until next Tuesday. Did we not also understand the importance of keeping top-secret military installations, such as his shack, top secret? This was a matter for the army as well as the police, possibly even the government; maybe some of his relations would have to know.

We were in the curious position of officially not existing and of possessing unofficial pictures of places that officially do not exist. But quoting Tweedledum logic at officials is rarely helpful as they are better at it. Usually you outface them nicely, firmly and attritionally until they crack and let you go. But instead, an extraordinary event took place. Emma started to blub.

Her Catholic-Irish toughness vanished and tears trickled down her face. She sniffed and a blob of snot fell out of her nose and on to her shirt. She wept. The official looked confused. Hysterical women were not regulation. No longer a matter for the army, this was now a matter for a handkerchief. He gave her back her camera and offered her a tissue. He garnered his resources once more. Still the situation was grave, he stressed. She had taken an unauthorised photograph and the film must be exposed.

Emma cradled her camera and looked at the button that would unclasp its back as if contemplating an abortion. Her eyes turned on the tear taps harder. 'Non,' she said, then blurted again: 'Non.'

The official tried the question of national security once more. 'Non.' Sniff.

'Why does she cry?' he asked me, and for the first time I saw that the ploy was working. Clever Emma. 'One cries in a war and when babies die, not about cameras,' he said.

Maudlin is as maudlin does. I began a maudlin burble in soft and indistinct French, stressing words like 'understand', 'seriousness', 'duty', 'poor travellers from a distant land', 'guests of your country', and rising to a crescendo: 'Never again . . . quite understand . . . tremendous gratitude . . . diplomatic relations restored . . . happy days and silly women.' Holding his limp tissue in his hand, his badge sagging from his pocket and a certain flaccidity in his epaulettes, he motioned us out of the door. And visas?

Just go.

We went south, quickly. By now we were just the three Land Rovers: ourselves, the Dust Busters and the Swiss Family Robinson. The Lads had forged ahead on the train with the by now unhygienic Dutch.

We drove through the Arguin Bank National Park, a resort of millions of migrating birds, and therefore one of Father's favourites. Pink flamingos and great chin-bagged slow flapping flocks of white pelicans scattered as we drove through them. Dippers, plovers and whimbrels pattered, legs blurring across the sand towards the water as we came near. Father had said look out for the slender-billed curlew, but then added that there was only one left and it was probably dead. We did not see it, or if we did, it was wearing a false bill. Bit sad, really.

Also sad was the sight of the pathetic sharks. The local people caught them in nets, hammerheads and blues up to six feet long, and cut off their dorsal fins while the fish lay gasping on the beach. The fins were exported to western civilisation to make expensive soup in funny foreign restaurants. The sharks were left to flap around on the sand until they died. Not so civilised.

Away from the beaches, the desert itself held life at night. The whistling yips of the jackal covens carried in the witching moonlight and the bright arc of the Milky Way. On the ground, bold and wide-eyed desert gerbils held scampering matches around our sleeping bags, unfussed by human presence.

By day in the desert there were few features in the landscape to mark our progress. We had seen our first camels in Morocco; in the desert proper we saw our first camel skeletons. Then, just as the Arab faces started to give way to the rounder, darker faces from the south, we passed our first acacias – those spiky flat-topped trees that stand bent like old men, backs to the wind – among the scrub of the desert hinterland. That was when we knew we had left the southern part of the Northern Sahara to go into the northern part of the Southern Sahara – and real Black Africa.

But not black enough. The sand still permeated every piece of kit we owned: cameras, sleeping bags, toothpaste – nothing was safe. Coffee came with two teaspoons of sugar and a teaspoon of sand. Seven maids with seven mops and the bitter tears of the carpenter would have needed a rolling contract and a large incentive package to get this lot shifted.

It was not, however, a problem for the Dust Busters. They, after all, owned a Dust Buster vacuum cleaner as well as brushes, two types of shower (one cold and one solar-heated), a GPS satellite tracking system to give their position and a gas-powered fridge. Michelle and Hazel dusted while Neil drove. GPS works by picking up radio waves from satellites to give a fix, a speed, an altitude and an ETA at Inverness Airport if you felt like it – an amazing piece of kit. All it lacked was the ability to say, 'Yup, still sandy out there,' to be perfect. It needs three satellites hanging overhead to give accurate information. Satellites, we learned, are like London buses: you can wait ages for one, and then four come at once.

Of other humans, we saw only enough to remark on the subtle change in their faces. But when we did see people, there was trouble. And it was always Achmed's fault.

Achmed offered a lift to a village chief we met. We pointed out to

Achmed that although we would be delighted to take him, we were already tight for space and the chief would have to travel on the roof of one of the Land Rovers. At this, the chief, a proud fellow in a blue *boubou*, lost his cool. 'Travel on the roof?' he shouted. 'I am not a monkey. I am not a dog. I am not a . . . a . . . pelican!'

But it was over the next incident that relations with Achmed fell to their lowest ebb.

If there was any talking to be done, Red invariably found himself doing it. He could embroil himself in a conversation of such pointlessness in languages so strange to him that officials and money-grabbers in all countries were left speechless and befuddled. It was difficult to tell whether he did it out of boredom, keen interest, or if he simply could not help himself. One of Achmed's sins was to guide us immaculately into a pay-and-display car park in a small village. There was no indication that it was a Mauritanian NCP, no sign saying, 'Have you paid and displayed?' So it was bad luck that it was there that the Swiss Family Robinson's Land Rover broke down. The parking attendant approached with a fine worth his week's salary.

Achmed then involved Red in conversation on a different topic – and bits of fried tuna on biscuits – with the village elders in a far-flung hut in another part of the village. Meanwhile, our situation in the car park was becoming more and more unpleasant. Each Land Rover had to be guarded front and back from marauding children and other shirkers while, at the same time, it needed three people to take apart Urs's steering column, which had seized up during the drive over one of Achmed's more entertaining dunes.

The parking attendant had called on all members of the village council not having tuna with Red to join him and press his case. They produced type-written documents, agreements from the last council meeting about parking regulations, and printed parking tickets with an extra zero added to the price in pencil. Four and a half million square miles of desert for us to stop in, and Achmed guides us unerringly to a metered zone.

The petty wrangle started to get ugly and there was still no sign of Red. 'There are many bosses here,' observed a laconic black guy, squatting nearby on the bones of a baleen whale.

It was all a little anxious but we finally escaped without losing Red or any money. We shored up the steering relay as best we could and drove off to look for the boy. We found him deep in his hut and deeper still into the South Africa Question and the Problems Involved in Fishing With Dolphins.

That night we camped outside the village, fending off jackals, gerbils and the ever-persistent parking attendant, and wrote a letter of recommendation for Achmed to show to his future potential punters. We took sore advantage of his inability to speak English, or read at all, I admit, and spiced it with words he might think were approving. It went like this:

TO WHOM IT MAY CONCERN:

Achmed took out party of three Land Rovers from Nouadhibou to Nouakchott through the Arguin Bank National Park. I am delighted to report that he is perfectly useless at his job and would barely make an excellent guide in a Butlin's holiday camp. It gives me great pleasure to name him Fuckwit of the Year 1994 for all activities concerning sand, Land Rovers and Sponging Anything He Can Get From Tourists.

I would hardly trust him to sit the right way on a lavatory seat and when it comes to guiding tourists, I doubt enormously if he could find his way out of a paper bag. The words piss-up and brewery spring to mind. If you value your clutch, your gearbox or your steering column, let him get as close to it as any sizeable bargepole will allow. In fact, if you continue to read this letter of recommendation, you will find yourself inextricably involved in a ceaseless round of parking attendants, strange men in blue clothes who compare themselves to pelicans, and a good chance of sinking into the biggest erg this side of Luxor.

There are nine of us in this party, from Ireland, England, Germany and Switzerland, and we are absolutely unanimous in our loathing of this paltry little man. We discard him entirely and wish you the very best of luck on your trip.

Yours faithfully, etc.

Gloating over the insult, we arrived at the bustle and traffic of

Nouakchott. It was a shock after the desert. George had to remember the rules of the road again – and then instantly forget them when he saw how everybody else drove. 'Indicating is obviously something only infidels do,' observed Red.

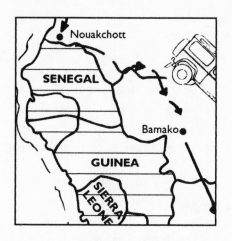

C h a p t e r 5

NANCY

Mauritania and Mali. Red, Emma, George and Me in Mistress Quickly. Neil, Hazel and Michelle in the Dust Busters' Land Rover. 200 days to the World Cup opening ceremony.

N ouakchott held us transfixed in a rabbit-like trance for longer than we had hoped. Our aim was to press on speedily to the greater rugby-playing nations of West Africa like the Ivory Coast, but somehow Nouakchott kept us back. In some ways it was relief after the long desert thrash, and a rest before the next 1,000-mile section to the Mali capital, Bamako. But mostly it was an effect similar to Alice's experience with the Red Queen: 'Now, *here*, you see, it takes all the running *you* can do, to stay in the same place.'

Luckily, in Nouakchott Nancy is all you need to know, rather like Jane Charley in London. Nancy is the answer to every dusty desert traveller's prayer. She is everyone's friend, is fun and has a family of four, from teens to twenties. She is polyglot. She is small, dark-haired, smiles all the time, is both mildly rounded and mannered. She was once English. She is now Mauritanian and honorary British consul. Nancy Abeiderrahmane can put you in touch with anyone, from government ministers to desert herdsmen. She is in love with her adopted country. She is its best British brochure.

Nancy is also fond of Mauritania's limitless capacity for whimsy. She told, with a twinkling eye, the story of the American cruise-liner that scheduled a stop in Nouakchott. 'Everyone was very excited,' she said. 'We hadn't had tourists here before and everyone knew that other countries had tourists, so why not Mauritania? The port held a special berth open. Unfortunately, a little trawler nipped into the space and was busy refuelling. The Americans spent the night anchored outside the port and then sailed away. They came again, but the same thing happened.

'The third time they came, they managed to dock, no problem. All the American tourists came ashore. All the taxis were waiting. Everyone was delighted until someone remembered that tourists need visas to enter Mauritania, so the Americans couldn't leave the port. There was a great kerfuffle and argument until someone else pointed out that it might be all right if they all left their passports behind, so that is what they did. Their day in Nouakchott was a great success, but at the end of it they all managed to get lost, and got into taxis to the other end of town. That is very Mauritanian.'

Nancy was born in England of a Welsh father who went to live in America and then South Africa, and a Russian mother who moved to Spain. Nancy followed her mother. She speaks English, Spanish, French and Hassini Arabic fluently and idiomatically. She lives in a house in Nouakchott with showers, carpets, even a cook and a television – and we were grateful to her for that.

'Actually, it's only a tent,' she said deprecatingly. 'Nouakchott is just a camp. They build the houses higgledy-piggledy up and down the sand dunes. There is no proper sewage system here.'

Nancy was married to the president of a Mauritanian bank. Britain needed an honorary consul and she was the choice of the then British ambassador to Morocco. But her husband was also a government minister, it was the time of the Gulf War and Mauritania is a Muslim country. Nancy, herself, is nominally a Muslim and wears the all-in-one wrap-up dress that all Muslim women wear. 'Really the women run the country,' she pointed out. 'They have all the gold stalls in the market. This dress, it's just a kind of modesty.'

Luckily for Britain, Nancy's husband left her and the path was clear. She held a Mad Hatter's Tea Party for other embassy women in Nouakchott to celebrate her appointment. 'Oh, it was so funny. Everyone in such silly hats,' she said. Then she added worriedly, 'But don't do anything like die, will you? That would be too complicated. Normally I just answer the telephone and say, "No, I don't do visas," and "No, you can't travel overland to Morocco from here."'

Nancy was last on the list of Things to Look Out For from my father. She marked the end of his North African patch, but she was at the top end of his Darwinian scale, having helped him to set up his Arguin Bank tours. She was a rock for us, too. I rang her as soon as we arrived.

'I have a cook,' she said. 'And a shower.'

No, no. We were tough travellers and were off to negotiate camping in the grounds of a local hotel.

The others were not pleased. 'I can't believe you said that, Charlie,' said Red. But I had accepted an invitation to lunch the next day, so there were three loud cheers for that.

Our herd of Land Rovers found the hotel, a large one by the beach, and the Dust Buster Michelle and I went inside to discuss a fee. It was strangely empty. There were a few Senegalese workmen asleep on the carpets in the large tiled foyer. It also lacked electricity. Michelle and I went further into the gloom in search of life. We came upon a fat man with a beard, and his thin and ascetic sidekick.

'Camping?' we asked.

This was a new one on him. He told us that he was the hotel's owner. Yes, it was undergoing refurbishment. It would be ready for a UNICEF conference next year. We told him that we were impressed.

'Camping is free,' he announced expansively. 'A gift.'

'Showers?'

'Showers are not free.'

The thin one showed me a shower. It looked like the refurbishment would be a big job. Just killing the cockroaches would take a while. By the time I came back, the fat one had already asked Michelle to marry him. 'He was very nice about it,' she said afterwards. 'He said I was pretty and he was looking for a fiancée.'

'That is very Mauritanian,' said Nancy the next day. We told her about the grasping Achmed. 'That is not very Mauritanian,' was her comment.

I went to visit Nancy at work. She runs a dairy producing the only pasteurised camels' milk outside Saudi Arabia. It won the 1993 Rolex Award for Enterprise. The milk is lighter and frothier than cows' milk, delicious, and is popular with Mauritanian men because it is so low in fat. Mauritanian women prefer cows' milk because fat, for them, is beautiful. It was easy to see which of the hotel-owners drank which. Michelle, I should add, is not fat, yet still strangely attractive to Mauritanian men.

The camels' milk comes from herds around Nouakchott. It is all milked by hand. How does it get to you without going off in this heat? 'Oh, the men run very fast with the buckets,' said Nancy. 'Actually, it is very difficult to make it go sour, much more so than with cows' milk. We have had great trouble making cheese out of it for that reason, but we have just managed to. We are going to export it to Fortnum & Mason, and Harrods.'

Running a dairy is a seven-day-week business. I cannot remember Jane Charley working a seven-day week. Nancy still found time to show us around. She took us to the covered market in the town centre. Everyone greeted her: 'Bonjour, Tiviski!'

'I was on television the other day,' she explained. 'Tiviski is the name of my dairy.'

She showed us beautiful black bangles decorated with intricate silverwork. 'No, they are not ebony,' she told us. 'They are black plastic drainpipes. The silversmiths found that the ebony kept cracking, and drainpipe is much more convenient. You can buy it in standard sizes.' There was leatherwork to buy there, too, all etched in tiny, detailed clever patterns. Biro work, it turned out, as Bic biros are much better for inking camel skins than the old-fashioned vegetable dyes and blood.

In the evening Nancy joined us at a restaurant, but had to leave early to go back to work. 'I think one of my men is cheating me,' she said sadly. 'There is a difference between the amount of milk I order and the amount I pay for, so I have left them to count the barrels. Unfortunately, one of the men I have left is the man I suspect.'

That is *very* Mauritanian.

It is also Mauritanian not to drink alcohol. After the desert trip we were gasping. We had asked about the chance of a snifter in our hotel. The thin man took me aside conspiratorially. 'I know a man who has wine,' he whispered. 'One bottle.' It was outrageously expensive. It would have had to have been Krug to be anywhere near worth the price.

In a roundabout way, we broached the subject with Nancy.

'Do they play rugby in Mauritania?' asked George.

'Oh no. No team games. No physical exercise at all here. They play a kind of draughts in the street with squares they scratch in the sand, but that's it.'

'Oh.'

'I think there is a French team at the Racing Club. You could ask there,' she suggested.

We went at once to the Racing Club. It was not quite the same as its grand namesake in Paris, where the rugby team drink champagne at half-time. In Nouakchott the Racing Club was a low building with a bar and some tennis courts. A bar? We looked again. It was a bar, all right. A bottle of whisky stood behind it, smuggled in through an embassy. Right, whiskies all round, and damn the exorbitance.

There was, I discovered, rather half-heartedly leaving the others burying their noses in drink, a rugby club in Nouakchott, and it was run by the French. A Monsieur Delaye arranged to come and meet me at the Racing Club the following evening.

I turned up to watch a group of French schoolchildren practising How to Be Rude to Native Staff at the bar while I waited. 'Hey, you, waiter. Coke. Now!' one shouted. But Monsieur Delaye was as good as his name. I inquired about him again. The Racing Club chairman I had spoken to the day before seemed rather confused. 'Monsieur Delaye? But he has nothing to do with rugby in Mauritania,' he said. This Mauritanianness was all-pervading. 'You must speak with Monsieur Voteau, n'est-ce pas, Mokhtar?'

He turned to the man named Mokhtar, a vast fellow with a Frank Bruno forehead and Muhammad Ali hands who was sitting beside him. 'May I present Mokhtar, Monsieur Jacoby,' said the chairman.

I shook Mokhtar's hand. It would be more accurate to say that

Mokhtar shook my hand, almost up to the elbow. 'Enchanté, Monsieur Jacoby,' he rumbled in Satchmo tones. 'Monsieur Voteau you want? No, no. I am in charge of rugby in Mauritania.' And at that point I left them, sanity still intact.

Nancy knew Mokhtar, of course. 'Such hands!' she said. 'He runs a hotel. I know a man who used to go to the hotel each week just for the pleasure of shaking hands with him.'

We had to leave Mauritania for Mali, which lay to the south, and then Ivory Coast. We also had to bid the Dust Busters and the Swiss Family Robinson farewell as they were driving to Dakar in Senegal. But Nouakchott had not finished with us yet.

Red drove into a pole. Not a man from Warsaw, as you will have worked out, but a metal spike in the ground. It put a hole in Mistress Quickly's radiator. It went well with the hole George had put in it the day before.

The story began with the oil-cooler that the Lads had thrown away in Dakhla and George had salvaged. It was a large hollow twisted lump of metal, bristling with more metal, which looked like part of a barbecue. It was meant to sit behind the radiator grille and cool the oil that flows through it. Finding the time to fit it was the problem. We could never quite settle enough during all our waiting at borders, because at any moment we might have to leave. So it sat under our feet. Somehow it managed to get under everyone's feet. It was jagged enough to scratch and tear, solid enough to stub toes and big enough to get in the way. It was also fragile, claimed George, so could not be left to jolt around with the luggage. There were times, I felt, when George could be insensitive.

George started by loving that car part. And it responded by loving George – or at least, it did not get in his way like it did in ours. George defended it against our chorus of disapproval. Meanwhile, it banged snidely into us and our belongings all the way across the Sahara. Then George came to fit it, and it turned on him. One of the sharper bits bumped into the radiator and holed it below the Plimsoll line. Pee-sosh-it. So off we went through the maze of Nouakchott's bigger open-air market, where you can buy anything from a pressure-cooker to a hand grenade, to find a welding shop and get the radiator fixed. The first time.

George had lost his patience with the oil-cooler by this stage, so we decided to get rid of it. Why not swap it for a pressure-cooker? We did not need a hand grenade. The man in the saucepan shop stroked his beard. He would have to ask a friend of his who was a mechanic whether it was worth it. That would take an hour. He would meet us in the sticky flyblown café at the end of saucepan alley and let us know. It was while parking the Land Rover outside the café that Red drove into the pole. An hour later, the saucepan man told us he did not want it. I expect a passing muezzin had said it was infested with evil spirits.

It had been quite Moroccan to try to sell tourists car parts that the tourists did not need. It was very Mauritanian to walk off the street into a bar, and ask the tourist if he had any car parts for sale. 'Tyres? Headlights? I see you have two headlights,' as if to say that two is at least one more than the legal requirement. But none of them wanted to buy the oil-cooler.

We went back to the welding shop in the afternoon. Its owner was glad to see us. And the work went on and on. It went on so late that George and Red went back to the home of Mohammed, the owner, and ate couscous with him. We offered him the oil-cooler in part exchange for the price of the work. Mohammed did not want it. We gave it to him as a present. As we drove away, Red reflected that Mohammed's shop would probably go bust now, or his wife would die – the curse of the cooler.

That cooler – and we were sure that it had a lot to do with that cooler – spawned an outbreak of stupidity in our party unparalleled before or since. Someone at the welding shop had pinched one of George's tools and he made great play of trying to find it in the sand when we went back to look for it next morning. That is not, however, the stupid bit. When we still could not find it, someone generously came in the car with us to show us the best way out of Nouakchott for Kiffa, on the Mali road, and he pinched my wallet. Africa is a continent of degenerate freeloaders like him, but perhaps only insofar as Europe is a continent of colonial bloodsuckers. That is not the stupid bit, either.

On the way to Kiffa we passed serried stacks of sand dunes, which are piling up behind Nouakchott and threatening to consume it. Normally the dunes shift harmlessly into the sea. Just one big storm might do it. Tired of sand, we decided to leave the main road and take a scenic route throught the more fertile plains around the Senegal River. That is still not the stupid bit, but the stupid bit started there.

The really stupid bit came after the fairly silly bit where we camped in the bush near the river, turned on the battery lights inside the mosquito net and started a gigantic ugly-bug disco. There were thousands upon thousands of flying insects, from tiny mosquitos, which whined like Stukas, to great flying crickets and lacewings which sputtered along like Sopwith Camels. I put up my own mosquito net inside the big one, but it served only to trap them inside. I woke up next morning on a mattress of – I do not joke – around 3,500 insects, based on a mean of twenty per square inch, including a large locust which had lost most of its limbs. Some of the small coleoptera might have been new to science. 'Right,' I said. 'Those of you not too legless to walk, carry the others home.'

The really stupid bit was further along the scenic route where the tarmac road stopped and we followed a track in and out of dry riverbeds, past smashed concrete bridges, in the drive round to Kiffa.

We picked up a guide in a rank little village called Mbout. He was an old fellow in a long blue *boubou*, nearly blind from dreadful cataracts in his eyes. He looked like a black version of Steptoe. 'You revolting old man,' we reminded him, but he had not been able to watch that programme. We did not want him to come, he just got in the car.

We came to a bridge, too wrecked to use, over a riverbed too steep to cross, and set off left, uptrickle and back towards the desert, to find flatter banks. At first we thought Steptoe knew the way. He waved his hand whenever we went off course and shouted, 'Hi! Hi! Ai-wish, ai-wish!' We blooming well wish too, mate. He led us in a great circle all afternoon back to just north of Mbout. We let him go.

But it was not close enough to Mbout that it was worth going back there. Nor was it exactly on the road. We had no water, apart from a gallon the colour of orange squash from a village we had passed. A gallon is the recommended intake for one person per day. Our gas bottle had run out, our food was going bad. And Red was sick. He had a huge thirst; he had to drink, but could not hold it down. It was not a good night.

The thought of running out of water was ridiculous, really. We were never more than twenty miles from a village and we had powerful pills to purify any water we obtained. But it was extremely demoralising. The worst of thirst is the feeling of panic. Each sip was treasured as if it might be our last. We stopped sweating and our tongues felt like bits of leather belt. I did not actually feel the others' tongues, of course, but mine did.

The next morning we left at 6.30am, heading for the main road to Kiffa. Some eighty miles later across open country and Cheshire cat tracks we hit it. There was much relief when we finally made it and a round of cold drinks that made the famous scene in *Ice Cold in Alex*, where they have their first beer for ninety monochrome minutes, look like a vicarage tea party.

Gradually, as we drove away from the arid regions and neared the Senegal River and Mali, tall cathedral rocks began to break up the dunes, and then a carpet of greenery crept across the mat of the desert. There was still a lot of sand, but more and more grasses and shrubs. These were proper camomile greens, jungle greens, still with the sunblasted starving browns underneath. It was an emptiness of tinder scrub, either waiting to catch fire, or already ablaze, or blackened and burned out. 'Take my breath awaaaaaaaaay,' we sang happily as we drove through the flames.

The wildlife changed, too. Hornbills with curious conky beaks flapped crazily, honking in and out of the kindling trees. They looked as if they had just worked out how to fly backwards. Other birds reminded you of English garden birds but the blackbirds and thrushes were irridescent blue and green, the magpies were the size of crows – or were the crows as gaudy as magpies? – and even the bright British goldfinch was outshone in vermilion. And then we were in Mali.

Black Africa begins at the River Niger, which slices Mali in two. All the signs were there: sick-smelling green sewers in the cities with bright red and blue dragonflies playing over them, sticky heat and the sound of automatic gunfire at night.

Bamako is the capital of Mali. The river that swirls through it, four times the size of the Thames, is spanned by low bridges. We crossed it on the Pont des Martyrs. There is a lot in Mali to commemorate the martyrs of colonialism. Concrete totems abound in the rural towns, like war memorials in England, and it was strange to see such harping on the past when what ails the country is the present. One might say the same of the English cenotaph but for Mali's poverty, exaggerated, as in Morocco, by lack of food, all killed by the heat. The land is more fertile than the desert land to the north, but Mali is a drought waiting to happen.

'Not really a rugby nation, Mali,' observed George.

He, Emma and Red had just been to a football match at the national stadium in Bamako – Mali v Angola. It ended in a 0–0 draw. Their eyes were still red.

'Emotional?' I asked.

'Tear gas,' explained Red. 'You should have come.' I had stayed behind to guard Mistress Quickly. 'We were sitting at the back out of trouble,' he added.

'It wasn't very lively during the match,' put in Emma, 'but little scuffles were bursting out all round.'

'And then there were the oranges,' interrupted George.

'Yes,' Red went on. 'Some of the supporters started throwing oranges on to the pitch after the final whistle, and the police returned fire with CS gas.'

George was perplexed to be on the receiving end of riot control. 'We shouted at them, "Not at us!" and then there was this panic crush to get out of the stadium.'

'One guy said that this was normal for a football match here,' said Emma. 'Thank God Mali didn't lose.'

The towns and cities we drove to in Mali were ugly, violent places. Soulless official buildings and barracks beggared with their concrete the private shanty-town houses. Concrete promotes beggary and shanties. The Tuareg rebellion in the north around Timbuctoo seemed to consist of mainly a gangster car-stealing operation. While we were in Nouakchott the Tuaregs had spilled over the border into

Mauritania and pinched, at gunpoint, the Jeep belonging to the head of the United Nations refugee programme. Mugging in Mali is a major industry.

The Dutch truck caught up with us in Bamako. We also met English overland holidaymakers from Truck Africa and Guerba Expeditions, all on a sixteen-week drinkathon to Nairobi. Between them, they had four people mugged in three days. On their last night, the Truck Africans boozed themselves blotto enough to decide to form a vigilante gang to stalk the streets in search of the villains. Not so sensible, we thought. Luckily, and unsurprisingly, they did not find any.

The villages, in contrast, were filled with people who could not stop laughing at us. Mali's country folk live mainly in round mud huts with conical grass roofs, just like the ones in the book we coloured in at pre-prep school in our geography chalking class. I warmed to the grass huts in Mali. My own green grass huts had been so successful, when I was six, that I coloured the tundra page and the pyramids page green as well. I failed my Geography O-level.

This village jolliness was infectious. We stopped at Sebabougou to ask the way to Doubabougou. Red strode from the car like a modern Stanley in shorts. The ladies in the millet field fell about with laughter. Red gave them one of his businessman's winning smiles. They hooted. He raised his hand in greeting. Tears fell down their faces. 'Doubabougou?' he said, seriously. They were gasping for air and rolling around. Even we were giggling in the Land Rover.

There was, we decided, a small chance that these names were fictitious. If a foreigner came to a village in Somerset and asked the way to Exeter, it might appeal to a schoolboy sense of humour to give him a list of towns to ask for on the way with names like Wotaplonker and Hiyafartface.

The roads in Mali had a sense of humour as well. Roads is perhaps too strong a word. They twisted amusingly then suddenly plunged wittily. They bumped and jolted merrily. They laughingly went at right angles to the compass bearing we wanted and then zigged playfully back again. Taking a Land Rover across them was like sitting on a skittish horse, the kind of horse it is difficult to sell, and they went on for the whole 1,000 miles, from outside Nouakchott right up to Bamako. Crash! would go the cutlery box. 'There goes the silver!' would go the cry. Bump! would go the plastic plates bucket. 'Mind the Meissen!' we would shout.

Bridges? 'Bridges, ha!' chuckled the Mali roads. 'See those bridges in Mauritania? Washed away in the first rains. Most of our rivers are dry most of the year anyway.' So every few miles Mistress Quickly nosed gingerly down crumbling riverbanks, ground across dusty riverbeds and elbowed up the banks on the other side.

Despite this problem with roads, Africa is a car-borne continent. Every journey in every city which does not require taking a wheelbarrow requires a car. Yet there are surprisingly few rattling along the roads between the cities. One reason for this may be the Africans' infuriating habit of driving until they run out of petrol. George spent half an hour trying to jump-start a Peugeot before its owner admitted that he was out of juice. It stands to reason that if you conk out in a city, you will never be far from a street petrol salesman, who will be standing by the road with a tall glass jar of four-star, glowing a dull evil ruddy, and a handpump. He can probably also give you a good price for oranges, paper handkerchiefs and the latest black market dollar rate. You do not find them in the countryside.

Every street in Bamako was like Oxford Street on a sweltering summer's day with Christmas-shopping crowds. It is an Oxford Street where people buy goods to sell immediately if they can, and where the bus conductors of the belching battling Bamabuses tout louder than the rest. The green and yellow taxis – 'Donegal colours,' Emma noted – find the best way to pick up fares is to drive into them first. During the argument that follows, the taxi-drivers can work out whether their victim needs to go anywhere.

African driving is based loosely on the original European idea. The same internal-combustion engine pushes passengers from A to B. In England, however, the fact that your car is on the same side of the road as another car means that you are both pointing broadly the same way. You might take that a little further and say that that shared intention breeds a certain camaraderie between you. Well, it does, compared to Africa.

First, rather than on the left or right, they tend to drive in the shade. Secondly, every other road user is an enemy, to be cut up, hooted, shouted or shrugged at. Swerving is obligatory. Headlights are optional. Brakes may be illegal in some countries. Engine oil and first and second gears are for wimps. Luckily, cars go so slowly and are filled with so many wives and grandmothers to act as airbags that personal injury is not an issue.

You would need a new edition of the Highway Code to explain the hand signals. The main ones involve hanging the left arm limply out of the offside window, knuckles trailing just off the ground. As far as we could work out, it meant any of the following: I am going to turn left; I am going to turn right; at a random point between here and Ougadougou I am going to swerve suddenly down a side road to visit my old mother and/or round a pothole and/or into a patch of shade and/or stop/accelerate sharply; I am going to flick the ash off my cigarette; I am quite safe in motor cars, apart from a tendency to grab passing cyclists; I need to air my arm; that shop over there is where I buy my wheelbarrows; and finally, please overtake – there is nothing beyond me except a twenty-ton truck overloaded to forty tons on its side in a large pothole blocking a narrow bridge around a blind corner. You get used to it.

The greatest danger to motorists in Mali, however, was the local constabulary. The police were an endless problem. Their nightly prayer seemed to be 'Give us this day our daily bribe.' And the pleasantry of human nature they had handed in when they picked up their uniforms.

It was the same every time. We would be flagged down by an officer. Another would be parked on his official moped, resting on the handlebars. A third would be in the official hut. The first would ask to see our papers. He would size up the interior of the Land Rover, assess what we were worth while we made every effort to look sallow and penniless, and then the shadow of a thin smile would cross his lips.

'You have committed a' – and they always lisped this last, holiest word – 'contravention.' Replace thin smile with a stinging glare.

It did not matter what we did, they always found something. And then it was into the hut to start bargaining for an hour. We normally paid a tenth of the first figure they pulled out of their peaked caps.

As revenge, we gave them extra presents of out-of-date pills from our clearance-sale stock of medicines. 'Take four of these,' said Red candidly to one, 'every one hour that you are ill. They are good for headaches, stomach upsets and sores.'   'And malaria?'

'Oh yes, and malaria. And rabies,' he added as an afterthought, though he did not expect our bent copper to believe it. Normally they were happiest playing with the little childproof screw-top plastic bottles.

Starting a shouting match was useless. Speaking any French was equally bad. George proved to be the best at dealing with them. He would drive them to impotent fury with his: 'Pardon? No, I don't speak French.' And they would subside fruitlessly and let him go.

A lot of the hassle revolved around not having the right tampons in your passport. Stop smirking there in the cheap seats. Tampon is French for stamp. My worst moment was with a frightful man in an equally frightful village south of Bamako. We started arguing. He started to speak rapidly and wave my passport in my face. My French could not keep up, so I put on one of my soothing grins. 'You think I'm stupid because I'm black!' he shouted. 'Certainly,' I replied, confusing for a moment the word 'noir' with 'Nioro', a small town we had just been through. 'Er, not,' I corrected. 'Absolutely not.' He went exocet, completely, and it took another hour and the help of a passing Peace Corps worker to calm him down enough to accept even a bribe from the former colonialist pig scum. By that time I was on the verge of telling him where he could stick his tampon. One always walked away from encounters like this in a state of disbelief, frustration and humiliation.

Western influence in Mali at its most explicit is based on aid and embassies. We saw two contrasting examples of this on our last two nights in the country. Both were foreign government-aid projects, one represented by a single Peace Corps girl, the other by a Danish company.

One day out of Bamako we were driving along when Red said: 'I think we just passed a white girl on a bike.' We were travelling on a road that was in the process of being built. The foundation was laid so we made good progress, but every now and then we came to a place where they were laying tar, or a great caterpillar truck blocked the way, so we had to turn round and drive back for a few miles to find a way round the obstacle. We made one of these diversions after Red's sighting, and five minutes later we passed the girl again.

'Definitely white,' said Red. So we pulled over and off he went to chat her up ('Red's scored,' we sniggered). Her bicycle was broken and was being towed by a local, so we knew she was likely to be indigenous. She was Peace Corps, Red reported, and had asked us all to stay. Beers all round, we thought. Actually, she lived in a mud hut in a village built entirely of mud.

Christine was a twenty-something Californian blonde, a Peace Corps volunteer who had left air-conditioned San Francisco for all this muddery. She had been living alone in a south Malian village for two years as part of a local education programme. Alone is not quite true, as Malian villages have little sense of privacy, but compared with them she was almost a hermit. Many Africans cannot understand the Westerner's obsession with privacy. There is a tribe in northern Cameroon which explains the way we draw our curtains and lock our doors at night by a legend which has it that we are really reincarnations of black sorcerers, and that we take off our white skins and sleep in the black. Fourteen people and seven children came round for tea with Christine the night we were there.

Mali is thick with children. It is a baby factory, and not one that would earn a British Standards kitemark. Christine worked in a village where infant mortality was running at twenty per cent, a crisis level. The Save the Children Fund people had recently come down from Bamako with a family-planning video. 'The people in the village loved it,' said Christine. 'Most of them hadn't seen a TV before, so they just sat and gawped at it. There was a bit of glare off the screen, too, and the audio was kind of fuzzy. I asked them afterwards if they understood it and most of them did. But they need their children to work in the fields.' Christine also explained that in Mali sex was the choice of men, rather than women.

The video failed to say where they could buy contraceptives, so it was lucky that Christine was on hand to tell everyone. Save the Children just showed the video and left. 'At least the instruction leaflet for the condoms has improved,' she said. 'It used to show a picture of someone disposing of a condom in a porcelain toilet. Nobody had seen one of those before. They thought the condom didn't work unless they had porcelain toilets.'

Mali is on the front bumper of the accident that is soon to hit the world. The human population is nowhere near saturation point, but it is thought to be growing at a daily rate of all the people who live in Bristol. And, according to the World Bank medium projection, in my children's lifetime, maybe yours, the figure for human population will reach eleven billion, and then it will follow precisely the pattern followed by every unitary population figure from fish in the sea to fleas on a dog. There will be too many people. Population will reach saturation. It will dive dramatically and hideously, climb again, fall less far, climb, and eventually even out to a sustainable level. This has not yet happened on a world scale, but when it does Mali will be one of the first countries hit. Looking at Mali you might ask yourself which of the Four Horsemen of the Apocalypse will do the dirty work. The Conqueror? War? Famine? Death? Whichever it is, we will have to get used to seeing a lot more stiffs.

The Malian way of life is simply encouraging the accident; putting a foot on the accelerator and not watching the road ahead. The benefits of Western civilisation will not be able to solve Mali's problem. Education, aid and diplomacy will not filter through in time. Perhaps it would be better if the first crash happened sooner rather than later, so that people could start rebuilding the world – if civilisation can cope with just standing back and admiring the carnage. Right now, Malthus would blink.

On a domestic level, Christine's hospitality was extremely well received. We went to her mud hut and ate rice and peanut oil with our fingers out of a huge washing-up bowl. It involved the same technique as *tajine*, but less of it fell into my mint tea. She had a loo (a hole in the ground) and a shower (a hole in the ground with a bucket beside it). Her parents had come to visit her from the States and had been amazed. It was great luxury for us.

The greatest luxury was to come. The next night we were on our way out of a town on the border when the police stopped us. They wanted a bribe, so they invented (thin smile) a *contravention*. Rather than pay it, we said we would go back into the town to the police commissariat. If we did that, our outraged officers would get no bribe, so we thought they might give up and let us pass immediately. We were calling their bluff. But no cigar, so back to town we had to go.

Guess who was travelling with us by this time? No clues. Give up? Jesper. It had to be. He had bowled up in Bamako and needed a lift to Ivory Coast. Passing a Danish aid project on the way to the commissariat, we decided to drop in on the strength of his presence in our party.

Jesper had an astonishing effect on the Danes there, who all had funny names too, like Karsten, Henrik and Knud. They were a boisterous bunch, mostly fair-haired. They would not have looked out of place in helmets with cow horns sticking out at the side doing a spot of looting and pillaging in England and Ireland. That was years ago, though. Now, thanks to Jesper, we were the long-lost mates. Nothing was too much trouble. Stay? No problem. Beer, steak and chips, showers (no buckets) and real Danish bacon for breakfast. Their generosity was equal to Christine's, but on a different level. Asgard is probably like this. It was a Night of the Long Hangover, but we did not mind. A big thumbs-up for Denmark.

Unlike the Peace Corps, this lot had everything laid on. They had no difficulty getting their fixers to fix our problem with the police. There were ten of them in charge of 500 locals digging pipelines for a new water supply for the town. Everything was air-con, servants and making the most in the European way of a miserable place – a little slice of Danish pastry for the African hard cheese. Some of them had been in Africa for twenty years. Christine made the best of her time by trying to go native, but her thirty-month posting was almost over. Nancy, by going completely native, I still believe had it right.

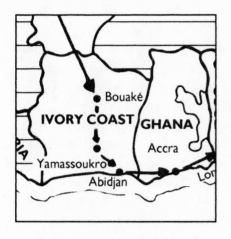

C h a p t e r 6

THE
ELEPHANTS

Ivory Coast. Emma, Red, George and me in Mistress Quickly are joined by
Jesper and later, Wicky. 185 days to the World Cup opening ceremony.

The big dribbling back stares through dim and blinking eyes at the rugby ball which is standing on the mound in the ground. A penalty kick. He has a broken nose and half-mast shorts. He takes one purposeful step back. Two. Three. Four. One step to the right. Run up to it, and boot. He misses the posts.

'Clapping a missed kick, that's good,' says Red.

There is an even bigger clap every time they kick it out of the ground altogether.

'It's actually a very slow pace,' comments George.

We are watching a match between two clubs, ASPAA and SIFCOM, in Abidjan, the capital of Ivory Coast, the next country after Mali. The pitch, sponsored by a company, like the teams, is rimmed with palm trees and a housing estate. The grass is thick, but lying doggo in the heat. The sun is burning in a hazy way. The players keep asking for water. An Ivory Coast flag snoozes on top of its pole, the same flag as Ireland's, but upside-down.

We were there as part of our quest to find out about the Ivory Coast national team, known as the Elephants. They won the African Zone matches in Casablanca to earn a place in the World Cup. Against the hopes and prayers of the bookmakers, they beat the favourites Zimbabwe and Namibia in the qualifying matches. They were to be the only African team in the tournament apart from South Africa, who, as host nation went through anyway.

Our first stop had been the national football stadium in Abidjan, which is rather like going to Wembley to ask for directions to Twickenham. So it was no surprise to be sent by a gang of enthusiastic locals to the Abidjan Tennis Club, the local Wimbledon, and from there to a hotel casino. Hotel doormen are famous for their knowledge, and this one was no exception. 'Rugby?' he said. 'You must ask at the US Embassy.'

A faint smile gathered at the corners of our collective lips. The Americans, however, were helpful. Sergeant J.J. Schroeder, with an accent born in the deep South, informed us that the Bar Maquis Paris was where the Abidjan Rugby Club repaired after training every Wednesday.

The Maquis Paris, chez Roland, was indeed imbued with rugby spirit. A corner of it was set aside as a shrine to the game, with cups, photographs of boozy evenings, pennants from visiting clubs – Dakar, Ouagadougou, and even, I was surprised to see, Mauritania. Roland put me in touch with the French, who run the national team. Oddly enough, it turned out that the rugby federation offices were in the basement of the football stadium, in two rooms and a converted loo.

Ivory Coast's qualification for the World Cup was a tremendous boost for the Ivorian national spirit. Everyone in the country was agog and abuzz with the latest news of their team, the first to reach the finals of a World Cup in any team sport. Even my taxi-driver knew about rugby. 'Now we are best in Africa. Soon best in world. We shall beat America,' he told me confidently. As the USA, minor gods indeed in rugby's Pantheon, hadn't quite made it to the World Cup, this remains to be seen.

ASPAA v SIFCOM is an important match, the Ivorian equivalent of Bath v Leicester in England. Although SIFCOM only has one

Ivorian international, ASPAA boasts eleven, with a total of forty-three caps. The little concrete stand is stuffed to bursting with a hundred supporters. Red, George and I are the only white faces there and everyone squeezes up to make room for us. Down below, two French coaches flap up and down the touchline shouting, and Emma hops in and out of their flightpaths taking pictures. Red is craning forward to look at the finer points of technique. We are trying to work out how much worse Ivory Coast are than Scotland, whom they will play in one of their World Cup matches.

'Back row don't go hunting to help the players,' he says. 'Go on, run it!' He sits up as the ASPAA fly-half jump-passes the ball down the threequarter line. The wing drops it. 'That was appalling,' says Red.

'They don't like running at people,' observes George.

'They're kicking it,' says Red. 'It might be because their . . .' pause for roar of clapping '. . . passing isn't slick enough. Go on, go on, go on . . . oh, no,' as ASPAA make a good run to gain seventy-five yards, then drop it.

ASPAA go long on shouting at each other, but short on piling in.

'Quick quick quick! pass the f. . .' says Red. 'Oh. Very good try.' ASPAA have scored. 'Charlie, that's called a try, when the guy sets the ball down there. It's like making a contract in bridge.'

The ASPAA number 13 converts it. The crowd ooh-oohs and whistles.

We found Abidjan a gem among the African west-coast capitals, which range in a line of five across a stretch of coastline only 400 miles long. Abidjan was high-rise and high-tech above the shanties and the shopfronts, in gleaming glass and steel, and proper tarmac roads. Accra, capital of Ghana, Lomé in Togo, and Cotonou in Benin were dustier versions. In Accra, Lomé and Cotonou the roads were mostly sandy, pocked with stinking septic ponds; palm trees grew on the wide streets where lime trees do in Kensington; no pavements, much; terrible traffic; painted plaster breezeblocked buildings, hardly over two storeys; no streetlamps, but a few striplights under some of the eaves; lovely warm temperatures in the evening, a relief after the day's heat; and a less lovely warm tang from the overworked sewers. Lagos in Nigeria, the fifth capital, was simply a ten-million-man hell.

Abidjan is the west coast's grandest commercial centre. Ivory Coast's late president, Félix Houphouët-Boigny, brought prosperity to his country between independence in 1960 and his death in 1993, and Abidjan boomed and bloomed. Houphouët-Boigny blossomed too, and may have become a little too big for his boots. He decided to promote his home village, Yamassoukro (pop. 500), in the centre of the country to capital city, and strove to make it look like one. It was a good effort, but it failed to convince the foreign embassies and businesses, which stayed in Abidjan. Yamassoukro now has a big 'To Let' sign hanging over it. We went there on our way from Mali to the coast.

The first you see of Yamassoukro from the north – from any direction, in fact – is the gigantic domed basilica poking out of the jungle. We were in jungle now, real rainforest; limestone cols and flats covered in veg and salad stuff and creepers hanging off high bushy trees. No sign of Johnny Weismuller, though.

The cathedral is based on St Peter's in Rome, which makes it about half the size of St Paul's Cathedral, so it was rather a shock to see it protruding over the palm trees. Houphouët-Boigny commissioned it to guarantee himself a place in the Catholic heaven. The Pope opened it in 1990. The old fellow must have scratched his bald pate a bit when he saw it. 'Jeez, look at that,' he must have said (in Polish, of course). The dome is a little lower than the one on St Paul's, but counting the huge gold cross on top it touches 550 feet, which makes the whole structure seventy-five feet taller. There is room for 7,000 people seated and 12,000 standing inside, and a further 300,000 standing on the Italian marble outside. That is room for more Catholics than there are in Ivory Coast.

Despite the towering pillars, the dazzling stained glass and the marble floors, Red and George were not impressed. 'Not very holy,' they agreed catholically. It lacked life. There was no Catholic institution attached to it, no sense of century-worn spirituality. The only people there apart from a dozen awestruck tourists – and Jesper, drinking Coca-Cola – were soldiers in trucks. It looked too new, the pews only just out of their polythene wrapping. But it also looked abandoned. It was the monster to Houphouët-Boigny's Dr Frankenstein, the Xanadu pleasuredome to his Kublai Khan.

It was mainly a resort for reptiles and insects. Agama lizards the size of a hand, gun-barrel blue with fiery orange heads and tails, loped like foxhounds across local obstacles as you approached. Up and down the gilt statues of the Virgin Mary and all over the Stations of the Cross. When not disturbed they behaved in the punch-drunk manner of retired army PT instructors. Knees up, knees up, hup-two, hup-two, along the top of the wall; nah then, has you were. Press-ups – hup-dahn, hup-dahn. Yes, sah? They tilt their heads and blink at you. Wot chew lookin' at, eh? Back to foxhound mode and stream away.

Hosts of migrating dragonflies hung around the trees and low ornamental hedges by the big empty car park, resting on their trip south with the harmattan wind. The harmattan blows Saharan sand into the air in the dry season to create a thick haze all along the west coast. We did not see the moon properly for days and the sun was reduced at times to an angry red ball.

The Basilica may not have been holy, but it was Catholic. Emma went cathocrazy, inquired about mass there – once a week only – met a nun, and found us a place to stay at the Catholic mission in the city. This was next to the compound of the presidential palace, again, built by Houphouët-Boigny, where we watched the presidential crocodiles being fed. No sign of Roger Moore.

The mission itself was a bunch of low city buildings filled with people all being terribly nice to each other, rather like a C. of E. coffee morning. But it was a good and comfortable night, and we were only bitten by mosquitos, not crocodiles.

Our billet in Abidjan was less pleasant. We camped by the beach in a concrete compound with broken bottles cemented into the tops of the walls. This was the Treichville quarter of town, a rough area. We knew it was fairly horrible, because every morning the male population went down together to the beach in front of us for a crap. They performed in concert, a symphony of excreta. During the day, nutty post-traumatic stress disorder sufferers from the civil war in neighbouring Liberia lurched into the camp and had to be ejected. One of them tried to sell George a lizard.

Treichville was nasty. How on earth we managed it I do not know, but these things happen so quickly in Africa: one moment Emma was calling her boyfriend Danny in Dublin from a grubby telephone booth in a back alley after the hours of darkness, the next there was a dispute over the price of the call, and the Land Rover was surrounded by angry locals. We pleaded and they shouted. We shouted and they pleaded. The booth-owner tried to snatch a book from the back seat as part payment, a weighty award-winning *History of Ireland 1912 to the Present Day*. I should have let him keep it, but I grabbed it back.

This was a matter for the police. Suddenly the area was plunged into blackness – another power cut. People started climbing on to the back of the Land Rover as we drove to the police station with the booth-owner. George slammed on the brakes, got out and ordered them off. They were furious, but George had been trained at Sandhurst to deal with situations like this.

The police station was as nasty and dark as Treichville, and as grubby as the telephone booth. It buzzed and boomed with humanity like an American police station when Hollywood is trying to prove that cops are overworked, but without the filmset wendy lights.

It goes, naturally, without saying, that tourists are rich, booth-operators poor, etc., and the kangaroo court found in the booth's favour. So we paid up, rang a stinging 'Merci, Messieurs', at them and stalked out. To no great avail, but it made us feel better.

This spat made us late for the big match. Not the ASPAA–SIFCOM match, but one in which Red and George were going to play. It was Wednesday evening after work and the Ivory Coast's French team, Lambert's, were playing a first-division black club called ASTP. It took place under floodlights on another of Abidjan's three rugby pitches.

Rugby in Ivory Coast started in the 1940s during the French colonialist period. It was always the white man's sport. After independence, the resident French made the first moves to create a true Ivorian national team. The federation was created in 1961. To start with the team was split, seven Frenchmen and eight Africans, and the French subsidised the Africans. This became expensive, especially for foreign tours, as more Africans replaced the French, and in 1974 the system was restructured and the first true national team was put together. The French formed their own club side, for which many of the original Ivory Coast team still play. They gave it the name Lambert's after the soap company that once sponsored them used a character called Lambert in a TV ad. 'Oh Lambert, you smell so fresh!' gushed his TV wife/totty. The French thought this was hilarious.

Lambert's was Bucolics Anonymous, infused with the kind of Depardieu shruggery found all over France's rural regions – the Camargue, Languedoc, Provence – and it is easier to shrug and gesticulate if you have the proper prop's shoulders to do it. We were asked along by just such a man, Jean-Michel. Give him pigtails, a moustache and a little tin helmet and he could have been Obelix. In the same and best Gaulish tradition we met nothing but good humour and generosity from Jean-Michel and his friends. He gave us the gen about Lambert's: 'Some of us played in the first division in France,' he said. 'Now we are fat, some are old. We cannot play as before, so we play rugby for fun.'

Lambert's were outpaced by ASTP, but there was *vie* in the *vieux chiens* yet, and not a few new tricks. 'Usually for the pack we are more heavy and more technical,' Jean-Michel told me on the touchline. He had injured his shoulder the week before so was sitting this one out. 'But as soon as the ball go out, we are finish – you understand?' he declared as the ball did just that. The ASTP right wing picked it up and ran for goal, but did not make it. The ASTP team all lost their tempers simultaneously and started shrugging at each each other, aping the French, but with ganglier arms.

George and Red joined Lambert's for the second half. George replaced Jean-Loup, who played for Ivory Coast in 1972. Jean-Loup's fifteen-year-old son was playing for Lambert's for the first time in this match. The oldest Lambert's player was nearly sixty. Geriatrix.

Red survived ten minutes of it on the wing. 'I've just lost too much weight,' he said, panting. 'Go on George,' he wheezed thinly.

George, I felt, was hampered by his hair. Since leaving home it had grown to a length the regiment would have frowned upon. He looked as if he was wearing a chrysanthemum on his head. It swayed and flopped in his eyes as he lowered his shoulders and made bounding charges into the rucks and mauls. Red, in the meantime, had grown a beard. By Abidjan it had gone beyond the stage of fashionable stockbroker's stubble and now had a Captain Haddock look about it, if not quite W.G. Grace. It was, we were delighted to see, bright orange at the gills, fading to a sun-and-nicotine blond around the mouth. The detritus of what he ate stuck in it from time to time – porridge oats, chocolate and what looked like bird-droppings, but was probaby a mixture of peanut butter and fried egg.

After the match the players stripped and hosed each other down on the pitch. 'I can't take a picture of *that*,' said Emma, aghast. George had enjoyed himself hugely. 'Some of those tackles,' he said between blasts of water, 'like hitting a brick wall.'

Once they were respectable again, Lambert's team headed out in a convoy of vehicles to go eating. Mistress Quickly chugged bravely but lagged behind. They waited while we caught up. Tonight's restaurant was not the Maquis Paris as normal, but one which belonged to one of the players, Bernard. It was opening night for his new venture, and Lambert's were invited to christen the place.

Roland came too. He was circumspect about chez Bernard in case it turned out to be competition for the Maquis Paris. Roland played Unhygienix to Bernard's Fulliautomatix. Bernard was a former French international.

We went in. Roland looked around him. The decor – all white – was a little strong, he observed sniffily. Some glasses of Côte du Rhône later I asked him if there was any rivalry. 'Huf, there is no competition between us,' he said emphatically, narrowly missing his wine glass with his mouth. 'This man, 'e 'as been my friend for eight years. Everyone 'ere is my friend for between two and eight years.' But he could not hide his delight when the main circuit tripped and the lights went out – and, again, and several more times.

Every time the electrics popped, Roland led a chorus of 'Appy Birthday to You', a rather mysterious choice, I thought. Surely 'Why Are We Waiting?' or even 'Lead Kindly Light' would have been more appropriate. In one of Bernard's blacker moments George slipped quietly outside. He came back clutching candles from the boot of the Land Rover. Huge success. Everybody cheered. 'The English are always organised – they have the candles,' shouted one. 'Yes, but the French have the condoms,' said another. More obscure Gallic humour. Roland pointed out that the meal would probably be more expensive now that it was candlelit. Bernard controlled his temper.

One of the men there that evening was Pierre Cassagnet, the father of rugby in Ivory Coast. A moustache, not tall, a prominent nose, yes, he was Asterix. 'This man is God,' a passing player had said to me when I met Cassagnet, dousing himself with water, on the pitch in the darkness. He had his own hose, but I doubt if that qualifies him for the post of God, even in Houphouët-Boigny's heaven. He is called God because he has been the powerhouse behind Ivory Coast's international success.

In 1980, Cassagnet took over as technical director of the Ivory Coast national team. He started work forming the team that would one day go to the World Cup. He retired in favour of Dominique Davanier in 1993, and now holds the title special adviser to the president of the federation. It is still his mission to develop rugby in Ivory Coast, and he is fanatical about it. He introduced the game to schools and teacher-training colleges all over the country.

I tried to ask him about Ivory Coast's chances against Scotland in the World Cup. 'It is not possible to talk of Ivory Coast versus Scotland,' he butted back. 'It is important for me to talk of where Ivory Coast sits in the sixteen nations. For me, that is more interesting and important. There were seven schools with rugby in 1980. Now there are 200, and that in a country without rugby heritage.'

As it was for Boo-Boo in Morocco, money was an abiding problem. The Ivory Coast federation's annual budget would barely buy one aeroplane ticket to South Africa. Luckily, Cassagnet had been able to bring in extra government assistance. The minister for sport was paying directly for the eighty staff, including coaches, involved in rugby in Ivory Coast, and for the eight permanent staff at the federation. As an incentive to the players in the national team, Davanier handed out cash to all who turned up to training. It would have bought each of them half a pint of beer in a London pub, but it was good money in a country where the minimum monthly wage would have bought only fifteen pints. It was hardly an issue in the world amateur v professional debate compared to the freebies and benefits that were going to players in South Africa at the time.

There was more subtle help from the French community. Companies in Abidjan who sponsored clubs like ASPAA or ASTP also tried to employ rugby players as casual labour. Despite the fact that Ivory Coast is the African west coast's big business centre, half the workforce was unemployed and there was no shortage of people wanting jobs. Jean-Michel was working for shipping agent SAGA. He explained: 'Sometimes our companies need workers. Now it is the cocoa season' – his ground-floor office near the port had a thick chocolatey smell about it – 'and we need people to carry bags. We take rugby players. We help like this.'

The next day, Jean-Michel took Red and me to visit the man Red kept calling the Grand Fromage ('Please, not to his face, Red' – 'Oh, all right'. Thinks: can I trust him?): Gervais Coffie, president of the Ivory Coast rugby federation since 1963. We went in Jean-Michel's car in an unaccustomed blast of air-conditioning. We drove from Treichville to the smart part of town, sprinkled lawns, swimming pools and servants.

If Cassagnet was rugby's God, Coffie was the game's Cronus. Under Houphouët-Boigny he had been secretary-general of the government and the fourth most powerful man in the country for the thirty-two years up to the president's death. He had been a close friend and confidante of the president for forty-five years. His house said it all. It was large and cool. There were staff, and the staff had cars. Rooms were filled with fetishes, those strange African idols, the glory of the hideous. Piped music played – jazz, classical and piano-bar – lift music. A wood-panelled interior, white walls outside, thick double-glazing and steel shutters rolled up but waiting for trouble. We sat in the garden around a table near a running machine.

Coffie himself came in. He was small and grinning, not the ravaged politician I expected. He wore little metal-framed glasses and a T-shirt. But the aura of power hung around him. He pulled out a large cigar and lit it. That is more like it. He reminded me of a mini Mugabe.

Later that week, another of the Lambert's players was fascinated that we had met Coffie. 'I don't think he is a killer, a real politician,' he said. 'He is too séductif.'

Coffie loved jokes. A friendly sheepdog ran up to him and tried to jump on his lap. He turned and looked at us. 'It is not a dog. It is a cat,' he said. Nobody laughed. Coffie laughed. Everybody laughed.

He called for drinks. They were poured. 'Santé,' said Jean-Michel. 'Slaînte,' said Red. 'Cheers,' I said. 'Er . . . bottoms up,' said Coffie. More laughter.

He does not play rugby himself. He never has, apart from one or two matches at school in France. He was not specific. 'When I arrived in France, I arrived in the south-west, which is the most pratique region in France for rugby,' he said. 'The first experience was at school in Périgueux. I was asked home by a friend. When I arrived at the railway station, the mother of my friend took our luggage and drove us straight to the rugby stadium to see a match.' His schooldays sparked a genuine interest in the game. Being president of the rugby federation is a feather in his cap, but it has been of no real political advantage in a country which puts football firmly first.

I tried Coffie out on the 'any chance of beating Scotland?' question that Cassagnet had so adroitly stonewalled. 'I am conscious that Ivory Coast is a young rugby nation,' he came back carefully. 'But in less than thirty years we have come a long way. From nothing to now is a long distance. We don't want to dream. We want to be realistic, to keep our feet on the ground and the ball in our hands. We will go as far as possible.'

First rule of dealing with journalists: never answer the question, in case that was what they wanted you to do.

What appeals to you about rugby? 'My family is big on football – we know internationals and some of my family are professional players – but after I discovered rugby in Périgueux and when I came back here I decided to look after rugby. There are thousands of people to look after football. I don't regret it for a moment. The feeling the people have in rugby, the spirit, the rapport, is most important compared to other sports,' he continued with greater feeling, spirit and rapport.

Strangely enough for a politician, he was actually passing all the lie-detection tests a journalist usually runs on his victim during an interview. Journalists watch for fibbers using long Latin-root words, like 'rationalisation' instead of 'going bust', and putting their hands near their faces, a subconscious signal that the fibber is in the process of fibbing. Coffie seemed to be meaning what he was saying.

Red asked: 'Gr ... er, Monsieur Coffie, what it is about rugby that appeals to the Ivorian character?'

Coffie paused. 'That is a big question,' he replied. Buy time and think, and do not just answer 'Getting into the World Cup, it's a nationalist kick.'

'Ivorian people like sport in general,' he said. 'I have nephews and cousins who play basketball and a brother who plays football, and relations who are presidents of the cycling, table-tennis and football federations.' No, not working. Try the stream-of-consciousness ploy. 'Speaking of rugby, it's the spirit of camaraderie, the heart, the human harmony that Ivorians like. Due to French colonisation, the French people have brought Ivorians to their sport. Little by little, rugby developed as more and more people were drawn to the game.' Thinks: that should shut them up.

No more questions, m'lud.

Right then, hit them with the political message: 'Félix Houphouët-Boigny was very respected,' he told us. 'He gave a message in 1971. He asked whites and blacks in the world to live together happily. Danie Craven, president of rugby in South Africa, gave the same message concerning the sport. Now both of them are dead, but it looks as if it is a spiritual message from God that Ivory Coast is going to the World Cup in South Africa. It is a symbol. It is a very good thing for humanity and for the sport.'

Coffie stood up. We all stood up. The interview was over. He was charmingly and eloquently sorry, but he had to race off. As well as the rugby federation, he was president of the Ivorian national ballet, and he had to go to a gala performance.

When he had gone, Jean-Michel gave his own view. 'In my

opinion, in other African countries if the foreigners leave, rugby will die. But not in Ivory Coast. There is a federation here. There are Ivorian referees.'

'That's probably why Ivory Coast is going to the World Cup in the first place,' said Red. 'It's the difference.'

Jean-Michel warmed to his theme: 'With my small experience and what I read, I think that during colonisation there were African people in the French colonies who wanted to be French citizens. The local people started to play pétanque and drink pastis. The good things and the bad things. The English just wanted to run their countries, to put the rulers on top, not to integrate.'

But then he suddenly feared that he had overstepped himself. 'You know, for outside vision it is important not to see me,' he said worriedly, 'but to see the Ivorians.'

So we went to see the Ivorians that Saturday, that ASPAA – SIFCOM match. As I take up the commentary it is still the first half. SIFCOM are driving and driving to get it over the line, but still they cannot score. ASPAA's greater strength is telling.

'All he has to do is fall over,' says George, fed up.

The touch-judge marks it off at ASPAA's corner. The ref says no, a twenty-two kick. 'That's definitely a dodgy touch-judge,' says George.

Boot and ruck. The ASPAA hooker helps a SIFCOM prop out from underneath it. The prop's boot has come off. 'They're definitely very polite,' says Red. The heat is starting to tell on the players by the end of the first half. Their kicking is more languid; they are pausing before scrums to wipe the sweat off their faces on to their shirt-sleeves.

George has some advice: 'Um. The blue and white team' – that's ASPAA – 'are quite well drilled setting up mauls. They can set up a maul well, but once you've got a maul set up you've got to roll it, which they don't seem to do. Or get big men running off it to suck in defence; make more room for the backs.' Pause. More advice: 'They don't know how to run into people. They don't know how to hit people. They don't have a wish to hurt anyone. It's a bit schoolboyish.'

Half-time.

'We do need to work at everything,' said Davanier when I met him in the football stadium's converted khazi, 'especially liaison between the players.' Nearly half the Ivory Coast national squad play for clubs in France. 'It is necessary to make more of a ménage between the group in France and here,' he added.

Davanier was not entirely impressed with the players' ability to pick up skills in France and import them to Ivory Coast. Cassagnet backed him up: 'The players who play in France play better,' he admitted, 'but they are more specialised, more stereotyped.'

For Davanier and Cassagnet, indeed all the Lambert's players, Ivory Coast's success in rugby was more important than France's. It was not a question of personal glory. They had the same genuine keenness for the Ivory Coast game that Coffie had. Jean-Michel pointed out that the West Africans are happier to integrate into the French way of life than they are into Englishness in former British colonies. It is also true, if rather sweeping, that the French expatriates try to get into the West African flow more than the English do, albeit on a grander scale than most Ivorians can afford.

We were lucky enough to go and stay in the holiday house of one of the Lambert's team members. It was not in his home country – it is the English who like to go home for their hols. There is more of a blur over what is home for the French in Africa. He was leasing it with some friends from a local village co-operative on the coast near Ghana, one of dozens of half-acre plots rented by expatriates and senior Africans alike.

Thierry, a doctor, had sat next to Red and George in Bernard's restaurant. Shortish, with dark hair and French black eyes, he looked like one of those admirable young Frenchmen from Médecins Sans Frontières who only find time to appear on the television when up to their elbows in some war victim's chest cavity. A young Getafix. He told Red about a fabulous stretch of coast he knew, fifty miles outside Abidjan.

'Marvellous,' said Red. 'We'll probably see you down there at the weekend.'

'Oh,' said Thierry. 'I thought I would use the house myself this weekend with my family, but do come down on Sunday for a few days.'

Red was embarrassed. He had not realised it was a private show. But he accepted Thierry's offer nonetheless, and off we went.

It had everything. Park the car. A long motor skiff buzzes over the lagoon with baggage and you on board. Land it, and a palm tree sandbar 200 yards thick separates you from the sea, where the water is warm enough to kiss you as fondly as it kisses its golden beach. There is just enough algae in the water to keep the costa property developers away, but not so much to make it stagnant. Only the palm trees are over one storey high.

In the middle of the sandbar a group of four double-sleeping huts with bamboo walls, real beds and grass-thatched roofs, and two smaller versions for shower and loo (proper European sit-down), surround a large central verandah hut with a kitchen. It came with staff: Jean-Pierre, a local who was so polite it embarrassed Emma. He banned us from the kitchen. If we tried to fetch a beer or make a cup of coffee he would come pattering up with 'Asseyez-vous, asseyez-vous,' and bring it himself. This exasperated Emma.

The waves were big enough to surf on. There was a surfboard, so we did not need the sand ladders we had been using through Morocco and Mauritania. The sand ladders are aluminium plates, four feet long, which go under the tyres to help Mistress Quickly out of soft sand. Up to then we had only used them for surfing, thanks to the Dust Busters' smart winch.

The sun was hot enough to grill you slowly like lamb on a spit, and the wind blew gently to take the bite out of it. The sand on the beach squeaked and creaked like snow in a pricey ski resort. I began to think I shall retire here.

There were fish in the lagoon which rose to the fly. I unpacked my Hardy travelling rod and went straight down to catch them, pretty green perch ribbed with orange, local name 'crap', which took with a bang on the surface, just often enough to make it sporting, but not so often to make it boring. They were confused by the fly to start with – 'You eat this stuff?' they asked – but soon got the hang of it.

I put the first one back. Jean-Pierre, who had taken a break from his usual round of cleaning, washing and infuriating Emma to appear at my shoulder, looked shocked – more shocked than when I had tried to teach him to make proper greasy fried bread that morning ('You eat this stuff?' he had asked). 'Please,' he said. 'You catch them and I cook.'

Most of the craps' splashing and rising activity took place in the middle of the lagoon, so a few days later I hired a boatman, Francis, and his pirogue, a long flat-bottomed canoe which he normally punted backwards and forwards across the lagoon carrying a cargo or coconuts and freshwater oysters. His price for the whole day was less than the fare for a short journey on a London bus. But as a ghillie he had a lot to learn. First off was about fishing flies. 'They don't eat this stuff,' he told me, looking at the Bloody Butcher suspiciously. He held it up to show to a gaggle of local women on the bank, who fell about with laughter. He reached over the side of the boat and scooped up a handful of hermit crabs, smashed them up, and put the meat on the hook. I could see his point, for crap definitely eat hermit crab. The water boiled around the baited fly like piranhas in *You Only Live Twice*.

I had trouble explaining that this was not sporting, so in the end I went for an attritional yet tactful system where by Francis would bait the fly, and I would dispose of the bait on the backcast and hope he would not notice until I had a bite.

Eventually he became bored and started to rock the pirogue: only so slightly that I could not tell him not to, but enough to make the fishing uncomfortable. The fly-line was also picking up the tar that sealed the zinc between the planks on the bottom of the boat, so we called it a day.

It was evening, a good time for fishing, too. They were rising fast, and big silver seafish were jumping like salmon. But the beauty of the place was best seen during the punt home. Curlews and pigeons made strangely English noises as the big tropical sun sank behind the mangroves and the palms, with raggedy clouds slicing across it. More jungly noises came from the great gold songbirds, gurgling warbles, and the hornbills, rocketing and swooping home to roost. As we landed the pirogue on the sandbar the mudskipper fish dashed for the mangrove roots and the last of the sunbathing ghost crabs hoisted their back legs and scattered for home.

Back in daylight at the SIFCOM–ASPAA game in Abidjan, the second half is just beginning.

'There's no aggression,' says George. 'They don't want to run into people. If I get a ball – and I know I'm not very good at it – if I can't run round someone, I try to run through him. I don't know why they're like that. They've got a low centre of gravity. Look, there's an example: the flanker gave away the ball too early. And the number 8 should have dropped his shoulder and run with the ball.'

'It's all very well this kicking for the corners and chasing,' says Red, 'but it doesn't develop any skills for the team.'

'They're not very fit. A very slow pace for the game,' says George.

'Ooh. Bit of a talk and a squabble,' says Red, sitting up. There is arm-waving on the pitch and the angry flash of white teeth; hands point down, palms up.

'There still only one try?' asks Red.

'Yup,' says George. 'They're not very happy. Frustrated.'

Red leans back on the concrete seat, legs up. George leans forward, elbows on knees, chin on hand. It is still hot. It is not bright – it is harmattan – but the sun is being cruel. The players' socks are slipping down in streaming sweat. Half a dozen chickens forage over the most tryless end. SIFCOM make a big push and the poultry look up nervously. ASPAA kick it away and they look down again.

Sixty minutes gone. 'What a boring game,' says George.

Sixty-five minutes gone. 'Can I have a fag please,' says Red.

Sixty-eight minutes gone. The ASPAA right wing takes the ball on a dummied left pass to the right and drives through. 'Oh, nice move,' says Red. It goes out to the left again. ASPAA nearly score. The crowd wakes up.

But way over on the right an ASPAA flanker and a SIFCOM lock are having a fight. Ooh-ooh, go the crowd happily. A spectator joins in. All three are sent off. Huge clapping, cheering and laughter from the audience.

❖   ❖   ❖

We lounged at Thierry's house on the coast for days, with a break in the middle to play more rugby and to pick up Vicky from the airport. And then we were five.

George's girlfriend, Vicky Parent, flew to Abidjan to join the party. She is Somerset, horsy, farmy, the best sort. George was happy. You could tell. As we were driving out of Yamassoukro he had suddenly burst out with his pronouncement on Ivory Coast: 'It's . . . um. Got everything we want in a country. Cheap beer, good coffee, rugby, and . . . beaches.' And Vicky.

It was bad luck, of course, that we had met Urs in Morocco. Anticipating his pronunciation, we rechristened her 'Wicky', and that is how she remained.

Red had had strong reservations about Wicky coming out. Arguments with George had gone on long into the nights and there had been numerous sub-committee meetings between Red and me and Emma in the privacy of the other side of Mistress Quickly to the side George was sitting at every camp from Morocco when George had first announced he wanted her to come. I was fearful for the party as well. Wicky would break up a perfect bridge four. But the moment I met her I knew I had been wrong.

The first thing we discover about Wicky is her giggle, which is remorseless. Once off it runs like a train with no brakes, pealing through all in its path. She was already well away at the Ghana border, where we camped on the way out of Ivory Coast heading east to Accra, and where the local military chose to do an extraordinary goose-step past the Land Rover in order to strike the flag at sunset. Huge squeak and snort from Wicky. 'Be Quiet Stand Still,' ordered the chief of brigade in the customs house. This was a solemn moment. Huk, huk, huk – snort – squeak. 'Quiet, Wicky,' we hushed. Hmffff . . . gn . . . hur, hur, hur. It was useless. George shook his head, and when George shook his head about Wicky there was no more a man can do. Luckily, the chief of brigade ignored her.

Wicky juddered with tremors all evening. We had to make camp on an asphalt lorry park with customs post and flagpole on one side, and freight parked and waiting to clear customs on the other, separated from us by a black and sticky sewer.

An object half the size of a cricket ball clattered on to Mistress Quickly's roof during supper. 'Good Lord! What was that?'

Emma knew the answer at once. 'A frog,' she said.

Hooo-hooo-he-he-he-he-ha. Quite a frog. Hmng-hng-hng-hoo-hoo. It turned out to be a rhino beetle with a six-inch wingspan. While Wicky cried with merriment it spent an unhappy evening doing pre-flight checks: flaps, ailerons; gunning its engines one by one; chocks away, spiralling whirring up to one of the lamplights, lesser insects falling aside in the jetwash, bashing the glass, losing it, flat spin, fire in the starboard tank: mayday, mayday – plonk – hitting the ground, stunned, and repeat.

Next it really was a frog, of sorts. Emma felt vindicated. Gug-gug-gug-fng, went Wicky.

When Wicky dropped gravel into the sewer muck, the giant poo toads raced up it. Thus, we thought, was their French name, *crapaud*, earned. Mmmj-mmj-mmjaah. Delighted, Wicky held a point-to-point for them, showering stones, which went splat in the slime, not plop, and the terrified toads hopped messily up and down the drain for her pleasure.

To her great credit, and worthy of a mention, her first action on arrival in Africa was to cut George's hair. She did it on the beach at Thierry's holiday house, and when she had finished, it looked like someone had murdered one of father's larger mammals there.

And the game? ASPAA against SIFCOM? There are still eight minutes to go before the end of the chapter.

Seventy-two minutes gone, and the ASPAA number 18 replaces number 5 on the left flank. High-fives as they run past each other.

Seventy-five minutes. There is a ruck by the stand. ASPAA have possession, almost rucking the SIFCOM hooker out of the way. He nearly gets passed to the ASPAA fly-half, but no, it is the ball. Down the three quarters in a push forward. Where is right wing? There is right wing. Takes it. Through SIFCOM defence like a greased pig, and it is a fifty-yard sprint as the crowd rises and cheers, and a stylish dive into the centre of the posts. The girls scream delight. And converted. This is more like it.

Kick-off. Slap. George (happily): 'That's what I mean by hitting somebody.' Out of the ruck, ASPAA again, down the left wing; they score again. Nice as pie.

'Quick ball,' comments George, 'and again it's the international players who set it up.'

The crowd chant the scorer's name. They spell it out in crescendo. And the try is converted. The roar dwindles to happy laughter.

'The crowd are enjoying it,' says George.

'It's like New Zealand, George: the Lions Test,' says Red. George knows what he means.

Four minutes to go and play hots up. Some of the SIFCOM team are jumping up and down in fury. It is behind the SIFCOM twenty-two. Their left wing tries a drop-kick. Misses.

'Oh, you donkey,' says Red.

ASPAA have it. They score again in the left-hand corner. The crowd stands, but they are not so impressed now. This is becoming normal.

The French SIFCOM coach is behind the line now with the rest of his team, supplying greater Gallic exhortations. ASPAA do not convert. The crowd settles down.

'They have got very good hands,' notices George of ASPAA after they have finished clapping their team-mate's failure. 'In fact, they've got all the necessary attributes physique-wise. The athleticism. But they don't have the skill level. Or the aggression.'

Seventy-nine minutes. Line-out to the left, ten yards short of the SIFCOM twenty-two. Maul, and ASPAA roll it. Out to the threequarters on the right. Picked up by the ASPAA centre, steaming down the middle. SIFCOM are nowhere. The crowd goes ooh-ooh-ooh-ooh. Plonked down behind the tryline. 'Perfect,' says George. It is converted.

'They've suddenly started playing,' says George.

The last few seconds. ASPAA try a few illegal moves, just for badness. The right wing kicks it, runs and lands over the tryline with it, bits like that. SIFCOM are indignant, but in terms of the final score it is futile. Final whistle, round of applause and no hard feelings. The score: 33–0.

'They've got a footballer's attitude to the game,' sums up George as we walk across the pitch back to Mistress Quickly, who is parked outside. 'Nancies.'

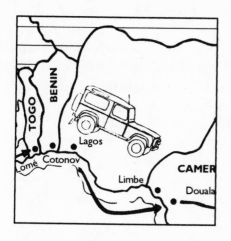

Ghana, Togo, Benin and Nigeria. George, Red, Emma, Wicky and me in Mistress Quickly. Jesper leaves us. 170 days to the World Cup opening ceremony.

Time was pressing on. Waiting to pick up visas, waiting to pick up Wicky and waiting for Wicky to pick up wisas took a month. Jesper tired of waiting after a week and headed off east. It left us only three weeks to get through Ghana, Togo, Benin and Nigeria to arrive in Cameroon for Christmas. Our hopes of making it through central Africa before the rains started were receding as well. We had told everyone we had met on the way, and everyone had agreed, and had told everyone else, that we would all meet in Limbe on the coast of Cameroon for Christmas, Sylvester, or Noël – whatever each language called it.

Getting to South Africa by road is easy, really. Go out of London and head towards Calais. Go right by the Sainsbury's there, left after the Houphouët-Boigny Bridge in Abidjan, then right again just before Jomo Kenyatta Airport in Nairobi; carry straight on down that road – you can't miss it. It is only political instability that makes it as complicated as that. When E.S. Grogan became the first person to travel the whole of the continent at the turn of the century he simply headed north from South Africa up the Zambezi and the Nile rivers and caught the packet home from Cairo.

So it was back into Mistress Quickly, and a sharp left turn east, heading towards the rising sun. Fired and inspired by the need for speed, we went through Ghana as fast as our cylinders could bear. The country flashed by. 'The trouble is,' said George, after some thought, 'that each country is like a wine-tasting. We stay there briefly, we taste it, and then we move on.' He was right, but in this case, with only a few shopping days left to Limbe, we had to race.

Ghana was once a British colony. I know a man who knows a man who has a labrador called Ghana – 'Small, black and independent,' he explains.

There were bits of little Englishness everywhere, some of them extremely small-minded. We were pulled over in a British-style speed-trap by policemen in British-designed fluorescent yellow vests with a white 'POLICE' on a blue background. They showed us the digital speed-gun reading: fifty in a thirty limit. We were so proud of Mistress Quickly. We felt for a moment that we ought to turn up in court and pay the fine just to have the ticket to frame and keep in her cab. Speeding! Clever old girl.

George was the first to come to his senses. He got out of the driving seat and went round to see the policeman. He had to go round because Ghanaians drive on the right. They used to drive on the left when the British were in charge, but the French dominate the west coast to such an extent that they had to change. A newspaper report announcing the change from left to right in Ghana once did the rounds. In keeping with the spirit of African driving, it went on to say that the process would take place 'gradually', which brought to mind several possibilities. For the first six months would only lorries drive on the right? Or could you drive on the right, but for a limited period have to give way to the right when approaching a roundabout? Or would you simply stick to normal African shade-driving, because that was what everyone else did?

'You have committed a criminal act,' said the policeman, who was fat and, of course, officious.

'Damn,' thought George. 'He speaks English.'

If he had spoken French it would have been so much easier.

George could have used the old 'Pardon?' routine. Instead he had to revert to his English technique: being rude to the man. 'What do you mean, "speeding"? . . . Well, there isn't a sign . . . Well, I didn't see it . . . What do you mean, "court tomorrow morning"? . . . Well, I am not going to be here tomorrow morning . . . I'm going to be in Togo.'

I listened, amazed. I could never get away with that. I am always polite to British policemen, though it is true that I always get nicked. George got away with it. The copper let him off with a warning. How did he do it? 'I know how they think,' said George afterwards. 'I did vehicle checkpoints in the army.'

As soon as we were round the next bend it was back up to fifty again, amid clouds of blue smoke from the exhaust. What we saw from Ghana's coast road had to be taken in at that speed, but luckily we found enough to amuse us.

Pastis and *pétanque* may represent the good and the bad in French culture, but the ugly was the French West African love of acronyms for company names, like ASPAA, SIFCOM and SAGA. We saw quite the opposite in company-name styling in Ghana.

We might have guessed it when we were in Ivory Coast from the minibus taxis that did the Accra to Abidjan run, packed to the gunwales with people and livestock, pausing only at roadblocks to allow the police to stiff the passengers for bribes. They all had marvellously plaintive mottos stencilled on the coachwork above their windscreens. Don't Envy me, Be Merciful, I Love You; the painfully optimistic Godspeed; the plucky Don't Give Up, and the more appropriate Who Cares, God Knows Why, and Six Feet Under.

There were small indications of what was to come in the first Ghanaian town we drove through. Maggie's Spot was next to Vera's Beauty Parlour – perhaps the two of them should get together – and just up the road from the church advertising the mildly blasphemous Clap for Jesus. Each sign above each shop was written in glorious funfair Punch and Judy script.

Then the signs went mad. The Lovable Soap Factory was outside the town where you could visit the dealer in Hair Cream & Hardware, or even the Madam de Madam 'It's a Matter of Cash' Jack of All

Trade. If, on the off-chance, Madam could not help you out, you could always drown your sorrows in the Time Heals Drinking Bar, or have a slap-up meal at the Don't Mind Your Wife Chop Bar. Perhaps they would serve you the widely advertised Star-Kist Tuna Simply Delicious It's Yummy.

Maybe only the bosom of the Church could help you. There is no shortage of churches in Ghana, all with new and improved formulae for getting you into heaven. The Joyful Christian Ministries Joyful Centre is opposite the hyperbolic Jesus of Nazareth SUPER Spiritual and not far from the Deeper Life Bible Church.

Some of the signs were slightly confused about whether their activities were secular or non-secular. The Divine Beauty Salon competed with Come To Joy Fair Where Sorrows Are No More. Unfortunately, there was no indication of what miracles Joy could perform for you. There was the God of Wonders Furniture Shop, or if you happened to have any vegetables on you, The Wonderful God Grinding Spot (Grind Your Tomatoes). Often omitted from depictions of the Stations of the Cross is the Calvary Rest Stop Burger Bar. Presumably it can create enough styrofoam to fill five baskets.

My own favourite was the bar its regulars know as Many Are Called Spot. I was about to go in to find out how many of those regulars answer to the name Spot, before I realised that it should be read as the 'Many Are Called' Spot. Few are chosen.

Some were just spelling mistakes or the result of unfortunate translation, and you could not help laughing at them because your mind was so tuned into it. The TV and video shop Radio Shark came in to this category, I hope, and White Horsie Whisky sidestepped local copyright laws nicely. The sign which read: 'Easing yourself at the beach is prohibited' could cover a multitude of sins. I hope the banner advertisement for Camp Meeting '94. Theme: Going Up Higher did not mean what it appeared to mean on first reading.

If you ever see a copy of the Accra Yellow Pages in a second-hand bookshop, buy it. Just opened at random it produced a parcel delivery firm called The Better Late Company Ltd (member of the Ghana Institute of Freight Forwarders) – 'Nobody does it better than BETTER LATE'.

Emma found a café in Accra called Kew Gardens: Come and Lick

Your Fingers. It was run by a lady afflicted with the madness of British-taught apology. In perfect English, perfect, that is, except for her squeaky, lisping voice, she greeted us: 'It'th thimply delithiouth, thank you, come with your friendth, thank you, and lick your fingerth, you're welcome, thorry.'

Enough of this frivolity. We wanted to get straight on to Togo for Nigeria visas. We had paused long enough in Accra to find that we could not get them there, and Abidjan and Bamako had been too expensive. It was because we were British. Diplomatic relations between Britain and our former colony were not good. Our Irish contingent had had no problem.

But first, however, we had to get into Togo, and the Ghana–Togo border was closed when we reached it. We hired the services of one greasy yet efficient local called Thomas. He had as much moral fibre as a green mamba, but he was on our side. He was our fixer, like Jane Charley in London. He had turned up wearing a balaclava in the cold before dawn among the spiritless concrete blocks of the border buildings where we were camping. 'Wake up now – this is African break of day.'

'Wha ...? Who ...? Whe ...? Issa quar'er t'six.' But he was persistent and we were too gaga not to hire him all the same. He was a little early, but he had wanted to beat the crowds of other fixers who would want our business. He waited crossly for us to brew our morning tea and coffee. We waited more crossly for the bribable officials to start work.

Women began bustling through in bright blue print skirts with swirly orange patterns, and unfeasible bundles on their heads. You do not need a wheelbarrow on the African west coast when you have a head. All goods and chattels can travel by head. We saw a fisherman carrying a shark, stiff as a plank; a man balancing a ceiling fan, which made him look like a mini-helicopter; a small boy carrying a bucket of water with so many holes in it that it looked as if he was carrying a working shower unit; and a short circular woman carrying a blue polythene-wrapped bundle of empty plastic bottles the same size and shape as herself. She looked like a giant blue hourglass. People walk beautifully with it, as elegant as camels, but they develop tough bull necks to cope with the weight which some of the less sporty British headmistresses might frown at.

Still we waited. We sat in the car. A dude in a wide grey jacket poked his face in the Land Rover window. 'Wah. EuroPEan. SaaVaa!'. He extracted his head and swaggered his shoulders off into the mass. We got out of the car to walk around and stretch our legs. Emma found a group of smiling nervous nuns to talk to, wearing white among all the colour and twiddling rosary beads in the face of all the worldliness.

At 8.15 am the Togolese minister for security and two burly army chiefs in sunglasses officially opened the border to a great cheer from the crowd. Apparently this does not happen every day. The border had been officially closed for eleven months. It made no difference to the amount of traffic going through, but the border guards were glummer. Their bribe income had halved instantly. The glums made them cross, and the crossness made them unhelpful, so they still made some money from us. Thomas doubted that we believed he was greasing the right palms. He came up to me as we drove to the line. 'This man will show you I have bribed him,' he said. The liverish guard wobbled up and angrily thrust a note in my face. His face said, 'Call this a bribe?'

Thomas was so successful, we hired him for the rest of our stay in Togo. There were more bribes and more waiting to come in getting our Nigeria visas in Togo, and we needed Thomas' help, but at least there was a chance they would give us the visas. Red went into the embassy in Lomé, capital of Togo, to sort it out. Mr Kio, the Nigerian consul (Visa Section) would not accept a direct bribe. His staff would, but he wanted greater glory. He wanted the honorary British consul to write him a grovelly letter begging him to allow us into Nigeria.

Jenny Sayer, the honorary British consul, who was as kind and as capable as Nancy had been in Mauritania, applied herself to our cause. She produced letters saying that we were who we said we were, that we would never wish to change and seek employment elsewhere, and that as far as she knew we were all close friends of the Queen, the Pope, and anyone else with cred Mr Kio could think of. She did it with a mildly resigned air. Mr Kio was always getting at her. Her air suggested that Mr Kio had once made a pass at her at an embassy party and that she had spurned him, and that he had had it in for her ever since.

It took three days of negotiation between Mr Kio and Red, Jenny and Thomas. The rest of us kicked our heels outside the embassy, waiting in case we were called in for interview. We kicked each other's heels. We even kicked the heels of passersby who annoyed us, such as the slightly unsteady man who came up to us while we were sitting waiting in the Land Rover, and told us that the reason we could not get a visa was because we ha-a-a-ad no fa-a-a-i-i-ith in Go-o-o-o-od. We advised him to go-o-o-o awa-a-a-ay. He put on a serene smile and started to tell us about his own fa-a-a-i-i-ith. We started the engine and drove round the block.

I began to hate Nigeria and Nigerians. Every day of the three it took us cost us more in time and brown-envelope money, and still there was no sign of the visas. I decided to look into finding a boat to Cameroon and skipping Nigeria altogether. The Irish could drive it. I saw myself asleep on the poop of a coaster, cruising across the Bight of Benin to the port of Douala in Cameroon and pottering up the coast to meet them at Limbe, well in time for Christmas. I also needed a break from the ever tossing and turning Land Rover, and I would not mind that much even if the other English, George and Wicky, did not come with me. The best chance of a boat was from the Benin capital, Cotonou, only a half-day's drive from Lomé.

Finally we left Togo, with Kio's staff paid off – and Kio perhaps with the hope that he could be in Jenny's knickers at the next party – and most importantly the necessary visas stamped firmly in our passports. Even mine; after all, I might not be able to find a boat. After the short hop in the Land Rover to Cotonou, a five o'clock start the next morning was arranged for the journey into Nigeria: another early morning, and another good reason for me to stay behind in Cotonou.

But I woke up slightly at a loss. The others had all left in the darkness, and I was in an empty campsite just outside Cotonou city centre. Mistress Quickly had been my world. There was no morning routine, no line of campbeds with me and Red and Emma trying not to wake and be first up, or it would mean coffee-making duty. No Emma finally being the first, and Red and I sighing our relief as we tried to catch a few more minutes' sleep. No George and Wicky to emerge later from their tent and ask if that coffee had been made. No argument with George about the finer points of making coffee with powdered milk (whether you wait until the boiling water cools down or not). And no resolution of the argument until after we had gone down the road to a street stall and ordered a slap-up local speciality breakfast, and felt strong enough to face the day. To console myself, I packed, paid and went into town.

The best way around Cotonou is on the back of a moped taxi. There is just enough tarmac on the roads to make good potholes, but not so much to prevent most of the driving being done through thick dust and sand. Hail a fellow in a yellow shirt with a number printed on it, sit on the back of his bike, and you're off, fishtailing wildly in the sand, the little wheels suddenly biting on the road and leaving you rueful about the next day's whiplash neckache. Every one a Sheen or a Knievel.

At traffic lights dozens of them stand revving: putter-putter-putter, whir-whir. The lights are red, but they are edging forwards and sideways, lifting the back wheel, on to the pavement; red to green, the motors scream and all eyes water in the monoxide fog. Off again, driving spoke to spoke, with you watching the front wheels jigging in and out of ruts, corrugations and other back wheels. At all times keep an eye out for brakeless parping container trucks bearing down with no-prisoner policies. Weave and whizz to where you want to go.

The other danger was from the hearses carrying the dead to burial which sped up and down the road with sirens rather than mourners doing the wailing. It was difficult to understand this sudden rush to commit the bodies, but it gave a certain dramatic flourish to a ceremony which has rather lost its way in England in an emotional tangle of self-indulgence and sympathy.

This made me feel better. Who needs friends when you have moped taxis? I spent a week simply zooming around on pointless errands. They seemed pointful at the time. There were plenty of boats going to Cameroon, and surely I could thumb a lift with one of them. I went to box-sized backstreet offices up rickety fire escapes and made friends with African shipping agents, some of them thin and sour, one of them charming, wheezing, joky and like a large toad. His tongue stuck out when he talked and I half expected him to start catching flies with it. He could not help the diesel shortage which was gripping Cotonou at the time. Nobody could. No boats were leaving the harbour.

I went to the port to see for myself. Outside it there were lines of cars stolen in Europe, shipped to Cotonou, and waiting to make a night run over the border to Lagos, where Nigerian government officials would buy them. Number plates had been stripped off, but there were still telling stickers from Dutch and German car dealerships on their back windscreens, and broken ignitions spilling wires on to the floor of the driver's seat.

The port itself was ringed by fortress walls to channel the visitors and matelots into the gently smiling jaws of the port police, who would let in anyone for a small consideration. Old tin-clad sheds on acres of concrete were served by rail and forklift trucks, all bonded warehouses, but unbonded as instantly as any cash appeared. Smuggling was not my interest, however.

I made for the row of ships docked against the harbour wall, from the enormous Scandinavian tankers to the tiny coastal odds-and-ends boats. Goods were rolling on and off at all times, timber, sacks of cotton, cocoa, tea, fish, and the smells mixing with the smell of oil and new paint on the hulls was knock-out. It caught you from the back of the throat, forcing a tracheotomy through the front, took you by the scruff of the neck and threw you backwards.

It was at that moment, though not that reason, that on my first visit to the place I desperately, urgently and knock-outly needed to go to the loo. One often needs to go to the loo on long car journeys, say, or walking the dog, or in town centres. You feel you have a minute or two's grace, maybe twenty. Sometimes you can enjoy the luxury of thinking, well, I can wait until the service station after next, or until I get home. This, though, was urgent. This was the 'gathering' that Christopher Lambert and Sean Connery talk about so solemnly in the film *The Highlander*. It came at me like the stab of a Kurgan's sword, and, like a stab, it stopped me dead in my tracks clutching my stomach. Unlike a stab, however it left me starting to sweat, to clench, and to think wildly, where is the nearest dunny?

It was just outside the port, in the café where I had had lunch,

400 yards away. I could see it over the concrete through the main gate, but all at once, as if I were looking at it through the wrong end of a telescope, it looked more like four miles away. The walk there was not really a walk. It was a wall-clutching stagger mixed with a stiff-postured slow march and ante-natal breathing exercises. This was what going into labour must be like. Every minute I was hit by terrible agony. And the minutes turned to half-minutes, and to spasms every few seconds, and I was only just through the gate. The policeman wanted to stop me, but one look from my pink and sweating face told him I was probably about to die of malaria, so he let me past. I took the last few steps as King Edward II would have done had they let him stand up after they stuck the red-hot poker up him.

The sour-looking waitress watched me with interest.

'WC?' I gritted.

'We're closed.'

'This door?' I ground.

'It's locked.'

Boot. Not any more. The timing was perfect. The fluid action of leaping past the splintered lock across the floor of the bog into a cubicle, dropping my trousers as I turned prettily on the ball of one toe, and hitting the loo seat with the speed of a driving-test emergency stop was balletic to behold. The next fluid action was less so. This was too much for the waitress. She went off to find somebody – a manager, or Dyno-rod, or someone. Too slow. I was out in under a minute and she never saw me again.

When I came back to the port after this exercise, I met the crew of a Russian ship. Another toadlike man but evil, with a face like a KGB torturer, disappeared from behind the salt-stained window on the bridge as I mounted the gangplank, and sent a thin and nervous bearded man down the steps to deal with me. This one looked like he had just escaped some cultural purge by claiming not to be able to speak English, and now the KGB wanted him to do just that. He was shaking so much he could barely talk. He almost cried when he learned that I was just a hitch-hiker. 'No, no, (thank Stalin) we are going straight home directly, and in some months (most inconvenient for you, sorry), when and before diesel arrives (and not a moment too soon), we do not know, we are waiting instructions, goodbye, dos vidanya (phewee).'

His was untypical of the reaction from the ship's captains I met – most were quite friendly – but their message was always the same. No, non, nein, nao, and any number of Gabonese dialects besides.

I booked into a cheap hotel in the town centre; unheard-of luxury on this trip. Mattress, ceiling fan, more than one storey, smiling staff to tend my every need – it had it all. I sat and drank exported Guinness in the bar next door on the first evening. It was run by a large and powerful Cameroonian lady whom everybody called Iseeya Mammy. Mopeds and cars were going home over the sandy tracks; there was a happy babble of local language; a mig-welder worked on a bench in the dust in the garage next door. George would have said at this point that it was an arc-welder, not a mig-welder, but George was not here. Even travel writers need a holiday.

A Canadian touring the west coast appeared in the bar. We did a crawl around other bars. He was a roofer from Alberta and showed me some Alberta holiday brochures he had brought with him. I was boozed enough to be enthusiastic.

And then it was morning. Judging by my condition, I had had a lovely time. I think I had also eaten some Extremely Hot Food. Ooh. Ow. And another thing: you cannot just lurch to your room and fall drunkenly on to your bed in Africa. You have to lurch to your room, then soberly and lucidly put up your mosquito net and spray it with antibug, and then fall drunkenly on to your bed. At least the mosquitos had hangovers as bad as mine.

Despite my drinking stamina hitting a disastrous new low, unmatched since school, I was back in the bar again that evening. I was alone, writing letters at a table, when a vast cross-eyed African prostitute sat down next to me.

'You alone? I will take a beer,' she told me through a mouthful of cassava paste she was chewing.

'Riddled,' I thought. 'Super job,' I said, and stood to leave.

It took me a few moments to pay my bar bill, and when I got back to the hotel she was sitting outside watching television in the courtyard with the hotel staff. They looked at me oddly. I could not work out why. I thought she must be a friend of theirs. I went to my room. She followed me. Help!

I told her to get out. She seemed to think she was staying. I said I was going to find something to eat, locked my door with her on the corridor side of it, and walked out of the hotel. The staff looked at me disgustedly, Iseeya Mammy at their head, arms folded.

The prostitute was following me. I walked briskly round the block, lost her, and came back. Who was *that*? I asked. We thought she was your friend, they said. I thought she was yours. Much nervous relief and no-score draws all round.

Time started to run out in Cotonou. There were about to be four days to Christmas, it was 500 miles to my rendezvous in Cameroon, and there was no sign of any diesel for the ships. I started to think about a land crossing. The hard-come-by Nigeria visa was solidly embedded in the passport, so it should be easy. The problem was working out how to pass through Nigeria without becoming a victim of its oft-gossiped crime, corruption and car crashes. I decided to go via the Peugeot 504 shared taxis that speed between Nigeria's borders, and to try not to get out until Calabar, close to the border on the far side, where passenger boats make the run over to Cameroon. If I held up the others by not arriving in Cameroon, and if that meant they would miss the gap in the Central African rains, I would be in terrible trouble.

The directions to Cameroon that Iseeya Mammy gave me were quite clear. She wrote them down. 'SEME BORTHE TO MASAMASA BOXSTOP LAGOS TO ABAR NIGRIA FROM ABAR YOU TAKE 504 TO CALABAR FROM CALABAR TO CAMEROON BORTHER'. I was ready to follow them to the letter, even the missing letters.

It was a bright blue early morning, that Christmas minus four days. The traffic was hardly underway, and the taxi fairly flew on almost all sparkplugs to the Benin-Nigeria border at Seme, a village which by day separates the noise and dust of Cotonou from the misery of Lagos, but which at this time was bathed in the kind of Bethlehemic calm you hear about in carols. It all seemed so easy. Stamp out of Benin and stamp into Nigeria.

Just thirty miles away in a suburb of Lagos – I am guessing, but bear with me – life was not so idyllic in the Musa household. Mr Musa had got out of bed and was struggling to get into a tight uniform as his wife lashed him with her tongue. 'Why,' he asked himself, as he had done dozens of times before, 'did I marry her?' He decided to skip breakfast, not that she was in any mood to make it for him, and marched out of his house, banging the door in frustration, to catch a bus to work. He normally took his dark blue 7 Series BMW, but the ignition had been faulty since he had bought it so cheaply from the man going through the border in it. He had done the man a favour, for otherwise, of course, he would have gone to prison – smuggling cars is illegal. Dark blue is far too hot a colour for a car in Africa, and anyway, it looked far better parked outside his house with a boy washing it from time to time.

Border business was picking up as I approached on foot. Raucous women with baskets on their heads offered to carry my bag through Customs if I had any dodgy items in it. I was busy sizing up the place so I said 'Thank you, no,' politely, rather than the normal: 'What? Give my bag to you? Do I look stupid?' The usual heat and sweat of funnelled humanity looked a doddle. Piece of cake.

Eight hours of arguing later, I realised that this was a cake I could have but could not eat. There was considerable argy-bargy getting out of Benin, where my expired forty-eight-hour visa from the week before made some easy money for Passport Control. I made no friends among them, thinking this would be the last time I ever saw them. Big mistake.

On the Nigeria side I was faced with a large, heaving bully who was standing outside pushing the locals to the ground. He gave me a shove in the stomach for not having a cholera vaccination on my yellow card. He was holding it upside-down. With hands in the air to calm him down, I pointed out that I had a perfectly valid one, administered only the day before by Nurse John Major RGN and officially stamped by her surgery which was called Made in Britain – Food Use Only in mirror writing. He let me through. He was just there to soften me up. The real bad guy was waiting in the office.

Mr Musa was a small, uninteresting man with British Rail side-burns. He was also chief immigration officer. I had overlooked him when I first arrived at the office. Instead I had made friends with a subordinate who played the trumpet in a local dance band.

This was my first affront to Mr Musa. He had not enjoyed his bus journey. There had hardly been standing room, and now he was looking for an argument to make him feel better. 'Here's one,' he thought. 'Tall, white, glasses – he'll do.'

Mr Musa convinced himself that I was a spy. One should never say the word 'journalist' to immigration officers. I did not. Instead I stupidly said 'publisher' when he asked, 'And what kind of businessman are you?'

'You have come here to publish about my government,' he ranted. 'You are a spy.' My passport was confiscated and a price tag equivalent to his year's salary put on it if I wanted it back. Damn his salary – this was several weeks of my budget. But getting the passport back was vital. There may have been no way into Nigeria without it, but there was even less of a way back into Benin.

I was taking a break from my argument with Musa when I allowed my new friend – let us call him Charlie Parker – to observe that I had two Höhner mouth-organs with me, and that perhaps I could play only one at a time, so did not need both. The concept of being a trumpet *and* a mouth-organ player sunk in. But no, he was too lowly to deal with Mr Musa, a man playing for higher stakes, or, more probably, steaks.

In reality I believe Musa needed extra Christmas cash. Let us continue the steak theme: I believe his wife had sent him out that morning to bring home the bacon or there would be no stuffing over the Christmas break. It was time to talk turkey.

We talked. The rule, at worst, settle on ten per cent of the asking figure for a bribe. We carried on talking, but it was not easy. I could only get in three sentences of pleading before he told me to get out of his office. At first I thought he did not mean it, but C. Parker kicked me under the table. Mr Musa was in a strong position. I had no passport, I was between borders, and there was not even a telephone to summon help. Mr Musa knew this. I spent a lot of time hanging around outside his office. Mr Musa was not ready to budge on price.

I thought of hiring a fixer, a Thomas. Many of them saw me

and offered their services. Mr Musa told me he was going home at lunchtime, and could we hurry up, please. I hired a fixer. This was my second stupid mistake. The fixer lost his temper with Mr Musa, which fixers should never do. Mr Musa smacked the fixer in the face, and then did him for assault. The last I saw of the fixer he was off to the nick in Lagos.

By now Mr Musa was in a bad temper. He had not managed it with his wife, but he brought up the bile for me. I paid the full price, some 700 times the going rate. 'Ooh, Nigeria is too tough. Everybody wants to eat dollar,' a rival fixer told me, glibly.

Mr Musa gave me back my passport with 'Refused Entry' stamped in red across the precious visa. He offered to issue another visa for the same price again. I turned it down. He told me how pleased he was that I would not be tainting his country with my seditious presence. I said thank you, just as we had at Treichville Police Station. What to do? Make a blood feud of it? Swear never to cut my hair until I had killed him? I clenched my teeth with Christmas cheer, fed up to the back of them, cut my losses and ran.

The Benin immigration were about to make a scene about my lack of Benin visa, but I barged through them with obvious white man's fury and hailed a taxi for Cotonou Airport.

Flying has made overland travel so much easier. If you take the centre of civilisation to be, say, Dick's T-Bar in Val d'Isère, as long as you can get to an airfield, you are never more than a day away from it. The overland truckie girl heading north who had caught cerebral malaria in Cameroon and had forty-eight hours to live if she was not treated was able to hop on to an aeroplane home to South Africa, recover, and rejoin her truck in Ivory Coast.

I walked briskly into the crowded airport building, ready once more to face and outface the officials. Surely they could not be as difficult as Mr Musa.

They were waiting for me – or so it seemed. They were pacing around in slavering packs, eyeing up their victims. As I approached them they raised their mouths to the ceiling and howled – arooo! Or, again, it seemed as if they did. My heart went down with all hands.

It became ridiculous. There was a flight to Douala in Cameroon that afternoon but it was full. There was a standby list, but it was warm to the touch with bribes. There were people on every square foot of airport floor, all hoping to go to Douala. You needed both hands: one to hand off the competition, and the other to hand out backhanders to the officials. The check-in was a scrum.

And today, lining up for the 17.05 Douala Handicap, a big field of luggage ranging from three-year-olds upwards. The race to run over just less than a quarter of a furlong and the going is lino. They are loading the last one into the stalls now. That's Christmas Shopping there, Christmas Shopping out of Market Stall by Taiwan Factory with Fat Lady in the saddle. She's in now. The check-in desk steward is here. They're under starter's orders. And they're off! First away it's Nondescript Box, Nondescript Box from Old Samsonite, and behind Old Samsonite it's Rucksack, the favourite Hand Luggage Only, Picnic Basket leading the rest of the field. They round the first turn and they're bunched up to the leader, Nondescript Box, tight against the rail. It's still Nondescript Box, owned by Local Chieftain, which won last year's Diamond Smuggling Stakes. Picnic Basket edging forward to challenge the leaders, and it looks like there's some barging going on between Old Samsonite and Rucksack, and that could be excessive use of the strap there by Fat Lady. Now, with only a few seconds to go, it's a big push from Hand Luggage Only from Nondescript Box, and here comes Rucksack – Rucksack from Hand Luggage Only – it's Hand Luggage Only – they're at the post – it's Rucksack – it's Rucksack by a nose. *What a finish*! And the baggage-handlers are on their feet as Rucksack, owned by Mr Charles Jacoby, is first to be checked in and on to the conveyor belt.

After that the hand-outs started in earnest. Luckily none topped a few dollars, but everybody had to have one. I even had to bribe people to let me see other people who were going to take more bribes off me. It was a bribe-frenzy. By the time I had bought the ticket, confirmed my standby seat, picked up my boarding pass and was ready to leave the country, the aeroplane was about to take off. It looked like the confetti scene at a guards officer's wedding as I ran through the departure gate past all the men in peaked caps, throwing away handfuls of the grubby little rags they call money in Benin.

Then the passport man stopped me. As he was the last in the line, he knew he was in a strong position. Ignoring the way the sky had turned black and the forked lightning played across my fevered forehead, he told me there was something wrong with my Benin visa. He was right, but there was no time to wait for him to work out what it was and cadge an even bigger bribe. I threw a couple of dollars at him, grabbed the passport as he was stamping it, and legged it. What he had not had time to work out was that, according to my passport, I had first entered Benin from Togo a week before, had not exited, but had been stamped in as if from Nigeria that morning and stamped out immediately, and without re-entering Benin he was allowing me to exit from Cotonou Airport. I felt he would only use that to his advantage.

The flight was remarkable. People were still trying to bribe their way on even as the steps were being pulled away from the side of the aeroplane. It was an Air Afrique stopping service which had come from Abidjan and was going on from Douala to Bangui in Central African Republic and Brazzaville in the Congo. It stopped in Lagos on the way to Douala. I saw the same stampede across the tarmac that I had been part of in Cotonou an hour before. But Nigerians are professionals. They make other West African bribery look like the silver collection after a low-church service. People were actually evicted from their seats to make space for a family trying to get to Zaïre for Christmas.

We were overloaded by now, and there was some murmuring from other passengers to the effect that we were bound to crash because of it. Laughable, I thought; overloading was the least of our worries. I was more concerned that the stewardesses, who were currently busy giving out bread rolls and beers to cushion the blow should we happen to come down, were patently taking it in turns to sit on the pilot's lap as we flew. The elderly African lady next to me in the loud print dress with pictures of South American toucans all over it, who had been praying loudly in French since take-off with her eyes closed, opened them for a moment when the beer-and-rolls trolley went past and grabbed as many as she could. Nothing ventured . . .

I did the same. Everybody did, and the stewardess ran out halfway up the aisle, to more muttering from the passengers in first class. One of them tried to start a fight but calmed down quickly when the captain drove into some turbulence. We survived the final approach to Douala and landed in a way that left the passengers in agreement that the pilot's mind was definitely on something else.

After an immigration procedure so easy it had me whooping with thanks in the arrivals hall and attracting the attention of the black-market money-changers and drunk taxi-drivers, I went into Douala and booked into a cheap hotel. It was, naturally, an all-night club and brothel as well, but I was too tired to notice, and slept solidly and dreamlessly until morning.

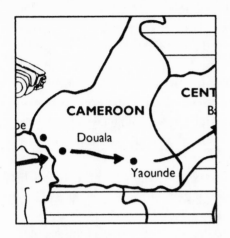

C h a p t e r 8

CHRISTMAS

Cameroon. Red, George, Emma, Wicky and me in Mistress Quickly. Jesper joins Neil and Hazel in the Dust Busters' Land Rover. Urs and Lara in the Swiss Family Robinson's Land Rover. Michael and Kay in the white Hanomag. Heinz and Christa in the red Hanomag. Steve and the truckies in the Truck Africa truck. 151 days to the World Cup opening ceremony.

Douala is Cameroon's main port town. Logs from the forests of Central Africa are shipped to carpenters, joiners and cabinet-makers all over the world from there, and some of the citizens of Douala have got rich on it. The city that grew around these citizens' businesses has bred hellish poverty for others. An old man in a brown ragged shirt and one-legged trousers stiff with dirt hobbled down the hill on a stick. The naked leg was so swollen with elephantiasis it looked like one of the tree trunks loaded on to Douala's ships. His knee was nearly as thick as his waist. The distended skin around his ankles spilled over his toes. I passed him to walk into town and find a bus for Limbe.

I stopped at the first coffee shop I came to. The worst of the hookers in my hotel had still been out looking for johns at breakfast, and I wanted to avoid them.

Who should be in the café but the Swiss Family Robinson, Urs and Lara. We were all surprised. Urs has a film star's face, high cheekbones and strong jaw, but a range of comedian's expressions tends to yoyo across it in moments of stress or amazement, which stretch and pull it to exhaustion. Try pursing your lips as hard as you can with a big frown on your forehead, then slam suddenly into your widest grin. Keep this up for five minutes, and hold a conversation while you are at it. Now consider doing it for the rest of your life. Urs did. Right now his face was rippling away like a wave machine. An incredulous 'Hello, Chorli,' was all he could manage to spit out.

But for all that, it was the same scene as Rabbit's return after his unsuccessful attempt to unbounce Tigger, with Urs and Lara playing the part of Tigger and me in the role of Rabbit.

. . . Tigger was tearing round the Forest making loud yapping noises for Rabbit. And at last a very Small and Sorry Rabbit heard him. And the Small and Sorry Rabbit rushed through the mist at the noise, and it suddenly turned into Tigger; a Friendly Tigger, a Grand Tigger, a Large and Helpful Tigger, a Tigger who bounced, if he bounced at all, in just the beautiful way a Tigger ought to bounce.

'Oh, Urs, Lara, I *am* glad to see you,' cried Rabbit.

There was a third person eating breakfast with the Tiggers, a German called Michael. It appeared that this trip was a politically sensitive time for the Swiss Family Robinson, and the background needs some explaining.

It all comes down to gossip. Let us go back in time and space for a moment to Mauritania. When they left us, the Dust Busters and the Swiss Family Robinson had gone off south to Senegal and worked their way round the coast of West Africa that way, while we, the Hoorays, went eastwards, back into the desert, and then south across Mali. When we met Jesper in Mali he told us some surprising news. The Dust Buster Michelle had fallen out with her boyfriend, the DB Neil, leaving, we guessed, his sister, the DB Hazel, to stare in the air and talk loudly about the weather, or equivalent. Michelle flew home from Senegal.

Part of Michelle's gripe was that she thought Neil fancied Lara. 'Not true,' protested Neil. But after putting the thumbscrews on Jesper, and he was reluctant to talk even then, we learned of the evening that they had all gone swimming in the sea together in Senegal. Jesper can take up the story.

'Et was after Mjichelle hed gøne. Everyone was – whjat is it? – skjinny-djipping. Is thet the wjørd?' Jesper was always keen to improve his English. 'Lara wjent out of the sea.'

'Why?'

'To tek a shjit? I djøn't knjøw. Bjut enywey, end then Njeil følløwed her.'

How romantic, we thought.

'We wjent bek to the cjampsite after the swem. But Njeil end Lara was nøt thjere. Thjen thjere was this sunset, end we were cjooking fjood – me, Urs end Hjazel – and E saw thjem togjether in frjønt of the sun – whjat is it?'

'Silhouetted.'

'Sjille-wetted. End E saw Njeil jump into these bjushes end Lara cem bek by hersjelf.'

'Why did Neil jump into the bushes?'

'Sjø that Urs didn't sjee hjim. End thjen he cem bek fjive minutes efter.'

Ah. Tactful.

George, Red, Emma and I talked among ourselves and decided that this witness evidence did not constitute a proper result. But we now knew that Neil was up for it. Jesper refused to be drawn on anything else. 'E'm only tjelling you what E saw,' he told us.

We knew that Urs and Lara were not actually going out, a couple, screwing – whatever you want to call it – but Urs did have a certain proprietorial air where Lara was concerned, so we were discreet when we met them. We knew also that Urs and Lara were not getting on together as travellers. They often spent their evenings shut in their Land Rover arguing with each other. This was unusual from a boy as mild-mannered as Urs and a girl as endlessly positive and happy as Lara, but we decided that the raised voices we heard were definitely reliable evidence. Then we remembered that the raised voices were speaking in German, which, being the dreadful language it is, meant they could easily have been reading love poetry to each other.

Douala was the proof, however. Lara was giving up the trip there. When I met them, Urs was about to drive her to the airport, and she was going to fly on to South Africa. Her replacement was Michael.

'The germans are unspeakable,' said Nigel Molesworth, but he had not met Michael. The same age as the rest of us, Michael had been travelling through Africa in a battered old Hanomag lorry with a friend called Kay. Kay is a bloke's name in Germany. They were taking time off from learning to be doctors at Gottingen University. They were completely charming, placid and reserved – all the qualities required for travelling. They were bright, too, and made you wish that the First World War had never ousted the Germans from their African colonies such as Tanzania and Namibia, because with men like Michael and Kay in charge, they would have made an excellent job of running them.

Michael always took our crass English jokes 'Two world wars and one World Cup – doodah, doodah' in good spirit. 'Ah well,' he would say, 'we made it to Paris twice since 1870. Next time, eh?'

Kay's girlfriend was about to arrive in Cameroon, and he wanted to stay on the west coast with her. On a whim and a prayer, Michael decided to go east with Urs. He may have looked at Urs's smart red Land Rover and thought it would be a better bet than his Hanomag, which was teetering on the brink of scrap by the time it reached Cameroon. At the best of times, Hanomag lorries look like a cross between a Willy Jeep and a dustcart. That Hanomag had seen its best times years before, just as Urs's vehicle had, though someone forgot to mention this. Had Michael not been so solid a character, he would have run screaming from Urs's Land Rover after a week, as this shed of a vehicle started to live up to that sobriquet by shedding its few remaining working parts.

I said goodbye to Lara as Urs and Michael stood up to take her to her aeroplane, and went back to my hotel to pick up my bag. We would all miss her butterfly lightheartedness and bright good humour, not least Neil. After they came back from the airport I drove with Urs and Michael, the new Swiss Family Robinson, the 100 miles back up the coast to Limbe.

This little resort town on the coast used to be called Victoria, and, grander than that, was formerly the administrative capital for the British Cameroons. It still has the odd vestige of this, such as its famous botanical gardens, which were being run by an angular young man we met called Jamie Ackworth. Jamie had a rather difficult Christmas, trying to balance having a wild time with us with the more sedate parties preferred by his white neighbours.

We were staying on a gently curved beach in a shallow bay six miles outside Limbe called, in typical Cameroon style, Six Mile Beach. It had chocolate-coloured sand, from the black ash of the huge, volcanic Mount Cameroon, which overlooked the town, and a blue lapping sea. It also had an oil refinery high on a cliff at one end, which only a month or two before we would have dubbed 'Tuareg'. But the refinery had a social club, which brought the twin benefits of uniformed guards for our camp and a bar in the clubhouse.

The party was in full swing when we arrived. Everyone was there. George and Wicky had pitched their tent under the trees by the beach where we were camping. Red and Emma had their campbeds under the tarpaulin awning from Mistress Quickly. The two remaining Dust Busters had their roof tent up on top of their Land Rover. There were two Hanomags, both as decrepit as each other, one Kay's and another belonging to an old German couple called Heinz and Christa. Truck Africa, strung with festive fairylights and parked at one end of the beach with their twenty people on board, made up the bulk of the gang. And there was a small, purple, tortoise-shaped tent in the middle of all this, which I recognised at once. It was Jesper. There was a huge amount of catching up to do.

Me: 'Neil!' Neil: 'Hello, Charlie.'

Me: 'Neil, what's all this I hear —'

Red: 'Charlie! How did you get here? I thought we'd lost you.'

Me: 'No – ha, ha – no such luck.'

George: 'Ah, Charlie.'

Me: 'Hello, George. Hello, daaarling.' (To Wicky, kiss on cheek)

Wicky: 'Hello, hello.'

Jesper: 'Hjello, Charlie.'

Me: 'Hello, Jesper. Now, Neil —'

Red: 'Hazel and Emma have gone off together to climb Mount Cameroon.'

Me: 'Have they. Have they. Now, N —'

Neil never said a word. He was not that sort of person. He and

Hazel were once the sort of children who would infuriate other parents' children by being so ideal. Both were good-looking, kind, dependable, generous, thoughtful and patient. They were characters from a Victorian children's morality tale, showing all that is good in human nature, the opposite of Struwwelpeter. So I gave up asking. Perhaps I would catch him drunk over Christmas.

Red told of the Hoorays' trip through Nigeria in Mistress Quickly. They had gone through with virtually no trouble. 'Not even at the border?' I asked. Not even at the border, he told me. One policeman had toyed with the idea of busting them for drugs after finding hypodermic needles in the medical kit, and then confiscating the needles in lieu of a bribe, but Red and George told him quite emphatically that with AIDS the problem it is, they were prepared to take the needles issue as far as the Nigerian President, so he backed down and went off to look for easier pickings.

Despite the lack of successful bribery, everyone was sad about Nigeria. The country was, they said, on its last legs. All the money it had made in oil in the 1970s was spent. The place had fallen to rack, and was now not long off ruin. George described how he had seen a lump of something on the flyover going out of Lagos. It looked like a dead animal. It was a human torso. There was a police check 200 yards up the road, and the coppers were obviously keen to ignore it. 'You saw that as well?' said Steve, the Australian who was in charge of Truck Africa. 'We saw it, and we went through Lagos a week before you.'

Steve was shortish, with dark standard-issue trucky hair which grew everywhere it could on his face. He was our master of ceremonies for Christmas; always a joke for the boys, always one for the girls if he had a chance. He had been driving trucks across Africa for years, and knew that to do it successfully, you have to be the boss. He was always bossing the other truckies. They took it well.

But Steve had a weakness. He fancied Hazel. He would not talk about it, but he went stupid and blithered whenever she walked near. And stupid and blithering things happened to him as well. If Hazel was in sight, whatever Steve was doing would go wrong, be it lighting a fire or opening a beer bottle, which normally he could accomplish with the flick of a Bic lighter. The best one was when a bird dropped a pile of guano on his head just as he had finally got her on her own, or at least as on her own as the thirty other people in the place allowed. He went off for a swim.

Jesper had, of course, made it through to Limbe only by luck and mismanagement. He had bought a bicycle and headed the wrong way out of Accra, got lost, ended up in a recently demilitarised village in northern Ghana, quelled a crowd of a hundred locals who all wanted to get into his tent to see what it was really like, found Danish aid projects and offices of the Danish shipping company Maersk all over the west coast and been invited back to all their managing directors' houses to stay, and finally arrived from Nigeria in a smuggler's speedboat which was outrunning but not outgunning a police launch close behind. He landed in a Cameroonian swamp and pushed the bike several miles to the road, where the Dust Busters, who just happened to be driving by, picked him up.

I related my Nigerian border troubles and everyone fell about with laughter; Jesper in particular thought it extremely funny, until Red started to tease him about some African floozy who had tried to pick him up the night before in a bar, and the fact that in trying to avoid her he had fallen over a chair.

'Don't give me djick,' he said. Red had explained to Jesper about the English phrases 'giving gip', and 'giving stick', but Jesper had not quite mastered them. His girlfriend was about to arrive from Denmark, and he was rather sensitive about the incident.

When the story of my troubles was translated for Heinz and Christa they laughed as well. We all learned to love Heinz and Christa. They were the only people over the age of thirty-five in the place. They spoke no English or French, only German, and were on a two-year tour of the continent. Heinz was wrinkled and bearded, like a troll or goblin invention of the Brothers Grimm. He was a heavy smoker, a habit which, aggravated by a bout of typhus fever, had him hacking and coughing through Christmas. He looked too grey for the kind of trip he and Christa were undertaking, but he always ploughed on in his boneshaking Hanomag. Christa was younger, and ran the logistics side of things. Heinz could be a little vague.

They were the first white people we met who really couldn't speak any language that we could. But like George with his French – or, rather, without his French – and his French-speaking policemen, Heinz and Christa had never had much trouble with local officials. Chatting with them was a problem for us, though, but we got through. Heinz had a battery-powered drill. We needed to put holes in a sheet of metal to rivet it to a large gap in the side of Mistress Quickly. Heinz was drilling these holes against the side of the Land Rover and not having much success. 'Nein, nein,' I said, 'drill it on the ground, it's easier. Neil, what's "drill it on the ground" in German?'

'Flooren boren?'

'Ja. Flooren boren, Heinz,' I said. Against all the odds, it worked – he did it.

I joined the party with great happiness. Steve was the first to announce that he needed to drown his sorrows that night, so the two of us and another truckie left at once in a taxi for Limbe. As far as drowning was concerned, Steve was already going down for the third time when the taxi arrived and he persuaded the taxi-man to let him drive. We veered and swerved into town, more on the verge than the road, and every other taxi we met we hooted and flashed and shouted. The taxi-driver thought this was hilarious. The other truckie and I sank low into our seats. But it was the Cameroon way through and through, and taxis all over Limbe waved at Steve in the street for the rest of his stay there.

Then the truckie and I had some beers as well. That night jumbled into a mess of debauchery and high living. Jamie Ackworth joined us for a bit. He had to: we broke up a drinks party he was holding for his dull neighbours and we were rude about their children until they went home. The four of us, and the taxi-driver, who could not resist coming too, lurched into Limbe's hospital to visit another of the truckies, who had gone down with malaria. The hospital was clean, cool and colonial, and the truckie was recovering well. We did our best to lower its tone, racing each other in wheelchairs, playing with the truckie's drip, writing rude messages on the clipboard at the end of his bed.

'You're drunk,' observed a nurse.

'Yup,' we rejoined wittily.

Red joined us. George and Wicky, Neil and all the rest met us in a variety of bars around town.

We stopped several times on the six-mile trip home to drink and dance. I tried to teach one ravaged old African woman to rock and roll. 'Yes, my brother,' her pimp told me, 'she is my mother. You want sleep with her?'

'Not poshible, old chap,' I replied after some thought. 'If I'm' – pointing to myself – 'your brother, and you're' – pointing to him – 'her shun, then she' – waving arms in direction of bar – 'musht be my shishter . . . er . . .' Pause for more thought. 'No, no, that'sh not right.'

He grew tired of this conversation and went back to the old African standby: get me British citizenship, get me out of this place. Like so many others with ambition, he had a Dick Whittington view of a Europe paved with gold. I tried to explain that I could not help him, but got badly stuck on words like 'ambashador' and 'shittyzenship'.

We moved on to yet another bar, the last of the night. It had to be the last of the night because of its tremendous floorshow. We stayed there until dawn to watch. It centred on us, the half-dozen last survivors of the evening, being white. A table was set aside for us. Beers were brought. 'Marvelloush.' More beers were brought, and on the house this time, in a burst of customer relations. 'Shmashing – thanksh.'

A ratty little man sat down next to us and tried to turn the conversation towards the Difficulty of Becoming a British Citizen. 'Thish man ish Trouble,' we observed to each other beerily and blearily. A big fellow by the bar, who was the local police officer, we later learned, took it upon himself to remove the Rat. But the Rat would not go. Our policeman picked up our rodent and tried to throw him out. On his way to the door the struggling Rat hit out at a group of people who turned and hit the policeman. The policeman dropped the Rat, who squeaked as he fell. The bar-owner went up to stop this shocking display in front of honoured guests. The policeman hit him. We settled back in our chairs to enjoy ourselves.

It was a time-honoured western-style brawl. Chairs were flying, tables were being knocked over, tarts were screaming and running for the door. Each scrap lasted a minute or two, with people in headlocks being hit by other people in bearhugs being hit by yet more people circling around and getting in an occasional haymaker or jab below the ribs. In the intervals the bar-owner came up to our table to make sure we were happy and our glasses were full.

The action scenes were great, but the best bit was the plot. Whenever everyone simmered down, the Rat would reappear at a side entrance. The first time the policeman spotted him, and barged his way through the crowd to get to him, but the crowd were having none of this, and laid into the policeman again. More thumping, and exit Rat quietly stage right. The Rat then appeared from behind the bar – he must have used a back entrance – and shoved someone into the policeman. The policeman hit the man, who fell into him, and off they went again, and again off the Rat sidled, out of the way.

It went on like this for two hours. We did not help. We were calling out encouragement. 'Ding ding, shecondsh out, round five!' and 'Wallop him!' It ended at dawn, when the Rat actually bit the policeman in the neck and the policeman arrested him. 'Boooooooo!' we shouted. 'Shame – shend him off!'

We were back in that bar the next night and the policeman came up proudly to our table to show off the doctor's certificate he had been given for his bite wound. We said in all seriousness that we thought he might catch rabies from it. He looked worried, then he laughed, but all the same he went off to the doctor again to check.

Nights like these were had throughout the holiday. The hangovers each morning were horrible to behold. Red, Neil and George were doing passing practice with the rugby ball in the sea. Red caught the ball from Neil, sent it spinning on to George, then turned round and threw up copiously. It floated like a multicoloured oil slick, you may be interested to know.

I bottled out early from the Christmas Eve wild night and went to bed, burned out. I had had a hammock made up in Cotonou, and had strung it between two trees at Six Mile Beach. I was looking forward to sleeping soundly in it for the few short hours that remained until Christmas morning.

At four in the morning I woke up to the sound of carol-singers. Not the most tuneful carol-singers, I thought to myself, and one of them sounds distinctly like Neil. They were a long way away, though, at the other end of the beach among the Truck Africa tents. 'We wish you a merry Chrishmush, we wish you a merry Chrishmush, we wish you a merry Chrishmush and a haaaappy New Year – tee hee, hee hee.'

'Mmmmmmmm,' groaned a tent.

I woke up properly.

They came a little closer.

'We WISH you a merry CHRISHmush, we WISH you a merry CHRISHmush, we WISH you a merry CHRISHmush, and a HAAAAppy New Year – hoo-hoo-hooo-hooo!'

One of them must be Wicky.

'Sod off,' said a tent more emphatically.

'Ooooooooooh. Shod off. Tee hee hee. She shaid shod off.'

Closer still.

'Look. There'sh a hammock. It'sh Charlie'sh hammock. Let'sh shwing it a bit.'

Oh, shit.

'WE WISH YOU A ME-RRY CHRISHMUSH – SHWING – WE WISH YOU A ME-RRY CHRISHMUSH – SHWING – WE WISH YOU A ME-RRY CHRISHMUSH – SHWING – AND A HAAAPPY NEEEW YEEEAAAAAAR – SHWING, SHWING, SHWING.'

No reaction. I decided that no reaction was the best policy. I groaned a bit, and tried to roll over. Luckily, I remembered that you cannot roll over in a hammock, but they were still swinging it into the tree, so they did not notice.

'He *musht* be awake by now.'

That was Red. I will kill Red.

'He'sh *pretending*.'

I will kill Emma as well.

They grew bored. 'Let'sh go and wake up Heinsh and Chrishta!'

It took them an hour to go to bed. The first rays of sunlight were creeping over Mount Cameroon and tickling the tops of the trees. It was a soft sunlight, and would not start burning for a few hours yet. Now I can sleep, I thought. Even the birds were not making much noise – probably too knackered after being woken up by those carol-singers. Or out of respect for the dead, I thought – me.

Crash! went the tree.

I woke up and rubbed my eyes.

Crash! it went again.

A troupe of putty-nosed guenon monkeys were holding a breakfast party right above me. They fed and fought each other for another hour, trampolining on the branches and showering me with twigs. I lay awake, wondering where I had left my catapult, and whether I could make the effort to get up and find it.

Just as they left, at six o'clock, an army helicopter buzzed the bay. I got out of bed and went off to make coffee.

A helicopter was appropriate for Christmas morning, I thought as I drank it, because a vague memory stirred of a long-lost newspaper article claiming that the pidgin English for 'helicopter' is 'mixter man 'e come Jesus Christ'.

Pidgin is an old slave language. It is so simple that it is confusing. We had trouble with it during our stay in Limbe. The word 'bush' for example, means any part of the country not built up. The word 'spring' they know from normal English as a source of water. And they understand 'rusty' because it is the cause of plenty problem not small small time when iron meets water. Unfortunately, in Land Rover engineering, springs and bushes make up part of the suspension, on which Mistress Quickly had received mortal wounds in Mali. Red made friends with an American missionary called Rusty who lived in the bush outside Limbe near a freshwater spring, and the two of them went off for a day to sort the problem out, Red's hangover permitting.

The chief guard at Six Mile Beach came up to me that day. I knew what he was going to ask, and my heart sank.

'Which side your brother?' he asked.

'Who? Red?' I replied.

'Brother with beard for face.'

'He gone for bush one time.'

'He done pass plenty time.'

'He gone look for spring.'

'He gone look for spring in bush?'

'Yes.'

'Waa. There is plenty water here.'

'No. He gone look for Land Rover spring. Spring and bush.'

'He look for spring *and* bush?'

'In bush, yes.'

'How he done that?'

'He gone to spring to find Rusty.'

'What small ting he have is rusty from spring?'

'Rusty is missionary,' I said in exasperation. 'You know, God, Senior Brother sort of thing.'

'Missionary is rusty?'

'Yes.'

'From spring?'

'Yes.'

'Waa. He no have missionary made from metal.'

'No. Rusty is name for missionary. He pass plenty time at house for spring. Small ting is also a spring. A Land Rover spring which is broken. And a Land Rover bush which is broken. And to get new bush and new spring Red has gone to Rusty who lives at the spring.'

'In bush?'

'Yes, in the bush. And pass one day there.'

'Waa. I see.' The chief guard walked off, scratching his head and mouthing, 'Spring for bush. Waa. Bush for spring. Waa.'

Pidgin has a wonderfully candid style. Every syllable is stressed equally, so every word sounds as if it comes from the heart. The cover-all word for contentment is 'fine', but this does not sum up its expressiveness. To say it properly you must put on a big grin, a general happiness with humanity, and pronounce it 'fiiiiine'. The taxi-driver who picked us up in Limbe on the morning after a big night to take us back to the beach lost his way. He also picked up some of his friends and relations who, since he was going that way, decided they could take the rest of the day off and spend it by the seaside. Taking a taxi is an easy way to get lost in Africa. The large and loudly dressed woman next to Hazel told her, sincerely and emphatically, 'This Man is Hiiigh-Ly Stuu-Pid.'

Steve made a huge effort over Christmas lunch. He bought two pigs and slaughtered them, and we contributed several chickens. The thirty of us sat down to eat on a long trestle table in front of Truck Africa, which was hung with tinsel.

We enjoyed it, but it was not Christmas. Definitely not. The Dust Busters produced a large Christmas pudding which their parents had given them, and I donated a small one from the toe of the Christmas stocking my mother made sure I took with me. Neil set light to them with bitter local brandy. We finished our meal, fat and homesick.

Why punish ourselves like this when we could be living quietly near Copenhagen, Dortmund or Taunton? Jesper was the most lonely. There were no other Danish-speakers on the beach. In the early evenings, he would take a chair down to the tideline and sit on it, a King Canute in the moonlight, and think of home. An aunt had sent me a Christmas card in the form of an advent calendar. It was a picture of Munich in the snow, with happy people roasting chestnuts and singing carols. Christa looked at it, and suddenly thought of home in Germany. She had made tissue-wrapped bundles of goodies for each of us, with a candle stuck in the top. They contained presents like After Eight mints. But Africa is too hot for After Eights. It is too hot and close and far away for Christmas altogether. The baubles on our Christmas trees were the dried grass nests of the weaver birds.

To ease their homesickness, two of the truckies had hired themselves happy Christmas hookers. They spent a lot of time in their tents risking everything from AIDS downwards. 'They must be mad,' said Red. 'Some of us are not impressed,' said a female truckie disparagingly.

It may have been the malaria pills that made us moodier. Mefloquine was the first drug invented to stave off malaria since the Vietnam War. People normally take Paludrine and Chloroquine, and die-hards just have a good dose of tonic water in their gins. Mefloquine was this year's wonder drug, marketed by the drug company Roche under the name Lariam. Back in Britain, the side-effects of this drug were getting a lot of press coverage These pills are what they call a prophylactic, a preventative, which everyone agrees is quite different from what everyone normally calls a prophylactic.

As well as our moodiness, we attributed our spectacular dreams to them. I saw two fantastically vivid Lariam-induced air crashes in the night. In one a Jumbo jet crashed into an oil refinery, and in the other a Hercules plummeted head-down, nose-first into a friend's house in Somerset. I caught an enormous Lariam fish. It was especially big because it had just swallowed my typewriter. Everything was larger and more Lariam than life.

The day ended with a trip into town to telephone home. Telephoning from Africa is fraught. Not only is it expensive, but the line is never clear and the distance makes it slow so when you talk you have to pause at the end of each sentence to wait for an answer. If you pause mid-sentence you find yourself talking over what the other person is saying. You do a lot of blithering on the telephone, and you never ask the questions you want to ask before the pips go or the line cuts off and you end up walking away feeling let down and isolated. It is disappointing.

When we drove into town that Christmas Day it looked like any other day. The market was going strong by the side of the dirt road, and people were shopping, albeit wearing slightly smarter clothes for church. The taxi-drivers were out in their usual numbers, lounging on their battered Fords and Peugeots by the road.

One of the taxi-men sauntered up to us as we walked into the telephone office, a low stone building with a tin roof and a wooden booth in one corner of its dim interior. He spoke American-film English. 'Hey, you!' he said. 'Don't you know it's Christmas? We *celebrate* Christmas in Cameroon, yeah, you know? Do you *celebrate* in your country?'

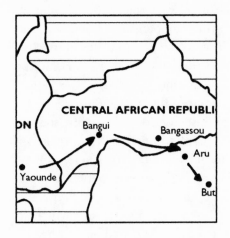

Chapter 9

CRIME AND PASSION

Cameroon and Central African Republic. George, Wicky, Red and me in Mistress Quickly. Are joined by the Peace Corps worker Jeff. Emma leaves Mistress Quickly. She replaces Jesper to join Neil and Hazel in the Dust Busters' Land Rover. Urs and Michael in the Swiss Family Robinson's Land Rover. Heinz & Christa in the Hanomag. 149 days to the World Cup opening ceremony.

N
EWS HERE UNNIGERIAWARDS PROCEEDED BORDER RE-
FUSED ENTRYWISE ACCUSED SPY LANDROVER INBROKEN
CAMEROON ALL CLOTHES TAKEN CHRISTMAS BEACH-
LOVELY TWO PIGS FOUR CHICKENS THIRTY PEOPLE INPEARTREE
UNPARTRIDGE PROCEEDING UGANDAWARDS ZAIREWISE SPEEDILIEST
GORILLA WARFARE UNSEE STOP. I started to adopt this old-fashioned
cablespeak to send faxes home with news. It saved money.

Our aim was to head directly from Limbe to the east coast of Africa. We would travel straight across Cameroon, where we knew the bribery, the crime and the roads were bad, straight through Central African Republic, where they were all worse, and as quickly as possible into and out of Zaïre, where they were the worst of all. The party was over until Uganda. This was the challenge that George enjoyed so much. This was the strain on all of us to which I was not looking forward.

The party broke up at Limbe. Truck Africa went off down the

coast. Steve shook us all by the hand, wrote rude messages on the backs of our Land Rovers with a marker pen, and fumbled a sad goodbye to Hazel. Jesper went off with Kay to await their respective girlfriends. The Swiss Family Robinson, the Dust Busters, Heinz and Christa and us formed a convoy and set off for the capital of Cameroon, Yaounde. Emma joined the Dust Busters' partly to spread the load, and partly to ease tensions that were starting to form among the five of us in Mistress Quickly. We left the sea behind. We would not see it again for another 5,000 miles.

Mistress Quickly was, indeed, robbed. It was dark when we reached Yaounde, an ugly smoggy city set on several hills, and we camped in the grounds of a Protestant mission, a small field around a church up on one of the hills. We had no chance to look properly at security there, but bedded down like pioneers in covered wagons fearing attacks by Indians, making a square with our vehicles. I slung my hammock from the roof-rack at the back of Mistress Quickly to Heinz and Christa's truck. During the night, just a yard away from my head, the villains silently cut the rubber bungy from around one of the small back windows and lifted out five bags, one belonging to each of us. Then they made off down the hill along the myriad paths in the scrub and dripping sewers, crashing through the thorns and sensitive plants, into the heart of the town.

Wicky discovered it. She was up first to make the coffee. 'Er,' – nervous laughter – 'I think we've been robbed.'

George sprang from his tent. 'Hmmm. Yup.'

Red and I joined him.

'Didn't you hear anything, Charlie?' asked George.

'Um, no.'

'I'm surprised they didn't ask him to shut up with all that snoring,' said Red. 'They're probably off now complaining to the Public Health.'

We had breakfast, and as one by one the others appeared we showed them the damage. We had to laugh about it; the only alternative was to cry. But it made us instantly racist. We prowled around Yaounde after that believing the worst of everyone. All Africans are crooks. You cannot help thinking it after one or two of them have robbed you. In the words of the song: 'I know the criminal classes suffer from social deprivation, but when my house was burgled all I could think of was castration'.

The most serious loss was Emma's cameras. All of them went except one. There were tears on the telephone to Dublin over that. A less serious loss were Wicky's washbag, containing bits like a small mirror and some contraceptive pills, and my bag, which held my only valuable item, my old school tie from Lord's of Piccadilly, the blighters. Wicky mentioned the mirror, and then said she hoped that police were looking into it, hfffg-hfffg-hfffg, hoo-hoo. I said they should be looking for a man with big tits passing himself off as an Old Shirburnian. Psshjjee-ee-ee-ee.

After combing the hill to see if the robbers had dropped anything during their escape (we found one of my socks), we went to make a report at the police station. This was a formality. The Cameroonian police were not going to do anything about it – how could they? But they knew they had to sign and stamp the report, and they knew that this was for insurance reasons, so they charged us for it. Red was spitting about it. We decided to leave Yaounde with all speed.

The last town we came to in Cameroon was Batouri, on the border with the Central African Republic. Batouri is a glorified trucker's café for the logger lorries trundling out of the Congo Basin. Nevertheless, it was New Year's Eve, and we needed a celebration to raise our dampened spirits, so Emma and I went off to recce the bars. We told everyone we would be back in an hour. Our convoy was parked in the compound of a small hotel. We were all camping but had rented one room for its bathroom. We used this system a lot, and it worked well as long as the hotel was grotty enough. Nice hotels did not like the look of us at all.

While Emma and I were away, everyone queued for showers. Neil and Hazel pulled out the box of smart clothes that they kept for Special Occasions. I never knew how they managed it. When we were caked in dust and dirt after weeks on the road, all looking like the American sandman monster, Neil and Hazel only had to polish their faces to a bright pink, and Neil would put on a sparkling clean silk shirt, and Hazel would step into a slinky number with light and bright colours in its pattern, and they would look like a fashionable couple plucked out of some trendy London nightclub. 'That's white, Charlie,' Red would point out in the pattern of Hazel's dress. 'W, H, I, T, E, remember?'

An hour later they were all ready. Heinz had combed his beard. Red, to our gratitude, had shaved his off as our Christmas treat. Even George and Urs did not look as if they would be thrown out of every bar we went to. But there was no sign of Emma and me. An hour turned into two hours, and they were just about to leave without us, when Emma walked in through the gates, looking unusually stiff. She was walking unnaturally carefully.

'He's drunk,' she whispered.

'Nonsense,' I said, tripping over the gateposts. 'She is.'

'Where,' asked Red, 'have you been?'

We both spoke at once. 'Well, there was this little bar' – 'Quite big bar, actually' – 'But it wasn't very good' – 'Oh, *that* bar' – 'So we went to the one next door' – 'That *was* big' – 'And had some drinks there' – 'And met a nice man who runs the petrol station' – 'So we might get some cheap diesel tomorrow' – 'We're sorry we're late' – 'So it wasn't completely wasted.'

The others thought it was. 'They need to lighten up,' Emma and I agreed in hoarse whispers as we trailed behind them out of the gates again.

The people of Batouri were taking New Year's Eve seriously. At the crossroads of the two main streets they had built a huge fire and set it ablaze. Groups of laughing, singing people wended their way drunkenly through more groups of people chatting or shouting happy greetings at each other. The whole crowd of black faces was coloured umber and amber by the light of the fire. We wound our way through this lot to find our bar. 'S'funny – I'm sure it was down here.'

'No. S'opposite way.'

'Oh well, this one will do.'

There were eleven of us, so we bought bottles of beer by the crate. We took one crate with us to find a restaurant, promising the bar-owner faithfully he would get his bottles back for the deposit. The place we chose, a bare concrete room with three tables which we dragged together, had the normal cheap fare of anything and rice. The waiter saw us coming, a large group of whites, with a look of amazement which turned at once to one of welcome, though we noticed his eyeballs clicking up dollar signs with the cartoon kerchiiing of a cash register.

We looked at the menu. Lucky we brought our own beer, we agreed – they don't sell it here. We ordered food. It arrived. We started to eat it. The owner of the restaurant arrived. The waiter was delighted. He could show what good business he was doing. He might be given a rise in his salary.

Not a bit of it. The owner was a Muslim. One sight of the beer bottles on our table and he flew off the handle. He was a tall man with Arabic looks and was wearing a jellaba. His skirts flapped round his waist as he stamped up and down in incoherent rage with the waiter, whose face had switched from proud to crestfallen. At first we did not realise what the problem was. Then we did, and we started to bolt down our food in case he took it away from us. The last of us were just wiping the remaining pieces of rice from the corners of our mouths when he turned and vented his wrath on us. 'Get out,' he roared. 'This!' He pointed at a beer bottle, hands purple and face shaking. '*Thiiiis!*'

'Can we have the bill, please?' asked Michael.

'Oooouuut!'

So we did not pay.

The evening went on, in and out of bars, and at street stalls buying fried meat and bread when we had the munchies. I missed the actual striking of the clock at midnight – I had fallen asleep. But I woke up an hour later, and walked out into the street again. At that moment, the others came up the road, sitting in the back of a pick-up with a dozen locals. 'Stop!' they yelled. The car slowed down to fifteen miles an hour, and I dived into it as it went past. 'We're going to a nightclub,' said Hazel. 'I think I'm feeling a little squiffy,' she added.

I was still disorientated after my sleep. 'Where are we?' I asked.

'Africa,' Emma said, waving her hand at the continent to indicate the area that she meant.

'But whereabouts in Africa?'

'Who cares?' said Red, grinning stupidly out of the darkness.

The nightclub was, incredibly, a real nightclub. It had the look of one of those glitzy, ritzy low-ceilinged conversions of a Victorian seafront house in an English resort town. Except it was almost bang in the centre of Africa. There was throbbing African music, the local stuff souped up on an electronic keyboard. It is uniformly dreadful across the continent, but this was better for being cushioned by alcohol. There were flashing coloured lights, a smelly dancefloor solid with Africans trying out all dances from the lambada to fully-clothed sex, and a terrace outside with chairs for those who just want a snog and a grope. Emma, Hazel and Wicky lasted a minute on the dancefloor before coming out complaining of rampant bottom-pinchers.

We survived a total of an hour in there. All the men tried to chat up Emma, Hazel and Wicky. Some of the girls tried to chat up Neil. One of the men tried to chat up clean-shaven Red. When he turned his attentions to Neil, we all felt it was time to head for home. We went outside. Our pick-up was waiting, still with a dozen locals in it. They were the same locals who had come with us. We suddenly realised that most of them had not been allowed in, yet they had waited politely for us. Perhaps Africans are not so bad after all. They dropped us off outside the gates of our hotel.

We went straight to a bar across the road for a chaser or two. One by one we faded, and left the bar to go to bed. The last four to return were Neil, Hazel, Red and Emma. I lay in my hammock and listened to them arrive. First Hazel and Red came in. I had to work out what was happening from the sound effects.

Clump, clunk, clunk – pause – fumble, zzzzip. Hazel climbing on to the bonnet of her Land Rover and opening the roof tent. Creeeak, creeeak, riffle, riffle, click, crash, tinkle. Red climbing on to the roof of Mistress Quickly to take down a campbed, and dropping it. 'Shit.'

Rumple, rumple, bump, 'Shit.' Hazel sorting out her bedding and hitting her head on the roof of the roof tent. Creak, creak, creak. 'Ffff-ing thing. Shit.' Red climbing down from Mistress Quickly and trying to work out how to put up the campbed.

Clump. Hazel settling down into her sleeping bag.

Silence.

'Bugger.' Red losing his temper with the campbed. 'Hazel? Can I come and sleep with you?'

Oh, Red. Cheap line.

Red, realising its cheapness: 'No, I mean in your tent.'

Does not sound any better, Red.

Something like: 'Mmmmmm,' from Hazel, or it might have been 'Mmmmmm?'

Clump, clunk, clunk – pause – fumble. Red climbing into the Dust Busters' roof tent.

Five minutes of silence.

Bump. 'Shit.' 'Hur, hur, hur.' Neil bumping into his Land Rover in the darkness, and Emma behind him, laughing.

'Hazel,' croaky whisper from Neil.

Pause.

'HAZEL!' Louder.

Another pause.

'Who've you got up there, Hazel?'

'Hur, hur, hur.' More laughter from Emma.

Silence.

'Who've you got? Is it Michael? Hazel? Hazel?'

'Hur, hur, hur, hur, hur, hur.' Emma.

'Have you got Urs up there, Hazel? Charlie, is it?'

'Go to bed!' Furious whisper from Hazel.

'Hur, hur, hur, hur, hur, hur, hur, hur, hur.'

Pause.

'It's Red, isn't it?'

'Hur, hur.'

'*Go to bed!*'

'I'm coming up to have a look.' Clump, clunk, clunk.

'Shut up, Neil.'

'Hur, hur.' Clump, clunk, clunk. Emma was going up too.

Zzzip. Neil closing the tent behind Emma. There are four of them in there now.

More muffled, a mixture of voices: 'Shut the f . . .' – '*Neil, go away!*' – 'Hello, Red' – 'Hello, Emma' – '*Go to sleep*' – 'Hello, Neil.'

Amazingly, none of them got off with each other. They were far too incapable for that. I know – I checked the next morning. They were in four sleeping bags, crammed in alternately head to toe. I woke them up with tea and inquisitions.

When we had all recovered from Batouri, it was time to leave again. The nice man from the petrol station charged us full price for diesel on the way out, even though we greeted him like an old friend. He had trouble remembering us from the night before. We drove on from there through the border into Central African Republic with minimum fuss and bribes – we were getting better at it by then – and headed for the capital, Bangui.

Bangui sits on the north bank of the thick brown River Ubangi, a tributary of the River Congo which forms the southern border with Zaïre. Bangui was laid out by the French during their time as colonists, and decorated by successive African dictators with triumphant arches and memorials, which serve only to cause traffic congestion. It is a haunt of muggers and aid workers, the second group making sure that the first is fed and clothed, the first also making sure that the first are fed and clothed.

We parked Mistress Quickly in Bangui town centre to buy some food. George and I got out of the car, leaving inside Red, Wicky and an American Peace Corps volunteer called Jeff to whom we were giving a lift. We'd taken as few vehicles as possible into Bangui itself because it was Robbersville. It was just us and the Swiss Family Robinson. Emma had gone ahead with the Dust Busters and the Hanomag.

While George and I were buying bread, a gang of children ran down the near side of the Land Rover, banging it. Red jumped out of the passenger seat on the off side and marched round to see what they were doing. Wicky and Jeff, both on the back seat, looked to the near side as well, and at that moment, someone put a hand through the off side window and grabbed George's wallet and camera, which were lying in the centre box between the two front seats. That is what we think happened: it was all so fast that nobody saw it, and we did not notice the loss until later. Luckily, not much money went, but another traveller's nail was banged into the coffin of an African town. We left Bangui as quickly as we had left Yaounde.

Jeff, from Tucson, Arizona, was a perfect example of a Peace Corps volunteer. He managed to mix complete fascination with the Central African way of life with a naïveté about why he was there. The Peace Corps exists to promote an American way of life, and that is not always a better way of life for locals. The Peace Corps is there to make Americans feel better.

Jeff was trying to teach the people in his village to build permanent fireplaces which were more economic on firewood. It was a question of perception. Jeff knew that as a Peace Corps volunteer, designing new fireplaces came into his purview. The Africans did not understand why Jeff thought a new kind of fireplace was necessary – the three rocks they normally used seemed just as good – or why he wanted them to save firewood at all, though they went along with it all.

On a more savage level, there are tribes in Africa which consider killing people perfectly normal. The Danakil in Ethiopia, for example. We, in the West, do not. Our influence through aid operations is curbing their killing, but their system works fine for them, and has done for centuries. The only problem with it now is that the modern notion of trade by air and by sea provides them with guns and bombs to make their killing more large-scale. There may be a question of redress, but is not always right to try to restore the balance by making them think in a more American way.

Certainly Central African Republic's dictators, and before them the French, treated the country badly, according to our culture, in the past. It was a place they could loot and pillage for its natural resources, from gold and diamonds to the rare antelope the bongo, which notables such as the French politician Valéry Giscard d'Estaing have been out to shoot. One of Jeff's Peace Corps pals cornered me in Bangui at the compound where we were staying. 'The point is,' he told me zealously, 'Central African Republic no longer wants to be France's unloved foster child, but America's well-loved ward.'

We did not mind. We liked Jeff. He was fresh from university and had a good sense of humour. It is part of American culture to go around the world showing off and being a hero. They turn all their team games into games for heroes. He was also a useful friend to have. He had already been in Central African Republic for several months. He lived in the town of Bangassou in the east of the country, the only exit point to Zaïre. Whites were not allowed to cross into Zaïre at Bangui, because the Zaïrean president's village was just over the river from Bangui, and the thought of too many Westerners there made him nervous.

So we drove on through the forest of Central African Republic. The logger lorries, great artics carrying treetrunks a hundred feet long, left for the coast carrying a hundred trees a day. The clouds of red dust they spewed from the road crusted the bushes on either side, which gave them the appearance of the silver-painted leaves of a Christmas wreath. The sweat on our faces trapped the dust until it looked as if we were all going as harlequins to a masked ball.

Jeff had warned us about the road-diggers. Piling down the dirt road we rounded a bend and slid to a cloudy stop at a thin sapling pole held across the road as a barrier. Behind it there were four children pretending to fill in a pothole. One of the older ones, maybe nearly six years, demanded money to let us through. There was one scrap of a toddler shovelling away with a twig and a look of such anxious concentration on its face that we gave them a coin. Most people, said Jeff, just snap through shouting abuse.

Kamikaze pullets and piglets dived under our wheels as we ploughed through the villages, and copycat snakes and squirrels did the same from the bush. Why did the chicken cross the road? To say most emphatically, we gather, 'Farewell, cruel world.'

The upland areas of Central African Republic were like some of the deciduous woods near my home on the Quantock Hills. It is the same red earth but dustier. The termite mounds are a giveaway too, and there are many more species – and spices – than on Lydeard Hill. Locals on the side of the road held up pangolins, the African scaly anteater, for us to buy and eat.

In the valleys, the rainforest blinds you and deafens you with greenery. Ferns and fronds splay upwards. Silver trunks rocket to a hundred feet and pop-pop in bright buds at the top. It is a firework display caught in a snapshot, with catherine-wheel palms, chinese-cracker creepers, billowing undergrowth on the jungle floor, booming blooming squibs of flora in yellow and mauve, and great round sunburst-flowering tree branches. There were huge butterflies in dozens of colours, especially cinders and embers of orange and yellow; some small in spiralling swarms around water as numerous as bees, and some so big you could feel the warm air on your face from their wingbeats as they flapped past.

The noise of the forest is not a pummelling babble, but a clever overlay of sounds, like a piece of jazz with all the sex and feeling of soul. It is muted during the day, but in the evening the crickets start up a catatonic snare-beat on the skins section. Then the rest of the world comes in on bass, box, and 'bone. There is a piu, piu, piu, piu, plelele, plelele, plelelo; a woik, woik, woik, and the whole gamut of arcade zap-game noises and ELO sound effects in between. Some are human, or human-invented demons, like the bird which cackles like a mad old woman. One bird sits in a tree and calls out testily, 'We're 'ere, we're 'ere, we're 'ere.' Then another will call the same from a hundred yards away. Then a third will join in. You want to shout: 'Will you make up your minds?' Frog choruses rasp and rivet through the night. Wicky and I sang Paul McCartney's frog chorus at them – 'Dom Dom-Dom Waaieeeai!' – but they did not understand.

The oddest sound came from the bushbabies. These little prosimians betray their innocent faces by screaming rhythmically in the small hours of the morning. It raises the hackles on your neck, a cry of splitting agony mixed with splitting pleasure, and would have given Macbeth's guards a thing or two to think about. We heard the bushbabies at their worst while staying at the Baptist mission in Bangassou. We could not go and stay with Jeff. He had to leave town for a few nights and come and stay with us. There was a good reason.

In Bangui, Red had told the story of the two truckies at Christmas who had picked up African prostitutes. 'I could not believe it,' he said, and then to Jeff: 'Do any of your lot delve into the local female population?'

At that moment I could see that the brick Red had been holding for some time had just slipped out of his hands and was dropping to earth in hideous slow motion.

'Er – yeah,' said Jeff. 'Some of us do – um – "delve" into the local population.'

Jeff was going out with a local in Bangassou. She was already engaged to a local functionary. Jeff called him, with a dreadful French accent, a fonk-shon-air. Jeff's accent was truly appalling. He had done the four-month French course required of him when he arrived, but was having trouble with the language. 'Sure we can eat,' he would say. 'Let's go down to the night mar-shay.' And, when we first met him: 'Are you guys going to Bonger-sue?'

The Bangassou girl chucked him when he came back from Bangui. She wanted to have babies and move to Tucson. He did not. He just wanted to complete his thirty-month stint making permanent fireplaces and eating out in night marchés. So, fearing reprisals, he moved in with us.

Jeff was not keen on the Baptists, even though they were American. He knew them and they knew him, and they greeted each other, but as soon as they were gone he told us how insular they were, how their children – and there was a group of two dozen of them – were not allowed to consort with local children. He resented their middle-American way of life, the way they cut themselves off with security fencing in a smart part of town from the people they were meant to be helping.

But I still felt they were no more nor less wrong in the way they helped the locals than he was. By being smarter and more aloof than the Peace Corps, they attracted a smarter kind of African – the fonk-shon-airs – to toe whatever line they were shooting, and Baptist-type fashions start at the top.

A gangly youth from the village turned up one morning in company with other village children. As a broken-English speaker, he tried to sell us grapefruit on their behalf. We were camped under a grapefruit tree, and spent much of our time avoiding being hit by the falling fruit, so we had to point out that even though we were white, we were not that stupid. Oh well, said the children, and he was a likeable fellow. He told us his name. It sounded like Maturing, so Maturing he remained.

Maturing talked Emma, Hazel, Wicky and me into going out on a pirogue trip down the Ubangi River to find hippo. We set out that evening to walk down through the village to the river. We quickly found that Maturing was a well-known figure in the village. People joined us, mostly related to him, and by the time we reached his hut, we numbered a dozen.

Maturing's family was even larger than we realised, and those both old and young enough to walk joined us as well. The trip started to take on a carnival atmosphere.

Then the local branch of Pickford's joined in. When people in the village move house, they ask all their friends round to pick up their belongings, and the whole lot sing and dance their way to the next house. We were on the route between the two houses involved in one such relocation, and as honoured guests took our places at the head of the hundred-strong column. Dogs barked, piglets squealed, chickens ran flapping from under our feet as the jolly throng jigged and jived through the village. Hazel taught them to conga, in the great Gerald Durrell tradition of educating natives. La doo-doo-doo-doo doo ha! La doo-doo-doo-doo doo ha!

We reached the river at last. The Pickford's procession had moved off in another direction, and we were left with the last of the gang of Maturing's friends and relations. They crowded round as Maturing showed us the boats. They were in the last stages of shipwreckedness, each shipping water and none with gunwale-to-water clearance of more than a few inches. Maturing assured us that the boats were safe.

The four of us slipped down the muddy bank into the least leaky one. Maturing followed in another that required as much baling from the inside as it did paddling on the outside. Other boats appeared from under the trees on the riverbank with other smaller relations in them.

'Chroist,' said Emma, in a rare show of blasphemy. She was holding her camera high in the air.

'. . . For those in peril on the sea,' sang Hazel.

'Hoo, hoo, hoo,' came back Wicky.

Even the rocky motion of paddling swamped the boat, which was now millimetres from the meniscus at horizontal. Hazel suggested we turn for home. We agreed. We abandoned the boats and all hope of hippo and slid back up the banks. Maturing was disappointed, but he had to admit that just the ripples from a retreating hippo would have sunk us, never mind a sustained attack. Hippo kill more humans in Africa every year than any other mammal.

Neil and I did our duty on the Sunday that we were at the mission and went along to the Baptists' prayer meeting to see what they were really like. We went to the home of a family called the Waltons. They had loads of children. The meeting had all the simple-hearted generosity and horridness of a community too small to cope with its own problems. In the chitchat beforehand each one was trying to out-charity the others.

'Have you seen so-and-so? He's not well.'

'Sure I saw him. I drove him to the doctor.'

'Sure, and I drove him to the doctor for a month last time.'

'And I took his wife a cake I baked.'

Then it was into the service. We were arranged in dark-stained wooden chairs in a circle around the papered walls of a small chintzy sitting room with a damp-sounding piano in the corner. A Baptist lady played the notes on it while quavering tremulous voices banged out hymns with words slightly changed from the C. of E. versions Neil and I knew. And then it was time for the sermon: a twenty-year-old tape-recording of a senior Baptist in Michigan bawling out the danger of Russian invasion. I caught Neil's eye, and buried my face in the Bible they had lent me, trying to find something unfunny. He was shaking slightly in his chair with suppressed laughter. It was all too solemn and small-minded. I was almost asphyxiating by the time we were let out of the door to cries of 'Good night. God bless.'

'Good night, John-boy,' Neil muttered under his breath and I had to run for the bushes that separated the Baptists' houses from our camp. 'What's got into him?' I heard from the distance.

Poor old Baptists. To their credit, they were friendly, generous, and all any individual among them would want as an epitaph is that he or she led a good and kind life, and they did.

We were staying with the Baptists partly for the security, but mainly for their workshop. Last-minute pieces of work had to be done on all the vehicles. We knew that Zaïre would loosen every nut and cog and George wanted to be sure that Mistress Quickly was up to it. While the rest of us scoured Bangassou for supplies of rice and diesel, he banged and wrenched and cursed his way through all her vital organs and finally wiped his greasy forehead.

'That will, er, have to do,' he pronounced.

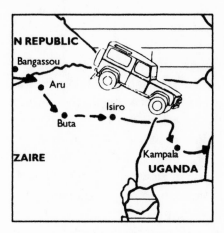

C h a p t e r 1 0

NDU TO ARU

Zaïre. Wicky, Red, George and me in Mistress Quickly. Neil, Hazel and Emma in the Dust Busters' Land Rover. Urs and Michael in the Swiss Family Robinson's Land Rover. Weirdo and Beat in the Turbo Twins' Pajero. 135 days to the World Cup opening ceremony.

Zaïre was a problem. From its border with Central African Republic at Ndu to its border with Uganda at Aru, it was a traveller's catalogue of corruption, terrible roads, mud and misery. One of the overland trucks had been stuck in Zaïre for two and a half months behind a lorry which was itself caught deep in mud. They gave up when their truckie punters mutinied and walked away. And that incident took place only a few months before we arrived.

To call the roads terrible does not do them justice. Take an unkempt brake, a dishevelled lonin, or the least likely-looking farm track you know and divide it by two. Put trees across it, put in holes big enough to swallow whole vehicles, and a liberal dose of rivers with shattered bridges, and you might be close. The average speed was ten miles per hour and the 'speediliest' only twenty.

The first 300 miles to the town of Buta were the worst for bridges. There were over fifty of them, most no more than two slippery logs at different heights from each other. We went over them as gingerly as we could. Red leaped into action at bridges. Get out of the Land Rover and march over it first, keeping a professional eye open for its load-bearing capacity and any structural weakness. Had we been in the Festival Hall, this is where the audience would have started clapping. Red reaches the other side of the bridge where the conductor's podium should be, turns on a toe and faces his orchestra. He raises his hands for a moment of pregnant stillness, then brings the Land Rover in, and conducts it across, a wheel on each wonky log. And if Red was a Beecham, Michael was a Von Karajan.

We were still four vehicles in Zaïre, but we had left Christa and Heinz behind. Their Hanomag was too slow. They met a Dutch couple in a Land Rover and set off through Zaïre with them instead. None of us liked the Dutch, so we were pleased that they were not coming with us. It is most odd that in Europe the Dutch can be some of the most fun people. Amsterdam is a great city. Germans can be difficult, sometimes really difficult, and as often as twice a century, but in Africa, we never met any but good ones. The roles were reversed.

Just as we were about to leave Bangassou, we met two more Swiss boys driving a Mitsubushi Pajero on an incredible journey south to South Africa, by boat to India, and then back to Europe via Pakistan along the Silk Road. These new Swiss were the most extraordinary characters. The same height, and short with it, they jumped in and out of their car, swung on the roof-rack and bounced on the bumper to give extra traction with cartoon-character energy, all quite unlike Urs. They did not look much older than sixteen.

Their names were Gothard – like the saint and his tunnel – and Beat. Now, Beat is a good name, so we went with that, but Gothard our Anglo-Celtic-Gaelic tongues could not cope with on a day-to-day basis, so we corrupted it to Got Hard, Go Hard, Guido, and finally Weirdo. 'Turbo Twins', we wrote in the dust on the back windscreen of their bourgemobile, 'Weirdo & Beat', and drew a picture of two monkeys.

Despite the physical obstacles, we tried to get through Zaïre as quickly as possible to avoid paying bribes. We met an overland truck which had been taken for a large amount of money in Buta. Among their crimes, they failed to have official Zaïrean insurance for their vehicle, and did not have two bottles of flyspray in their cab, only one. We knew how serious a crime this was. In Central African Republic, we had nearly had to pay up for not having two red breakdown triangles in our cab. Between all the cars in our convoy we managed to raise two, and while the police were walking down the drivers' windows checking with the drivers, Neil was running from one passenger window to the next carrying the triangles.

Buta, directly on our route, with no way round it, was the Zaïrean immigration officers' Charybdis, and their chief officer, whom we dubbed the Beast of Buta, their Scylla. The Beast of Buta was a legendary figure among the travellers we had met. Like all immigration officials, he worked in a large crumbling Belgian colonial building, like the ruined Indian temple which was home to the Bandar Log in Kipling's *The Jungle Book*. Creepers crept in and the Beast and his staff occupied any rooms which had any part of a roof left. Little wooden doors to the old Belgian pigeonhole system of bureaucracy hung off on rusty hinges.

So we approached Buta cautiously. Although there is no way round it, we found a local who could take us through the one back street which avoided the immigration officer. We decided to opt for this subtle approach and hired him at a cost of one cigarette and an out-of-date guidebook to Morocco. 'Poor bloke,' said Red. 'He is going to spend his whole life yearning to go to Morocco.'

It is not easy being subtle when you are in a convoy of four noisy diesel-engined cars and other traffic is practically non-existent. In the 300 miles from Ndu we had passed only one other car. We did our best, creeping into Buta with the engines on whisper and maintaining radio silence. Then a back wheel on Mistress Quickly broke a plank on one of the bridges, and the car crunched downwards a foot and jammed. It was similar to that Pepsi-Cola advertisement where the lorry is about to go over the cliff. The other back wheel lodged on a girder, but started to slip slowly, and bits of rotten bridge began to fall into the water twenty feet below. It was out with the high-jack at high velocity and up with the back. We slipped the sand ladders under the wheel and managed to winch her off.

All thoughts of subtlety went out of the window. The whole population of the northern suburbs of Buta had gathered to watch, and surely now the Beast must know we were coming. We doubled our average speed and raced for the town's eastern edge and freedom.

There was a barrier across the road. Hell and tarnation. Men with machine-guns and tin hats. This is normal for immigration staff in Zaïre, but luckily it was only a police check.

They told us to hand over our papers. We gave them a packet of cigarettes. They agreed that our papers were in order, but they said we would have to go back into town and visit Immigration. We gave them a pair of sunglasses. They said they thought there was a possibility that Immigration was asleep. We agreed that that was a possibility. They said that he could be woken up. We gave them a sachet of self-tanning lotion. The irony was wasted on them and they said no, on second thoughts, he would not want to be woken up. Not yet, anyway. Marvellous. Could they raise the barrier now, please? They looked at it. Oh yes. The barrier. There was something else, though . . . a solar-powered calculator, yes, that was it. Up went the barrier and they gave us a smart salute as we raced off.

We put as many miles as our springs could bear between us and Buta that evening. For a sum the same as his salary per car, so four years' worth, we were sure that Immigration would send out a car or a bike to chase us. We even thought of demolishing a few bridges behind us to slow his pursuit. But Immigration did not need to send a car. He had a radio. When we arrived at a village that night there were six immigration officers waiting for us. Their chief waved us down. Bugger, bugger, bugger. Did we not know that it is illegal to drive at night? he asked silkily. Right. Plan B.

This was our latest ruse to deal with officials. We had all found to our enormous cost that you cannot get angry with Africans in peaked caps. Neither do they listen to reason. So we invented Plan B, which was where we sent in what we called the Wham Team, George and Michael. George's hair had grown and he was starting to look once more like artists' grisly impressions of Piltdown Man. In the regiment he would have looked odd; in Africa he looked frightening. Michael's job was quietly and politely to translate whatever the official was saying from French into English for George, whom we all called Chief for this purpose. George's job was to shout at Michael: 'Tell this man that that is unreasonable/not true/not legal and that we are within the

law/under the limit/friends of the ambassador [delete as applicable]'.
Michael would then quietly translate this to the official.

George would only ever get angry with Michael, who played
the stool pigeon, and would gradually win over whatever ounce
of sympathy the official had been blessed with as a child before
he began to aspire to a uniform. It was Oscar-winning stuff, and
never failed.

It worked a treat on the village immigration chief. The Wham
Team wore him down to an utter muddle. He said he would come
back in the morning and sort it out. He meant, of course, to hold us
up until the Beast of Buta turned up himself and did us over properly.
Foolish man. Our wheels were rolling a quarter of an hour before
dawn the next morning.

The Pajero belonging to the latest additions to our convoy, Weirdo
and Beat, the Turbo Twins, was loaded with groovy add-ons. The
ceiling of their cab was a forest of switches, controlling lights, music,
and no doubt action as well. George gave them a powerful spotlight.
It reduced our weight and increased their happiness.

'Holy cracker,' said Beat. 'You don't get this in Switzerland.'

'Wayahooee,' said Weirdo.

'Japtrash,' said Neil.

Neil drove a heavy 130 Land Rover. Mistress Quickly was a
109. You do not have to be a Land Rover buff and barely a
mathematician to work out that that made Neil's grander than
ours. While George, Urs and the Turbo Twins buckerooed in and
out of the ruts and holes, Neil drove safely and ponderously. Neil
was going to South Africa to look for a job flying Dakotas and
boatplanes. He wanted some fun before inevitably, as he saw it,
he became an airline pilot. He had already been offered a job
smuggling contraband into Nigeria, but had turned it down on
the grounds that it was possibly the wrong side of too much fun.
If you are reading this book on an aeroplane and the intercom kicks
off, 'Good afternoon, ladies and gentlemen. This is your captain
speaking. My name is Neil Jackson,' then you are in the best of
all hands.

'Great British cars, Land Rovers,' said George proudly.

'*German* cars,' pointed out Michael, referring to BMW's bargain-basement buy-out of the Rover Group.

'They were British cars when these ones were built,' said Red stoutly. All our Land Rovers were built in Solihull, in Warwickshire before the days of the West Midlands.

There was healthy rivalry between the cars. Beat watched Neil ford a deep stream. He was concerned. 'If his motor stops he is pretty shitty off,' he told George.

Beat picked up English expressions, we never found out from where. These Beatitudes, as we called them, included 'great stuff' and 'seize the day'. Occasionally he would slip up. He liked the 'mountain-ious scenery' and felt he could 'get the hang out of it'.

'It is so hard to drive over the congregations in the road,' he told me loudly one Sunday.

'Corrugations,' I corrected.

'Yes, connorgrations.'

Beat never just said anything, he always shouted it. And Weirdo shrieked and screamed an accompaniment. When Weirdo sat with us in Mistress Quickly he caught odd-shaped beetles, bugs and slugs to show to Wicky, who chortled at them. Otherwise he sat, farted and howled with laughter. Red and I formed a theory that the municipal borough council of the Turbo Twins' home town had put up the money for their Africa-Asia trip to cut down local noise pollution. They were delinquent teenagers.

Despite being so placid, Urs was the biggest cowboy among the drivers. He quickly took the record for annihilating the wildlife. In one day he scored a goat, a snake and a piglet. I can vouch for this because I was in his Land Rover. I was there because Beat was in my place in Mistress Quickly, and Michael was in the Pajero. Michael was in the Pajero for its greater comfort. He needed comfort because Urs had reversed into him the night before, knocked him over and knocked him out.

The next day Urs hit a tree and crushed his front wing, and then he hit an oncoming lorry. In the total 900 miles across Zaïre we met only half a dozen other vehicles so hitting one of them showed surprising talent.

The Turbo Twins' Pajero was the most comfortable, but the Land

Rovers the more capable. The Land Rovers were able to hold a steady course and to grip the greasy logs over rivers where the Pajero slipped off. Then it was a shouting and yodelling match between Beat and Weirdo as to whose fault it was, the driver or the conductor.

We never really drove in the European sense in Zaïre, except on a few short upland stretches. It was more of a 900-mile controlled slide. George's elbows flew as he spun the steering wheel in and out of the edges of holes that we would only have half filled had we fallen in.

Right. This is turning into an activity book. If you shred a dockleaf and stuff it up your nose to get a good snort of chlorophyll, chainsaw a foot off one leg of every stick of furniture in your drawing room and spend a month jumping between chair and table you can drive through Zaïre in the comfort of your own home. If you can persuade your friends to throw buckets of muddy water and damp twigs at you the same time, while shouting, brroom, brroom, all the better. 'Gob on you,' said Wicky when her hip and my head clocked the same altitude on the back seat. 'Gob on you,' I said when the Land Rover bounced back the other way. Shake it down baby, twist and shout.

We laid bets on who would tip over first. It was, poor old girl, Mistress Quickly. Wicky and I had to escape through a passenger window as she lay burning on her side. But it was not as exciting as it first sounds. Wicky and I were in the front of the car and Red was sunning himself on the roof. Wicky drove up the lip of a large hole and slowly the Land Rover tipped. Wicky and I viewed the approaching ground with a chorused 'Whoooops.' Red jumped clear, sustaining the only injury we could diagnose at once, a broken flipflop, and with everyone's help we soon had all four wheels back on the ground. Oh, and the burning was just a bit of oil which had spilled on to the engine.

'None of you English got angry when the car went over, no? I would go spare if it happens to me,' said Beat.

Even after Buta, bridges were difficult, because they started to get bigger. From the rusting girders over some of the Congo's bigger tributaries, you could play Poohsticks with oil-tankers. On one hundred-yard relic of a railway age we found a message scratched into a girder. It was from the Lads, who had passed this way a month before us. 'We built this bridge, you lucky bastards.' Our advice was: keep the day job – you are better at batting and bowling than bridge-building. But that was uncharitable: it had been hammered in that month back to a standard shattered state by lorries. We rebuilt it. Heaven knew what it would be like when Steve crossed it in his Truck Africa a week after us.

Huge overloaded lorries swayed through the mud in Zaïre with an elephant's gait. They had to keep moving or they would stick and block the road, and, people said, sometimes for weeks, as that earlier overland truck found out. The lorries had to stay in the ruts or the whole shebang would slide sideways and roll. They never picked themselves up like elephants, though. If you wanted to pass an overturned lorry, the only way was through the forest with an axe.

In some places, the roads looked like riverbeds which had grudgingly agreed to halt their flow of water until we had passed. In others they were a line of puddles. 'You'd think they could do something useful like join up and make a river,' said Red as we sank into yet another.

George was happy with the adversity, it was clear. He started humming snatches of 'Zip-A-Dee-Doo-Dah' and wore a knotted red and white spotted handkerchief on his head like a subway Guardian Angel vigilante.

The rest of the party did not fare so well. After successfully digging his Pajero out of one hole, Weirdo dropped the high-jack from the roof and cracked his windscreen. Beat lost his temper in three languages: 'Merde, scheisse, this really pisses me off. That cost 600 dollars Swiss francs.' He threw his shovel and mattock to the ground. Light blue touchpaper and stand well back.

Beat blamed Urs, who was standing next to him. Marvellous. A continental argument, rather like Bosnia. A panoply of expressions flashed across Urs's face as Beat laid into him in German, French and anything else he could think of and without drawing breath. 'Always toujours you make us go trop schnell schnell vite and not stopping so now we make a mistake, huh? You on some kind of mission?' Then more rattling and gabbling in Beat's own-style Esperanto.

It did us good. Up until then Mistress Quickly had been holding

Least-Favoured Land Rover status for slowing everyone down. We could now hand that accolade to the Swiss.

It was raining. It was muddy. It was miserable. It was not the worst of the Zaïrean rains, but it was enough that tempers could snap in an instant. You really see the worst in your fellows. Roll on Kenya I thought. Michael stood away from the argument with the same expression of jilted condescension on his face worn by the Bundesbankers on television when everyone started pulling out of the ERM. It rained a lot in Zaïre. Not a drab English drizzle, but a proper pelt – and even that, we were assured by the locals, was not real Zaïrean rain. At night you could look up at the stars and the permanent harvest moon and feel sure that it would be dry until morning. Within a few seconds a diaphanous gown of high clouds would cover the naked moonlight, followed by puffy organza cumulus, and then an ugly black smock which would shed gallons of water on you. The only warning was a few moments of damp air when your skin felt like warm blotting paper, and a sharp cut of cold wind. Somehow it always found its way into the bedding, and you could not stand up from the campbeds or hammocks because of the red muddy rivers that ran beneath them.

For the first time we could not stick our elbows trucker-style out of the car windows and tan our elbows. The forest was too thick, a wall of stems. Unlike in Central African Republic, we could not see the jungle for the trees. Giant bamboo clumps sprouted upwards and outwards, supporting the forest canopy like a fan-vaulted ceiling. Dead leaves jigged and jitterbugged in the earthen wash behind the wheels of the car in front. By the side of the road, whenever there was a gap, termites had built mounds, some like giant mushrooms, and some the Lilliputian versions of the Carpathian Mountains that range across the Hammer House of Horror.

The butterflies were even better than in Central African Republic. They came in colours louder than the worst crop of bow-ties at a May Ball or among any member of nuclear scientists and advertising executives, whirligigging around water in polka-dot patterns, lozenges and wavy stripes.

The jungle was so spectacular that there was no majesty left for the African black kites, raptors which flapped around humbly like carrion crows. They were dowdy creatures, roosting around villages looking for an angle on a chicken. The locals ran at them, shouting and arm-waving when they tried a heist, and the sight of a kite struggling to take off from the ground is not attractive for a bird capable of soaring and wheeling over mountaintops. The chickens bore the scars of these attacks on scrawny plucked necks and kept as tense an eye on the sky as we kept on the ranks of Zaïrean officialdom we tussled with.

Buying diesel in Zaïre was a tribulation. The only people who could afford to buy diesel to sell to us were the officials. But official diesel was so expensive it could only be bought with unofficial money – that is, money that we had not declared on entry to Zaïre and which we did not have to exchange at the punitive official rate. And unofficial diesel was cheap enough to buy with official money – yet we could not get a receipt for unofficial diesel for our official currency declaration forms that would be valid. Either way, the blighters could put us in prison.

Luckily, the officials were greedy enough for money to agree to meet us halfway on this point. We would arrive in a town and enter a kind of bureaucratic amnesty where we would be allowed to buy unofficial diesel with unofficial dollars from officials who were acting unofficially. Once the handover had been made and we were happy that the diesel was not overly diluted with kerosene the officials would revert to being official again. They would question us closely about whether we had dared enter their country with unofficial money despite the full knowledge that we had.

There is a good rumour as to why Zaïre should have such an appalling economy. Apparently the president of the country put the printing job for the new note with his head on out to tender. A South American won the contract and printed US$100 million worth. This was enough, the president reasoned, to see Zaïre through to the end of the century. But he reckoned without the South American, who ran off a further US$200 million on his printing press and came to Zaïre and spent it.

In one town I made the mistake of changing US dollars into the Zaïrean currency on the black market. Due to the staggering rate of inflation in Zaïre, just a few dollars bought me a plastic sack full of

Zaïrean notes. It was impossible to hide this amount of illicit currency in the Land Rover in case it was found and we were fined, so we ended up throwing handfuls of the stuff away, keeping only a bit to help with the daily barter for food that we undertook in the villages we went through.

Driving through the villages one felt rather like the Queen. Locals lined the track, cheering, waving, smiling and shouting 'Toodi! Toodi!' which was as close as they could come to 'tourist'. They were always flabbergasted and delighted whenever they saw a girl driving. It was tricky to reconcile the pop-star treatment we received from the locals with the utter unpleasantness of the government officials. In a curious salute, the villagers held up a few spare bananas, eggs and pineapples which they hoped to sell or swap. Some of them begged cigarettes by putting their hands to their mouths. Hazel always blew a kiss in return. We all learned the Windsor wave, the slight rotation from the wrist, as any movement more energetic became tedious and tiresome.

Buying food was not easy. Near the towns, the locals took money in exchange for goods. We found that foreign coins were perfectly acceptable. Any foreign coins, in fact, as long as they had big numbers on them. Mauritanian ouguiya were highly prized. 'It would be funny if in 140 years the world's finest coin collection suddenly emerged from Zaïre,' observed Red. 'If the family which, up until then, had been known as "stitched" became millionaires.'

Cigarettes were a harder currency than these 'dollars'. One smoke bought a bunch of thirty bananas. And plastic pots with screw-top lids were the best bartering tools of all.

We would arrive in a village and spot a small girl holding up an egg. We would stop and open the window. Others with bananas, pineapples or small cherry tomatoes would press forward, crushing her out of the way. We would motion them aside and beckon to the girl, who would be pushed forward, hugely shy. Wicky would take the egg and examine it. She would look across at the rest of us sitting on the edge of our seats. Was it all right? we wanted to know. She was the expert. She would nod. She would get out of the car, and George, Red and I followed her out, looking as if eggs were as far from our minds as anything, and we had no desire whatsoever to eat today. The little girl would still be holding up the egg, and the village would have formed a semi-circle around her.

'C'est combien, pour l'oeuf?' I would ask in a bored way.

They would not understand my accent.

Wicky would bend down to the girl and show her a plastic pot, cleverly combining disinterestedness with a weary oh-well-if-I-must look. She would then count to ten on her fingers. Ten eggs for one pot. There would be a one-second pause as the enormity of the village's trading position sank in, and then the place would explode like a big run on the pound in the London International Financial Futures Exchange.

Everybody had eggs to sell. The village swarmed with runners finding chickens and squeezing them for more eggs. Wicky magicked more plastic pots, and all four of us started shouted bargaining. We should have been wearing LIFFE blazers. We could hear hens squawking in agony in the background.

Suddenly Wicky would shout: 'Stop!' She would have been offered the first egg from under a broody hen. She could tell because it was still warm. It had taken us a while to learn that as far as the villagers are concerned, if the stupid foreigners wanted to give away valuable plastic pots for eggs, they could even have the ones with chicks in. At that point we would cease trading, the floor would close, the computer screens blink and die, and the dot-pixel futures and options board fade away to nothing. It was back in the Land Rover and on we drove.

We camped in the villages whenever we could. We would stop in a likely-looking clearing and asked to see the head man. He was always delighted. Quite apart from the novelty, there were the trading possibilities. His village were happy too. Quite apart from the trading there was the thievery they might get away with.

Everyone in the villages loved the entertainment. It was better than a soap opera to crowd around our square of cars in the darkness and watch the battery-lit floorshow in the middle. It was like *Neighbours*, or more probably *Dallas*. They would remark to each other about the curious techniques we used to prepare our food, and possibly make some lewder comments, for every now and then the crowd would erupt into stifled sniggering.

They never interacted with us unless invited. There was a strong imaginary proscenium arch between the audience and the players. One village we stopped in was an exception. We were cooking chillis. I was chopping them with a penknife. I absentmindedly paused to wipe my eye, and instantly I felt a burning as if some one had thrown nitric acid in my face. I could not open the eye, and sat there rubbing it, to everyone else's cruel laughter, for some minutes. Eventually our audience, which numbered around forty, could stand it no longer. They nominated a man who could speak French to tell Urs, who spoke it best, to tell me to rub my eye in someone's hair.

'What?'

'Rub it in somebody's hair,' repeated Urs.

I looked around with my good eye at the ghastly array of greasy mops and matted curls I was dining with that night. Even Hazel's hair, normally immaculate, was not showing its usual shining lustre.

'Whose hair?' I asked, still clutching my face.

Urs asked the man, who said 'son ami' to Urs, who said to me, 'your friend.'

I hoped that this was not a Good Samaritan-style test. I hoped the village were not going to judge me for choosing a white person's hair over a black person's hair, or girl's hair over boy's hair. It was a moment of somewhat baleful symbolism. I picked Emma. She was not enthusiastic, which the crowd thought super.

But it worked. I stood up from Emma, and the pain had gone away. Her hair was a little gungy from my tears, but it was worth it. I blinked and grinned at the crowd. Aaaah, they went.

We were all friends after that. They produced a guitar, I produced my banjo ukulele, and the evening began to sound like a bad Boy Scouts' jamboree. Neil's guitar came out, and raised the tone once more to a sustainable level. At the end of it we went to our separate beds happy and bonded. We dreamed fruitful dreams about a world where blacks and whites could live in harmony, even if that was bad luck on the various other shades of red, yellow and brown. We even woke up in a kind of hazy contentment, rather than to a strained bicker over who in which vehicle was having the best breakfast.

But somebody, *somebody*, had been into the camp at night and pinched a bag of grapefruits from the Dust Busters, snitched a plastic jerrycan from the Turbos, and swiped Urs's expensive mountain boots. We registered our disapproval with the chief of the village, a weedy man in a brightly coloured sarong.

'Oh, bum,' he thought, it was obvious.

The villagers started to go rhubarb, rhubarb, rhubarb – or, in their own patois, papaya, papaya, papaya.

'But Something Has To Be Done,' said the chief, and set off to find the tea leaf.

An aide rang the village bell, a rusting lorry-wheel hub which went clonk, clonk, and summoned all the adult males. Cassava, cassava, cassava, they muttered. The gathering gathered. Banana, banana, banana. A child produced a spanner and dropped it surreptitiously at our feet, but it had not been stolen from us. No one was coming clean. Someone was lying.

Time to bring out the local polygraph lie-detector. Not quite as advanced as that, in fact; more a kind of Ordeal by Palm Frond. Two men held two bundles of palms to make a swing door. All the males had to approach, say out loud that they did not do it, that they were not there, and then walk through the gate with arms raised.

The chief looked on sadly. He was having to exercise his authority, and he was not sure he had any. Luckily, his aide, a shifty-looking fellow in a loud shirt, took charge. He made sure that every male went through the palm fronds, even unto the last village idiot, telling the truth, the whole truth and nothing but the truth. They all did it. Still someone was lying. Tomato, tomato, tomato. Yam, yam, yam.

'What now?' thought the chief.

'House-to-house search, chief?' suggested the aide.

'Right,' said the chief. 'House-to-house.'

They went through every one of the twenty-three mud huts in the village, lifting up the eaves of the dried banana-leaf roofs, emptying prized plastic pots, and digging through the ashes of the fires with their feet. Everyone was Holmes, Poirot and Clouseau. The house-to-house yielded nothing. Someone was Moriarty. And still he did not own up. Pineapple, pineapple, pineapple.

The chief was flummoxed. The aide scratched the curly black hairs on his head. 'Now what?' thought the chief wetly. 'The foreigners are not happy.' Grapefruit, grapefruit, grapefruit. Someone edged forward to the aide and had a word in his shell-like.

'Ur,' said the aide, which translates as 'Aha'.

'Ur?' said the chief. 'What?'

The supergrass had found a clue. The last village idiot lived in a hut at the unfashionable western edge of the village. The supergrass had spotted not one set of footprints along the road marking his progress in the morning, but two identical sets, and another going in the opposite direction. The village set off for the hut as a man, a pack in cry, feathering along the scent. How they picked it up is hard to tell as they had all walked that way and back during the search, but how they picked it up is immaterial. Urs went with them – it was his boots that were missing, after all.

'I just went to the hut,' he said afterwards, 'and a few guys went off into the forest and they came back with the stuff.'

But Urs was not convinced that the village idiot was the criminal. 'They said he had already stealed a jerrycan from an overland truck, but I think they just wanted to show us they found a guy, and the whole thing with the footprints was a mad thing.'

But it was too late. The pack had found, the stag was brought to bay, and the huntsman had him in his sights.

Reprisal was instant and ugly. They tore down his hut. They pushed the walls in and the banana-frond roof came down in clouds of daub-and-wattle dust. They punched and hit him. They tied his hands behind his back and they kicked him. They carried him down the village back to the rest of us, waving the stolen goods and baying and screaming. His two wives were begging for mercy.

The village ignored them, and dropped him at our feet like a carcase. Blood was trickling out of his mouth, his eyes were swollen, a flap of skin was hanging off his temple, and there were welts showing through rips in his shirt. He was not moving much. They carried on beating him up in front of us. Every man had a kick at him. One man stamped on his head and more blood spurted out of his mouth. They smacked him with sticks. He was too damaged to cry out. Another man picked him up and nutted him.

'Enough.'

It was the aide who said it. We did not say it. We could not intervene. It was a crime against us, but the punishment was meted out within the village. We cried mercy, but there was to be none until his body was pulp. Honour was at stake, face was not to be lost – except most of the idiot's face – but the greatest aim of this violent show was the public maintenance of public morals: an occasional lynching to keep the peace rather than a fair and just system of law.

When we discussed it, Red pointed out that had the idiot produced the stuff a week later, he would just as likely have been given a slap on the back from his fellows, and a general well done, keep up the good work. But because he was caught red-handed, or framed red-handed – in mob rule it is not important which – it was mob rule that came to bear on him and he suffered. The aide told us to leave the village. The idiot was being taken over the road to the meeting hall, where someone had strung up a rope to hang him.

Another person who suffered in Zaïre, but for quite different reasons, was Wicky. Insects adored Wicky. Perhaps it was her pale schoolgirl complexion. From the tiniest bug to the largest wasp, they chomped and spiked and stung all her exposed skin. While the rest of us went around in our shorts in the heat, Wicky had to dress up as tight as an eskimo.

Worse still, she scratched the bites. In the heat and the wet, some of them went septic and became tropical ulcers. Sometimes she looked as if she was about to cry with the pain, and once she could not walk at all at the end of a long day, and had to be lifted into bed. But being Wicky, she always managed to find something funny to take her mind off it.

Michael was called upon to treat her. He did so assiduously, making appointments for her every morning and evening, and because he was only learning to be a doctor he was able to do it unencumbered by medical expertise.

Hazel was Wicky's nurse. Hazel looked after all of us. She always had a sweet word – when Wicky's running sores were stinging, when Michael had been run over – a soothing glance and a cooling touch. Everyone in every car felt niggled at some stage in Zaïre. Hazel always stayed unflustered. Neil snapped that she had locked the back door of the Land Rover before he had finished in it. Cool. Neil groused that the Land Rover was unlocked at the back, and he wanted to go to bed. Still chilled. Remarkable Hazel.

Tropical diseases are revolting. The man with elephantiasis in Douala was the worst single case I saw, but the villages in Zaïre were thick with sickness. A lot of people had balloon swellings on their throats. This was cyanide poisoning of their thyroids, caused by eating too much cassava, and the treatment was iodine. Simple. But they did not have any. There were deformities, too. Loads of them. More than you would imagine the afflicted could survive. Bad luck on them, and worse luck on them because their kinsmen often treated them little better than mules. They looked like minor characters from *Star Wars*: gawping, blithering, blank, hunchbacked. There were withered limbs, wasted bodies and minds, inbreeding victims. Many had Bill Clinton Campaign T-shirts. He will be delighted to hear that his presidency has not been completely futile.

The scenery started to break up towards the end of our journey through Zaïre. There were gaps in the jungle. Through the greenery of one, Wicky, feeling better by now, spotted a granite tor. Terrific. We stopped at once and most of us climbed Mount Wicky for a view of a liquid orange sunset over the misty jungle, for a flange of baboons to watch us, and for a frolicking rock hyrax to be oblivious of either troupe, group or whoop. We saw granite tors all around us. We wondered how we could have missed them from the road. And there were even African black kites practising putative soars and wheels. The grey granite faded into a distant blue and beyond it was another, softer, grey, the Blue Mountains, the range that separates Zaïre from Uganda. We set off again with renewed hope, for the cool morning to this sweaty nightmare was not far away.

Once up in the Blue Mountains, we left the torrid zones of jungle and the landscape started to become closer in looks to Kenya's Rift Valley moonscape, the cradle of man. At last we arrived in Uganda, muddy but unbowed. I had not felt so grubby in years. Our clothes were not so much unwearable as untenable. My socks were trying to mate. ·

It did not stop us celebrating on our first night in Uganda. We were through. It seemed incredible. So bribe-hardened were we that the last border crossing at Aru had been a walk in the park.

This was also farewell, for the Swiss Family Robinson wanted to push on at speed to Nairobi, and the Turbo Twins to head south to see the gorillas in the Virunga Mountains. It would leave just us and the Dust Busters to head towards Nairobi at a more leisurely pace. But celebration was the key. And, what was more, there was a Five Nations rugby match on the BBC World Service that night, England v Ireland, or as we had it, George and me v Red and Emma. We found a bar in the Ugandan border town and took over a low and poky room, with peeling whitewash, warm lager, cobwebs and geckos on the walls. The four of us arranged ourselves on either side of a low wooden table with the radio in the middle. The rest sat on other tables to be shushed loudly during exciting bits. Wicky and Weirdo sat in the corner laughing at each other.

The radio was hopelessly indistinct. You could hear hard consonants from the commentator, like Bs and Vs, but it faded into a crackle at every try: 'Bphhhz . . . vcrrjjxcrr . . . pt . . . pt . . . *Score!*'

'Goal!' shouted Emma. 'Zjooooeeew . . . phngjjb' – 'Shut up, you lot' – 'Sssssss . . . brrrr . . . stjjjjx . . . as we just mentioned,' it went.

Nevertheless, we worked out that both Neil Francis, the Irish second row, and Martin Johnson, English second row, were stretchered off, tit-for-tat, and the final score was 20–8. To England. *Engerlaaaaand!*

'I just don't believe it,' said Red.

At that moment, a deputation of senior African officials came into the bar to visit us. We froze in our seats. This had to mean a bribe.

'Good evening,' said their leader in English, and introduced himself as the town mayor, then his chief clerk and his chief of police.

We muttered good evening in return, still frozen.

'We have come to welcome you to Uganda.'

This was a bad sign.

'May we ask where you are staying?'

'No.'

'We must know for security,' the mayor continued smoothly.

'Outside the town,' said Urs.

'To the east,' said Neil. North, south and west were all in Zaïre. Obvious, really.

Silence.

At this the deputation realised that they were going to get nothing out of us. 'Thank you,' said the mayor. 'Enjoy your stay.' And they left.

We did some realising, too: that they were genuine; that they were honestly concerned for our welfare; that they were actually keen to welcome us; and that they did not want any money for it. Bloody marvellous. Welcome to East Africa.

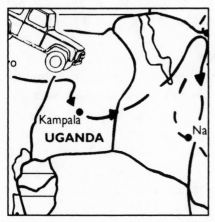

Chapter 11

THE
HEATHENS

Uganda. George, Wicky and me in Mistress Quickly. Red, Neil, Hazel and Emma in the Dust Busters' Land Rover. 125 days to the World Cup opening ceremony.

We arrived in the Ugandan capital, Kampala, for the ninth anniversary of Yoweri Museveni's sweep to presidency, which ended decades of genocidal government by criminals like Idi Amin and Milton Obote. As Robby Rodriguez at the Land Rover garage fixed Mistress Quickly's alternator, he recalled the final grisly days of the final grisly dictator's rule. The centre of Kampala had been cordoned off. Rodriguez was stopped at the roadblock on his way into work, but he knew the officer on duty so was able to persuade his way through. 'You won't like it,' the officer warned.

Rodriguez drove along the bypass, swerving every few yards around the bodies of looters and some of the unlucky soldiers who had been shooting them. It was a sickening sight, a revolting noise when he failed to swerve hard enough, and his wheels were splashing through puddles of blood. He reached his garage. It was a ruin, and of the 160 trucks he kept there for sale not one was left. The routed, retreating government army had stolen every vehicle they could find to flee north to the Sudan. Burned-out Russian tanks and armoured personnel-carriers littered those country roads when we drove through.

In despair, Rodriguez drove on into Kampala city centre. It was the piles of corpses on the steps of the post office that finally made him turn round and go home.

Extraordinarily enough, Kampala returned to normal the next day. The city scrubbed itself down and presented an as-if-nothing-has-happened face to the world. All the bodies were cleared up overnight, and all the blood washed from roads and walls. Museveni had started as he meant to go on.

Now, nine years on, Uganda has one of the fastest-growing economies in Africa, and the only trace of those troubles in the fabric of the city are a few high pockmarks of bullet-holes on some of the buildings. You can hardly believe it ever happened.

In a flat at the top of one of these buildings lives Peter Dow, a white and an old Africa hand of the handiest kind. A chartered valuation surveyor, he has done stints elsewhere in East Africa in Tanzania and Zambia, but returned to Uganda in 1992. He had first moved there in 1969, but left in 1972 after Amin came to power. Uganda has not played as a national rugby side since then.

Peter is a confirmed and fulsome expatriate and a rugby player, like so many others, no class withstanding, who will have to bite their tongues on retirement to England if they are not to be dubbed Africa bores, yet who on home soil abroad are valuable and fascinating, bright and vital, and leave you with the hope, both reverent and irreverent, that they will never have to live at home on what must be foreign soil to them.

Peter played centre for Kampala Rugby Club in the late 1960s, and in 1971 played for East Africa against Cork Constitution. Those were his headiest of heydays. Playing for town clubs like Brentwood or Cheltenham when he lived in England never quite matched being part of a side that represented a quarter of a continent. It was a thrill and a razzmatazz he could not conceal. He was not exactly a rugby buffer, but he was a great reminiscer. 'Well, in the old days . . .' he would start an anecdote, and '. . . I would like to see that now,' he would end it.

'Well, in the old days we could go back and forward to Kenya because the Uganda Police School had to do training flights in an

old Caribou, which yawed because of its ridiculous tail section all
the way to Wilson Aerodrome in Nairobi.'

He laughed as he looked at the black and white picture of the
ungainly aircraft parked on the tarmac at Entebbe.

He leafed through old photograph books of great matches, and
the yellowing newspaper reports that went with them. 'That's Dickie
Evans, that one. He was a centre with me in Kampala. He was fast,
yes, he was fast; a lovely ball-player. He lives in Nairobi now; runs a
company called Homegrown, and all his top executives are ex-rugby
players. You should go and see him. I'll give you his number. You
should speak to him.'

Rugby is a luxury. It did not survive in Uganda with the anarchy
of Amin's rule, nor while the equally nasty Obote was in charge. It
staggered to its feet with Museveni's takeover, and there are now
five teams in the Ugandan league, three of them in Kampala. The
expatriate side, the Heathens, dominates. The main African side is
the Kobs, named after a kind of antelope, like the Impala team
in Kenya and the South African Springboks. In 1993 the national
basketball team, the Rhinos, formed the Rhinos Rugby Team. The
ANC, the anti-apartheid organisation exiled from South Africa under
apartheid, also had a team in the Ugandan league. 'I thought the ANC
was a good ingredient,' said Peter, 'but they were a bit physical, let
us say.'

The best of them, the Heathens, Kobs and Rhinos players, came
together as one team for the first time in 1994 to enter the Enterprise
Cup, a knock-out competition for all the first-class clubs in East
Africa. Kampala Rugby Club had won it every year towards the
end of the 1960s, and were then undisputedly the strongest team.
In 1994 Kampala beat Kenya Commercial Bank and lost to another
Kenyan team, Mombasa. But when Mombasa came up to Kampala
to play the match and Peter had the pleasure of entertaining them,
it stirred some of his memories of those old days in the 1960s.

'It was very good for Ugandan rugby,' he said of the match. 'But
it really was terrifically popular in the 1960s. We used to get big
crowds down there,' he said, pointing vaguely out of the window
towards where the Lugogo Stadium now stands.

Rugby, with golf, sailing and a soccer team called the Diplomats, is the main game of Kampala expatriates today. But it is not what it was prior to Uganda's inglorious gory days. In part, Peter blames the strength of the Heathens. They win the league title year after year, and there is little competition for them. It is not such good fun. 'Kampala Rugby Club used to be comprised of Wasps and Hornets, two even sides which united for the Enterprise Cup or Kenya Cup matches,' he said. 'I would like to see that now.'

Uganda is not cured of its old ills yet. Protection is vital, and all businesses in Kampala keep a man or woman with a gun on the front door. These range from men in uniforms with Uzis outside Barclays Bank to more ragged people with battered Lee Enfields strapped up with wire guarding lesser institutions. The nice lady sitting behind the counter in the bookshop pointed me to the trashy novels section with the muzzle of her Kalashnikov.

A gun-happy country, Uganda is also an alcoholic country, so it is not surprising that bullets are sprayed around a bit at night in drunken bursts. But Kampala is no Bamako. This is friendly fire, shot off in high spirits and a general feeling of happiness that the bad old days are over and that cheap beer and economic recovery is here to stay. That does not stop the population diving for cover whenever a gun goes off. And so it was that the Heathens nearly caused a coup.

Every year the Heathens warn the Kampalans of their main fund-raising event, a 5 November firework display, with advertisements in all local papers proclaiming: 'There is no insecurity.' The fireworks annually attract 1,000 expatriates to an orgy of toffee-apples, mulled wine and aerial bangs – 'a bit incongruous for Africa', as Peter put it.

Last year the ads did not hit home. The fireworks went off with spectacular racket, a lot of locals hit the deck, fearing yet more civil war, and several nearby defence units went on full alert.

Luckily, nobody was shot, but the Heathens had some explaining to do afterwards. 'It was mainly rockets. It was really quite fantastic,' said Peter of the display, though with no shadow of regret. He played down the criticism.

Dominic Symes, in contrast to Peter, was an old Africa nutter. He was not the slim ascetic Foreign Office type normally associated with the name Symes, but shortish, roundish, bearded and bespectacled. He ran an orphanage, a banana farm and a bursting African social life from a small hut in 130 acres outside Kampala. He had gone native.

We met him in the street on a Wednesday. On the Thursday he picked us up to take us to an island he bought for fun on Lake Victoria. We learned that, although Dominic's plans could never quite be called 'best laid', they could go wrong in just the same way.

When he picked us up there were already twenty people on board the back of his pick-up, including his local magistrate, Bukulu, and some of his orphans, who wanted a ride into town for the fun of it. Bukulu could not stop the local police from picking Dominic up for running an illegal taxi service. He certainly drove like a Kampala taxi-driver, using his horn, I began to suppose, as a kind of echo-location device.

The whole raucous lot of us quickly met problems in getting to the island, namely that the last boat had already left, so we went back to the farm, stopping on the way to pick up several gallons of banana wine, cigarettes, two cabbages, an eight-piece drum band and a troupe of dancers and their costumes. The engine gasped and wheezed the last five miles over dusty tracks through banana plantations with over forty of us on board. The noise was terrific, as all the artistes were warming up in the back, in the cab and on the roof. Red sat under a pile of children going through a rainbow of interesting pastel colours. He was suffering one of his post-Zaïre hangovers.

As soon as the pick-up ground to a halt, wheels pressing firmly against arches, the drummers and dancers leaped out. Red went and lay down.

The drummers went at it with a more relaxed look on their faces than the Mohammeds of Imlil, but with much more speed and noise. Tak-te-tak-te-tak-te-tak tak-te-tak-te-tak-te-tak tak-te-tak tak-te-tak te-tak te-tak. A simple fiddle played a tune like a warped record of an Irish jig with a scratch that keeps bouncing the needle back to the same place.

More activity for you. Stand up. Bend your knees slightly. Stand on the balls of your toes and stamp your heels, each twice, in time to the drums, and keep it up for hours. Do this with a colobus monkey skin tied around your bum and make that bum revolve crazily, as if you were waving an extra limb. That is the really tricky bit. While all this is going on downstairs, hold your arms out like the branches of a tree and put a serene Buddha expression on your face. 'Our girls are not hinged like that,' said Neil in awe as we sat in wicker chairs and watched them dance like this.

Neil loved African girls. No, not like that. Only to look at and talk to. Every chance he could he would, as he put it, 'rap with the locals'. He spoke passable Swahili, and they loved it, especially the prostitutes in the bars, even when they knew he was not a scorable proposition. He learned obscure terms of endearment in Swahili like 'I love you like roast beef,' and 'Your nipples point to six o'clock.'

Dominic was a mining engineer and a computer consultant, but only when he needed the money. He was brought up in Kenya. 'When I first came to Kampala I joined the rugby club and would go out and spend 100,000 shillings a night,' he told us. 'But the honky way of life isn't quite right for me. That would feed 200 kids.'

He was looking after 340 children when we saw him – 'No, 347 after the car accident last week. We go down to about 300 in the malaria season. That's just this district.

'I give them quinine and antibiotics. If they break a bone I send them to the witch-doctor. He is good. I came off my bike at 180 kilometres an hour – multiple compound fractures, the works. The doctors in Kampala said amputate from the knee. The doctors in Johannesburg said amputate the foot. The witch-doctor here gave me something to smoke and rubbed the bones sticking out back into place. I can't use one of my toes, but I was back on my bike in three weeks.'

It was the wars that started this acceleration of orphans; it is AIDS and large families that keep it up.

Bukulu was a charming, modest man in his thirties and one of the few between the age of thirty and sixty we saw in Dominic's district. We asked Bukulu how many children he had.

'About ten, really, sort of,' he said.

'And wives?'

'Three, sort of.'

'And girlfriends?'

'Sort of.'

Laughter all round. 'So what's it like in heaven?' asked Red, now recovered. More laughter.

Bukulu saw no reason to take AIDS seriously. 'Doctors tell us not to sleep with women, but doctors get AIDS too,' he said with impeccable African logic. Bukulu subscribed to the pan-African live-for-today ethic that we saw everywhere. A man could work for years to rise in government, and then blow it all and be sacked for taking a one-dollar bribe. A woman could happily knock off a known AIDS victim thinking to herself, well, that gives me eight years, and I could die this year of malaria.

'There is a hundred per cent death of all between children and grannies,' exaggerated Dominic, ignoring the living proof of Bukulu. 'Basically, we're squatting in all the vacant houses.'

Dominic does his best for the children, and in exchange they are his workforce and provide his home. 'I pay cash for schools and meat at weekends,' he says. 'No. He's not very bright,' pointing at one child who was pouring us tea. 'He's thirteen and I am taking him out of school this year because I can't afford it. It's arbitrary. I read the reports and say, you, you and you can go to school; the rest of you, no.'

He is tremendously enthusiastic about his adopted country. Like Peter Dow, he remembers the golden days of the 1960s, but unlike Peter he sees their imminent return. 'Uganda in the 1960s was the pearl of the continent. The Switzerland of Africa. And we will be again. Maybe next week.'

It all seemed ideal. George was turning over in his head possibilities of working in Uganda, maybe setting up a dairy farm. Dominic fell over himself with encouragement. 'We are a racist society. You have a great advantage – you are white. You can have a couple of PHDs in dairy farming as bellhops and 300 kids to make sure your cows' bottoms are shining every morning. You can have a staff of ten per cow.'

We made it to the island the next day. The Sese Islands are scattered near Uganda over Lake Victoria, the world's largest inland lake, which sits in the centre of the continent and feeds, among others, the Nile. We crossed the equator for the first time, and for the first time by boat. On seagoing ships this traditionally involves a ducking on deck. Luckily we all forgot this, or it would have been bilharzia all round.

Bilharzia is a bug which lives in water snails and breeds in everyone else. To stop us from catching it, porters waited at the port, just south of Entebbe, to carry our belongings and, we were apprehensive to discover, us on their shoulders to the waiting boats. Nobody fell in, though Wicky was shaking so badly with giggles that her porter had trouble finding his footing.

We stayed in the Seses with Bukulu for far longer than we thought we would. Even without Dominic's disorganisation, we failed to find a boat back, and then it was a weekend, and so it went on. Luckily, the island was fabulous. It was heavily forested with a small grassy hill rising out of the middle. Dominic's children had cleared a camp at one end, a mile across from a small fishing village on the other side.

The trees grew in the island forest like large companies on a stock exchange ought to. The giant Sese spiders festooned their upper branches with silky influence like corporate executives, seeking whom they may devour, sometimes each other. They sat in hundreds, each in its own muslin covering of web, waiting for opportunities. Other smaller spiders sat at the tops of other smaller trees, aspiring to the mighties above them, willing their own tree to grow faster and looking for a gap in the echelons, but always keeping one eye on the younger whizzier spiders below them.

There was fishing in the lake. Wicky caught a small fish, a tilapia, with a hand-line, and we killed it, lodged a pebble inside its stomach to weight it, and punctured it with large hooks until it looked like a punk. We towed it behind Bukulu's small canoe all round the island, but never caught the huge Nile perch we hoped for. We nearly caught a black kite which dived at it, but we stopped paddling and let the fish sink until the bird went away.

The kites were always on the make, grabbing fishgut from the shoreline around the village and bullying the magnificent fish eagles, who disdained these raids, their giant black wings and royal white heads swooping above us on powerful thermals and updraughts. Even the little ibis, egrets and divers took a more professional approach to hunting than the thuggish kites: using the drifting platforms of water hyacinth as mulberry harbours to launch attacks on the cruising fish. They skimmed the brown water, in and out of the islets, in search of a quick scoop. And the pied kingfisher went from hover to flick-spin crash-dive splashdown to pull out fry. The kite protection racket tried to mob these fish out of them. Red called them 'the local hard birds'.

Camping on the island was not completely comfortable. It was not the kites, thankfully. They did not flock down and demand money with menaces. It was something smaller than the kites. It was the ants.

They were dreadful. The jaws of the soldiers that defended the workers were so strong that once they had locked on to you, even if you pulled the abdomen and thorax off, the head still stayed, pinching into your skin. Locals use them to stitch wounds. They were the most indestructible ants we had come across. 'These aren't ants.' said Hazel, trying to squash one at breakfast. 'They're Terminator termites. Look: I keep standing on this one, and he keeps reforming back into an ant again.'

They marched in ranks a couple of inches wide and we never saw a head or a tail to their columns. They may have just been several concentric circles, going round and round the island. We felt them as soon as we landed on the beach, and ran slapping for cover when we did. They were the bane of our stay on the Seses.

But the worst of their tenacity was reserved for George. He and Wicky had pitched their tent in a clearing right in the middle of the rest of us. It was a good tent, with a flysheet, mosquito netting and a rain cover. With pinpoint accuracy, the ant column wound its way through the rest of us as we slept, marched up the sloping wall of George's tent, found the only hole, which was the metal ring on the roof where the pole poked through, and squeezed, individually, into the tiny crack between pole and ring. Two commando battalions and a tank division had silently got inside.

Wicky woke up to feel something on her face. Sleepily, she wiped it off with her wrist and it landed on George's face. 'Yeeeeow!' he shouted, and sat up. 'Torch, Vick – where's the torch?' he said urgently.

Wicky tried to ignore him and go back to sleep, but he shook her awake again. She handed him the torch. He switched it on, and saw that the inside wall of the tent beneath the hole was a moving carpet, that one battalion had established a headquarters at the foot of his sleeping bag, and that the other was just about to launch a parachute drop from the ceiling. The tank division was busy building an emplacement in his washbag. He leaped out of bed, grabbing Wicky, and flung himself and her out of the door of the tent, barely pausing to unzip it, just as he saw the ladders go up and heard the whistles blow in the trenches for the big push. Unfortunately, he landed on an ant supply-line outside, so there was more cursing and slapping.

He and Wicky spent the rest of the night wiping out the invading army, using all the tactics and strategy George had learned at Sandhurst. By morning they were exhausted, and slept until lunch.

Finally we found a boat. We returned to Kampala ready for the final leg of our eastbound trip to Nairobi. After that it would be a straight run south to South Africa on tarmac. The hardest and the harshest part of the journey was over.

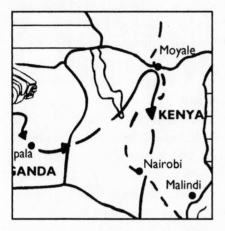

Chapter 12

TEAM TALK

Kenya. Neil, Hazel, Emma, Red and me in the Dust Busters' Land Rover. George and Wicky in Mistress Quickly. 108 days to the World Cup opening ceremony.

'Horrible Tom, Horrible Tom, do you read? Over.'
Crackle, crackle, fuzz from the other end.
'Horrible Tom, Horrible Tom, Horrible Tom?'
More fuzz.
'Bwana Tom?'
Crackle.

The African radio-operator and I were standing in a low-ceilinged room in a functional white-painted farm office building which carbuncled out of the green flatlands surrounding Lake Naivasha, an hour's drive north of Nairobi.

'He is not answering,' said the radio-operator unnecessarily.

I decided to give up and call later. The walk back to the others was down a straight dusty farm road, past the security man at the gate – called an *askari* in Swahili – over the railway line that runs north all the way to Kampala and south through Nairobi to Mombasa on the coast. It was called the Lunacy Line by detractors when British contractors built it with labour imported from India at the turn of the century.

The others were waiting beside the main road outside the Delamere Dairies farm shop which sold Emma and Hazel delicious cold yoghurts while Neil and Red fixed the puncture on the Dust Busters' Land Rover.

'Delamere,' I had thought when we stopped there. 'Delamere, Delamere, Delamere. That rings a bell.'

I had met Tom Cholmondeley some years before when he had been at the Royal Agricultural College in Cirencester. He had been learning how to run his father's farms, which I knew were somewhere in Kenya. His father – it all came back now – was Lord Delamere. Tom was the Honourable Tom, or the Horrible Tom, Horrible for short, as his African staff cannot pronounce the word 'honourable' and they insist on being polite.

Neil and Red finished tightening the wheelnuts and we drove on into Nairobi.

Neil, Hazel, Red, Emma and I were all in the Dust Busters' Land Rover. It was a happy state of affairs born of unhappiness. Since Kampala, Red, Emma and I had been honorary DBs. The Hooray team had not, in the end, survived the vicissitudes of Zaïre and had broken in two. Mistress Quickly herself, we discovered, was almost in two pieces as well, as George found more and more haemorrhages and tumours in her vital organs. The trip was falling apart.

The end began with niggles. These were the sort that niggle as much because you know it is petty to be niggled as they do in themselves. Cracks that had hairlined between us from the start and widened imperceptibly all the way down from Europe wrenched us apart in Zaïre. Travel had beaten the team. We all felt disappointed.

The biggest battles were between our strongest players, Red and George. The first was over who should do the driving. George, in charge of Mistress Quickly's wellbeing, thought he should do it all. Red, worried in case George became ill and could not drive, thought he should do some in case. Driving through Zaïre needed special skills. It was an easy issue over which to fall out – after all, driving in mud is fun as well. We all wanted to do it.

'Charlie, I can't go on,' said George finally, one half of a deputation with Wicky on a dark night in Central African Republic. I felt like the conciliation service ACAS. 'We're going off on our own,' he added to drive the point home.

Wicky backed him up loyally. George did not like saying things like this. 'You know that Red always wins arguments with George. He is better at arguing,' she said.

'Oh. Right. I'll talk to Red,' I told them.

'I can't believe George is being so *childish*,' said Red crossly later, and carefully within earshot of Wicky. 'I'm not going to back down.'

'No. Quite. Awful, isn't it? I'll talk to George.'

'Red is always trying to score points off me,' said George when I got him on his own. 'I'm not going to back down.'

'Absolutely. Terrible. I'll talk to him.'

The next morning, a warm morning as always in Africa, dawned frostily in our camp. But George and Wicky were still there. They had not left. Between the few words that George and Red spoke to each other could be heard the tinkling sound of breaking icicles.

Wicky had thawed overnight and the two of us sat on the back seat of the Land Rover for the rest of Central African Republic stifling giggles and writing messages like 'I think they should go into the forest and hit each other' so as not to break the arctic and antarctic silences in the front seats.

Emma, niggled by George over his military manner and thoughts on Ireland, had already joined the Dust Busters' Land Rover in Michelle's empty seat. Neil and Hazel were, as ever, delighted to help.

There were more arguments to come. Whether we should abandon Heinz and Christa before Zaïre, or whether we should let them come with us and slow us down had George and Wicky vigorously defending Germany against the rest of the world, including Michael, a German. I joined the rest of the world as soon as I saw which way the wind was blowing.

George's petulant outbursts, the pee-sosh-its, were now enraging everyone. Wicky siding with George maddened Red, and it infuriated him more that he was irritated by it. Red and Emma, who never backed down in any arguments, condemned them. My sitting on the fence at all opportunities made the others spit. Squishiness like that is hopelessly annoying in a team. Yet we lasted longer than most. And the show had to go on. We solved the difficulties by swapping around between the Land Rovers and the Pajero throughout Zaïre.

The niggle is an invisible force. We hardly ever saw it when it troubled other vehicles. Yet it was a more frequent occurrence for one of the others to come to one of us and ask to swap seats for a day. On one occasion, after an unfortunate failure to communicate on the part of all the factions involved, we had Beat and Weirdo driving alone together in Mistress Quickly in strained silence, George and Wicky driving the Pajero and the rest of us crammed into the other cars.

The Hoorays had spent a few days apart between Kampala and Nairobi and we greeted each other joyfully when we met up again, but it was not long before hostilities were resumed. Red wanted to sell Mistress Quickly, and told George so, early one morning before George had performed his breakfast ritual. ('Below the belt, that,' I agreed with George.) George pointed out that the idea was to drive on to South Africa. Emma's firm intention had only ever been to go as far as Nairobi, where she was due to meet up with her boyfriend, Danny, soon to arrive. Emma was out of the equation. Wicky and I hovered in the background. 'It's rather tactless to be talking about this in front of Mistress Quickly,' Wicky said.

It took some weeks, but at last the situation was settled happily. George bought Red's share of the Land Rover. Red was keen to stay in Nairobi and find a job. He liked it there. George and Wicky limped on south, hoping the poor old girl would make it. If not they would sell her on the way. Her top speed was now down to thirty miles per hour.

The reconciliation was merely the wearing off of the effects of Zaïre, a kind of poison. But that poison had contaminated the tears of our Lady from Lourdes with which Emma first blessed our travels. Others who have done this trip in the past say that they loathed their travelling companions by the end of it, but have been the closest possible friends in years since. One of those others was Gavin Bell, an old rugby-playing friend of Red's from school, who lived and worked in Nairobi. He had driven from Abidjan to Nairobi some five years before to raise money for the World Wildlife Fund, and the relationships on his trip had suffered in exactly the same way as ours.

I wanted to know about rugby. Every white in Kenya knows some white who knows or does anything, and Gavin took Red and me to rugby training at a sports club near the hotel where he worked. Gavin did not play any more due to injury, but trained assiduously to keep fit. Nairobi is a first world city in that respect. The session was almost all white, the players yomping up and down and round and round the pitch in the evening light, and then back to the bar for beer and bonding afterwards. 'It's a bit cliquey,' Gavin admitted. 'The whole of Nairobi is cliquey. I like to stay on the edge of all of the cliques; not be involved especially with any of them.'

Gavin's father, Gordon Bell, was heavily involved in rugby in Kenya. He played for East Africa on tour in the copper belt in what is now Zambia in 1962, and captained a UK tour in 1966. In 1968 he became coach and chairman of selectors of the Rugby Football Union of East Africa, and in 1972 its chairman. He is now a trustee of the RFUEA, a Kenya Old Fart, and that is meant respectfully.

When Gordon left school in 1952 – The Prince of Wales School, now called Nairobi School – the dominant clubs in Kenya were Harlequins and Nondescripts in Nairobi, made up mainly of the professionals and civil servants out there running the empire, and the club from Eldoret, a small town in the west of the country which had a strong South African community, the *voortrekkers* who had come to Kenya in search of a new life. Gordon played for his old-boys side, which became Impala Club in 1956. Most of these clubs have made great efforts to attract black players since independence in 1960.

'Impala Club is still going,' said Gordon sadly. 'Rugby's not. Rugby has gone.'

Despite his position, Gordon does not believe that rugby has much of a future in Kenya. Like Peter Dow, he harked back to the heydays of the 1960s, when the East African side was a match for teams like England and the Springboks passing through Kenya and the rugby-club system fulfilled a strong social purpose. 'Rugby was a very good way of meeting people in a short time. It was a well-run organisation,' said Gordon. 'I am a pessimist about its future because now it is not so well run. People who run it now want kudos.'

Like Gordon, Dickie Evans stays out of national rugby. 'People just use it for politics,' Dickie said. 'Rugby is for life – friends for life – people who are mercenary about it are wrong.' Dickie was the rugby man I went to see on Peter Dow's recommendation. He is a rugby junkie, and more upbeat about the game than Gordon. He is also an astonishing businessman.

Dickie came to Kenya from Cornwall as a civil engineer in 1969, working on United Nations projects. He was once selected for Cornwall, but could not play because of injury, a regret of his. Now aged fifty, he is running a group of four companies, including Homegrown, the largest grower and exporter of flowers in Kenya, an industry which at the time was Kenya's biggest foreign currency-earner. Every night thirty tons of Dickie's flowers fly to Europe, one and a half Jumbo jets'-worth. His companies sponsor the Nondescripts, known as Nondies, and Mombasa Rugby Club on the coast, and he personally sponsors Penzance and Newlyn in his home county, Cornwall.

Dickie is not universally popular in Nairobi. He is a little too successful. Many people are jealous of that, and some accuse him of sharp practice. But dogs are well known for eating other dogs in business.

He employs only rugby players in key positions in his companies. Both his co-directors are ex-Kenya players, and he has four generations of East Africa captains on his staff, including himself, spanning twenty years of the team.

'When you've been at the bottom of the pile with someone, under pressure, you know who to trust,' he said. 'People who work here have to be man-managers. They have to be adaptable, hard-working – which goes with training – and they have to have a sense of humour.'

Dickie had strong views on the game going professional. In fact, Dickie would have strong views on almost anything. He talked in world terms. 'Has Wimbledon depreciated by going professional? Ivan Lendl's one regret when he retired was that he hadn't won it,' he said. 'I cannot see that top players being paid top money is going to have any effect, as long as the referee remains in charge. I don't think it would affect amateur rugby in the least. It's the cream rising to the top.'

The author and Abderrahim Bougja, President of the Moroccan Rugby Federation.

Red in a pirogue at Assini Mafia, Ivory Coast.

Lara from the Swiss Family Robinson somewhere in Mauritania.

The Dust Busters in Nouakchott: Michelle, Neil and Hazel.

The author in Morocco.

The Dust Busters in Zäire.

Christmas at Limbe on the coast of Cameroon. Steve from Truck Africa is bearded, seated left foreground.

Gaborone Rugby Club celebrates South Africa's win over Australia in the opening match.

Red guides Weirdo over a bridge in Zäire. Michael is in foreground, the author left and Mistress Quickly behind.

From left, Urs, George and Red try to fathom the author singing in the Sahara.

Hazel and the head of a gnu.

The train across Zambia to Lusaka.

Wicky is carried to her boat in Lake Victoria, on the way to the Sese Islands.

Red sleeps off Christmas in Limbe.

The author and Red admire the crater in Mount Longonot, Kenya.

Emma reaches the top of Mount Cameroon, shortly before Christmas.

Derek Pringle in the Sahara.

A camel gets a lift in Morocco.

Ronda in Spain.

Camping at Christine's mud hut in Mali.

Wildebeest and a hippo in Zimbabwe.

A local post office in Mauritania.

Mistress Quickly crosses a bridge in Zäire.

The author crosses a bridge in Zäire.

Red coaxes the Dust Busters across a bridge in Zäire.

Mistress Quickly advances across a bridge in Zäire.

Mistress Quickly goes through a bridge outside Buta in Zäire.

Camping in the Sese Islands.

Red practises rugby skills on the coast in Kenya.

George and the author lost in the Western Sahara.

A bobby boots a ball off Cape Point, near Cape Town.

Roberta and Justin at Segera in Kenya.

Giraffe in Zimbabwe.

Paddy on a cattle truck with one of the Horrible Tom's staff at Moyale, the Kenyan-Ethiopian border.

The author and George, the surviving members of the team, on Cape Point, near Cape Town.

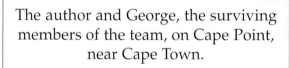

The Horrible Tom and his staff handing over cattle to the Ethiopian government at the Kenyan border town, Moyale.

George tries to open the door to let Wicky and the author out of Mistress Quickly as she lies on her side in Zäire.

Red guides the Dust Buster Neil into deep water in Zäire.

A local watches us pick up a parking ticket in the middle of the Sahara Desert, in Mauritania.

David playing cribbage at the Dunkley Inn, Cape Town.

The author revolutionises the fishing industry in the Congo Basin by using artificial flies.

The author and his catch.

From left to right, Paddy, the Horrible Tom and the author, outside the Kitale Club, Kenya.

The Elephant's coach Dominique Davanier and his team doctor talk to a player at an Ivory Coast training session in Abidjan.

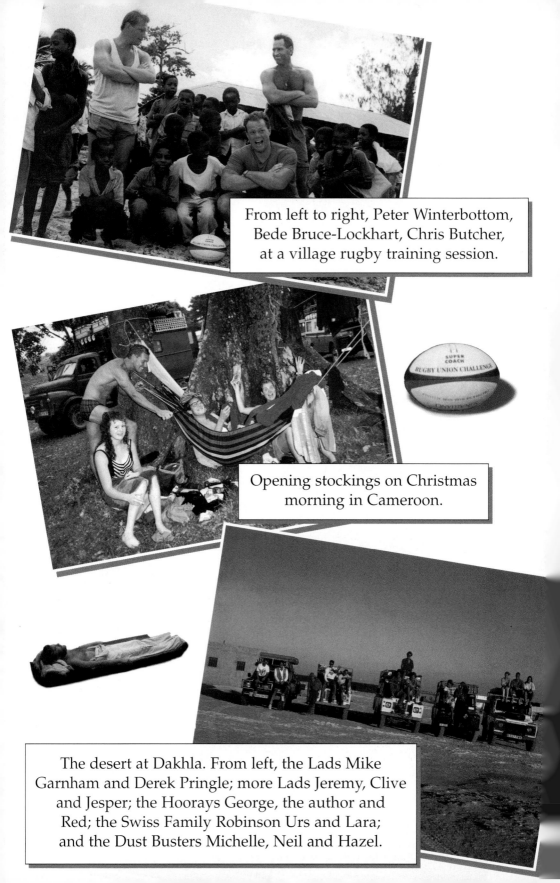

From left to right, Peter Winterbottom, Bede Bruce-Lockhart, Chris Butcher, at a village rugby training session.

Opening stockings on Christmas morning in Cameroon.

The desert at Dakhla. From left, the Lads Mike Garnham and Derek Pringle; more Lads Jeremy, Clive and Jesper; the Hoorays George, the author and Red; the Swiss Family Robinson Urs and Lara; and the Dust Busters Michelle, Neil and Hazel.

From left, the author, Bukulu, Emma
on the Sese Islands in Uganda.

Having supper with Nancy in Nouakchott.

Steve from Truck Africa reliving
the birdshit incident with
Christmas trifle, Cameroon.

Grubby in Zäire.

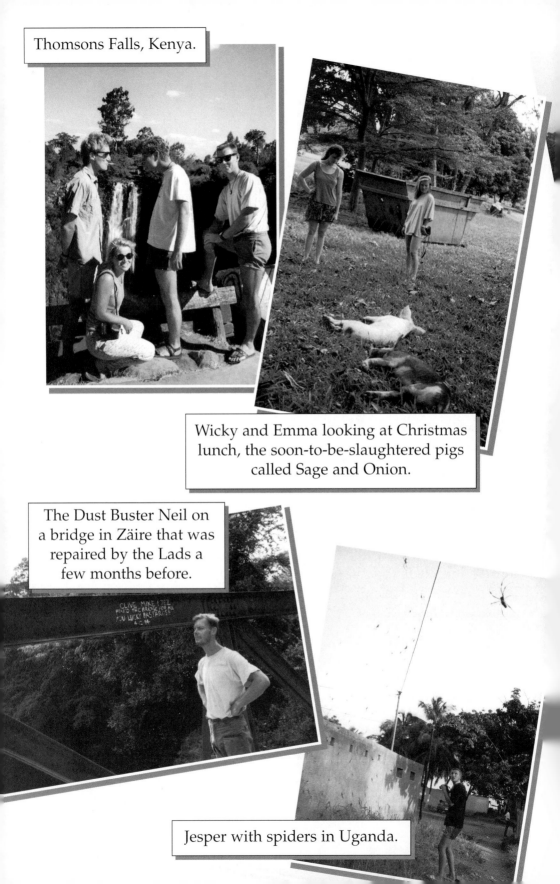

Thomsons Falls, Kenya.

Wicky and Emma looking at Christmas lunch, the soon-to-be-slaughtered pigs called Sage and Onion.

The Dust Buster Neil on a bridge in Zäire that was repaired by the Lads a few months before.

Jesper with spiders in Uganda.

On a granite coll in the Congo Basin, Zäire.

Spiders on the Sese Islands.

Emma not keen on lunch (It took us months to train the cane rat to do that).

Zäirean polygraph lie detector. The men of the village had to walk through these palm fronds and say they did not steal from us. The man in the shell suit is the chief's 2IC, who had a man beaten to death for us.

Bede Bruce-Lockhart at a training session in Zimbabwe.

Peter Winterbottom, Chris Butcher and Bede Bruce-Lockhart at Victoria Falls.

Peter Winterbottom meets a local scrum machine.

Chris Butcher falls in love with a local.

But professionalism versus amateurism was not being debated in Kenya – the game has too low a profile there. The only country in Africa which would benefit from professionalism was South Africa. There was not the money anywhere else. Even soccer players in Kenya were only just talking about going professional.

'Professional football is one of the reasons I don't think rugby will survive here,' said Gordon Bell. 'Rugby just doesn't attract the Africans, and there isn't enough money. Nondies and the other clubs used to survive because there was an endless supply of civil servicemen in their twenties coming here. All that keeps Nondies going now is second-generation Kenyans, sons of fathers coming back.'

At games in Nairobi, most of the blacks sat in the stand while the whites went to the concrete seats on the other side of the pitch. Gordon said that in the old days it had been the other way round. 'There is no racism in the game, but races tend to go to their own and Nondies is mostly white. But there is big antagonism in the crowd watching rugby between blacks and whites. I refuse to go because of it.'

Nairobi was not a good place in that way. Called locally Nairobbery, the city was, at worst, a seething septic tank of crime and abuse. Mugging was rife. Wealthy people – white people – lived in the highest of high security in quiet suburbs. Their houses were fortresses of paranoia, especially those of the expatriates. The residents, those whites with citizenship, were a little more relaxed about it all. Coils of razor-wire around lawns were disguised by rose bushes and flowering bougainvillaea and patrolled by *askaris*. There were *askaris* at every gate, striving to look suspicious of visitors, and embarrassed when visitors turned out to be real visitors. They were not always armed, as they were in Uganda, but many carried bows and arrows, incongruous with a Securicor uniform.

Complaining about your *askaris* is a national pastime. Being an *askari* suits the streak in the third-world equatorial African that likes to sit in the sun not doing much. Gavin's *askari* was not there one afternoon when he returned from work. Gavin hooted at his gate impatiently. No movement. He hooted angrily. Nothing. He gave a last furious hoot and the gate was opened by the terrified man, who had only gone off for a pee. 'If you *ever* leave this gatehouse again you are fired,' stropped Gavin. So the *askari* never did leave, not even for a pee. When I last saw him, Gavin was debating whether or not to relent.

In Nairobi blacks preyed on whites, whites sought revenge on blacks, and everyone went for the Indian population. There was an armed gang of blacks going round hijacking cars. It was serious. The white community might be small, but there were two people at rugby training alone who had had their cars pinched by these men in the previous month. One of them had been driven at gunpoint up to Naivasha, where the carjackers dropped him off, and stylishly gave him a few bob to catch a bus home. Less stylishly, four days later and a hundred yards from where this fellow was held up, they shot dead a young woman dropping her child off at nursery school.

Nothing could be done about it. Someone recently shot a robber who turned out to be a high-ranking policeman, much to the government's embarrassment. Worse still, but not brought up officially, a white saw a black stranger driving a friend's car. He followed discreetly through Nairobi city centre and watched the man drive into State House. The car, of course, had been stolen. The thief must have been in government.

Car theft may be about money, possibly jealousy, but the tension is also maintained by young white men who go out on purpose to beat up blacks or Indians. There is a story about an incident late one night at a Nairobi nightclub. A few whites had been walloping a few Indians. The Indians got together, called in reinforcements, bribed the *askaris* to lock the nightclub doors and set about the whites. Jolly good thing, too, most white people said. Not really, said others who had just been chased round Nairobi National Park by a gang of drunken Indians wanting to beat them up.

Some people are brought up this way. The housegirl is the lowest of the low in staff hierarchy. Some fourteen-year-old white boys got together in a friend's house armed with porn videos while his parents were out. They made the black housegirl come too. 'Do *that*,' they told her, watching the videos, 'or you're *fired*.' Nairobi, however, was East Africa, and for that I was grateful. The city centre, the worst part, was fine as long as you kept any bag you were carrying close to your chest and concentrated hard on who might be in your pockets. These stories of interracial strife were available to us because we spoke English. Commentators on French West Africa say that the social system is much worse over there.

And it was only ever bad in Nairobi. Out of town, the country had a mild us-and-them feel about it, but country people all over the world know that they have to rely on each other. At worst white farmers referred to the *watu* – 'the people' – as 'the neighbours', just as the spymaster George Smiley called Soviet intelligence 'the neighbours'. It was 'the neighbours' who were responsible for stealing fence wire and telephone lines and snaring the wildlife. The *watu* called all whites *mzungu*, Swahili for European. Everyone claimed it was, if not a term of affection, just a term, but it always sounded aggressive and offensive. 'Hey! Mzungu! How are yooouuu!' they shouted from the roadsides as we swept past in cars with the windows wound up three-quarters.

Dickie Evans was more cautious about racism in rugby than Gordon Bell. 'We've had multiracial rugby here as long as I can remember,' he said. He was more keen to talk about the blacks' abilities on the pitch: 'The Africans were fit and fast when I was playing, and still are, but their forward technique took time to develop. It's still a struggle to find Africans big enough to play, but they're great on the outside.'

'It was predominantly a European game,' Gordon said, 'and the Africans always played football. Now they are joining the clubs and they can be very good when they put their minds to it. Their big problem is bulk. But the racial side of the game disturbs me,' he emphasised. 'I wish Nondies had encouraged young Africans to join. Harlequins and Impala did it very well. But it may be too late now.'

Kenya's rugby is in the doldrums – Gordon knows that – yet Dickie is a win-only man. He wantes to bring it back, and he paid for the late David Protheroe to come over from England and train Kenya before the last World Cup in 1991. It was too little and way too late. Kenya did not even make it to the African Group qualifiers in Harare. Their hopes for this World Cup were demolished very early on by Zimbabwe and Namibia in Nairobi.

Dickie was unimpressed by the break-up of our team – George, Red, Emma, Wicky and me. He used it to expound upon a wider theme. 'From where I sit, no win, no respect, and the beer always tastes better if you win. I am stunned that Damon Hill should be made Sportsman of the Year when he only came second. If you take that forward into your professional life, it's all about quality. I get amazed about people in public life who get caught in bed with people – where's their pride?'

Comparing us to Cecil Parkinson was a little steep, but I could see his point. Red and George were leading largely separate lives at this stage, while I shuttled between them, looking forward to the time when I could disappear into the bush for a bit.

I went racing with George and Wicky in Nairobi. George owns a racehorse in England and he was keen to see how Kenya played the sport of kings. Wicky went because she was missing her horses. I went for the entertainment.

The Ngong Races, on the road out to the Ngong Hills, was just like the best of British summer racing, only with guaranteed sunshine and more of a family feel. Rich children were parked on clipped lawns with nannies in groups. Parents wandered from parade paddock to the main stand. In atmosphere it was all far removed from Nairobi city centre, just a few miles away. Each horse had any number of staff to look after it. There were even the necessary seedier concrete bits by the bookies and the Tote for smarter racegoers to decry before nipping down and slipping a few shillings on Lucky Boy.

The racecard was a little confusing. We worked out the horses' names, but the codes for each horse were in a different order from English races. We thought each horse's age was its draw number, and struggled under the misapprehension that the owner was the jockey. Not knowing any of the horses racing anyway, this system worked well until we came to a maiden fillies' handicap in which most of the runners were owned by syndicates.

'Some of these horses have an awful lot of jockeys,' said George, confused. 'This one's got six.'

'And they're all going to be loaded into stall number two,' gurgled Wicky.

The finer points defeated us until the end. It may have been a maiden race, but most of the horses seem to have won several times in the past, according to the card. The horses crashing down the turf were magnificent, even though the ones we chose were as defeated as we were. We left before the last race and went back to the campsite.

By the time Red and George had kissed, made up and signed their Treaty of Versailles, I had made plans to take my tin helmet and retreat upcountry from the firing zone. I made contact with the Horrible Tom at last, and asked if he had a fence I could sit on somewhere out of the way for a bit.

'Fences?' he hooted. 'We have hundreds of fences. We have fences enough for *58,000 acres*. Come and sit on all of them.'

So endeth the second leg, Ivory Coast to Kenya, and beginneth the third, Kenya to South Africa.

PART II

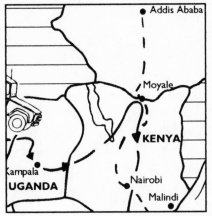

Chapter 13

THE HORRIBLE TOM

Kenya. 90 days to the World Cup opening ceremony.

T he next day came up frabjously, a shouty cracker of a morning. The sun bounced into view. I laughed merrily as the small green tropical birds that lived in the tree above my hammock tried to drop small green tropical messes into my coffee. I was in that campsite in Nairobi, my last campsite of the trip. From here on in I reckoned to stay with friends all the way to the World Cup.

The pressure of time suddenly eased off. The race to get through Zaïre before the rains began was over. That was always going to have been the hardest part of the journey, and we had now made it through the challenge that George enjoyed so much. If we had arrived a week later in that country we could have been a month late into Uganda. We could have stuck in any mudhole there for days had the floods begun. With that in mind, George admitted that he felt slightly robbed.

The tone of the trip had changed completely. I planned to stay in Kenya for a while and then potter slowly southwards on trains and buses visiting friends along the way. There would be no more concern about the vehicle, about whether she was too hot, or too cold, or consuming too much oil, or too little, or where we might find the next garage that actually had diesel to sell us. Feeling a mixture of relief and sadness, I left that campsite fairly sure I would not see Red or Emma or George or Wicky again before that other life, England, began in July when the World Cup was over.

There was the joy of the cold shower and the ecstasy of the colder shave. Even the sight of the drunk African unconscious in the sewer as I walked out of the gate brought a feeling of happy oneness with humanity. And the memory of the infant who had jumped up and ripped my watch from my wrist just the day before as I sat in the Land Rover at traffic lights merely induced a sense of hazy laissez-faire. Nairobi could be like that.

Today was the day that Georgina was coming to Nairobi. Georgina was my girlfriend, who had sustained the trip for me that far with Encouraging Letters and News of Her Horse. She was flying into Jomo Kenyatta Airport on a British Airways flight from London. I took a bus out there.

Not seeing someone for so long makes one apprehensive. She might have changed. She might be a monster. I probably had changed; maybe I was more monstrous. The feeling gripped the guts with uncertainty. I arrived on time to meet the aeroplane which was, equally un-Africanly, on time as well.

Georgina walked into the arrivals hall, the same as ever, tall, beautiful (goes without saying), and, best of all, chutching a bottle of champagne in one hand. Clever girl.

All I could do was blither at her.

'Helloooo!' she called.

Gibber, gibber.

All of a sudden it seemed so unlikely that we had reached this far. Georgina's arrival, so much looked forward to, was the trigger for the full magnum impact of the trip to hit me. This was, this really was, Nairobi. The journey from Madrid to here had taken five months, and that was moving fairly speedily. From here to South Africa could take as little as a week if necessary, and there were another three months to go before the start of the World Cup. Let's party. We took a taxi back. Pop, went the cork. The blithering simmered down.

Our first stop was an unpleasant hotel, the Hermes, quickly

redubbed the Herpes, whose only advantage was its nearness to the railway station. We had to stay in Nairobi for the first night. Experience had taught me that Georgina was prone to sudden fits of tiredness. She would live life at several mach, then announce that she was a trifle weary, and in under a minute would be fast asleep. She made it to the hotel with a few seconds to spare. I went off to organise train tickets back up to Naivasha.

We left the Herpes Hotel with relish the next morning in order to head north to one of the five most important events in modern Kenyan history. The other four are Karen Blixen, Joy Adamson, Jomo Kenyatta and Julie Ward. We were off to Happy Valley, ranged round Lake Naivasha, in and out of the Aberdare Hills and up to Mount Kenya, written about by James Fox in his book *White Mischief* and subsequently made into a film.

Happy Valley is not what it was. The wild-child fast-car twenties and thirties, which slid to an ugly halt in a Nairobi suburb with the murdered Lord Errol at the wheel – a crime which has dogged Kenya for over half a century – depended on several criteria. To be a truly happy white in Happy Valley you had to have a past, the kind of past that gave you no future in your home country; you needed few cares or inhibitions and, despite the amount of sex going on, no children to speak of – certainly none to speak to.

James Fox dug up a perfect Happy Valley quote during his research into the Errol murder. It was from a chap about an incident in Nairobi's Muthaiga Club in 1928: 'Well, there is a limit,' he said, 'even in Kenya, and when someone offers cocaine to the heir to the throne, something has to be done about it, particularly when it is between courses at the dinner table.'

If you fitted in with all this, and a title would not go amiss, then you could come to Happy Valley and pursue your interest in fast women, slow horses and fattening cattle from a heavily overstaffed house. People can be so grand in Kenya. The staff of one's staff can have staff.

The necessity to have as few children as possible meant that there were few descendants of the true Happy Vallyers left when I was there. They hid upcountry in their ranches or down on the coast near the sailfish and the marlin. They made occasional forays to Nairobi or Mombasa airports to go salmon-fishing, skiing, or attend Oxbridge, Sandhurst or Cirencester. They did not go around murdering people.

Horrible Tom was one. His late step-grandmother was the Diana played by Greta Scacchi in the *White Mischief* film, whose surnames during marriages over the years included Delves Broughton, Colvile and Delamere. She was, by all accounts, the sort of person of whom the equally late Queen Mary remarked in a rare yet prudish show of humour, 'My name, too, has changed several times during my life, but while mine have been by accident, hers have been by enterprise.'

Happy Valley was a story of whites at play. The rest of Kenya is a catalogue of blacks at war. The train journey to Naivasha was amusing for being riven by intertribal conflict.

Kenya has many tribes, which fight whenever they feel they can get away with it. Two of the most dominant are the Maasai and the Kikuyu. The Maasai tend to be tall and lean in looks, and are noted for being some of the best cattle-herders in the country. They hate the Kikuyu, a shorter, fatter people who run much of the business in Nairobi not already controlled by Indians and whites.

President Moi of Kenya comes from a tribe closely related to the Maasai. When rumours of his death spread across the country at around the time we all arrived in our several Land Rovers, a number of his tribe were beaten up and their businesses burned down. It had looked serious from Uganda. Dominic had advised us not to go to Kenya until the fighting stopped. We decided that this was just standard Dominic melodrama. Happily for the clan Moi, the punch-ups and arson turned out to be a small price to pay as the Kenya shilling crashed against other world currencies, only to make a miraculous recovery when Moi made his own equally miraculous reappearance. Members of his family reportedly made large sums on foreign exchange-dealing that week.

The tribal war on the train was between our steward, a Maasai, and our cook, a Kikuyu. Georgina and I had a first-class compartment on the overnight train to Kampala. Rattling along extremely slowly, it would take only two hours to get to Naivasha, but even so we had been issued with meal tickets and bedding tickets. The Maasai fellow was the first to come, shortly after we had pulled out of Nairobi Station and begun the long climb up on to the eastern scarp of the great Rift Valley. He took our meal tickets and our order for supper – chicken supreme followed by treacle pudding.

We waited for an hour. From the top of the scarp we watched an orange ice-cream sun melting into the mountains on the other side of the valley. When the last of the light had dripped away, I went to find the food. I found the cook, the Kikuyu. 'Will you bring food?' I asked. To English ears it sounds rude put like that, but 'bring this' or 'bring that' is a normal command in East Africa.

'Yes, sah, sorry, sah,' he apologised. The word 'sorry' is a great palliative. Africans apologise for events they have nothing to do with. I could bang my head walking into a room and 'sorry, sorry, sorry, sorry,' would echo around as if each man there was personally responsible for local doorframe-sizing.

Ten minutes went by and nothing came. I stood up and walked out of the compartment to meet the Kikuyu in the corridor.

'Coming, sah, sorry sah.'

He followed me back into the compartment. 'What you like on the menu?' he asked.

Georgina and I looked at each other.

'Chicken supreme,' she said.

'Followed by treacle pudding,' I added.

'You give me meal ticket now?' he asked, writing down our order.

'No, we gave it to the steward.'

'Steward?' Some thought. 'Yes, sah, sorry, sah, I'm coming.' He went off.

Confusingly, Africans use 'I'm coming' to mean that they are going, but will return at some point in the future.

Another minute went by. We heard a hushed but heated argument in the corridor. And then the Maasai knocked on our door. He was cross. Waiting was his responsibility, he felt, not a Kikuyu's.

'What you say to that man?' he asked.

'We gave him our order. You were too slow,' I said.

'I'm coming,' he said, and shut the door.

More muffled arguing. The door opened again.

It was the Maasai.

'Have you brought the food?' asked Georgina.

'I'm coming *now*,' he said frantically as he retreated.

The argument faded down the corridor. Five minutes later the Kikuyu appeared with the chicken supreme. Not to be outdone, the Maasai appeared with the bedding. With the difference in height, they stood shoulder-to-elbow in our doorway and glared at each other.

'Food first,' I said. 'We don't need bedding. We're getting out at Naivasha.'

'You must have bedding,' said the Maasai.

This argument was not being run along European lines. I could see it slipping out of my control. Time to be tougher.

'Right,' I said. 'You,' the Kikuyu, 'put food down there. You,' the Maasai, 'here is ticket for bedding. Take bedding away. Bring treacle pudding. And you,' the Kikuyu again, 'bring coffee. Now go.'

'I am coming,' they chorused, and left.

To my surprise, the chicken stayed behind, the bedding left, and the treacle pudding and the coffee arrived in the right order.

We arrived at Naivasha and spent the night in a tourist cottage by the lake to the drowsy sound of crickets and frogs, rustling papyrus plants and thumping, grunting hippos. The next day it was back up to the Delamere Estates farm office to radio the Horrible Tom. He lived half an hour up the road on the largest of his father's estates, Soysambu, which stretched all the way around one of the Great Rift Lakes, Elmenteita. He sent a car down for us.

Our driver was Bernard, a shortish African not unlike the Bond villain Whisper in *Live and Let Die*. He drove slowly and talked indistinctly. He chose one gear and stuck to it all the way. He never attempted to overtake, except with maximum possible risk to life. Georgina held the dashboard tightly and my foot kept trying to find the imaginary passenger's brake pedal.

People are always crashing cars in Kenya, where drink-driving tests and MOTs hardly exist. We passed a minibus-taxi on one hairpin bend with its chassis so twisted from previous pile-ups that it was creeping crablike along the road.

On the verges of the tarmac, game browsed and grazed unperturbed. There were herds of zebra, Thomson's gazelle and impala.

Beyond them our eyes feasted on a British orderliness in the fields. This was so much easier to live with after the tangle and mess of Zaïre. There was wheat and there were cattle. I could see why settlers wanted it to look this way: to keep control. This was a place where people grew flowers in their gardens for fun. It was not a continual battle to keep the flowers outside their gardens. This was a place where the sons and daughters of bwanas and memsahibs could go to smart prep schools, like Pembroke at nearby Gilgil, wear immaculate uniforms, and 'Good afternoon, sir' you nicely. Kenya was like an English shire county which, inexplicably, I had never visited before. There were farms and small towns and the same sort of friends lived there.

We rounded a bend on a contour in the hill and saw Lake Elmenteita spread below us, hemmed by saltflats showing high-water marks like the rings in the trunk of an old oak. It was spotted with thousands of pink flamingos. We were now in Soysambu.

'That is Lord Delamere's house,' said Bernard, pointing to a dot on a distant hill across the valley.

Ten minutes later, at a steady forty miles per hour, he pointed out another dot, the Horrible Tom's house, and we turned off the road. We drove through the gate, past the *askaris* who lived in a house there, and for another five miles along farm tracks through the estate around the edge of the lake. Herds of antelope mingled with cattle in the grassland.

Tom's house was a large bungalow with outbuildings for guests and more houses for staff behind it. From the verandah, over a small garden ringed with trees, the view led down over dry grassland fields to the lake, but so exhausted you with the stunning beauty of the place that it was an effort to drag up your eyes to admire the hills on the other side of the valley.

There were birds splashing around in a birdbath in the garden – sunbirds, lovebirds, even starlings so gorgeous that a visiting English songbird would be moved to say, 'Phwoor! Wor! Look at the plumage on that!' Tom was keen on birds. Lake Elmenteita had recently won the world forty-eight-hour birdwatch, clocking 298 species and beating the favourite, a site in Ecuador.

Tom had other friends from England staying with him at the

time. The Delameres never stopped having people to stay. The house party was going strong when we arrived. We were greeted by Jamie, David and Ding-Dong, and we were all in the drawing room drinking Scotch when Tom walked in. Georgina jumped up for an affectionate greeting. The two of them had been at Cirencester together.

Tom, in his mid-twenties, was practising being a patrician. Eton and Cirencester teach you how to receive orders. Now he was learning to give them. He had the imposing look he needed. Taller than me, his fair hair crowned a face led by the Delamere nose. In the old days it had been a dominating proboscis. These days it was like a retractable Roman nose which jammed halfway between in and out. A hill at one end of Lake Elmenteita matched it so perfectly that its local name had been replaced by a new one, Lord Delamere's Nose. Putative pregnant Delamere wives have to study it carefully in order to produce the necessary sound stock.

Jamie was a roaring booming exuberance of man. He combined foppishness with the manner of a drill sergeant-major. 'Dahling,' he could command Lady Delamere across the room at supper like a declaration of war to her husband, and then in similar tones, like a colonel (retd.) describing his part in Tobruk, tell a long and rakish story about a grandfather called Boffy who was rude to people all over Knightsbridge and St James's and, according to Lady Delamere, who knew him, was 'vi-yery like Ji-yamie'.

Tom's mother, Lady Delamere, whom we met later, had an electric metal-melting smile that she combined with the ability to pronounce 'tapestry' as 'ti-yepestre'. She had a warm and highly developed sense of humour, enhanced, I decided, by a spell as secretary of the white rugby club in British Guyana, but in other ways, size and manner, she was more like the Queen, only younger. She was married to Lord Delamere, taller, thinner and rather older who, as Jennings might describe Darbishire, was the sort of chap who Always Talked in Capitals. If that was the case, then Tom tended to talk in *italics*.

The other guests, David and Ding-Dong, were young Fulham marrieds. Ding-Dong was an immaculate woman, so good-looking and well-groomed you expected a loudspeaker in the parade paddock suddenly to announce: 'And the prize for the best turned-out wife goes to number 2, Ding-Dong', while at the same time you noticed how dirty your own fingernails were. David lived in an equally ordered world, but his depended on organisation and un-African disciplines like Observing Dress Codes or Being On Time For Breakfast. It left him wide open to the love of Jamie's life: practical jokes.

Jamie had been a talented fencer at school. He now walked with a stick which he could use accurately, sometimes painfully, possibly lethally, and always with a snort, hoot or cackle of laughter. He adored pranks of any kind. They ranged from the slapstick to the meticulous. On the day she was due to fly home, Georgina and I were talking glumly by the pool at Muthaiga Club. We were easy meat for Jamie, and with a prod of his stick helped by a shove from David, we at once found ourselves in it and Jamie and David standing cackling above us.

But Jamie's best effort was aimed at David. The groundwork had been laid a month before. As I was there it was expanded to include me. It was, he asserted, an old Maasai tradition to eat a strip of the stomach lining of the first zebra whose kill you witnessed.

One of our first daytime entertainments was to go and see zebra being shot. It is illegal to shoot any ground game in Kenya unless you have a licence. Tom has one, and we went with him to watch. Georgina was not wildly keen on the idea – it smacked of gunning down horses – but zebra are vermin on Soysambu, like rabbits. We drove in a Land Rover down to the back of the farm and stopped at what Tom charmingly called 'a paddock'. It was fenced, he was right, but an Exmoor hill farm could have fitted inside its acreage quite comfortably. There were sixty cattle grazing there, large friendly animals with lumpy shoulders that are a result of crossing Friesians with Boran. There were also 1,000 zebra in herds, munching the much-valued grass near the tree-line. Tom shook his head despairingly.

He ran a game-meat dealership at Soysambu called Fair Game with a slaughterhouse just outside his compound. There the carcases of game from the farm came to be skinned and jointed. Big bald-headed blotchy-faced marabou storks hung round in groups waiting for carrion. They looked like out-of-work actors at someone else's first night. They stalked around with effete luvviness and the look of those who have spent their lives trying too hard to keep their outsides looking young and beautiful while stuffing their insides with junk and rubbish, and have long since lost their last cosmetic battle. They flapped from ground to tree with the noise of someone beating a carpet, and shook the branches when they landed.

Fair Game was one of several pilot projects set up by the Kenya Wildlife Service (KWS) to see if allowing limited shooting licences to provide game meat was feasible. The government of Kenya was forced to ban all game-hunting apart from bird-shooting in 1977 following pressure from the international community, but with the benefits of culling more firmly in the international public consciousness – conservation, not preservation, of animals – KWS wanted to see if giving game animals greater value to landowners would increase the quality of herds.

Tom, a keen naturalist who maintained a 7,000-acre game sanctuary on the estate, was convinced. 'If game is *worth* something to the economy, it is less *likely* to be slaughtered out of hand for food. Landowners will *protect* their game more,' he said as we bounced across the brown grassy field towards our targets.

Game accounted for thirty-five per cent of the biomass on Lord Delamere's estate. Cattle, sheep and goats made up the other sixty-five. This mix worked well as game animals often ate different plants from cattle. 'Thomson's gazelle eat *short* grass, which cattle cannot, and eland browse on plants like *seneccio* which give cattle *liver cirrhosis*,' Tom had told us over breakfast that morning. 'Dikdik eat lots of *small plants* which cattle cannot *including*' – he looked across his lawn crossly – 'garden plants.'

Every dawn and dusk the little dikdik gambolled in the garden, but only when the dogs were shut up. Tom had two dogs, liver-coloured German short-haired pointers, Chaos and Artu. They were bullies. He called them 'the Brotherhood'. They might not have actually worn jackboots and Jerry helmets, but they were Nazis, the local Gestapo. No other dogs were safe and the game trembled for miles. We did not take them on this shoot. And when we took them on any bird-shoot they disappeared on twenty-four-hour dikdik missions.

Until it began to have a real cash value, most landowners cursed the game on their ranches. Now that it did, Tom welcomed the fact that since game-cropping had started at Soysambu, and despite recent years of drought, the total game population had increased from 12,000 to 14,000. This compared to 11,000 head of cattle. Tom admitted that there had been no visible improvement in the cattle herd on the farm, but he said that Fair Game had helped to improve the farm management.

'There has been a *vast improvement* in the running of the farm, because we are always going into *nooks and crannies*,' he informed us. 'Petty crime is down, like people stealing fence wire. There is no poaching now, and because there is *money* in it, we can afford to *pay people* to remove snares.'

There were some snares still around. It is not a pleasant way for an animal to die. I found one Thomson's gazelle lying by the road, gasping out its last, with a piece of looped fence wire tight around its midriff. It had managed to pull the wire free from the post where it was anchored, but internal bleeding was killing it.

'Another advantage of game-cropping,' added Tom, 'is that we are enjoying a much closer relationship with KWS, who wield *tremendous* influence here.'

KWS stood square on the side of caution. It was a long and difficult process for Tom to get a licence. Every year KWS officials come to count the game and then, taking into account rainfall and vegetation, work out an annual quota. This normally comes to between ten and twenty per cent of the count of each species. In 1992 there were 2,000 head of zebra on the farm when the KWS people came, and the original cull quota was 400. In 1994 there were 1,000, and the quota went down to 100. The difficulty with KWS's census was that during this time there were an estimated 15,000 zebra shuttling between all the farms in the area, depending on the weather and the availability of grazing. Tom noted a total of 8,000 on Soysambu for some months in 1994, and consequently cursed his reduced quota.

Using around 3,500 rounds, Fair Game was taking 1,200 zebra, eland, buffalo and gazelle off the estate every year, totalling sixty-five tons of carcasses. The company sold the meat to hotels and restaurants in Nairobi, and the lower-priced cuts of meat through local markets.

We went to various spots by gates along the 'paddock' and parked

Tom's Land Rover. Then, whoever wanted to go would walk with Tom quietly up the fence line, downwind of the herd, to a range of around 200 yards. Some of the zebra would stop eating, look up and stare at us, ears pricked forward, trying to work out whether we were dangerous.

This was not sport as a truly tricky stalk is sport. This was vermin control. But the excitement of that long walk was palpable. We spoke rarely and quietly. One sudden movement would spook the herd into a rush gallop in a clattering cloud of dust. The sight of hundreds of large animals charging in one swift mass through the dry field was jaw-dropping and gobsmacking. Barely breaking stride, they would slip through wire-strand fences, kicking up tussocks, sometimes just a few yards from us, and disappear up and over the hill.

If the herd was still there, the two of us would sit or kneel at the firing point. Western civilisation tends to teach that it is barbarous to kill animals in this way, especially when an electric shock or a bolt-gun in a slaughterhouse seems so much cleaner, yet the primitive excitement you feel levelling the cross-hairs of the telescopic sights at the animal's heart, just behind its shoulder in the Y of its stripes, comes from beyond and above what you know to be civilised behaviour.

For the benefit of us, the inexperienced shots, Tom demonstrated how to lie on the spiky grass, rifle strap wrapped round his elbow, pointing the gun halfway sideways from the perpendicular of his body. He brought the muzzle up. 'Normally we shoot it through the vertebrae in the neck,' he said, *sotto voce*.

An old stallion with blacker stripes than the rest regarded us curiously from the middle of a small group of zebra. Tom breathed more slowly, once, twice, three times. Hold. Crack-dmm, went the gun.

The herd took off, startled. The stallion stood, stunned. A new sensation was running through his body and mind, which was fading fast as the blood supply ceased from his heart, pierced by the lead bullet. He staggered, wide-eyed. His instinct told him he had to stand. Staying upright was all that could save him. He fell, kicked, and died.

Tom and I stood up quietly. Tom spoke a few words of Swahili into his radio. The Delameres always carried radios, and relayed messages to each other via the permanently manned Soysambu control station. We walked soberly over to the kill. Behind us, David started the Land Rover and drove up. Everyone had been watching through binoculars.

Another Land Rover came towards us over the field. It was the Fair Game bloodwagon, driven by Tom's Maasai staff, which had been following us discreetly. He had just summoned them. This, now, was Jamie's finest hour. 'Stomach lining!' he was calling rudely between shouts of laughter as he stood out of the roof hatch of the Land Rover with Georgina and Ding-Dong beside him. 'Stomach lining!' He looked like a cross between a panzer commander and a porn king.

Tom turned away to smile, cleared his throat for seriousness, and ordered his staff to start the gralloch. Out came a long knife, and one of them sliced the belly of the beast's carcase. The innards spilled out. More Swahili from Tom, and the chief cutter looked at him oddly. Tom repeated it.

'Well,' thought the cutter, 'if that is what the *bwana* wants, that is what the *bwana* shall have.'

He cut two thin strips from the wall of the zebra's stomach, wiped the half-digested grass off them, and handed them to David and me. David looked at me. Moot one, this.

'Suburban not to,' reminded Tom honestly.

David put it gingerly into his mouth. So did I. There was a brief sensation of supermarket sliced cold ham and I swallowed it whole, thinking happier thoughts. David retched quietly to himself.

'Enjoy it?' asked Tom.

'Oh, yes,' I answered bravely.

The cutter held up another piece. I looked away.

Jamie exploded with earth-shaking laughter. 'Gotcha! Ha, ha, ha, ha, ha!' he bawled. He was crying with mirth. 'Joke!' he mouthed, gasping. 'It was a joke!'

David and I regarded him grimly.

'A joke?'

'A joke! Ha, ha, ha, ha, ha, ha!'

The others, in on it, were in stitches. Even the Maasai were chuckling.

'I thought it was a tradition,' said David gravely.

'Oh, it will be,' said Tom. 'It's going to be from now on.'

'Bastards,' David and I agreed solemnly. 'Absolute bastards.'

We ate the best of the zebra steaks that night on a barbecue. It was delicious, a strong beefy flavour – 'The *only reason* people eat beef is because cattle are easy to *domesticate*,' pointed out Tom – but David and I refused seconds.

In between brief forays out of the farm organised by Tom for us to see Kenya, we spent our week by the Delameres' swimming pool. Tom and his parents could not have been kinder to us. At the bottom of that kindness there is an inbuilt fear in white Africans of other whites slumming it in Africa. Roughing it is fine, but slumming it, no. If you look even slightly slummy, they ask you to stay at once. It was the most ideal week.

Jamie captivated Ding-Dong and Georgina. 'They are my super-models,' he thumped. 'Claudia and Elle, and I am Yves.'

Wherever he went it was with a 'Come on girls,' and each of them would attach herself to an arm. He had them swimming and sunbathing to synchronised order. If not quite nonplussed, David and I were far from plussed.

There was a bad moment for Tom when David and Jamie reported that some of their travellers' cheques had been stolen from their bedrooms. Things had been swiped from Tom's house before and he blamed the staff. It only took a telephone call to cancel the cheques, but Tom was furious, and when angry, he used a colourful but extraordinary array of language. He stormed from room to room. You could hear him shouting at his guests in various parts of the house: 'They're just *taking the piss*! This has happened before, fuck monkey. Fuck monkey *and* shitalump. I ought to line them up on the lawn and sack them all.'

'Why don't you shoot every third one until someone owns up?' we suggested.

Tom looked keen on the idea for a moment, but then frowned as he remembered the drawbacks – the police, murder charges, that sort of thing.

In the end he sacked the housekeeper, Mary. It was a hopeless situation. None of the staff would admit that they had done it, but they knew that justice would be remorseless. Slowly more and more of them made Mary the scapegoat. It was nearly for her own safety that it was better that she went. Other staff were stoning the door of her hut in Tom's compound. The Delameres have learned to be ruthless in this respect. Soysambu alone employs 250 people who support a further 4,000 living on the estate. It is like running a small town.

The week came to an end with a drive down to Nairobi and a night at Muthaiga Club. The whole party was leaving. Only Tom remained at Soysambu as I drove the gang to the airport.

The club system is still strong in Kenya and Muthaiga Club is the daddy of them all. Any overnight trip to a town upcountry came with a search for the whereabouts of a local club that reciprocated with one's own. There were lists on the walls of all of them of *personae non gratae* who had not paid their bills at reciprocating establishments.

Muthaiga Club reciprocated with hardly anyone. It was too smart for that. It was a settlers' club, unlike the Nairobi Club, which was set up as a civil-service club. It was not possible to be a member of both.

Muthaiga is the Bel-Air of Nairobi and the club is the best bit of it. Through a porticoed entrance there are staff to the left and staff to the right as you walk in. There are pigeonholes and noticeboards for members and their sports clubs. Turn left and there is a quiet reading room with the latest papers and magazines from London, like *Shooting Times* and *Horse and Hound*; turn right for a dining room which goes on to a verandah and into a garden; turn right again, and a bar demanding jacket and tie after 7.30pm leads you back past a library into the lobby again. In more obscure and secret rooms there is a billiard table and a men's bar, where women are forbidden and chaps can go to grunt and bond in peace. Cameras are not allowed in the building in case anyone is photographed with someone they ought not to be, bringing to mind the old saying, 'Are you married or do you live in Kenya?' Money is completely taboo. Everything is signed for on chits by members and accounts are settled at the end of the month. Outside the club building, there is a swimming pool with a series of almost identical old ladies cruising up and down it daily, all full ahead like frigates.

We had a whisky night to celebrate the departure. Georgina flew out that evening and the others the next morning. I came back from dropping her off at the airport in another blithery mood. Perhaps it is just airports that have this effect. Jamie made me play backgammon until shortly before the next dawn. The staff, used to this behaviour, stayed up to keep us stocked with more whisky.

When it came to the walk back to the cottage in the grounds that Jamie had rented, we found that neither of us could. Jamie had the advantage of his walking stick, but the hundred yards we had to traverse were almost impossible. I kept stopping by bushes in the herbaceous borders to sit down. I desperately wanted to be sick, but was not even capable of that. Jamie, meanwhile, was making even slower progress and roaring commands to staff who had by now gone to bed. The journey took half an hour, ten minutes of which Jamie spent trying to get over the step to the cottage. I was under a nearby shrub, egging him on between hiccups.

'Bloody thing,' he boomed at his stick.

'Come on shport, it'sh a doddle,' I offered.

'Damn the bloody f . . .'. Huge effort.

'One shmall shtep for you . . .'

'F . . .' Heave, and he was over.

'Hic.' I had a few glasses of water before bed.

It was a quiet Jamie indeed we led lamblike on to the aeroplane the next day.

I retired at once to Soysambu for hangovers and moping.

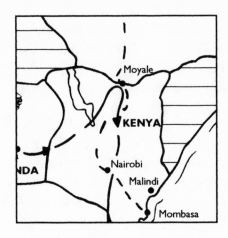

Chapter 14

A MONTH IN
THE COUNTRY

Kenya and Ethiopia. 80 days to the World Cup opening ceremony.

I drooped around Soysambu for a month. Tom was tremendous at organising *entertainment* to take my mind off *things*.

'Ethiopia,' he said. 'Let's zoot.'

Tom had to drive north to the Ethiopian border to deliver ninety cattle that the Finnish government had bought from Lord Delamere to present to the Ethiopian government. After that he planned to drive on to the capital, Addis Ababa, pick up his girlfriend, Wendy-Woo, who was coming out for a week from England, and drive south at speed to Nairobi to put her back on an aeroplane. It was a 1,700-mile round trip.

The other man coming was a friend of Tom's called Paddy, another white Kenyan. Paddy was a character. An almost permanent house guest at Soysambu, he lived in a world halfway between confusion and amusement. He was vague about where he came from.

'I live in, er . . . Nairobi? Um. Mombasa,' he told me. 'Somewhere between the two.'

Paddy was not keen on company for company's sake. If it arrived he preferred to slope off for a sleep.

'I think there are people rocking up for tea,' he would say. 'Um. I'm just going to shirk about for a bit.'

'Right-o,' I would tell him. 'I'll skulk here and see them.'

'See you after the skive.'

So the three of us arranged to set off north in a Land Rover borrowed from Tom's father – Tom's needed parts at the time – in convoy with several large lorries full of cattle. We were to follow the Rift Valley towards the deserts of Kenya's Northern Frontier District, and supervise the handover. We would stay in clubs all the way up while the drivers and staff made their own arrangements.

It was when we were about to leave that I realised I did not have an Ethiopian visa. Tom sent Bernard and me on a fast drive to Nairobi to visit the Ethiopian Embassy. There the sour lady behind the desk told me it would take twenty-four hours. No time for that. I bought her a bunch of flowers and she issued one on the spot. Bernard then hurtled me, more speedily than he had ever done before, 200 miles north to catch up with the convoy, which had left at dawn. The next day was a more relaxing drive, allowing me to take in the incredible scenery of the approaches to the NFD.

The Rift Valley is the Jerusalem of the natural world. Physically it is quite ordinary to look at, just a bigger version of many other East African valleys with more than normally stunning views from the top of its escarpments. Parts of it reminded me of the Vale of Taunton Deane, but a super-enhanced version and without the M5.

The rift's glory is its heritage as the birthplace of mankind, for which we must thank the excavations of Louis and Mary Leakey in the 1950s. This is what gives sanctity and symmetry to its raggedy rocks, its rascally twisted acacias and its dirty rugged hillsides. The first words spoken on earth were spoken in the Rift Valley by Homo habilis 3.5 million years ago. I am a big fan of words. And it was H. erectus, only half a million years later, who kicked off culture, and what anthropologists charmingly call 'stone technology'. Just as the sombre hills of Glencoe in Scotland resonate to the throes of the Macdonald massacre, so the Rift Valley has a sense of the earth's court mourning for the birth of man.

H. habilis to H. erectus to H. sapiens, handyman to upright man to thinking man – not a million miles from Shakespeare's seven ages of man: the mewling, puking infant, whining schoolboy, sighing lover, jealous soldier, round belly'd justice, lean and slipper'd pantaloon and, 'in second childishness, and mere oblivion, sans teeth, sans eyes, sans taste, sans everything'. It gives a dreadful inkling that we may end up crippled man.

In the south, the natural perfection of the Rift Valley was marked by the sores of agriculture that I so admired after Zaïre, crossed by black bloody weals of roads, and buildings the scabs of modern civilisation. In the north, spinneys of dusty whirlwinds hundreds of feet tall arched and twisted across dry red cakey deserts iced with chocolate volcanic ash and sprinkled with sugary white salt. The deserts along the rift fault-lines are decorated with small extinct volcanos.

It has Hollywood qualities. In remote northern Kenya you could meet a tribesman in the bush carrying a spear and dressed in a bright red cloak straight from Central Casting's wardrobe department, a drop of bright blood on the dry brown scrub. And, just like at the flicks, he would speak perfect English.

We passed oases in the Didagalgalu Desert, magnets for goats, camels, donkeys and their herders. Tribesmen walked their beasts towards these palm-ringed holes through a wash of mirage on the sand. With all legs lost, they looked as if they were punting boats along with their spears.

This was not Eden. You got Eden down the road in the south of the rift at places like the Aberdare Country Club and Treetops, and you could have it landscaped, weeded and served with Pimms. The rift proper was the palm of God's hand.

We made it to the border and started the lengthy process of Customs and Immigration for ourselves and our cargo. Somehow, another steer had found its way on board one of the trucks. We were sure we had left with ninety cattle, but now there were ninety-one. Tom was keen to hand them over and be done. Perhaps he said, the extra beast was a present from Lord Delamere himself. Ethiopian bureaucracy being what it is, he had a day's form-filling to achieve this.

The cows were unloaded and spent that day on a dusty patch of ground staring around with those expressions of absolute stupidity that pass for fear in the bovine universe. The drivers and staff organised water and doused the cows liberally all day to keep them cool. At last Tom came out of the final office of the day, rubbing his hands. We could leave.

Going into Ethiopia, we discovered a country thick with landscape. The views blasted us to blasédom. And the road was amazing. It had been built by a civil engineer who obviously had designs on Silverstone and the Nurburgring. Tom was itching to take his motorbike the 800 miles from Soysambu to the Addis Ababa, and to break any existing world records in the process. When the rain fell on the road, as it did in light showers in an early start to the year's rainy season, skeins of steam rose and drifted, and cut and curled in our wheels.

Ethiopia is not like Kenya. In Kenya the views are carefully orchestrated by the KWS to leap out at you. Many people think that Kenyan roads are badly designed, with poor visibility approaching bends, bridges and brows, in order to increase the road deaths and keep the population down. My theory is that the Kenyan roads are designed that way on purpose to give tourists titillating miles of climbs up many dull gulleys and through tedious trees, and then to wow them with a sudden view at the top of such drop-deadity that they are instantly reduced to tears. Ethiopia was more like the Cotswolds. There were great views all round all the time.

'Excelente,' said Paddy, in a Paddy kind of way.

'MBA,' said Tom, in awe of it. 'Miles of Bloody Africa.'

Tom had a way of breaking your line of thinking in conversation with the most appalling one-liners and puns. We would be in the Land Rover and 'Moo . . . moove out of the way!' he would shout at a herd of oncoming cattle. 'Or you will be *cowed* into submission.' Whenever possible he would observe that there was a zebra crossing.

Even worse were his non-sequiturs. We could be chatting about the political situation in Bosnia when, excitedly: 'Oh look, oh look, oh look, a *plastic-lined irrigation channel*. That's one of the *wickedest* things I've seen,' and just as we turned our minds to that one: 'And *look*, the swallows are migrating.'

There were birds everywhere. South of Addis Ababa there was a line of lakes which attracted dwarf bitterns around its reedy shores, pygmy kingfishers flashing like blue jewels as they flew with small fish in their beaks. Colonies of white-breasted cormorants sat on rocks offshore in the Rift Valley lakes. They stood, heads up, some with wings outstretched, as if a Victorian photographer had arranged them in attitudes for a school picture. They made a noise like a convention of dentists trying out new gargling techniques.

We abandoned the clubs once we were into Ethiopia, and slept out in the bush, but we treated ourselves to a hotel in Addis Ababa. Tom and Paddy were as happy asleep on a tarpaulin in the hills as they were in the Hilton: men who could walk with both baboons and bourgeoisie. The Hilton was not quite so happy with us, though. There was dismay at the reception desk when we arrived. It is a chain of hotels which upholds the most European of standards, and to arrive with sand in our hair and diesel oil on our shirts was a test for them. It was only our Europeanness, faintly visible under four days of stubble, that saved us.

Wendy-Woo was waiting for us when we arrived. She was a kind of Hazel, endlessly good-humoured, especially with Tom, who tended to *do* things *suddenly* and *surprise* people. She had been at Cirencester with Tom and Georgina. They were all old friends.

I had met her before she was going out with Tom. Now that she was, I could not help studying her nose for potential genetic influence. Cleopatrian, I noted, good conk.

Wendy-Woo, you may have noticed, is an odd name. Tom lived in a world inhabited by people with silly names. Ding-Dong's real name was Adrienne. Just after she left a Snoo (Deborah) came to stay with the elder Delameres. Even the tough and sunburned white Kenyan who flew the crop-spraying aeroplane was called Flip-Flop.

Addis Ababa was good-looking in the centre, but the Hilton made sure its guests saw as little of the locals as possible. What we did see – poverty and architecture, the two most obvious facets of African low ethics – combined ruthless Christian orthodoxy with more cut-throat Marxism, a hangover from the old Ethiopian government. In order to get back to Nairobi in time for Wendy's flight, we turned the Land Rover round and set off after one night there.

Despite the good roads, we did terrible damage to Tom's father's Land Rover on the way back, prompting more terrible language from Tom. 'Shanks,' he said. 'Shanks, monkey tits and dog's ringpiece.'

The front prop-shaft broke at the universal joints, the viscous coupling on the fan stopped working so the fan would not go round, there was an oil fire on the turbo, the handbrake cable snapped, and a short circuit that we could not track down finally drained the battery.

'Not importante,' said Paddy, who knew about cars.

Still, we made it back to Soysambu, thanks to Tom and Paddy's engineering skills. Not thanks to Paddy's driving, though. He had a maniacal streak in him. Normally quite calm and shy, he could not resist overtaking other cars, whatever the danger. He flew down the last of the Kenyan roads towards Soysambu on the right side of the road, which was wrong, past long lines of traffic. Lorries piling along in the opposite direction flashed and hooted him all the way, and he reacted by taking to the bush and driving along the verge. He was proud, he told us, of having driven the length of the Uhuru Highway, the main dual carriageway through the centre of Nairobi, on the wrong carriageway at night with his lights off. It surprised me that he was still alive. He is the only driver to whom I have ever found myself saying, 'Stop the car. Get out. I'm driving.'

After that, Paddy, now in the passenger seat, treated me to a long discourse on Crashes He Had Survived. He was just telling me that the most common cause of accidents in Kenya was driving into the back of slow-moving lorries when he shouted, 'Watch out, Charlie!' as I came to the point of no return doing just that. I slammed the wheel hard to the left and slid sideways along the road until we were virtually under the lorry's exhaust pipe before the tyres gripped and pulled us safely into a thorn bush. Mollified, I let Paddy do the driving after that.

We found Soysambu bereft of cars. Tom's own Land Rover still lacked parts, and Bernard had decommissioned the farm's last remaining Peugeot 504 by driving it into a zebra. Bernard belonged to Tom, so all in all Tom had Some Explaining to do. 'These boys,' said Tom, irritated. 'They've got the *most* sexually active fingers in the world. Touch anything and they fuck it.'

Tom went down to Nairobi with Wendy-Woo and Paddy. He left me at Soysambu, and for fear I would mope, he lent me a motorbike to go and see the animals in the game sanctuary.

There was a giraffe there, the sole survivor of a disastrous operation to bring several to Soysambu from nearby Lake Nakuru National Park. When a giraffe falls over it is likely to die. Naturalists explain that this is due to its gastric juices spilling up its long throat. All but one of them expired while being herded into trucks and driven the forty minutes down the road. Unfortunately, they had to be moved – there were already too many at Nakuru. But officials at the Nakuru end chose a lousy shipper. It was more good proof that wild animals can be managed, if managed properly, but cannot be herded around like farm animals.

The remaining giraffe was a tremendously elegant animal to see. If camels should be sent to top English girls' schools, then giraffes should be the preserve of the more exclusive Swiss finishing schools, purely for their ability to canter. The Soysambu giraffe's pace was immaculate and seemed so slow I wondered if it was really moving at all.

The goldbugs were swarming off Lake Elmenteita. They were buzzing in the evenings with the vigour of Neagh fly around the lights on the verandah, and the dining room resounded to the click-click-click of them bouncing off the ceiling at supper. They were toenail-sized beetles, coloured an ochrous burned umber, and they only appeared for a short season each year, which was marked mostly by the soft but sickening crunch, crunch, crunch as anyone crossed the verandah. If you hit a swarm while riding a motorbike around the farm, the view through your helmet was like that moment when Captain Kirk hits the hyperspace button and the stars on the screen of the *USS Enterprise* blur for a moment and zoom past.

I sat on a rock, next to leopard fewmets, staring out over the flamingos on the lake. These flamingos did not move much in the heat of the day. When the gang had been there, we had formed a theory that they were really inflatable, and that the Fair Game staff were employed by Tom to pump them up each dawn to attract tourists. But staring from rocks with whatever humour definitely comes under the heading Moping.

Live animals not the answer? Go and see dead animals. Tom sent me on a night drive with Fair Game to watch them lamping and shooting Thomson's gazelle. I joined the team in darkness. There were two men in front for driving and gralloching and three in the back, me, the lamper and the shooter.

As we drove along the farm tracks, aardvark pottered ahead of the Land Rover, ignoring the headlights. Cape hares dashed under the wheels of the vehicle while jackals watched from the background, waiting for victims. What looked like hot coals bouncing through the hilly grass and shrub turned out to be the eyes of spring hares, known locally as Gilgil kangaroos, jumping ludicrously along on their hind legs. God must have been joking when he made them.

We quickly came across a herd of the gazelle. The .22 that the staff used performed well on the night drive. The whole process, from sighting, through firing, cutting the gazelle's throat, the gralloch, and putting the carcase into the back of the Land Rover, took a best time of less than a minute and never more than five. In one case it was so speedy that the two men in the front who leaped out to do the gralloch forgot to put the handbrake on. The vehicle started to roll rapidly backwards downhill. Of the three of us in the back, two were too busy holding gun and flashlight so I was compelled to leap on to the roof of the cab and swing, Dukes-of-Hazzard style, through the driver's window to apply the brake.

The gazelle, dazzled by the lamp, were easy targets. They sensed danger, but were not sure what it was. Whenever they started to run away one of us would give a wolf-whistle and they would stop and stare, giving a clear shot. It took an hour to make up our night's quota of six.

I left Soysambu for two long weekends to visit other ranches. Long weekends in Kenya really are long. There is only a momentary feeling of guilt every Wednesday as the previous weekend merges into the next. Lady Delamere sent me to see a tea and coffee plantation owned by a friend of hers called Dowson. His house, on a hill above Nakuru, overlooked the rich green ranks of serried tea bushes with pickers in headscarfs plucking the yellow leaves from the top. The green became startlingly opalescent at dawn and dusk.

Dowson made great efforts to show me his crops, and took me on a trip up to a national park next to another lake, Bogoria, where hot springs bubbled out of the ground. The sounds of these little geysers ranged from the spluttering of an old engine, pinking louder than the pink of the flamingos in the warm water behind, through the noise of a big fuse on a whizzbang rocket, to the most terrible indigestion. There were large angry baboons in the trees by the lake, like packs of arboreal rottweilers, and in among the kudu a teddy-bear-faced waterbuck appeared, more cowish in looks than an antelope ought to be.

The whites I met in Kenya were addicted to watching game. It was a novelty for me, but you would think they would get bored with it. So much of it lined the roads. Every opportunity they could, however, they would take a week off, Wednesdays notwithstanding, to go on safari.

Another animal enjoying the spa was a monitor lizard, three feet long, waving its tail from side to side to swim along just offshore. As we drove past, ugly warthog with sticking-up tails – radio-controlled pigs, Dowson and I agreed – scattered from the fresh waterholes that feed the lake. Their ferocious tusks belied their fear.

The next weekend trip was to go bird-shooting at a ranch called Segera, almost as large as Lord Delamere's, which sat directly beneath white-capped Mount Kenya on the Laikipia Plateau, where the African sun shone on a cool windblown scrubland and the sky was so immense you wondered if you were not too close to heaven. My hosts were Roberta Fonville, whose family own the place, and her fiancé, Justin Mayhew. On the first day, Justin and I went out with guns and dogs.

We surrounded a tree, inasmuch as it is possible for two people to surround a tree, where a guinea fowl and a vervet monkey sat side by side on the branch, watching us. The guinea fowl had been planning its evening roost there, and now stuck its head up on the end of its long, grey, mottled neck to work out what we were. The monkey had a more nonchalant air. It was just passing through, it seemed to say, and was simply keen to know which way we would be passing so that it could carry on passing in the opposite direction. A stand-off.

The monkey made a decision and moved suddenly. The guinea fowl took off like a corn-fed pheasant too fat to rocket. Bang, went my twenty-bore, and bang went Justin's twelve, and down it came.

'Your bird,' said Justin.

'No, yours I think.'

'No, no, really,' and so on, until we forgot exactly where in the little wooded and thicketed cut with the stream running through it the bird had fallen. We searched and searched, spiking and scalping ourselves on the thorn bushes and swearing. We put Justin's dogs in, a motley pack of two: a standard poodle so enthusiastic it had been under general anaesthetic three times in the previous six months to have inch-long thorns removed from its paws, and a rottweiler who betrayed his breed by barely being able to say boo to an Egyptian goose, let alone a guinea fowl. They had no luck.

More cursing later, Justin observed: 'Do you know, I think the monkey picked it.'

I think he was right. There were one or two of the bird's distinctive blue-grey feathers with white polka-dots leading away from a point in between the two points that Justin and I variously swore that it had fallen, and there was no sign of the monkey.

'Partial to a bit of guinea fowl, monkeys,' said Justin. 'Come on, Tumbu! Shella!' calling the dogs. 'I'll bloody lose them to a leopard one of these days,' to me.

We went back to the ranch house; another of those perfectly designed cool-by-day and not-too-chilly-by-night one-storey buildings, like Tom's and like his parents' house, with a large verandah on which to drink sundowners and look out over a clipped lawn across the plateau at the mountain, which tinged to flamey colours in the evenings.

As well as the shooting, there was game to watch in abundance at Segera. I had the 48,000 acres to myself. There were horses to take out to go and see the wildlife, which included elephant, lion, cheetah, hippo, oryx, giraffe, leopard, and a rare melanistic leopard, black all over. If I had not liked quadrupedic transport, I could even have watched elephants from the safety of the swimming pool, Roberta told me, as they kept breaking into her garden, tearing up the lawn, leaving huge piles of dung, and frightening the staff.

I was most conscious that my six months on the continent of Africa had so far been bereft of elephants, apart from the Ivory Coast rugby team. There had been plenty of signs – steaming dung, chewed-up trees, and crops trampled only minutes before I arrived, but never the real article. I was not to see one at Segera, either, even though the second-largest herd in Kenya, 400 animals, had the farm as part of their territory. The only elephants I saw in the whole of the trip in the end was a Lariam-induced herd in my dreams sitting on the chairs in Tom's house complaining about Bernard's driving. You could not allow yourself an obsession if you were on Lariam. It always came back to haunt you.

Never mind. There was always the bird-shooting, and it was good. It was all walked-up, extremely rough, and extremely sporting. The bag limit by law in Kenya is twenty-five gamebirds per day, excluding duck.

Enter the man Marcus, a straight-talking white Kenyan who had been a KWS warden for fourteen years, had shot it all from poachers downwards, run a rhino sanctuary, was a director of the elephant charity Tusk, and was now in charge of game-management on Segera, a kind of game-harbourer-cum-security-man. He had learned his Swahili on the coast where the language is at its most fluent. Marcus spoke it flawlessly, and too fast for most upcountry Swahili speakers to understand. As with many white Kenyans, Swahili words crept into his English sentences.

He stressed the sporting value of the place. 'The beauty of Africa, bwana, is that you walk through the bush and you have wild birds coming up in every direction. They've not been fed. They've not been put down. They're wild. It's unpredictable, and you are also on a game walk. If you come across a herd of elephant, you go round them,' he told me.

The second day's shooting, with Marcus, was more organised and efficient than the first day's walk round with Justin. He knew more precisely where to find the birds. We used the cool of the evening and the advantage of twilight. We started at four o'clock in the afternoon and went on until dark at seven.

The three birds we were aiming for were the guinea-fowl, which were the size of a big broiler chicken; the yellow-necked spurfowl, which were more bantam-sized, and the smallest and most sporting of the lot, the crested francolin, which were like little partridges. Marcus got especially excited about the francolin. 'You get coveys of them,' he said, 'no more than five or six. They go into a bush, you creep up polepole – slowly bwana – you chuck a rock in and out they come: fast, furious and fun. I have seen people come to Kenya who are used to shooting driven birds and who can't hit anything here for two days.'

The best part of the francolin-shooting was that they sat tight until we were ready to shoot them. Neither of the other species did. Marcus, driving his Land Rover, could be herding the guinea fowl towards the guns like a wacky version of *One Man and His Dog*. The guinea-fowl could suddenly decide that this was the moment to take off, and they sailed over as if someone was throwing heavy grey pillows in the air. The guns all roared and the birds thumped down dead, and when the noise died away and even the runners had been picked, we could walk over to any bush where we had seen the francolin scamper for cover and do Marcus's rock trick. Frrrrrt! Out they came in all directions, and for a second our world was a blur of wings, feathers and burned powder.

The yellow-necks, for cunning, lay halfway between the guinea fowl and the francolin. They sat by the side of the farm tracks. We got out of the car when we saw them, loaded up, and walked towards them with all the easy charm of a thieving vervet monkey. They looked at us worriedly, and started to edge away. At fifteen yards we gave them a winning smile. Some of the more panicky among them started to run. We started to run. They took off, and at that moment we had to be ready to stop, safety catch off, and shoot.

Marcus was a staunch rough-shooting man. 'My policy:' he said over supper on the last evening between mouthfuls of eland, 'if you want to come out here and shoot something, you work at it and you appreciate it. If it's not there, it's not there. Shauri ya mungu – it's the hand of God.'

Marcus ran the game-cropping at Segera. His story telling grew more excitable as the evening went on. He told me about animals he had shot and how much it hurt him to do it. 'Right here, man, right here,' he said emotionally, clasping my hand and striking my chest with it. 'I had American students here, bwana, and I took them to watch me down a zebra, and I said, "Come with me, but don't you cry." We got out in the field. There was the punda – the zebra. Bang!' He slapped his hands. 'Down it went. And bang!' He slapped his hands again. 'I finished it off with a .22 in the head. But still it kicked' – he put his arms and legs out straight and rolled backwards on the sofa to show me how – 'and I turned round and one of the American girls was crying, so I took her by the hand' – he grabbed my hand again – 'and took her up to the zebra and I said, "Look at it. Now cry. Go on – cry." Because I do, every single fucking time man, I kill an animal, and when it goes down, and it lies on its side, and it looks over its own shoulder at the blood that is pouring out, sometimes three feet in the air, man, and it can't believe it, I cry. And in all my years of hunting I have only let two wounded animals get away.'

I retrieved my hand, which he still held tightly. We had drunk well that night, and Marcus was full of stories.

He was trying to raise a baby zebra at the time. The zebra was convinced it was an Alsatian, like Marcus's five other dogs. It was Marcus's lissom blonde girlfriend, Annabel, who looked after this canine-style ungulate. She had taught it to accept a head collar, which it did not think much of at all at first – none of the other Alsatians wore head collars after all – and hoped to teach it to take her for rides. But it was a male, so likely to turn out aggressive. He already bucked slightly shirtily when I patted him on the rump, but he loved company and used to lay his head on people's laps for an ear-scratch, blowing bubbles of pleasure. If no laps were available, he would walk up to men and butt them in the balls to create one. Ouch. He was just the right height.

Marcus had found him in the grass after he had culled the foal's father, an ageing stallion. Marcus had not noticed him at first. The foal's mother kept coming back to the scene of the kill, despite Marcus shooing her away. He thought she was being loyal to the late leader of her herd, and his mind was on other matters, like the gralloch. Eventually another younger stallion came up and claimed her for his herd, and that was the last Marcus saw of her. It was then that he discovered the foal, only a few hours old in the grass. That was the real reason the mother had been back, but she was not coming any more.

Zebra foals memorise their mother's individual pattern of stripes in their first three days, and do not leave her until weaned. Sometimes they can accidentally imprint on the wrong zebra, and then they starve to death. This one plumped for Annabel's floral-pattern summer frocks, and would now not let her out of his sight without loud complaints.

On another tack in the conversation, Roberta told me about the difficulties of owning property in Kenya. She was shorter than Annabel, dark-haired, and always candid. Her biggest problem was staving off buyers for her farm. If a politician ever fancied owning Segera, all he had to do was turn up and say, 'I am going to buy this place,' and offer whatever paltry sum he felt like. She had had that problem within the last year, and had had to say how honoured she was that this powerful man was taking an interest in her farm. But, she said, he would have to meet certain conditions towards the estate workers which, she and Justin made sure, were unfulfillable. That was the only way out.

Roberta's family had only been established in Kenya for twenty-five years. That made her vulnerable. The Delameres, with a century of history in Kenya, enjoyed a higher profile. It was not so easy for politicians to grab their land. Roberta had had one badly frightening experience. A Kikuyu businessman put together a consortium of three busloads of people to buy Segera, and then waltzed off with their money. These people, not realising what had happened, came up to Segera in their buses to claim the land they thought was theirs, and to split it up into a hundred small plots. They were angry to find the old white owners, Roberta and Justin, still there.

To quell them, Justin and Roberta had to make speeches along the lines of: 'My friends. You have paid money for this land to a businessman. This man has not paid the money to us. You must not be angry with us. You must go in your buses to see the man you paid.'

Roberta said that it was a terrifying ordeal. It could easily have gone the other way, and the crowd could have turned into a lynch mob. But at the end of it everyone was happy and cracking jokes with her. 'The African has a strong sense of fairness, you see,' she said.

Lord Delamere was resolutely against this turning of the old huge estates in Kenya into small plots. 'It is just Not Efficient to farm like that,' he said bleakly. But it was a popular dream among Africans to own their own acre, their *shamba*, with a hut in the middle of it in which to live out their days.

When I came back to Soysambu, I discovered that Tom had disappeared. One moment he had been in Muthaiga Club, the next he was reportedly in Italy for a week. I was alone in his house with his staff, and since Bernard had been sacked over the Peugeot/zebra incident, there were none left who could speak English.

Lady Delamere asked me to check that Tom's cook, Wangi, had been feeding Chaos and Artu. Wangi was a short and extremely ancient retainer whose only contribution to conversation thus far had been a dirty old man's laugh – 'Hurr, hurr, hurr.' He had explained Tom's disappearance to me with the words: 'Horrible Tom – hurr, hurr, hurr – Itagli'. Communicating with him was tricky. Using my *Tourist Guide to Simple Swahili*, I accosted him outside his kitchen.

'Jambo, Wangi.'

'Jambo, bwana.'

Draw breath and start as you mean to go on: 'Now listen here, Wangi: mbwa kali.' I had seen *mbwa kali* on gatepost signs in Nairobi with pictures of dogs on them, and I guessed that one of the words meant 'dog'.

'Uh?'

Artu and Chaos trotted round the corner into view at that moment, fresh from some outrage of larceny or genocide.

'Mbwa, mbwa!' I gesticulated at them. It was a lucky guess.

'Ndiyo, mbwa iko.' Yes, there is a dog.

This was the difficult part. I consulted my phrasebook.

'Mbwa kula nyama?' Dog eats meat?

'Ndiyo.'

Pause. 'Ngoja kidogo,' I told him. 'Wait awhile.' I think this phrasebook was written in 1930. More frantic fluttering of pages. Oddly enough, the book had no complete phrase for 'Are you feeding the dogs?' so I had to construct it from others in the Eating Out section.

'Kuna nyumba ya kula yako utuletee mbwa?' Perhaps 'Does your restaurant serve dog?' wasn't quite the right thing.

'Hapana. Hurr, hurr, hurr.' ('No – ha, ha, ha.')

Wangi was shifting nervously on his feet. I was getting more desperate.

'Hakikupikwa ya mbwa kutosha.' 'That dog is not cooked enough.'
'Uh?'

This was my last chance. Wangi was about to run away.

'Wewe mbwa nyama.' 'You are dogmeat.'

He backed rapidly into the kitchen. I gave up, and waited for Tom to come back to sort it out. I noticed that Wangi started to avoid me now, and preferred to leave meals out and call me to them from the safety of his kitchen.

The last of Tom's post-Georgina rehabilitation techniques consisted of boozing sessions and that, again, was where clubs came into their own. Tom and I stopped off at the Gilgil Club, near Elmenteita, on the way back from Nairobi one evening for a swift one. Tom's new driver waited in the car in the car park.

We really meant to be quick at the time, but then I met someone I had met in Nairobi three weeks before, and Tom met an old friend, and I met someone else who, coincidentally, had been at prep school with me, and more old friends of Tom arrived, and we stayed for supper, which was a bit like school dins, and I got into a game of poker over whisky in the bar afterwards, and so it went on. The driver wisely went to sleep.

It was one of those twenty-to or twenty-past the hour moments, and the hour was not much under three, and there were still a dozen people at the bar. We came from several different countries, too – England, Tanzania, New Zealand, Kenya and Northern Ireland – a caustic mixture. Then there was one of those really spooky coincidences: a rugby ball appeared at our feet from behind the bar just as a gap in the conversation took place. Less than a sip of whisky later a Tanzanian had it spinning through the air towards a New Zealander. The Kiwi passed it to a Kenyan, who sent it down the English line until it missed the Irishman at the bar and broke some empty beer bottles. Oh dear, we agreed.

To keep the ball away from the bar and prevent further damage, the Irishman suggested we throw it at the dartboard and try to dislodge the darts stuck there. On the first throw the rugby ball missed, but it took out a lightbulb and neatly skittled some more bottles on a table. A tennis ball appeared, and a hockey ball. People started throwing empty bottles, bar stools and beer crates and the floor was ankle-deep in glass.

The old barman, Kanga, still padded around on it in bare feet. He was as much a fixture as the club building itself, and had seen much worse behaviour in the old days.

We started setting up targets for our missiles. We sang terrible rugby songs that we made up on the spot as we did so: 'Seven-and-fifty Old Farts sitting on a board . . .'

I scored a widely applauded two out of three on beer bottles balanced on the dartboard from behind the bar with tins of tomato juice. But the high point was the effort of the Kenyan, who emptied his revolver at them. He missed, but they came down anyway as the wall shuddered with the impact of the bullets, which set off dogs all over Gilgil. We sang some more; we had snowball fights with all the ice from the freezer. I smashed a bottle on the bar like in the films, but I cut my hand quite badly, which never happens in the films. We drank the bar dry of whisky and left a chit for several crates of empty beer bottles – 'That way we won't get into shtrouble,' slurred Tom, even though the room looked like the inside of a bottle-bank. We carefully removed the slugs from the wild west display above the dartboard to destroy the evidence in the hope that people would believe that Gilgil was simply suffering from extra-large tunnelling termites that year, but equally carefully I accidentally left the slugs and spent shells in the till.

Tom and I were the last to leave. We woke up the new driver, asleep in the car, and he woke us up when he had driven us home. It was dawn again.

Tom's parents raised their eyebrows fractionally at supper that evening when he told them of events at the Gilgil Club. Lady Delamere had already told me that I looked 'pi-yale and i-yinteri-yesting' when I had surfaced at lunchtime.

Lord Delamere recalled the story of the Large Boer Lady who had dropped her Beretta automatic pistol down the loo By Mistake at a smart lodge during the Mau Mau terrorist uprising in Kenya in the 1950s. It went off several times, embedding shattered porcelain in her backside. Other guests laid her out on the billiard table and picked out the porcelain, while she complained loudly in Afrikaans that she still needed to go to the loo. 'Very Unreliable, those Berettas,' said Lord Delamere.

Both Lord and Lady Delamere had much on their minds at the time. On occasions like this, when their son was in trouble with the Gilgil Club committee – like the time when he rode his motorbike around the dining room – they treated him with only slightly more mildly doting exasperation than normal.

This was a prevailing attitude in Kenya. I began to think that white Kenyans were different in attitude from people from home. They always noticed what people did, but they never judged it. Gossip was rife – everyone loved it – but no one ever said, when they discussed how so-and-so had sacked/knocked off/murdered so-and-so else, that he or she was necessarily good, bad, right or wrong to have done it. Lord Errol, Karen Blixen, Joy Adamson, Jomo Kenyatta and Julie Ward were all events to be merely noted, not judged.

There was only slight surprise about the lad from Nairobi who went to London with a few pounds in his pocket to find a motorbike to drive back to Kenya. He tried to double his money in a casino but lost the lot, so he stole a bike instead and drove back across the Sahara as far as the desert country Chad. There the French Foreign Legion stuck a gun to his head and advised him to turn back as there was a war going on. He reached Niger, another desert country, where he sold the bike and flew home.

This attitude meant that you could go to Kenya and be as loopy as you liked. Nobody would condemn you for it there. Yet it made the white Kenyans some of the most naturally well-mannered people you could meet. There was none of the fear of being judged that forces manners in England.

Lord Delamere was far too busy to worry about Tom. As well as running the farms, he was president of a railway, the Elmenteita-Tokyo-Boston Railway Company Ltd. It reached neither Tokyo nor Boston, yet, but he had high hopes for it. The line consisted of 600 feet of HO-gauge track capable of running nine trains. He was addicted to it. Every evening after supper he would retire to a building he had had put up specially in the grounds of his house, and work on it. He owned a British Rail guard's cap which he wore while peering over jigsawed chipboard scenery and control panels, talking all the time of 22-Ohm resistors and Straight-through or Halt circuits.

Lord Delamere's mornings were similarly regimented. Before breakfast he would take his dogs, two vast yellow labradors and an ill-disciplined mongrel, for a walk in the field that stretched for three miles in front of his house towards the lake. Anyone going with him would be treated to an informed but tongue-in-cheek commentary on the State of the Farm. 'Look at My River. It is down to Four Months a Year. It used to run all the time. It's the Africans who have done it, cutting down the forest at the top. They should all be Shot, or Flogged.' Or: 'I have three types of Frangipani in My Garden, each with a Distinctive Smell. Here, smell this one. Indian Hair Oil in a Cinema, don't you think? This one? Expensive Indian Lady's Scent. And this one Something in Between.'

Lady Delamere's life at the time was fraught with running the Elmenteita section of the Kenya Safari Rally. This event, run over the three days of the Easter weekend, was a tough 1,500-mile route of dirt tracks upcountry all around Nairobi. There were time controls along the way, and Lady Delamere was in charge of the Elmenteita control, a job she had enjoyed for several years.

Tom and I went with her to look at the site she had planned for her administration and catering tents, a rocky outcrop on the far southern edge of the estate by the road. We climbed it with a picnic tea basket packed by Wangi, who had been embarrassingly relieved when Tom came back.

Peace hung over the Rift Valley there. A herd of impala, partly hidden by bushes, munched dry grass at the foot of the rocks. Guinea fowl foraged, thinking it may be time to find a roostable tree. On the drive back to the house, a melanistic leopard, black tail up, bounded out of the high grass and out of our way across the road. Lady Delamere gasped. 'That's the fi-yirst mi-yelanistic one I have seen in thi-yirty-one years,' she declared.

Quite a special black cat to cross one's path. I decided to stay in Kenya for the rally.

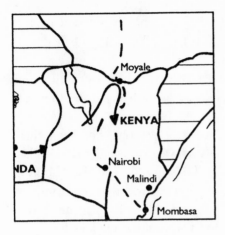

Chapter 15

A NIGHT ON THE TOWN

Kenya. 40 days to World Cup opening ceremony.

Erik asked me to come along as part of Des's service crew over the three days of the rally. I had to be at Simon's house at the foot of the Ngong Hills at 11am for a 12.30 start in the centre of town on the Thursday before Easter. I'll introduce you properly to Erik, Des and Simon in the next chapter, because we haven't quite got to the rally yet, and, as it turned out, I nearly didn't get there, either. For me, Day 1 of the rally started at Day O, when I went out to the Carnivore Restaurant, which claims to be the largest in the southern hemisphere, the night before with Luigi, who got drunk.

I met Luigi through Tom. He was managing a factory on behalf of Italian investors and the Cheshire Homes, which employed disabled people in Nairobi to tie flies for fishing. Luigi, the Horrible Tom, Emanuele and I had all been trying them out trout-fishing on the River Malewa, which slides and floods down the hills that overlook Lake Naivasha with the volcano Longonot and the Hell's Gate National Park in the distance across the Rift Valley.

This stretch of river, around 6,500 feet above sea-level, was owned by Emanuele. It held good fish up to four pounds and wild claims in the seedier club bars of monster twenty-pounders that had snapped rods with a shake of their mighty heads and hospitalised anglers through exhaustion after hours of fruitless fighting. We had four miles to play with, fly-fishing only.

We gathered at the treehouse that overlooked the river: all in our twenties, two of us fair-haired and English-looking, the other two shorter, darker and definitely Italian. An ibis got up and flew to one of the orchid-covered trees which had struggled out of the high, thick bush along the riverbank, and went 'yarr, yarr' at us indignantly. They were Thomson's orchids, like Thomson's gazelle and the Thomson Falls, the three swansongs that every great African explorer wanted to achieve. In turn, a black coucal, looking like a Frankenstein cross between an eagle and a cuckoo, fled from under a yellow flowering bauhinia bush, and scared two black river duck into showing us a clean pair of speckled backsides.

To call it a treehouse is a little optimistic as it was not quite finished when we were there. Since the success of Treetops as a tourist attraction – and Treetops has been established so long that the young Princess Elizabeth heard of her father's death and her succession to the throne while staying there in 1952 – everyone has put up a house on stilts overlooking a pool where game can come and drink water as the punters quaff gin and tonics. Tom was even considering building a village on stilts on land his father owned at Lake Naivasha and inventing a new indigenous tribe to live there wearing traditional dress designed by Versace and offering theme-park-style crocodile rides.

Emanuele's treehouse was modelled on one Tom had already built on his own game sanctuary. Emanuele was enthusiastic. It was going to have beds in it.

'Eet is very good to sleep around,' he told us, waving an arm at it.

'Sleep outside?' we suggested.

'That ees what I said.'

The Italians are so well settled into Kenya that Happy Valley should be renamed Contente Valley. They have long been known at the game-fishing resort of Malindi on the coast, dubbed Milan-di by Red when he was turned away from one hotel bar for not being

Italian. Red was down there entertaining his sister and friends who had come out on holiday.

'Who was here first?' he asked the hotel doorman.

'Vasco da Gama,' was the icy reply.

But in a burst of mid-century aggression the Germans were in the process of ousting their former Axis allies from Malindi. In turn, the Italians were fleeing in droves to the island of Zanzibar off Tanzania – ironically, itself a former German colony – near the aptly named Mafia Island. It was a German who caught the 1,250-pound blue marlin at Malindi while I was in Kenya, the largest caught off the continent, and one-and-a-half times the Kenya record. Unfortunately, he did not qualify for the record because, after five and a half hours fighting it, he had to retire exhausted, fainting and vomiting, and pass the rod to someone else.

Thankfully, the British still held all the records for antics in Happy Valley, such as our shoot-out in the Gilgil Club. According to legend, Tom's great-grandfather, Lord Delamere, used regularly to shoot up the fashionable spots in Nairobi, and it was to him that Kenya owed her first trout. In 1904, Delamere wrote to that other famous early Kenya settler, E.S. Grogan, to say that the whites who were then living in the country wanted to see wheat in their fields and trout in their rivers, and that if Grogan could sort out the trout, he would deal with the wheat. Grogan imported frozen trout ova from the UK, and that is how, ninety years later, we came to be fishing for them.

Armed with Luigi's flies, and after careful observation of weather conditions and fly hatches from the treehouse, viewed mainly through the bottom of a beer glass, we went down to the river.

The Malewa is as overgrown as a Cornish stream. Unlike by a Cornish stream, a black and white colobus monkey was strolling elegantly through the branches of a tree as we arrived, dangling its long plume tail and disdaining the banana trees and flame lilies that tangled the riverbank. A rotting half of a dead python lay on the path as a memorial to some battle in the night. The Italians, the home team, instantly agreed that it had been killed by a leopard. The visitors more modestly suggested a mongoose.

Just as for Tumbu and Shella, there was always the slight danger of leopard for unwary fishers. Normally the cats stayed well out of the way, but the local village's were complaining that they had seen one take a three-year-old child the week before, and the KWS was planning to come up and do some trapping.

Leopard or mongoose, it had done considerably better with its python than we did with our fishing. None of us were experts at the sport, and the overgrown banks of the Malewa quickly defeated us. There was swearing in three languages – Italian, English and, in moments of desperation, Swahili – as we reached into the thorns to pull out flies.

The next problem was the spate. Heavy rains following the years of drought had turned the Malewa into a rich soup and the fish did not appear to be hungry any more. There was not a rise to be seen.

After a couple of hours we retired to the half-built treehouse to consider our position. The rain came on again, a five-minute spell of thunderous drumming water on the tin roof. Just as it finished, as instantly as it had come, and we were about to call it a day, there was a rise.

I saw it. The others did not believe me. They left me to address it alone. They went off to get ready for the party that night at Iain and Oria Douglas-Hamilton's house beside Lake Naivasha. The Douglas-Hamiltons are famous for their work with elephants, and for their books *Among the Elephants* and *Battle for the Elephants*. Oria is Italian.

My fish had, of course, to be on the wrong side of the biggest gomphocarpus bush, a kind which traps even the wary on the pale green spiky balls that hang from it. And there was just a thin green line of reeds and rushes disguising the water's edge beyond it. I surreptitiously crept along the path, tripped over and slid down the bank with the sound of a thousand hippos, and froze.

Swirl. There it was again. These fish are stupid.

Hemmed in on all sides, I could manage only a flick of a rod's length of line, which fell on to the rise in an ugly pile. I stopped still again. Nothing moved. I was just lifting the last of the nylon off the water when up it came, looked at the fly, a last-resort small black job, and was about to turn away when the tension and frustration of a day of no fish made me strike hard and foul-hook it, but in the cheek.

Foul-hooking a fish means a strenuous fight. This trout took off like a pinball and bounced off the underwater roots and obstructions, winding them round with the line I let him have. Then he chose to jump, and pulled his web apart as he did so, leaving me free to pull in line as quickly as possible.

I had no net, so had to make it to the nearest clear patch on the bank, ten yards away, where Emanuele normally launched his little rowing boat. The first step forward brought me crashing to the ground, tripping again on a root, so I crawled it on two knees and a hand, dedicating the other hand to keeping the rod tip up. The fish must have been well hooked, however foully, for it did not come off despite this treatment and despite its energetic skip along the surface of the water. Once on clear ground I could haul him in and beach him. A mighty cheer: he was a rainbow trout of nigh on one pound.

Emanuele sent a driver down to pick me up. We had to go straight away. I changed speedily as Emanuele laughed cruelly at my catch. We drove down the hill to the party.

The Douglas-Hamiltons owned a beautiful house, needless to say in colonial style, but not in the normal bungalow format. It was more like an English country house in shape. It sat in parkland by the lake. Iain flew his light aeroplane in to land on the airstrip in front of the house, just as the sun was setting beyond the hills around, the last of its light burning the tall tops of the papyrus on the lake shore a glowing red and yellow, and the first of the hippo were pondering on coming out of the water to graze the grass.

The party was the usual round of boozing and feeding you find in England, but with different weather, so perfect in Kenya for parties, and the moon was full and bright.

Tom said loudly, in usual Tom-style, at 2am: 'Let's go for a drive.'

Emanuele had predicted drily that Tom would say, 'Let's climb a tree,' so I was quite relieved.

The two of us raced off around the park in his Land Rover, now mended, and down the airstrip to the lake. A herd of hippos which had been feeding in the garden charged ahead of us back to the safety of the water. It would only have taken a shove from one big angry male to tip the car over. The moonlight put a lovely silver-blue shine on their huge grey backsides lumping through the long grass.

We left them in the lake and zooted, to borrow Tom's expression, back to the party, playing the game on the way where the passenger has to take over the driver's seat while the driver gets out of the window, crawls over the roof of the cab, and crawls back through the passenger window. Repeat, keeping the car going as fast as possible.

Red gatecrashed the party with, of all people, Jesper. Despite the split a few weeks before, it was good to see Red. I had been beginning to miss my old travelling companions. But I had no plans to rejoin them. Red and Jesper had got lost several times on the way from Nairobi, and by the time they arrived people were starting to grab the available beds for a few hours' sleep. Within a few minutes they had woken everybody up by starting a water-fight in the kitchen.

Jesper had reached Kenya in typical tortuous manner. He had followed the same route as us into Zaïre, but, having no transport, had had to try to rely on lifts from the few vehicles on the road. He had heard that there was a bus leaving from Buta. But there was so little traffic going that way from the border that he spent three days walking the fifty miles to the town. He was so exhausted when he arrived that he did not notice the thief in the night who stole most of his money as he slept. Then the Beast of Buta fined him a large sum for a currency-declaration contravention.

Starving and with no money, Jesper somehow managed to find a job in Zaïre and earn some. Zaïre is hell – there are no jobs there – and we never found out quite how he did it. Next he found an aid flight leaving for Nairobi, and hitched a ride on it. Jesper's guardian angel must be on the verge of a nervous breakdown. Red found him wandering aimlessly around Nairobi, and brought him back to stay at the friend's flat where he was staying. Jesper was now keen to learn how to be a diver on the coast, and his girlfriend was coming out to join him.

Jesper had learned some more English from Red before the party. The last I saw of him, he was leaning against the wall amusing himself by chatting up a girl whom Red had already identified as a target.

'What's your name?' he asked her.

'Siobhan,' said the girl.

'Is thjet e njame, or e sjexually-transmjitted disease?'

'Very witty, Jesper,' said Red, walking away.

The next morning I went back down to Nairobi with Luigi, and that is when Erik asked me to be service crew on the rally, and that is when Luigi, Emanuele and I ended up on, as I have mentioned, Day O in the Carnivore Restaurant.

Luigi had already had a few by the time we arrived at the Carnivore, a large hall out of town, like a barn, with tables stretching out of all the doors and a dancefloor. In fact, it is fair to say Luigi was off his face. We boozed and caroused there and at a neighbouring nightclub called Psy's to dreadful seventies music but with lots of fun people, mainly white, of course. It was not an act of apartheid – it was, as Gordon Bell observed, that races like to stick together. Luigi, however, was not fun. He was starting to be offensive. He was lurching and staggering. Everyone told me to take him home.

It took an hour, but by 4am I had got him into a taxi and we drove away. Luigi was behaving like a small child that did not want to go to bed. He fell asleep once we were moving. I paid the taxi-driver extra in advance in case Luigi woke up and threw up.

Unfortunately, I was not entirely up to the mark either. The twenty-minute journey took an hour as we kept losing our way. When we got there we tried all the drives along the road where Luigi lived to work out which was his house. We even tried the right one, but neither of us recognised it.

The taxi-driver started to get a bit fed up. After going round in several circles he told me to flag down a passing car full of white people and ask if they knew where we lived. I did, and two equally drunk sixteen-year-old girls said, 'Yesh, of courshe we know who Luigi ish: follow ush home.'

On the way, Luigi suddenly woke up and said he needed a walk. I told him, 'Be quiet, we are following thoshe girlsh home.' The taxi-driver foolishly turned round and locked Luigi's door to emphasise the point. This hurt Luigi's Italian pride, always the last bit of a continental to get really comatose, and he unlocked the door, opened it, and stepped out as we moved along at a steady twenty miles per hour.

The taxi-driver looked at me. Both of the taxi-drivers swam in front of me for a moment, joined briefly like Siamese twins, and then moved into focus. 'Leave him,' I said, not thinking that letting an incoherent, possibly injured, Italian lie in the middle of a Nairobi road during the hours of darkness could possibly be a bad idea. So we drove on to the girl's house.

'Where'sh Luigi?' they asked.

'He shtepped out of the taxshi,' I told them.

Peal of girlish laughter. 'We didn't know him anyway!'

We sneaked into their house, trying not to wake the dogs. The girls were under threat from their parents of being grounded if they came home after 2am. It was now nearly 6am, and T minus five hours until I had to be at Simon's house for the start of the rally.

I woke up on Day 1, two hours later – T minus three hours – in a spare room, to hear a grown-up, possibly their mother, walking around the house.

'Where am I?' I wondered.

The door to my room was open, so she had probably looked in to see who I was. I had no desire to see who she was and have to explain myself. Luckily, within a few minutes I heard a car starting and moving off down the gravel drive, so I guessed she had had to go out.

I quietly pulled on my clothes, fell over, stood up, and tiptoed out into the hall and through the kitchen, carrying my shoes for extra silence. The cook caught me. 'Don't you want to say goodbye?' she asked me briskly, arms folded, blocking the doorway. These Africans always spoke English when I did not want them to, and only Swahili when I did.

'Er – not really.'

'Come and say goodbye,' she said – or demanded – propelling me out of the kitchen and down a corridor. She banged on the door of the girls' room.

No answer.

She banged again.

Not a sound. Thank goodness for that.

'Well,' I gabbled, 'I don't think they are going to wake up and I don't want to disturb them and I really must be going and thank you so much and I'm off now and so goodbye,' and shot off down the corridor, out of the kitchen door across the lawn, pulling on shoes and kicking excited dogs out of the way as I ran, slowing to a walk to 'jambo' the *askari* at the gate cheerily, and out into the road.

Then I had a sudden realisation. I had exactly the same problem as the night before: I was lost. Except now it was T minus two and a half hours and no taxi. I started to walk down the road until I came to a main avenue. Had I turned left there I would have recognised Luigi's house within 200 yards. As it was, I turned right.

It was agonising, because it started to dawn on me as well that Luigi could easily have been run over or mugged or murdered, had he survived the fall at all. Five miles later at T minus one hour I found a house I knew, belonging to one of the people I'd met at Psy's who had suggested I take Luigi home, and that is where my luck changed. Luigi's car was parked outside with the keys still in it. Nobody was awake in the house apart from the staff, so I scrawled a quick note to the effect that I had pinched it, and pinched it.

It took a mere ten minutes to find Luigi's house from there, and luckily he was in it, asleep, fully clothed on his bed. His staff were pleased but perplexed to see me. They said that Luigi had come in at 6am and told them all that someone had stolen his car. They could not work out what I was doing with it.

It took some time to wake Luigi up, and still the minutes were ticking away. He kept opening his eyes, looking at me blearily, and closing them again. Then at last, with his eyes closed, he put his hands into his trouser pockets and asked: 'Deed I geeve you all my money last night, Charlie?'

'No.'

'Then I've been robbed.'

I was relieved to hear that that was all.

At that moment Emanuele drove up to see how unwell his friend was. He had made his own way home the night before. A few words in Italian woke Luigi up properly.

It turned out that after landing on the tarmac, Luigi had tried to walk home, had got lost, and had ended up chatting to two *askaris* who agreed that it was not a good thing to be walking around Nairobi at that time of night and let him kip for an hour in their hut before walking him home. Luigi was not clear whereabouts along the way he had been robbed, or whether his money had just fallen out of his pocket, or if he had spent the lot – and it was a lot – on drink the night before.

At T minus ten minutes, Emanuele kindly agreed to drive me to Simon's house twenty minutes away.

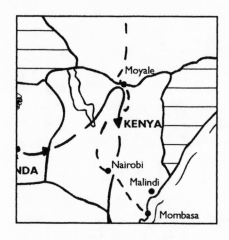

Chapter 16

THE KENYA
SAFARI RALLY

Kenya. 39 days to the World Cup opening ceremony

P ay attention. I am going to introduce you to some new characters.

Des, the first, was tall, slim, fair, curly-haired, quiet and calm to a degree, and a racing driver in the 1995 '555' Kenya Safari Rally. Mark was shorter, formerly a jockey in Sussex and at the Curragh, but quite the white Kenyan. Mark was Des's navigator. He peppered his dialogue with Swahili like Marcus at Segera.

The others, including me, were service crew. The most important man was Simon, a medium-sized fellow of slightly roundish figure with prematurely greying hair – you will see why. Erik was taller, louder and South African, but with no trace of an accent. Big Tom, as opposed to the Horrible Tom, was the largest of the lot of them, six foot six and tapping on the door of twenty stone, an expatriate Welshman who worked selling railway parts around East Africa. Peter, the accountant, was the opposite: he was the shortest, with only a slightly spreading figure and glasses. Peter was also an expatriate. He had given up accountancy in London to come and work in Nairobi. Sean, the eldest, was fiftyish, from Kent, and now managing director of BMW's salerooms in Kenya. And then there were the caterers, Luisa and Katrina, who were the youngest, in their early twenties.

In 1995 the rally was an amateur race. Normally it is one of the World Championship rallies, but each year one country takes a year off and this year it was Kenya's turn. There was still plenty of sponsorship around – British and American Tobacco's 555 cigarette brand was the main source of funding – and all the big car companies entered vehicles, but the event was imbued with bags of extra amateur spirit.

Des's entry only came about because, in an amateur kind of way, he had persuaded Simon to do the engineering side – that is, to build the car. He had caught Simon with his proposition in a vulnerable moment in a swimming pool on the coast in the small hours of New Year's Day. Des had entered the rally before, but had not yet finished it.

His Range Rover, drawn number 101, had the magnificent Rover 3.5-litre V8 engine. Inside, Simon had stripped out extraneous features and installed an intercom for driver and navigator, a radio, and special bucket seats with racing harnesses.

We had radios as well. As service crew our job was to meet Des, Mark and their car at various points around Kenya, refuel them with food, drink and petrol, check the oil, and to help Simon tie on any bit that looked like it was about to fall off. Luisa and Katrina were there to make sure that everyone had enough food, beer and cigs for the trip.

The rally followed a route starting and finishing in Nairobi each day. It went round the Maasai Mara south-west of the city on the first day, a third of the way to the coast on the Mombasa road on the second, and halfway north to the Ethiopian border the third.

Day 1

Everyone had arrived at Simon's house by the time Emanuele dropped me off. Most of us were rally virgins. There was a feeling of nervous expectation, a young-mum-to-be-ness about that morning. We stood around in groups and chatted, trying to keep out of the way of Simon and his engineers, who were running backwards and forwards wielding tools that looked as dangerous and outlandish as a ninja knife collection. George would have been jealous of this lot.

Simon's house was one of the large country bungalows that whites like to inhabit in Karen, a Nairobi suburb at the foot of the Ngong Hills named after Karen Blixen, with plenty of acres for extra buildings: staff cottages, swimming pools and tennis courts. In the background there lurked high fences and *askaris*. Simon had appropriated one of the buildings as a garage for the car and all the shelves were stuffed with spare parts. He was still frantically wiring in horn and headlights when I arrived, ready for the off an hour later. Even when Mark and Des strapped themselves in, started her up, revved the huge engine and drove away, spitting gravel from under their wheels, Simon's spanner was tightening the last nut. He pulled his hand away just in time. 'I'll finish it at the next service,' he said, wiping his brow with an oily hand.

It was lucky car 101 made it to the start. Of 141 entrants, only seventy-five passed the beady eyes of the rally scrutineers, who did a kind of MOT on each vehicle to make sure it was raceworthy. Simon spent the whole rally in a jangle of nerves, worried that a part would fall off, anxious that a fuel line or a brake cable would snap, and terrified that for some reason or other the car would not finish. He absolutely refused to let alcohol pass his lips until the end, whether that was the last triumphant chequered flag in Nairobi or an ignominious roll into a muddy ditch.

Simon's advice at the final service meeting had been: 'For God's sake, Des, take it slowly. I just want you to finish. That would be a result for me.'

Mark, the navigator, backed him up. 'Slowly, slowly, bwana, polepole,' he told Des seriously. 'That is the way.'

This was unusual coming from Mark, one of Kenya's wildest characters. He had a jockey's height and the kind of slightly wizened race-hardened yet little-boy's face that goes with it. We could always tell when he was drunk because a grin would spread aross his face, his eyes would open wide and his eyeballs would roll slightly upwards. He was noted for falling face-first into food at parties, and his favourite trick at Psy's nightclub was to climb the wall by the men's loo, punch a hole in the ceiling plaster, climb up through and along the attic, punch another hole above the disco and drop the fifteen feet down on to the dancefloor.

The rest of us took the rally a lot more lightheartedly than Mark or Simon. Erik gave the three support cars for the service team the radio-call signs Big Knob 1, Big Knob 2, Big Knob 3, and the rally car itself The Big Knob. Des, of all of us, was the most laid back. He was a good and fast driver, and though he did not brag about it, he knew it.

My first job was with Big Knob 2, driven by Sean with Big Tom in the front seat. We went out of Nairobi and down the scarp of the Rift Valley towards the Maasai Mara. It was a straight tarmac road an hour long on the valley floor. Zebra and hartebeest grazed the coarse brown grass on the verge, in and out of constant reminders to Enjoy Coca-Cola.

These parks were wasted marketing opportunities. What about a discreet KWS logo genetically engineered into the stripes of every zebra? Or hyenas which, instead of their short rising yips, hummed an easily identifiable jingle? Or those redundant marabou storks to flap about with their attention-grabbing rasping wingbeats trailing banners saying, 'The Man-eaters of Tsavo welcome Abercrombie & Kent'?

Game parks had been a revelation for Wicky when she had seen her first one in Uganda. She hunted with the Devon and Somerset Staghounds at home. 'The D&S would have a field day with this lot,' she commented as we watched the antelope from the roof of Mistress Quickly.

Watching a buck running alongside you from a Land Rover is the best way to appreciate its grace. Its back legs provide power, the front legs are the shock-absorbers, and it lifts its haunches clear over all in its way. It is hypnotic, and in time you start to think it is moving in slow motion, which is an illusion caused by the animal's 'do-you-call-this-speed?' langour, and the way it keeps its head still as it moves, like a top freestyle mogul-skier.

As Big Knob 2 approached the service area we could see rocketing clouds of dust from rally cars coming at right-angles to our section on dirt tracks. These were the first of the specially built team cars from the main event – Subarus, Toyotas and Mitsubishis – which had helicopters in their support crews.

Des and Mark were competing in the classic event – the home-maders – which followed behind. It was a smaller class, and as well as Des's car, it included three other Range Rovers and a Land Rover Discovery.

Below the classic cars on the list of entrants were the historic cars, including an Austin Healey Sprite, a Triumph 2000 and a Ford Mercury Comet.

Despite the poor roads and poorer driving, cars last well in Nairobi. Due to its altitude the atmosphere there contains barely any salt to rust them. The Sprite went on to win the historic event by dint of being the only finisher.

Big Knob 2 reached its position, a piece of flat ground on a hill overlooking the hinterland of the Mara. There were service teams along the road on all the available flat areas. They ranged in clout from the Toyota team, which had several cars and vans and space to land its helicopter, to some of the local drivers in the classic event, who had struggled to find a few family and friends to turn up in an ancient pick-up with a couple of cans of oil and petrol and an old spare tyre. Big Knob 2 was rated somewhere in the middle of this lot. Sean's car was laden with tools and jerrycans and carried two spare tyres on a roof-rack. Wisely, Sean also brought folding chairs and a large supply of wine to supplement our rations. We sat in the sun and we waited. And we waited. And we waited. We drank, we dozed, we chatted. We were out of radio contact with the other Big Knobs, who were then scattered all over south-western Kenya doing the same as us.

The Toyota team's helicopter landed and took-off a couple of times fifty yards away. That was fun. We did some chatting about that. A spotter aeroplane came over at a hundred feet. Also fun. Unfortunately for the pilot, we later discovered, he was warned by Kenya Civil Aviation for reckless flying, and not allowed to buzz the track again.

It was like the waiting we had done in Mistress Quickly in the Mauritanian desert, except with wine. There was always the imminence of action, the chance that The Big Knob would arrive and we would have to leap out of our seats and carry out the service. It was impossible during this waiting to settle down comfortably enough to do anything but mooch. So we mooched.

Rally cars shot by at intervals, as did boy racers from Nairobi, most of them Indians, who viewed the rally as open season on crazy driving and speeding. So they sped. They followed the rally track and got in the way. Their little 1.2-litre engines whined at max revs while the great Cosworth growl of a Ford rally car changed down to avoid and overtake them.

An Austrian car pulled up in our service area in the late afternoon. These Austrians entered the rally every year. The driver was exhausted. Both driver and navigator had so much dust in their mouths they could barely talk. The navigator asked if we had something for cleaning contacts as his engine was misfiring. Some rally service crews sign contracts to say that not only will they not drink for the duration, but they will refuse to help any other competitors than their own. Not Team 101. Cheers, cheers, cheers. Sean produced WD40 to spray the engine and we gave them Ribena with straws, which they squirted into their mouths. They thanked us wearily but warmly and were quickly off again.

That is proper amateur spirit, we congratulated ourselves, even though Big Tom told them he thought Austria was part of Germany. They had no energy to find that comment funny, we noticed.

After that, I got the banjo out and we sang the usual medley of Disney hits. A group of passing Maasai children stopped and joined in with their peculiar Maasai dance: group jumping on the spot while grunting. The sun was setting now. With the rally cars roaring by, kicking up kisscurls of loose earth on the road which fell inwards behind their back wheels as they raced away, and the dancing Maasai, it was a thoroughly modern African scene.

At last the radio crackled into life. It was Mark. 'Big Knob 2, Big Knob 2, do you read? Over.'

'Big Knob, Big Knob, this is Big Knob 2. Loud and clear, over.'

'We are . . .' (pause – Mark was concentrating) '. . . just coming off the escarpment. Will be with you shortly, over.'

'Roger, wilco Big Knob. But don't *ever* call me "Shortly". Out.'

Now the excitement started to build properly and we were out of our chairs instantly, shooing away the Maasai and arranging the jerrycans. Des and Mark came in a few minutes later. It was dark and we had put the red and orange flashing torch on the roof of Big Knob 2. They slid to a halt off the road and on to our dusty flat patch. Big Tom and I smacked open the petrol cap and started pouring in the four-star while Sean checked oil levels. We wiped all the windows, mirrors and headlights. Des and Mark were caked in Mara dirt, tired and shaken up after a day of driving at speed over rough ground, but still remarkably relaxed.

'How do you feel?' I called at Des over my petrol can.

'Gritty,' he grinned, showing white teeth under his dirty face.

It was all over in another couple of minutes. Des and Mark sank the last of their Coke and sandwiches, strapped in, headlights on, and were away with more billowing dust in the battery arcs that we were using to light up the service area.

After that we simply packed up and followed them slowly into Nairobi. Although we had not really done anything that day, we were exhausted, even those of us who didn't have hangovers. I went to stay with Sean. He lived alone in a large house in the Muthaiga part of town, though I was in no condition to notice it. We collapsed into our beds at midnight.

Des and Mark were running third in their class behind the Discovery and another Range Rover. Simon was ecstatic.

Day 2

It was a seven o'clock start at Simon's house the next morning, Good Friday. I was in Big Knob 3 this time, with Peter the accountant and Katrina the cook. The race was going down towards Mombasa on the coast, south-east of Nairobi, and back.

We had a couple of services to carry out. One was out in the wilds near a village called Olepolos. The other was to be late in the evening back on the road into Nairobi, near the airport.

The Mombasa road, long, straight and busy, is one of the most hair-raising rides in East Africa. Cars go faster east of Zaïre. I had been down to the coast with George and Wicky earlier on during my stay in Kenya, to the small fishing and tourist town of Malindi. It was before I had heard of the rally. I wanted to catch a sailfish, another of Kenya's great sports.

Erik sent me there originally. Erik and Des owned a fishing magazine in Nairobi, and Peter was their accountant. Erik wanted me to go and see at first hand just how good big-game fishing in Kenya could be.

The Malindi Sea Fishing Club was an attic room with a big bar and bigger windows. It is just across the road from the pier, which juts out across the silty beach and into the Indian Ocean. Between the pier and the club was the scaffolding where the day's big fish were brought back to be hung, weighed and photographed with proud punters, and then sold to the local fish market. All fish caught belonged to the boat, not the fisher, so this extra money from the market financed the crew. What the punters shelled out for their day went to pay off the loans for the boat, and the skippers lived off the difference.

The boats themselves were magnificent; sleek and white, and decked out finer than spacecraft. They were moored mainly in Malindi's badly sheltered harbour, protected from the worst of the weather only by a reef. Every year one or two sank at anchor in the storms. They had twin engines, a cabin, cool bags of Coke and beer, sonar to show shoals of fish swimming underneath, and room for up to ten rods out of the back. These trailed poppers and streamers wrapped around slices of bait fish, bubbling along the surface. Manufacturers gave these metal and plastic lures wacky names, like Blue Cavitator. These, and dummy lines of bright plastic squid, attracted the fish.

Only two or three people fished on the boats at a time. They were ferried out from the pier in launches provided free by the fish-dealer who bought the catch.

The skipper sat in a wheelhouse like an eyrie and kept an eye out for signs of fish, either jumping, or flocks of seabirds diving for small fish on the surface which showed there may be bigger fish below, or, as a last resort: 'Where we were yesterday looked pretty good.'

My host, a man called Cheffings I had met in Nairobi, had his own boat, a more modest version of the above, with room for a total of four people and six rods. Cheffings was a tall, softly spoken man. He had, as Arthur Ransome in *Rod and Line* describing a carp-fisher wrote, 'a strange look in his eyes. I have known and shaken hands respectfully with the man who caught the biggest carp ever landed in England. He looked as if he had been in heaven and in hell and had nothing to hope from life, though he survived, and after six years caught an eighteen-pounder to set beside the first'. Cheffings and I were after even greater quarry.

We set off before dawn in the freezing cold. Cheffings' houseboy had packed sandwiches, cold drinks and a thermos of coffee. Despite my early-morning bleariness, I remember an explosive sunrise in pink and orange over the dark blue ocean.

There were three of us on board, including the boatboy. He normally worked on one of the commercial boats, and Cheffings was pleased to get him. He did everything for us. He cut slivers of bait from yellowfin tuna caught the day before, wrapped them with wool on to spangly lures and put them over the stern. Meanwhile, keeping up a steady seven knots, we headed for the best sailfish area, five miles offshore. Dolphins cut in and out of our bow-wake, avoiding the big steel hooks trailing twenty-five yards behind us.

Just as we came to the patch that Cheffings was looking for, a glassy, rubbery piece of sea on the edge of an underwater shelf, there was a bang, and one of the rods started jiggling in its holder, line stripping off the reel at a huge rate. I just had time to glance up and see a long blue spike, the bill of a sailfish, poke and waggle out of the water where the lure was.

The boatboy jumped up, all senses locked on to the rod – luckily nobody was in the way – and grabbed it out of the holder. He gave it half a dozen sharp jerks to lodge the hook in the fish's mouth. It was all happening at once. I have a memory of Cheffings shouting, 'Take it, Charlie' – and the boatboy passing it, and the next thing I knew I was into the fight.

On its first run it felt as if the line was tied to Mistress Quickly, which George had inadvertently driven over a cliff. I looked down, jammed the butt of the rod into my pelvis and razed the first layer of skin off my fingers trying to slow the heavy brass reel, which was minging away to itself.

The boatboy was reeling in all the lines to my right. The fish cut right, I was pirouetted a quarter of a turn right, and the boatboy ducked with the last rod just in time as the line sliced the air just above his head.

The fish turned sharply and began heading back for the boat. Cheffings was at the wheel trying to keep it behind us. I barked my knuckles reeling in to try to keep the tension on the line. The fish's bill broke the water and cut it in a shark's-fin V towards us. Phrases like 'Keep reeling,' and 'You're going to lose it,' from Cheffings floated into my concentration.

As the fish came to the boat it dived, a bubbling opal-green torpedo at two fathoms, and it passed just below the stern. I was yanked half a turn to the left and pulled to the other side of the boat.

The boatboy grabbed me in a hug around the waist. 'Now,' I remember thinking, 'is really *not* the time.' The reel went into reverse and the line whistled away with the fish. 'What on earth is the boy trying to do?' crossed the small part of my mind not fully fixed on the fish.

He was trying to fit me with a belt with a plastic plate at the front in which to place the rod butt and save me from certain hernia. I could not look down, so did not work this out until it was in place.

The fish was a hundred yards out and did another flick-turn to come back to me. Another, more exasperated, 'You are going to lose it,' from Cheffings. I was buggered if I was. Almost literally, too, as I jumped backwards to save the line tension and knocked the boatboy over. I did not notice. He stood up and tightened the straps on my belt as I pressed him against the wheelhouse.

The fish jumped. Time stood still. Everything – the sun, the compass needle, Cheffings and the boatboy – stopped in my head for a second which lasted an hour. Cheffings' last 'You've lost it' rumbled in my ears like a tape played too slowly. The fish, blue and silver, extended its sail and hung, arched, standing on the water on its blue forked tail. Double-buggered if I have. I dropped the rod tip like a good salmon fisherman and felt the jolt as the fish landed on the line. But the slack saved me. It was still there. The clock started ticking again.

That was its final moment of freedom. From then on, even with more deprecating comments from Cheffings, it was mine. There were more jumps; there more runs from the boat at the point of gaffing it. But after a quarter of an hour it was flapping on the deck, and at last, swiftly, lifeless. I collapsed on to a welcome bench and a beer, loosened the belt and let the boatboy do the rest. Only fifty pounds, not a big fish, but a first fish, so worth three times that weight – which, incidentally, would pip the Kenya record by five pounds.

The rest of that day in the boat passed quietly. Sailfish jumped, some synchronised in pairs, with quite astonishing beauty, and bills appeared at baits, but none hooked properly. At the end of the day, tired and happy, I hauled in a dorado, an odd-shaped fish which looks as if someone has forgotten to put its head on, but that was that.

After our return to harbour and disposal of the catch, I celebrated at bars with names like the Driftwood Club and Ocean Sports, known locally as Open Shorts. There were German and Italian couples there out looking for sexual adventures with the *watu* – yes, both sexes. This was Africa; one can do anything in Africa. And it fitted in with *watu* majority thinking on sex as something you do at any opportunity with anyone who is available.

For the trip back to Nairobi there was a bus from Mombasa, and the only seat available was at the front, next to the driver. I could see why everyone was reluctant to take it. It gave you a full cinematic experience through the giant front windscreen of how bad drivers on the Mombasa road really are, not least our own driver.

Bus drivers who crash and kill people are normally lynched on the spot by angry surviving passengers. Consequently, there are no African bus-drivers around with experience of a bad crash, and they drive oblivious to the danger of other road-users. There is a popular theory that bus-drivers assiduously keep fit so that if they can still walk after a serious accident, they can flee into the hills faster than their passengers. The local name for the Kenya Bus Company is the Ministry of Death.

Back on Day 2 of the rally, Peter was having none of this nonsense. In normal life, Peter was a quiet fellow from the south of England. His job was to look glum daily on behalf of Des and Erik's company accounts. On the safari rally he was a man possessed, a beer never far from his lips, and behind the wheel of his car he was a one-man mission to teach the rest of Africa to drive properly.

But Peter whizzed as wilfully as Paddy, shouting rude words at other road-users and inspiring as much fear in Katrina and me as a bus-driver. The more we complained about the quality of his near-misses, the nearer he came to them. He took one roundabout by shooting between the cars on it like a King's Troop gun crew galloping a chain loop or a scissors pattern at the Royal Tournament. Katrina and I agreed that we were not nervous passengers, but this was the limit.

We found Olepolos and were able to stop the car. The Angel of Death, who followed Peter everywhere looking for pickings, stalked off cursing. We were still alive.

We had another long day in the scrub with a speedy few moments when Des and Mark turned up. 'Need eye-drops,' was Des's comment today. Once again, he and Mark were stained with dust from the road. Everyone had been expecting mud all over the course from the recent rains, and the big teams had hired all the available local safari companies as mud crews to stand by near the black spots. Almost every white resident in Nairobi who owns a four-wheel-drive vehicle calls himself a safari company. There was not much mud on the course in the end, but the dirt was sticky enough to cling to every surface. You could not read the big number 101 on the side of the Range Rover.

While Des and Mark sped off on another dirt-track leg, Big Knob 3 opened up its throttle for the run back to Nairobi. There were crowds lining the road from the airport in, and other traffic was slowing down to avoid them. Not Peter. His foot went down and he corkscrewed through the jamming cars, abusing everyone on the way, and never, on principle, stopping for roundabouts. Katrina and I hid under our seats, partly from terror and partly from embarrassment.

'None of the dents in this car are mine,' Peter told us cheerily as he scraped between a minibus-taxi slowing up in the fast lane and a party of picnicking Sikhs on the side of the road. Big Knob 3 was Peter's battered company Volvo.

We were surprised that he did not overtake any of the rally cars which had to use that road. The rally cars had timed sections on dirt roads and then half-hour slots on tarmac between the tracks when the pressure was off but when they had to find time to complete their services.

The rally cars always took the tarmac fast, if not quite as fast as the timed sections. The local-hero driver, Patrick Njiru, in a Subaru, managed to roll his car several times on the tarmac and had to be helicoptered to hospital. Ooh, went the crowd, who had wanted him to win the main event. In fact after spending a night in for observation he was fit and well the next day, but his car was not. We saw it concertinaed by the side of the road.

Part of Peter's need for speed between Olepolos and Nairobi was that Big Knob 3 had run out of beer. He wanted to get back to town in case the off-licences closed early because it was Good Friday. We made it by the grace of several gods, bought the necessary alcohol and were back in position on the forecourt of one of the factories along the airport road by dark.

The factory would not let us use its lavs. They had been reserved for the Subaru team, the blighters. There are not many trees in Nairobi, and Peter desecrated and fertilised the few there were as soon as he had had his beer. We had to declare exclusion zones around most of them.

There were trees further out on the Mombasa Road. Big Knob 2 had been a hundred miles down there near the Tsavo National Park, and came back in darkness in convoy with another team's service crew. Suddenly three tyres between the two cars blew out. *Watu* had put nails on the road so that they could do some mugging. Two cars containing eight people were too many to mug at once, however, though the locals rustled around behind the trees while Big Tom swept the area with the service-arc lights and the others changed the wheels.

All three Big Knobs gathered for the last service of Day 2. Simon was frantic. He could see victory, which for him meant The Big Knob simply completing the rally course, and he was scared to his wit's end that Something Would Go Wrong.

It did not, however, and Big Knob went piling into the second finish, refuelled and refreshed, to let us go home to another midnight bed.

Des and Mark had moved up to second place in their class. Simon was delirious.

Day 3

Something was bound to Go Wrong on Day 3. Simon knew it. His oily fingernails were down to their quicks. He was a calm and delightful man in normal life, but his fuse had shortened over the previous forty-eight hours.

It was going to be a long day, too. After an early start, the rally wound over the rift escarpment and into the valley northwards, past Soysambu and Lady Delamere's Elmenteita passage control, into the Cherangany Hills as far as Lake Baringo, and back to Nakuru for midnight. It would be dark, but this drive was through scenery as beautiful as any in Kenya. When Georgina, normally a toughish soul, had seen the view from the tops across the Kitali Valley, she had cried. There was to be a two-hour rest at Nakuru, and then the run home to Nairobi. We reckoned we would be finished by 4am – if the car finished at all.

The day started badly on our drive out of Nairobi, in convoy, on our way to Nakuru. We had an extra service car, which was useful, but its turbo blew out, which was not, so we limped into the Rift Valley Sports Club in Nakuru and left it there. This also meant we could have a few drinks at the club bar – not Simon, of course – to help us decide what to do. Erik and Peter started drinking their beer with greater intent. Finally we transferred all people and as much kit as could be carried into the other Big Knobs.

I was in Big Knob 1 with Erik and Simon for Day 3. Big Tom, in Big Knob 2, and I began playing with the radios: 'Broadsword, this is Danny Boy,' we called each other (*Where Eagles Dare*), and 'Breaker, breaker, one-nine, this is the Rubber Duck,' (*Convoy*).

Big Knob 3 went ahead to a refuelling stop near the Cherangany Hills. Big Knobs 1 and 2 followed behind. We were two miles away from them, looking out for them on the right. The correct way for Erik, driving Big Knob 1, to pass that information to Big Tom in Big Knob 2 was to say: 'Ghost Rider, you are 3,000 yards to bogey at zero-niner-zero degrees. Call the ball. Over.' (*Top Gun*).

Big Tom: 'Roger, Mustang. Permission to fly by.' (*Top Gun* again).

Charles: 'Negative, Ghost Rider, the pattern is full.' (Still *Top Gun*).

Big Tom: 'Wheeeeewsh.' (Noise of overtaking, as in *Top Gun*).

Simon (stressed), taking the mike: 'Er, guys. We're getting close. Let's keep the airwaves clear.'

Erik's right hand came quietly out of his window, below the sill out of Simon's sight, and made a small masturbating movement. Big Knob 2, behind us, dissolved into laughter. Luckily for Simon's blood pressure, they did not broadcast.

Peter broadcasted, happily, all day, mostly to himself, as the Cherangany Hills blocked much of the transmission.

Peter: 'Thish ish Big Knob Thingummy calling anyone with a shmall dick. Eshpeshully Erik. Hello? Hello? Ish there anybody out there?' (Pink Floydish, that last part).

Peter even broadcasted when all three cars were parked in the same place. He sat in Big Knob 3 wittering away to himself. 'Shomeone come over here. I need a bonk.'

Simon was on the verge of walloping him, but he controlled himself and stayed on the verge, by the road, where he stood mournfully willing the rally car to appear. By then it was midnight. The day had gone surprisingly smoothly. Des's comment of the day had been: 'Grubby. Glad we got goggles today.'

The car had developed no faults that needed repair beyond tightening shock-absorbers, replacing headlights and tying the rear bumper back on with a piece of wire. Any parts which had ever needed changing came straight off Big Knob 1, Erik's own Range Rover. And when these ran out, Simon started raiding Sean's Land Rover Discovery, Big Knob 2. Neither Erik nor Sean were overwhelmingly pleased. But they had their own missions. Erik was psychotically intent on always being near beer, and Sean, who had for many years lived in South Africa, where the barbecue, called *braai* in Afrikaans, is a way of life, wanted to find a good butcher open that Easter Saturday. At one service stop we were treated to the sight of

Sean and Big Tom, who also liked his meat, racing backwards and forwards along the road in front of us in Big Knob 2 between local towns, scouring for entrecôte. We had visions of them kidnapping a cow, strapping it to the roof and bringing it back for slaughter, but they found a butcher which could supply. Simon did not eat much. By midnight he was sweating with worry.

'They should have come through,' he said blankly.

We tried raising The Big Knob on the radio, having persuaded Peter to let us have the airtime. There was nothing. Simon paced up and down. We milled around uncomfortably.

At 1am there was life: 'Crrr . . . crrr . . . Big Knob. This is . . . crrr . . . crrr.'

Simon grabbed the mike. 'Where are you? What's going on? Has anything happened?'

Mark was getting closer, so the reception was clearer. 'Receiving you, Si. Has this section been cancelled? Over.'

Simon turned to the rest of us, grouped around the radio in the darkness. 'What the hell is going on?' he demanded of us.

'Something's happened,' said Big Tom, obviously.

We had seen a few cars go past into Nakuru, but not many, and only from the main event, not the classic section. We were waiting five miles out of town. We guessed that it had been sticky for everyone.

Simon: 'Mark. Where are you? Over.'

Mark: 'We're on the main Baringo–Nakuru road.'

We stood there, stunned. It was the wrong road.

'It's over,' said Simon to the rest of us. It was a horrible, terrible moment. They were way off course. They should have been coming in from the hills above Nakuru, not along the valley floor. 'Fuck. It's over,' he said again. 'Mark? You're on the wrong road. Come straight into Nakuru and we'll meet you there. Over.'

The radio went dead.

'Mark?'

Nothing.

'Mark?'

Still nothing.

'They must be behind a hill,' suggested Erik.

'We'd better keep a car here until we make contact,' said Big Tom hopefully.

Simon sent Big Knob 1 off to Nakuru to get a clearer signal, and as an extra measure dispatched Big Knob 3 up the hill to try for a signal there. Si was so disappointed. He opened his first beer. Months of work destroyed on the last section of the last leg. He was nearly crying.

Time went by. Simon sank a few melancholy beers. We tried to say things to cheer him up like, 'I blame Peter', or 'I blame the government'. Big Knobs 1 and 3 reported radio silence at their ends.

'Strange,' we all thought, but not aloud.

Simon had more beer, but more tentatively now. He took to standing by the road again, staring up it at the hills lit by the moonlight. Simon stood there for an hour, just staring, a beer undrunk in his hand.

We were becoming concerned at this silence from The Big Knob. One moment they were so clear, the next they had vanished. Erik thought they might have had an accident. I said they had probably been captured by aliens. Nobody thought that frightfully funny. Big Tom said the unthinkable, the unhopeforable, that they had turned round and gone back into the section again; we knew that they never used their radio in a section because they had to concentrate.

'Even if they have,' Simon pointed out to Big Tom sadly, 'they'll never make it. They'll be time-barred.'

Simon looked shattered, and despite a few jokes on the surface, deeply, deeply disappointed. We could only sympathise, but we could not feel the heartbreak of all his work going down the plughole.

It was 3am. If they had been on schedule they should have been into Nakuru, rested for two hours and out again half an hour before. Three of the cars in the classic section had gone through by now, two Range Rovers and a Land Rover Discovery in first place.

Then Peter's voice came over the radio. He was up at the last passage control time-check on the hill.

'Damn him. Drunk,' we thought.

But he was sober for a moment. 'They're through!' he shouted.

'They're through passage control! They were two minutes from being time-barred.'

Hearts, now mended, leaped to mouths. Simon gaped. He put down his bottle quite carefully, turned round with wide eyes and yelled a yahoo into the night sky, the kind of cheer that bounces off stars.

Within five minutes Mark and Des were with us. Not knowing how much time they had before the final check in Nakuru itself, Simon did not let them off the road, took one look at their knackered expressions, one listen to the note of their engine. 'OK?' he shouted over it. Des nodded. 'Go, go, go!' and banged the roof to speed them on their way.

Big Knob 1 picked them up on the way into Nakuru, and guided them to the check. They made it; then turned round directly to go to a service we had set up at once on the way out of town for the easy tarmac run to Nairobi.

Everyone was so happy. Simon was back in full engineering swing again. Peter was pissed. He nearly got a punch in the hooter for filling up the petrol tank until it overflowed on to Simon's face as Simon worked on a rear shock-absorber underneath. Good spirits prevailed. It was a delighted drive back to Nairobi.

At 5am rally car 101, The Big Knob, mounted the stand outside the Jomo Kenyatta Conference Centre in Nairobi, with flags flying and Safari Rally banners all around. It was a heady moment. Des and Mark stood on the bonnet and opened a bottle of champagne. They had come fifth in the classic class. Lady Delamere was there. Simon made me pipe the car up the ramp on the banjo. He really was crying.

What had happened in those hills? we all wanted to know. First, explained Des, it was the mud, and as it was the last leg, most of the mud crews had sloped off home, bored. All the cars got stuck. Des lost his shoes in it. There were some *watu* standing around watching or desultorily pushing a few of the cars. Des took a rational approach. He found the local chief and offered a couple of thousand shillings to get all the *watu* working on his Range Rover. That was a lot of money. One whistle from the chief and the whole village were putting their backs into it, leaving other cars floundering without any help. In the end, only twenty-seven of the total of seventy-five competitors in the main, classic and historic events finished.

That was what had lost the time. Then there was the wrong turn, which put them on the wrong road. As soon as they had heard Simon say, 'You're on the wrong road,' Des had slewed the car round and back they went, ignoring the radio, just concentrating on finding a route once more into the timed section.

We all went for breakfast at Muthaiga Club. It was an orgy of alcohol. It started at 6am and went from downing depth-charges of green chartreuse in wine glasses sunk into pints of Tusker beer, through shots of any kind of spirit, bottles of champagne, bloody maries, to throwing everyone into the swimming pool.

For his size, Big Tom showed a remarkable turn of speed in chasing Peter into the pool. Peter, we felt, deserved the first ducking, yet he slipped through tackles 'like a greased pig', as Big Tom put it; that Big Tom who set off after him like a knight of legend, weighed down with armour, and making a trundling five knots over short distances on a heavy horse. He was not, as those legends have it, capable of 'pricking o'er the plain', yet it was a good example of our man's lumbering acceleration. We had to wait before we could catch Peter near the swimming pool again.

We were exhausted but euphoric. Erik's bloodshot eyes sported two shades of red: crimson from lack of sleep and vermilion from alcohol.

It ended at teatime. I lay down on one of the sunbeds by the pool, issuing strict instructions to the staff there not to disturb me, and went off into the deepest of all sleeps.

I woke up at 7pm and, true to their word, they had closed the place around me, shut the bar and put a cover on the pool, and had not woken me up. I got out by rattling at the staff entrance. Sean, who had found the energy to play golf that day, came to pick me up. We went out to supper as a celebration, but were only able to doze in our soup. It was time for bed.

The next day was solid party as well, culminating in the Safari Rally Ball at the Hotel Intercontinental. Everyone was there – the Austrians, Paddy, Lady Delamere, though Horrible Tom was away in

South Africa. Big Tom came. I wore his spare dinner jacket, several sizes too large.

Big Tom nearly got away with stealing the giant 555 Safari Rally sponsorship sign behind the band. It was ten feet square and enamelled on metal, so would have looked lovely over Simon's workshop parts emporium. The Toyota team had just tried to half-inch it, but had been caught by the Hotel Intercon duty manager. He had had it propped against the wall outside his office. Big Tom went up, posing as an official from British & American Tobacco, and told the manager that he was not happy with the way the sign was being treated, and could the manager bring it to Big Tom's car at once. The manager loked perplexed. Most Africans hate feeling responsible for decisions like that.

'Look, I'll sign for it,' said Big Tom, 'if it makes you feel better. Bring paper and pen.'

Unfortunately, at that moment a real BAT man turned up.

'If anyone is going to sign for anything it is going to be me,' he said pompously, and guided the manager into the office.

That left Big Tom guarding the sign outside by himself. The Toyota crew were standing around nearby. 'If I were you,' he told them, 'I'd take it.' They did.

Mark was on flying form again after his three days' enforced sobriety. His eyes were up at top-floor level, only just beating the corners of his mouth. We went across to the Intercon casino, and on the way through found him chatting to a Sikh boy on a sofa. The poor lad, a little lost in the noise, obviously thought Mark was just being nice to him. But we could see Mark's eyes fixed firmly on the boy's turban, which he was about to grab. To a man, we pounced on Mark and swept him protesting away.

At the end of the evening we manhandled Mark into a lift in the multi-storey car park. He would not get out when we reached the floor where we'd left the car, and disappeared off to another floor. We called the lift again, but when it came back it was empty. We went off to look for him, some up and some down. I found him on the fifth floor and lured him back into the lift by saying he could use the emergency telephone. Luckily he could not, as somebody had already stolen it. We got him home at last.

There was more partying on the third night at Luisa's house, but it all ended with a bang. At 2am Mark felt the urge to drive the rally car from the party to Psy's. There were five of us in it, two in the back and three in the bucket seats in the front. A mile from the party and drunk as ever, he took a left-hand corner too fast.

'Triple caution left!' we sang out, just like real navigators.

The car went on to two wheels and was about to roll. The front offside wheel found the grass on the verge and started to slide. It righted the roll, but the car was out of control, beyond steering. It hit a high garden wall and stopped.

A thirty-foot length of wall disappeared into dust and clouds of mortar, and the noise, at the speed we were going, was like a bomb going off. The two girls in the back were thrown around like dice in a shaker. One of them chipped a leg bone. No one else was hurt. Mark became instantly less drunk. We reckoned, rightly – we were lucky – that nobody had seen us, so Mark drove the car back to the party in acrid clouds of burning leaking oil, and the rest of us walked it. It was an expensive accident for Mark, and the end of his celebrations. The next morning, out walking off their hangovers, Katrina and Luisa saw the Indian owner of the wall staring, flabbergasted, at the rubble. They had to turn away to hide their giggles.

Des and Simon were not happy, though both characteristically calm about it. They had almost expected Mark to do it, even though their orders to him had been: (1) 'Don't drive the car when drunk, Mark,' and (2) 'On second thoughts, Mark, don't drive the car.'

I left Kenya shortly afterwards. I expect Mark did too.

Zimbabwe. 32 days to the World Cup opening ceremony

C ollin and the interviewer, Farayi, were sitting next to each other behind the glass wall in the radio studio at the Zimbabwe Broadcasting Company's flash offices near the Borrowdale Racecourse in Harare. They were at a table with a large square microphone on a stand between them. They were recording the Friday-evening sports programme.

The studio operator called them on the intercom: 'Move in, please.'

'I'll be on his lap soon,' protested Collin.

'OK, that will do. Stand by.'

He played to the end of the last taped interview, and Farayi cued in: 'Thank you for that from Bulawayo. Staying with rugby, I have with me Collin Osborne, director of coaching and development at the Zimbabwe Rugby Union. Collin, you must be very excited about the arrival tomorrow of Peter Winterbottom.' He pronounced it 'peterwinterbottom'.

'Er . . . good . . . er,' said Collin. 'He'll be here for a couple of days holding training sessions, meeting schoolkids.' He gathered tempo. 'Yes, he's second to none. He was captain of Harlequins in London and has played for England and The British Lions. He is the most-capped forward in English rugby history.'

'That's good,' said Farayi. 'And, Collin, tell me: why is peter-winterbottom here when he plays for England?'

'He doesn't play for England any more.'

Silence in the studio, followed by a hearty roar of laughter.

'Sorry, I'll try that again,' said Farayi.

The studio rewound the tape, and cued: 'Stand by.'

'Collin, tell me: how did peterwinterbottom get to Zimbabwe?'

Collin explained the trip. Winters was travelling for two months from Tanzania to South Africa with another former England international and Harlequins forward, Chris Butcher, a Scotland squad and London Scottish back Bede Bruce-Lockhart, and a Sky TV cameraman. The three rugby men had all played for South African teams in the past, Winters for Transvaal, Butch for Natal and Bede for Durban Crusaders. Their mission was to raise interest in rugby in East and Southern Africa and to raise the profile of and money for the Richard Langhorn Trust.

Richard Langhorn, or Langers, a Harlequins player, had planned to drive the whole way through Africa with Winters to the World Cup. They organised a sponsored Land Rover and the trip was all set. But at the end of November 1994, Langers went into hospital for an operation to correct a back problem caused by a rugby injury. While under anaesthetic he had a heart attack, and he never came round.

Langers' death was a tragedy, but Winters knew that his old friend would have wanted him to go ahead with the trip anyway. So Winters set up the Richard Langhorn Trust, a fund which pays for handicapped and underprivileged children to enjoy the sports Langers enjoyed, like rugby, cricket and sailing. In just six months the trust had raised as much as a useful city salary. Winters marshalled Bede, Butch and the cameraman as travelling companions. He knew that Langers' ghost would be with him all the way as well.

Zimbabwe was the last country these four were to visit before South Africa and the World Cup opening ceremony in Cape Town. Collin, a former Harlequins coach and an old friend of Winters, had been organising talks and training sessions for them to give in Zimbabwe. There was a day to go before they arrived and he was frantic for publicity for them, which is why we were at ZBC.

Collin's history made him somewhat unique in Zimbabwe. A black West Indian, born in St Kitts, his family moved to England during the great immigration of the 1950s when the Conservative government implored the colonies to supply Britain with factory workers, bus-drivers and dustmen. He was brought up in Birmingham. His childhood ended with Enoch Powell's Rivers of Blood speech and the racism that followed on the streets thereafter. He trained to be a PE teacher and played centre for Moseley Rugby Club for six years. He had a Lenny Henry Brummie accent and though forty and bearded, he looked late twenties. Being English, he thought like an Englishman, which surprised the locals, and was endlessly exasperated by the African never-never mentality.

Collin first came to Zimbabwe in 1984 to teach at a government school. He was offered a three-year contract in 1987 by the Zimbabwe Rugby Union, which kept him in the country as a coach. In 1990 he returned to England to do a stint as a Quins coach, and in 1993 came back to Zimbabwe with another three-year contract.

This time his brief was a little different. Zimbabwe has every chance of being the second-best national rugby team in Africa after the Springboks, but it will take a generation before the country has a chance of being the best. Collin was brought back in order to spread the message of rugby across schools by coaching coaches and holding rugby clinics all over the country. He belonged to that breed of man in Africa, like Bougja and Cassagnet, whose jobs are to be the apostles of rugby.

I met him first at a schools tournament in Harare. I had sped south from Nairobi through Tanzania – not pausing at snow-capped Kilimanjaro – and Zambia – avoiding the Victoria Falls – by train and bus to find a letter waiting for me in Harare. It was from Emma, who had been there with Danny only a fortnight before me. They had since flown back to Ireland. It read: 'I took some pictures of the Zimbabwe national team a few weeks ago & came back yesterday for a match between Zimbabwe & South Africa – 15–50 – took plenty of pics. Their trainer (Zim) is Collin Osborne – he used to train Harlequins in England. I said you were around soon. I've even been to a few league matches in Bulawayo & where have you been, Charlie – fishing?? Do get in contact with him as he's a lovely guy & mention me the greatest, smallest photographer ever & he'll remember.'

With a recommendation like that I had to call. Collin had a mildly preppie look about him as he sat on one of the long wooden benches around the Prince Edward School rugby pitch. He was wearing brown cords, brown loafers, a pastel shirt, a cricket jersey over his shoulders and a panama hat with a stripy Harlequins band.

It was a bright afternoon with a light breeze blowing. The main pitch was rimmed by politely rippling jacaranda trees, and under them school chairs and benches for the gently rustling spectators. The floral patterns of the ladies' frocks looked like a kind of flowering poinsettia against the trunks of the jacarandas. They drank from Prince Edward School crested cups with saucers, the kind of tea which tastes brown and progressively lukewarm as the day wears on, just as school tea ought to.

The old pavilion at one end of the pitch was a one-storey colonial building with blooming bougainvillaea tendrilling over the verandah, hung with baskets of petunias. 'Yes, petunias,' confirmed the old white fellow on the other side of me from under his trilby. 'There was a music-hall song about that,' he added drowsily.

White puffy clouds drifted quietly above the thunder of the boys in boots on the field, a sound as peaceful as cricket in this climate. It was not as tropical here as Ivory Coast. Light applause and a murmur of appreciation greeted each try touched down on grass as clipped as a croquet lawn. 'Who *is* playing in this match?' asked the old fellow. This was rugby purely for the sake of the game.

Harare, as cities go, was tremendously refreshing in this way. It was the first truly first world city centre I came to in Africa. It had drug-pedlars on the streets, as subtle as their European counterparts. It had 'salad garnish' in cheap restaurants translating, in the best British tradition, as a lettuce leaf, a quarter of a tomato and three crisps. Huge sparkling office buildings lined wide litter-free pavements and four-lane tarmac. People queued in post offices in an orderly manner.

'The whole city is very well planned,' said Rasna, an architect I met.

'They've really thought about avenues and things.'

These avenues are cleverly planted with trees and bushes to make them burst into synchronised colour at different times of the year. From mid-September to October the jacaranda and the agapanthus flower a gorgeous purple. The yellows and the oranges take over in January with the cassia tree, the flame tree-like erythrina, the feather-duster tree, which is also called touch-the-sky, all the deep orange-coloured flamboyants, the oleander and the yellow wattle, a mimosa. When I was there, these January trees were still out due to the odd nature of the rainy season that year and the recent drought, but they were being challenged by avenues pocked by the pink and white of the bombax, which has the potbellied trunk of a baobab but is covered in thorn, a bauhinia, the Himalaya cherry, and the bougainvillaea. These were more in keeping with a climate that had become drier and dustier after Kenya.

The rugby festival was for fifty-seven schools. Odd how that number keeps cropping up in rugby, isn't it? It was a pre-season look at players. Teams played fifteen a side and twenty minutes each way. Collin was there to see how his high-density team was performing. A high-density area in Zimbabwe is the same as an inner-city area in Britain or a township in South Africa. These children had few sporting facilities at their schools, and Collin was pleased and proud of the way they had taken to rugby. He had arranged a sponsor for them, a local pork-dealer called Colcom, and had built up the team from nothing.

Clive Barnes, headmaster of Prince Edward School for the last ten years, was an imposing, tall white man. He was friendly to me, a grown-up, but I would hate to be expelled by him. He had a lot to say about the development of rugby since Zimbabwe's independence in 1980, and the change for many schools from white to black overnight.

'Before independence there was almost no rugby in black circles,' he said. 'Most of the white community believed that the black boy would not take to rugby. That was a fallacy. This festival is almost ninety per cent black, and that's good, because they are the future in this country. The black boy loves contact sports, against everyone's beliefs, and he has opened up a much more fluid, running rugby, which is currently very popular. The back lines are almost exclusively black because of their pace. I run cricket in Zimbabwe schools, and there is not so much interest in it as in rugby. I'm a great believer in black sport. If I don't believe in it, it won't happen here.'

Back to the bench. Collin sat and chatted about Zimbabwe's defeat by Ivory Coast in the African qualifying matches and about the current state of Zimbabwean rugby. But his mind was clearly not on the interview. 'Look at that,' he raged. 'That number 10 keeps kicking the damn ball – and not very well. Sorry. Where were we?'

'Ivory Coast.'

'Well, I will give Ivory Coast credit,' he said. 'A lot of them play rugby in France. They're not mugs. They're quite streetwise. We're gentlemen here. I understand it's the same in business in West Africa. If you watch our schoolboy rugby, you'll see how gentlemanly it is. The staff take tea in lounge chairs. This translates to an attitude on the pitch. When we go to an international match we stand back a bit. We don't know how to cope with it. You won't see raking here. But I'll take nothing away from Ivory Coast. They won it fair and square.'

Collin's attention wandered towards the action on the field: 'Ach – look at it. They're still putting up the same basic pattern as I taught their coaches. They haven't got any further. And as soon as they're under pressure, they revert to type. They're fragmented. They're not disciplined. They come out of the changing room fired up for the first fifteen minutes, and then they lose discipline.'

Where were we? 'I blame the Rugby World Cup organisers. We had to play three internationals in five days. Who else had to do that? It was penny-pinching. RWC said: "Let's gather in Morocco and have a tournament."'

As an aside: 'Morocco played very well in front of their king. They suffer because they lose their players to France, just as we lose our best players to South Africa.'

Number 10 kicks for touch. 'I mean, that sort of thing,' said Collin furiously. 'I just can't see the point of it. And tackle. *Tackle*. The tackling's too weak.'

Collin returned to the point. 'I explained to RWC that it was unfair to do it this way. It is *medically* unsound with all the pressure and so much at stake. We were only allowed a squad of twenty-six, too. We lost our fly-half and a centre in the first ten minutes of the first game, versus Namibia, and then a flanker. We were down to a squad of twenty-three immediately. There were only two on the bench! We were buggered for the rest of the week.'

The opposition score. 'Oh. Oh my godfathers! This is *typical* of Zimbabwean rugby. The fly-half was under pressure. Everyone is just *standing around*. There's a scrum-five yards from the line. No support. Ach.

'Rugby has so much significance in these schools. It's a macho thing. When a school wins everyone has a spring in their step, girls and boys. There is that status attached to rugby here – Eton and "chaps". One school, Churchill, has a full pipe band to bring them on to the pitch. It was a whites-only school and there were fears that when it went black that sort of thing would stop, but it carried on. They love it. The people here have assimilated the whole rugby package. The players speak Shona. On the pitch they speak English. They call the line-outs in English, even though they only speak Shona.' Collin stared at the play as he talked. 'Oh for G . . . for f . . . *knock him backwards*! That's jellybaby tackling. It's so easy: if you are ever in a situation where you don't know what to do, pick a guy in a different-coloured shirt, dip your shoulder and run *at* him.'

Collin returned to the point once again, and rounded it up. 'It would have been nice to go to the World Cup but it came at the wrong time. 1995 is the centenary for rugby in Zimbabwe, and we have too much on this year. We're in the B section of the Currie Cup in South Africa, which guarantees ten matches a year, as well as touring sides coming here, like Scotland A, New South Wales and South Africa Rural XV. In the old days, because of the political situation down south, we were not allowed to compete internationally, even though we had no contact with South Africa at any level in rugby. We used to be begging people to come and tour here. Now we're turning them away.

'Have you heard that rumour going round Harare that Ivory Coast can't afford to go to the World Cup and we have to go instead? I don't know where it started. I wish people would stop spreading it,' he added.

'In September we're hosting the All-Africa Games, and eight rugby teams are coming to compete as an exhibition sport. They are split into two pools of four. The second pool is Zimbabwe, Namibia, South Africa and Ivory Coast. There is a great determination here to, let us say, redress the balance.

'Look. Number 10 has kicked it again. He's done the same thing all afternoon and he still hasn't succeeded. Does he think that because he's done it eighteen times they won't expect it a nineteenth?'

As the pioneer column marched a hundred years ago on Matabeleland and Mashonaland – what would become the country Rhodesia and later still Zimbabwe – bringing Cecil Rhodes' trade plans, they also brought rugby, a hidden import. National rugby is now split between Matabeleland in the south of the country, and its capital, Bulawayo, and Mashonaland, centred around Harare. Collin complained that the politics between the two can be petty, but it is not the same political game they play in Kenya, for example. And inter-regional matches are more exciting for it.

More difficult is persuading blacks to take a part in the organisation of the ZRU. Until 1995 there were no black administrators at the ZRU, but President Robert Mugabe of Zimbabwe heard about it and forced them to take someone on. It was a sop to what post-apartheid South Africa now calls the BCI index – blacks, coloureds and Indians, and their ratio of jobs to those of the whites.

'Blacks did not play rugby before 1980,' explained Collin. 'They could not, because the white government only gave them football pitches at their schools. None of the blacks who are at the top of their professions and have the time to work for the ZRU, a voluntary organisation, have sufficient interest in the game. That is why we are planning for future generations.'

Clive Barnes is on the Sports Commission of Zimbabwe. 'It was sad that we had to force the issue about blacks on the ZRU,' he said. 'Up to now we have never convinced blacks to make a financial commitment to rugby. It's not part of their psyche. They think the money will come. But I don't think the young black people I am teaching will agree with these shibboleths. We are fifteen years into independence. It will take another fifteen years.'

The white old guard in Zimbabwe wear rugby as a badge which, post-independence, they are keen to award to their new black leaders, just as in the Ivory Coast. This kind of cultural shove is normally resented by blacks in charge, but Mugabe knows the importance of rugby in Zimbabwe, and for the second World Cup in 1991 he sent this Coffie-Gervais-style message to the Zimbabwe rugby team competing in Ireland:

As I pass through the United Kingdom on my way from the United Nations headquarters in New York, USA, I would like to take the opportunity to wish you, members of the Zimbabwe rugby team, success in your matches. Though famous rugby heavyweights are among the teams ranged against you, I am convinced that your experience, exposure and training since 1987 have seasoned and prepared you for this long-expected encounter.

In wishing the Zimbabwe rugby team well in their World Cup campaign, I am happy to note the tremendous development of the sport among the young of all races in Zimbabwe since independence. Rugby has become the fastest-growing sport in our schools and is, perhaps, the most integrated of our sporting disciplines.

The numbers of teams participating in the current contest, their geographical distribution and national diversity is indicative of the popularity of the game. I am indeed happy to note that in you Zimbabwe is ably represented.

I trust, also, that the team will be good ambassadors of Zimbabwe. Sport has a crucial role in our life – it inspires us to further the cause for peace, friendship and solidarity, not only within our borders, but the world over.

Good Luck!

R.G. Mugabe
President of the Republic of Zimbabwe

Mugabe could, everyone agreed, be a little bufferish on occasions – he tended to bang on a bit – but the message was well meant and happily received.

The schools festival ended, and Collin started making his huge efforts for Winters' arrival. On the big day, he brought his high-density boys to the national ground which was inside the police training school in Harare, next to State House and Mugabe's palace. Collin even called in favours with a ZBC TV film crew to cover Winters' training session.

Winters and his lot were supposed to arrive at nine in the morning. At ten, the ZBC crew turned up. There was no sign of Winters. Collin was going spare with fury. They recorded a desultory interview with Collin, but his mind was elsewhere.

'Collin is going to kill somebody,' commented Paul, a national coach, as Collin was seen stomping up the stairs to his office to make more desperate telephone calls.

At eleven the TV crew left. Collin was biting the carpet in his office in between making calls to try to track Winters down. At half-past eleven Winters arrived.

The first sounds in the silence after the engine of the minibus switched off were those of Bede and Butch sparring.

Bede: 'I broke your knee.'

Butch: 'No you didn't.'

Bede: 'Yes I did. You put your leg forward, and I broke it.'

Butch: 'You did not.'

Bede: 'I could have done.'

The four big men fell fighting out of the van.

'Hello, mate,' said Butch to me, breaking it up briefly. 'We had a puncture.' A lie-in, more likely. 'I'm Chris Butcher, this is Bede, this is Muppet.'

'And this is our mute,' said Bede, indicating Winters, a thickset, quiet man with the look of a Yorkshire farmer.

Collin had already warned me that Winters did not speak often. 'Winters never said much on the field as captain of Quins, but he had a way of looking at someone and saying quietly: "Let's go." And they knew he meant it.'

'Hello, Coll,' said Winters when Collin arrived.

Collin had been dismissing his high-density squad. His temper was fully restored, and he was delighted to see his old pals.

'Sorry. Puncture,' explained Winters.

'Hi, guys. Not a problem. Look, we've got to go on to another training session now, a hundred kilometres away.'

They set off at once. Winters sat stone-faced in the front of their minibus next to their driver, who was starting the engine. By the time they moved away from the ZRU ground, Butch and Muppet in the back had already wrestled Bede to the floor in two arm-locks. The minibus was swaying visibly, and cries of pain were coming out of the windows. Bede was stronger than both of them individually, but not together. They increased the pain until he promised not to get them back. But as soon as they let go, he jumped on Butch. In the end, the most damage was done to the driver, who was an incoherent wreck by the time they returned that evening.

Muppet, the Sky TV cameraman, was ex-forces, Royal Engineers, a hard-man freelance travel-the-world photographer. He had the same energy and Tigger spirit as Emma. His curious name was earned in an incident when he was aiming a .458 at a baboon in Zambia, but missed and hit the main transformer for Victoria Falls, plunging the little tourist town into darkness. 'Muppet' is army-speak for foul-up.

Muppet had organised a Sky TV crew to film Winters' departure from Twickenham carrying messages of goodwill from the Fifty-Seven Old Farts to the South African Rugby Football Union, and Winters' arrival in Cape Town for the opening match of the World Cup, and he was shooting footage of the journey in between. The trip had been the kind of mayhem that I learned to expect from these four. They never got their Land Rover in the end. The sponsor pulled out, so they flew to Tanzania, to Dar Es Salaam – 'A shithole,' commented Muppet, 'no rugby there at all' – and from there spent some time on Zanzibar, just off the coast. Then it was off to the Maasai Mara in Kenya for the African lions to meet a British Lion.

In Nairobi they coached the local Harlequins team, and then flew south from Nairobi to Lilongwe in Malawi, missed a connecting flight, and took a taxi to a lunch in their honour at Blantyre. That is like taking a taxi from Birmingham to Manchester. Winters, normally the most silent of people, had to make a speech.

'He wouldn't shut up,' said Butch. 'We were signalling him – hoi, enough, sit down – but he wouldn't listen to us.'

'Bored them rigid,' said Bede.

They played a charity match in Malawi, Bede on one side and Winters on the other. All the other players wanted to nobble Bede and Winters. Bede, as ever, enjoyed himself hugely, throwing the ball in the air as he crunched through potential tackles and catching it afterwards, or passing it around his back.

One player tried a rough piece of tackling on Winters. Big mistake. At the next opportunity, Winters, with the ball, ran towards this man. Just as he reached him, Winters passed, but the follow-through of the pass caught the unhappy man neatly in the solar plexus, leaving him doubled up.

They also went out fishing for tigerfish on the Shire River – 'Didn't fucking catch anything,' said Butch – and managed to lose the car keys of the brand-new 4x4 they had borrowed. They broke the door open, tore off the dashboard and hot-wired it. It did not go down well with the car's owner. It was Muppet who lost the keys, so he was fined heavily during that evening's drinking games.

Then they chartered an aeroplane to Zambia, where they went to the Roan Antelope Club in Ndola, in the copper belt, famous for having the highest uprights in the world, 110 feet tall. Next they cadged a lift to Harare – where I met them – and from there were headed south to Bulawayo. Finally it was up to Victoria Falls, a flight down to Johannesburg and a drive to Cape Town. For their arrival in Johannesburg, they had organised a sponsor to let them have four Harley Davidson motorbikes for the day. They were delighted about that. 'Can we have four women with baby oil rubbed on their tits as well?' asked Bede.

After that Muppet had to go back to England to start his next project. Bede was needed in London by his employer, Rank Xerox. Winters planned to stay and follow his old team around with Butch before going back. Butch wanted to stay in South Africa and look for a job.

They had seen a lot of rugby so far. In a rare serious moment, Butch aired his thoughts on it all. 'Rugby's fucking dying in Africa, mate. And I think it comes down to money. There just isn't the corporate interest. Dar Es Salaam in Tanzania, it's non-existent. Take Malawi: they've got two teams, Lilongwe and Blantyre, and they're all expatriates playing. None of the locals are coming through. And every year there are fewer and fewer expatriates. They're going to have one team soon. You can't have it elitist like that in sport, mate, unless it's a game like polo, which is sponsored by rich individuals who like it that way. At the Roan Antelope Club in Zambia they're really keen. I played for ten years all over the world and I have never seen a pitch as good as theirs.' He shook his head. 'Middle of fucking nowhere, mate. And the mining companies have taken a dive there, so there isn't the sponsorship. I think all the money that is going to come from the World Cup should go back into developing the sport in countries which need it, not to countries like England or South Africa.

'Look at Zimbabwe: traditionally very strong as Rhodesia, and still strong in schools. England schools are good, but Zimbabwe schools fucking tan them every time. Zimbabwe *needs* the money, mate.'

Their trip had been organised by another Wendy – nothing to do with the Horrible Tom – who ran Team Talk Promotions in London, a company specialising in just this sort of operation. Wendy was from Bulawayo, so this was her home patch. She was an athlete, too, and had represented both Zimbabwe and South Africa in the high jump at school. Originally the lads had tried to work out a route through Africa for themselves. Then it was, 'Wendy, mate, could *you* do it?' from Butch.

She said that the biggest difficulty in the planning was that the four lads would meet, agree that one of them would call her about, say, insurance, and the next morning she would get four consecutive telephone calls.

'Wendy, mate,' (Butch) 'what's the score on insurance?'

'Urh, Wendy,' (Winters) 'what are we going to do about insurance?'

'Do we need insurance, Wendy?' (Bede.)

'Wendy, we've got to have insurance.' (Muppet.)

'Guys, guys, guys,' she told them. 'Sort out what you want, and then just one of you call me, OK?' So they put Butch in charge of planning liaison; an odd choice, as Butch, of all of them, was the most clueless about where they were at any time.

Collin had organised a kind of chat-show event that first evening in the ZRU headquarters. Winters and Butch were to field questions from an adoring public while Collin played Terry Wogan. Chairs were put out all over the wooden floor of the big club room, around a grand array of trophies and photographs from Zimbabwean and Rhodesian matches spanning the century.

But Collin's publicity let him down. In the end only a smattering of people turned up, mostly Collin's rugby friends in Harare. Luckily, among them was the man who opened the bar, so we all stood and drank instead.

Collin did not mind. The previous fraught days setting up Winters' tour of the country had been so exhausting that, curiously, they had killed any care he had had that any of it would work. He was just happy to see his mates from England again.

I had spent the afternoon at Harare Sports Club watching a local match, and, in a frenzy of self-publicity, had been interviewed by the ZBC radio commentator about my trip through Africa. The show nearly did not go out as a kick from the twenty-two sent the ball sailing up high above us, sitting obliviously on the stand in the sun wearing headphones, and down on to the radio transmitter unit between us. Luckily my shouted 'shit!' did not go out on air. The commentator carried on without drawing breath.

I met Paul Rendall, the ex-England prop, at that match. He was touring Zimbabwe with Bracknell Rugby Club prior to going to South Africa for the World Cup. The Judge, as he is known, was pleased to hear that his old team-mates were in town, and came to the ZRU that evening with some of his new team.

'It's like an England reunion,' smiled Collin.

It meant that the lads could get back to their standard habit of sparring and scoring points off each other. There were many points to be scored off Bede.

'You're fat,' Winters, Butch and Muppet had unanimously told Bede at the start of the trip.

'I am not,' he had countered, but to show that he could, he had gone on a diet for a bet, and was not allowed red meat or bread.

Zimbabwe is famous for its beef. Two joints of it were laid out on a table at the ZRU that evening for us to help ourselves and make into sandwiches with sticks of bread. Bede watched us eat with watering mouth before retaliating. He took the bottles of horseradish sauce and chutney and a spoon and ate all of them. 'Look at me,' he complained, slurping sauce. 'I'm down to eighteen and a half stone.'

I wanted to go to Bulawayo, the same direction as Winters and his lot, and I cadged a lift with them. The next morning we started the trip south stopping the Winters Roadshow on the way to hold a training session for the Zimbabwe national squad. The place Collin had chosen was called Gweru, an unregarded little town halfway between Harare and Bulawayo, so neutral territory for the Matabeleland and Mashonaland players. It was miserable there. 'Gweru' must be a local word for bad weather.

'What is this?' complained Winters in the drizzle.

'Fuck this,' said Muppet, holding his camera exasperatedly. 'Viewers want pictures of Africa in the sun.'

'It's always like this in Gweru,' said a Zimbabwean physio. 'Or else it's unbearably hot.'

Despite the weather, the Zimbabwean team were pleased to have a player of Winters' stature with them. The coaching, tackling practice for the forwards against team-mates holding tackle bags, went ahead with Winters calling mainly monosyllabic instructions, but he was more talkative than normal. 'That's good. That's good. Take it on low. Low. Take it on. Hit. Hit. Guys, you've got to keep talking, hey? You've got to keep talking to each other. It's still very loose. You're not the biggest forwards who have ever played rugby. It's got to be tight.'

The Zimbabweans were keen to show off and gave it their all, so much so that Butch, watching from the touchline, feared they would injure themselves. 'It's always a recipe for a fuck-up, these tackling things,' he said quietly.

They survived unscathed however, and cheered Winters on his way to Bulawayo, where we were staying the night. Bulawayo was a flat-looking town, known locally as Skies, for its enormous African skies. Life started, as far as science knows, 2,700 million years ago near Bulawayo. The oldest fossils recorded are the remains of algae found in a quarry there. I am a big fan of life.

Our digs were fixed up by Bulawayo Wendy. We were going to stay at her mother's house. Wendy's mother was a 'whenwe' – prone

to suddenly saying in exasperation, 'when we were Rhodeeeesia . . .'
There are whenwes all over this part of Africa. What Wendy failed
to warn us about were her aunties, who also lived there.

Auntie Viola was eighty years old and could be quite rowdy. Auntie
Dorothy was a slighter version of Auntie Viola and more austere, but
with a pale and daring puce rinse. They spent much of their lives
arranged on comfortable chairs around the patterned carpet of the
front room of the house in the suburbs of Bulawayo.

We sat on more chairs around the room. It was evening, and
Wendy had supplied us all with beers to drink. She was remarkable
at doing that. Butch introduced Winters to the aunties.

'Auntie Viola. AUNTIE VIOLA' – you had to shout – 'Winters
is a very famous English rugby player. He is the most-capped
forward ever.'

There was a moment's silence as this sank in.

'Does he play for Aston Villa?' quavered Auntie Viola. 'I have a
sister who lives in Birmingham.'

Butch looked stunned. Winters was not sure what he had heard,
but the words 'Aston' and 'Villa' had filtered through his much-
cauliflowered ears. Muppet and Bede rolled on their backs with
laughter.

'It's not FOOTBALL, Auntie Viola, mate, it's RUGBY,' said
Butch.

'That's men running round a field after a ball, isn't it?' she
demanded of Auntie Dorothy. 'It's all the same to me.'

'I don't think you should have any more brandy, Viola,' commented
Auntie Dorothy.

By now Winters was laughing. When that happened, his whole
inscrutable face creased into action: 'Wa-ha-a-a-a-a.'

'Good to see him laughing,' said Auntie Viola. 'He doesn't laugh
much, does he?'

Bede started playing up to the aunties. He had been a professional
wrestler in the USA before coming back to England to play rugby.
His name in the ring had been Lord Villiers, his image the kind of
toff the American public love to hate. His catchphrase chant had
been 'Ea-sy-ea-sy-ea-sy.'

In the Maasai Mara, the four of them had used the Lord Villiers tag to advantage. It started accidentally, but there were some girls from New Zealand staying there who bought it completely. 'Is he really a lord?' they asked.

Bede was happy that his wrestling had been replaced by rugby. 'They're very good athletes, those wrestlers, but to be perfectly honest, a lot of it's stage-managed and faked,' he confided.

The aunties did not hear him say this. They loved the wrestling.

'Now, Dorothy, she never misses it on the television,' said Auntie Viola. 'I sit here with my book and look up to see when it's all over.' But later: 'Ooh, I did love that Giant Haystacks,' she admitted.

Bede showed the aunties some more of his warm-up tricks, flexing muscles and looking angry. He took off his shirt for them. 'He *is* a big boy,' observed Auntie Viola. Bede sat down heavily at this. His mock surprise was slightly spoiled by the cracking noise as the back of the chair broke off.

'Never mind, never mind,' said Wendy.

Bede got out the Freddie Kruger rubber mask they had brought with them. It covered the whole of his head, and he looked more frightening and disfigured wearing it than the original character from *Nightmare on Elm Street*. He chased the terrified African staff round the house shouting: 'Here comes Freddie . . .'

What the boys did not realise is that 'mask' culture in Africa is strong. Many black Africans believe that when you don a mask you actually become that character. One evening at the Victoria Falls Hotel Bede was wearing it and stuck his tongue out at the waiter bringing his gin. The waiter, wide-eyed, dropped his tray of glasses and skidaddled. The others had to explain quietly to the head waiter that Bede had been burned badly in a fire, terrible tragedy, that sort of thing.

The mask was, as everything was to those four, the subject of spoof and fine. Any of them who wore it was allowed to assume the character of Freddie Kruger completely, but was not allowed to admit afterwards that he had been the one in the mask. He had to pretend that he had just left the room for a few moments. If he forgot, and referred to whatever Freddie had been doing, he had to down a beer. It was a drunken parody of African belief.

At one stage, Bede, Butch and Winters thought that Muppet had lost the mask in Harare. Muppet denied this strenuously. He said he had never had the mask. It would have meant a fine – a downer – if he really had lost it. The memories of the downers after losing the keys to the 4x4 were still clear in his mind. Then Butch found the mask, and agreed with Winters and Bede to hide it in Muppet's bag. Winters would demand that everyone turned out their bags to look for the mask. When it fell out of Muppet's bag, there would be fines. But before Winters could do this, Bede and Butch cunningly hid the mask in Winters' bag instead. 'It's a double-bluff,' said Butch. 'Don't tell him, mate, OK?' This behaviour was continual.

The next day we were due to go and coach schools in Bulawayo. But shortly after breakfast, Winters was trapped by Auntie Viola and Auntie Dorothy.

'Do you remember the war?' was Auntie Viola's opening gambit.

'Urh?' said Winters deafly.

'I don't think he remembers *that* war, Viola,' said Auntie Dorothy, looking Winters up and down.

'I remember the war,' said Auntie Viola. 'Ooh, they were frightening days. Birmingham was the worst hit. Birmingham and Coventry. I remember the night Coventry was burning. It was like daylight in Birmingham . . .'

Winters woke up to the conversation and sank low in his chair. The top of his sloping cranium barely touched the embroidered antimacassar draped behind him.

'My son was born during the Battle of Britain . . . We were evacuated when a time-bomb dropped in the yard of the pub fifty yards away . . . I worked in a factory . . .'

Poor Winters. He might have been unfazed and unfunked by all the capped forwards in the world, but in a room with a patterned carpet surrounded by aunties – and these aunties were the highly surrounding kind – he did not stand a chance.

'Have you been to Blackpool? I've been to Blackpool. Ooh, the illuminations were wonderful. And the big dipper. I was scared as anything when I got off that. Those men used to go up on it with you for all that lovie-dovie stuff, but I was too scared . . .' It went on and on. Nobody would rescue him.

❖   ❖   ❖

If the Zimbabwe team were happy with their training session in Gweru, the schools teams were overwhelmed in Bulawayo. The lads spent an hour with some primary-school children. 'Har, har,' cackled Bede in his Freddie Kruger voice as he went out on to the pitch. 'I'll teach 'em rugby: beer, tobacco and womanising! Har, har, har.'

The primary school was so large that Muppet was drafted in to take a group. The four coaching styles were quite different.

'Five press-ups when you catch the ball,' Winters ordered his children.

'Er, guys: aggression when you pass, OK?' suggested Butch at his.

'Left, right, left, right, left, right,' shouted Bede cheerfully. 'Old Macdonald had a farm . . .' he sang to them.

And '*Smile* when you catch the ball,' commanded Muppet. 'Look *happy*, men. *Biggest* smile in the *universe*.'

The children loved it. As far as they were concerned, Muppet was as big a rugby star as Winters. They all asked for his autograph afterwards. 'You have brought us the skills of ruggaby,' said a passing schoolmaster, grinning.

Zimbabwean English was surprising. I expected funny words and phrases from the blacks, like 'ruggaby', or, when you asked a question to which they did not know the answer, the reply: 'I am not the one.' But even the whites would say odd things. It was the South African influence creeping in. They said, 'Is it?' when you made a comment, any comment, and 'Hey' at the end of a sentence.

'How is it?' they would greet me.

'I am *fiiine*,' I would answer, recalling Cameroon. And perhaps: 'Did you know that Peter Winterbottom is in Zimbabwe?'

'Is it? He's a good player. Hey.'

'What?' I asked the first time.

'What?'

'You said, "Hey."'

'Man, everyone says "hey" at the end of the sentence.'

'Is it?' I said.

It was the lads' last day in Bulawayo, and for Wendy and Collin, the end of their part in organising the trip. We went to a bar after training. Bars in Zimbabwe are cursed by dress codes, and this one was no exception, despite its nastiness – jackets, ties and no jeans. We were the only people wearing sweaty T-shirts and shorts in a room full of suits – Bede had had a word with the management and they had quickly seen his point of view.

Collin had been suffering a hard day battling with Africanness to spread the word of rugby. 'The trouble is,' he said, 'national players here treat rugby as a hobby. There is no *need* to represent their country, unlike South Africa. I remember telling a guy he was selected to play for Mashonaland. That's half the country, the last stage before the national team. He said: "No, I'd rather go waterskiing and out on the lash with my mates."'

'He gets my vote,' said Bede. Then, on second thoughts, 'But I suppose only if that's the exception, not the rule.'

'We don't have the depth of players here,' Collin complained. 'In England there are more clubs than we've got players. If every player, from schoolboy upwards, was a club, England would still have more. Even if you're a shit selector in England, you just wait for the players. It's survival of the fittest.'

'What's going to happen to you when the game goes professional? Will you lose players to South African teams?' I asked.

'It's happening already,' replied Collin. 'A number of players have gone to South Africa. There's one lad, an Under-21, outstanding talent, who has already been approached by Natal. Professionalism will be terrible for us. And countries like Romania, who are on the verge of developing real quality, will lose out. The emerging nations will always find it difficult if they haven't got the money to sustain the game. Look what happened to football teams like Dynamo Kiev in Russia when football went professional. You never hear of them now.'

'It's going to happen, mate,' said Butch.

Winters nodded.

'Winters, I don't think you're drinking as much as the rest of us,' observed Bede suddenly.

'Urh?'

'Yes, mate, you or Muppet,' confirmed Butch.

'Fuck off,' said Muppet.

This was a cue for a reaction. Winters, unexpectedly eloquent, responded: 'OK, what about that time when Muppet went to bed, and you two went out, and I stayed drinking with the others until you came back?'

'We were out drinking,' reasoned Bede.

'What about the time you went to bed early, and me and Bede and Muppet stayed drinking?' said Butch to Winters.

'Fuck off. I did not go to bed early.'

Bede: 'You did.'

Butch: 'You did, mate.'

Winters: 'I did not. All right, how much earlier did I go to bed than you?'

Bede: 'Half an hour.'

Winters: 'And how many beers did you have in half an hour?'

Butch: 'Must have been a couple.'

Winters: 'A couple? Oh, excuse me. No, lads, you're right. I've lost, I've lost. I'm two beers behind you now. We've got two weeks left. I'll never catch up.'

But they made him down one all the same.

'Hey, Charlie,' said Bede. 'I hope you're writing all this down for your book.'

I was not sure how I could. They kept my hands full of beer bottles at all times. 'No, no.' I replied. 'Just talk closer into the flowerpot.'

Winters: 'That's typical of you, Bede: always looking for publicity.'

Bede: 'I am not.'

Butch: 'Yes you are, mate. Wherever there's limelight, you're in it.'

Bede: 'Fuck off, Butch.' He threw a playful punch at Butch at around, I guess, eighty pounds psi.

Butch did not react – it was uncool to flinch. 'No, you are.'

Then there was the cigarette game. Bede, Butch and Winters had all given up smoking for the trip. They were all gasping for a fag, but none would renege on the bet.

Butch plaintively tried to find a reason to do so. 'We are on holiday, you know.'

Wendy put a Camel cigarette in each of their mouths and I held a lighter up between them. The flame reflected off the sweat of desire on their faces.

'You go first, mate,' said Butch to Winters.

'You're team captain. You have to,' argued Bede.

Winters leaned forward on his bar stool towards the lighter. Butch and Bede leaned forward too. Then they all leaned back.

Butch, to Bede: 'You were going to do it, weren't you?'

Bede: 'Fucking wasn't.'

Butch: 'Do it again.'

Winters leaned forwards again, watching the other two closely. The end of his cigarette was almost in the flame. The others were exactly the same distance away, eyeing each other. Winters went a millimetre closer. Butch and Bede held their breath so as not to be tempted.

Then Winters straightened up suddenly and spat out the Camel to laugh. 'Wa-ha-a-a-a-a-a.'

Butch and Bede took the unlit cigarettes from their mouths reluctantly. 'You bastard,' they said.

It was time for Wendy to take Bede, Butch, Muppet and Winters to Bulawayo Railway Station to catch their overnight train to Victoria Falls. They knew they were cutting it a bit fine. We had already had three for the road. 'Just one more,' Butch kept saying.

They all squeezed into Wendy's tiny car, with her at the wheel. Like most cars in Bulawayo, it was of uncertain age and definitely doddery make. Films about the struggle in South Africa, like *Cry Freedom* and *Worlds Apart*, were always made in Bulawayo because producers knew that there they could rely on a ready supply of period cars. With a combined weight from the five of them totalling around 1,000 pounds, plus bags and cameras, the wheels were pressed hard against the arches and there was a nasty smell of burning tyres from the friction as they drove away.

They made it to the station just as the train was pulling out. Wendy, the athlete, sprinted ahead for the tickets, leaving the keys in the car – but there was no time to buy tickets.

Muppet, the keymaster, locked up and followed the rest, laden with cameras, as quickly as he could. But there was no time for tickets. Butch, Bede and Muppet dived on to the moving train.

'The keys, Muppet, give me the keys!' shouted Wendy, running alongside the train.

'The what?' called Muppet.

'Throw the keys!' yelled Wendy.

'Oh yes. The keys.' He tossed them over.

Winters was still pounding down the platform with his luggage, keeping pace with Wendy. 'You will come to Vic Falls this weekend, won't you Wendy?' he asked.

'Winters!' she screamed, 'Get on the fucking train!'

'But you will Wendy, won't you?'

'Of course I fucking will, now *on* the *train*!' She opened a door for him to leap into a carriage after his bags.

'Oh shit,' said Wendy. 'The money! Boys, the money!'

Wendy had taken all their available Zimbabwean dollars to go and buy the tickets. She had not bought the tickets and she still had the cash. Now they had nothing – not even a clue where they were going. Butch had asked Wendy several times where they were supposed to be staying.

'Victoria Falls Safari Lodge,' Wendy had said.

'Right, mate,' he had answered vaguely, and then a few minutes later: 'What did you say it was called?'

'Honestly, Butch, it's not that hard: Victoria Falls Safari Lodge.'

'Right, mate.'

She was fairly sure they would ring her up the following morning to ask again if, of course, they had not lost her telephone number.

Wendy drove back to find me and Collin in the bar. She looked drained. 'They've got no money,' she sighed. 'They don't know where they're going. God, I'm going to miss them.'

Collin nodded. He had enjoyed their stay more than anyone. He was tired of African lackadaisical attitudes in his job at the ZRU. And he was tired of having to preface even the simplest remark to his staff and players with an explanation of its meaning. He would miss them, too.

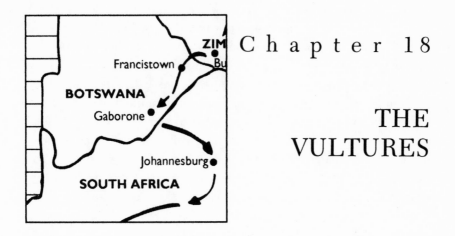

Chapter 18

THE
VULTURES

Botswana. 0 days to the World Cup opening ceremony.

'**B**otswana Rugby Union,' said Angus, doing his centre-of-attention bit, 'the Vultures, are unbeaten in international Tests.'

'Well . . .' said Marcus, like Angus a member of the Botswana team.

'Yes,' admitted Angus, 'well, we've only had one Test match in our history, against Kenya.'

'But we beat them,' added Terry, a third member of the team. 'Only now we can't afford to go on any more tours.'

'We're going to retire now,' said Angus, 'undefeated.'

We had gathered in a low white-ceilinged brick-built conference centre in Gaborone, the capital of Botswana, to watch the opening ceremony of the 1995 Rugby World Cup and the match between South Africa and Australia, the Springboks against the Wallabies.

The match was in Cape Town at the Newlands Stadium in front of 44,000 people. Our event was being run jointly by Gaborone Rugby Club and Cresta Hotels 1,000 miles to the north in front of sixty people. There were lines of tables angled towards a five-foot-square projection screen, and four smaller television screens around the room.

Everyone was infected and infested by the hope that South Africa would beat the defending champions that day. The men secured the best seats. Girlfriends grabbed the next-best seats. Their white faces were painted in the green, gold, red, blue, black and white of the new South African flag. Mothers stood at the back with children. Other children bounced on a bouncy castle outside, minded by a large but deflated Botswanan rugby player, waiting to be relieved by a mother. There were five black waiters and one white one who was painted in the colours of the flag as well, and when the lights went out for the screening he gave up his job to sit down and watch.

Gaborone, known as Gabs, is a low blue-skied brick-built city in a country with barely enough population to sustain a small market-town economy. But per capita it is the most prosperous country in Africa. Botswana sits snugly between Zimbabwe to the east, Namibia to the west and South Africa to the south. It is a beautiful country. It ranked for me alongside Kenya and Ethiopia as the top country I visited in Africa. Johannesburg is four hours' drive away from Gabs. We watched the match on South African TV.

The lights went off and the televisions went on. The beers were lined up and the heads turned round to the screens. The commentators started rattling off player statistics. Séamus O'Neill, the fifth man on our table and older than the rest of us, was shocked. 'When I was playing rugby, my optimum weight as a flanker was the same as Fergus Slattery, seventy-eight kilos,' he said. 'Look at them. Fuck it. The flanks are all over six foot and a hundred kilos.'

Séamus used to play for Matabeleland in the 1980s. Angus Boxshall-Smith, Terry Livingstone – a great-great nephew of Dr David Livingstone, and tired of the 'I presume?' jokes – and Marcus Lubbe were wearing the Vultures' World Cup T-shirt with all the flags of the competing nations and a cartoon vulture in one corner captioned, 'Waiting in the wings'. They have played for the Vultures since the team was formed.

The Vultures' history is short. Surrounded by countries with some of the longest rugby histories in the world, somehow the game never came to Botswana. In 1975 a man named Mike Small started throwing a ball around on Wednesday evenings with a couple of mates. It was a good excuse to go boozing afterwards. But the idea caught on, especially among the diamond and copper mines who had the resources to build facilities, and in some of the remote Afrikaner farming communities. Gradually more and more clubs, or 'groups' as Smally calls them, appeared. There was never a year when all these clubs managed to find enough players: Botswana is just under half the area of South Africa, but has less than five per cent of the population. Gabs RC is still the only club to have two sides. It has been an exclusively expatriate sport.

The game also suffered from the great distances involved in crossing the country to play matches. Maun RC in the Okavango Delta, 400 miles from Gaborone across the Kalahari Desert, still fulfils its fixtures. They think nothing of an 800-mile round trip to play a match.

The most convenient clubs for Gabs RC to play were in South Africa, but the years of sanctions against their next-door neighbour made that a touchy subject. 'I don't know how you're going to word this,' Smally said to me. 'I assume you know about the politics here. But we used to pack our kit and go to South Africa shopping with the wives. We played when we got there because we just happened to have our kit.'

The national squad, the Vultures, is drawn mainly from Gabs RC for convenience. Smally was stunned when they beat Kenya. He was manager of that tour. He is now president of the Gaborone Rugby Union. 'Kenya made the mistake of underestimating us,' he said. 'They were 20–18 ahead and we scored with our final kick. They threw the ball around – lovely rugby – and it certainly lifted our game. But we won in the dying seconds.'

In the opening match of the Rugby World Cup, another national team made the mistake of underestimating the opposition. But before the whistle was blown for the kick-off, there was the showtime television paraphernalia of an emerging nation showing off to be watched.

There were examples of South African culture to warm up the opening ceremony in Cape Town. Some people said that there was no such thing as South African culture. Others, later, said that you had to have been there. On television it looked sugary and laughable. Zulus danced on the turf at Newlands in the manner of a New Zealand *haka*. Black people in wellies, vests and hard hats did the gumboot dance. 'It's amazing to watch,' said Angus. 'Amazing' was not the word which sprang to mind. Next on the programme was a gang of vaudeville boppers which conjured up the worst excesses of the *Black and White Minstrel Show*. To end it up, representatives of the national teams competing marched into the stadium and there was a walkpast of totty from around the world. A rugby ball was passed down the line of all the players, becoming heavier and heavier with symbolism, until it reached a small black boy at the end of the line. Gabs Rugby Club players – big, sensible men in normal life – were lapping it up.

'That's the future of South African rugby,' said Marcus gumptiously.

The little boy carried the ball to a podium, where stood an Old Fart from the World Cup organising committee, a white, next to Nelson Mandela, now an honorary Old Fart, we guess, as that floozy belted out the rocked-up version of 'I Vow To Thee My Country' on the Newlands tannoy. In the background, behind the podium, stood what looked like South African presidential secret agents, all wearing sunglasses and white Rugby World Cup T-shirts. Someone had obviously told them to mingle.

Nelson made his speech welcoming the world to his 'rainbow nation'. Gaborone was too close to the white, conservative, Afrikaner areas of the northern Transvaal to shed many tears of emotion, but nobody applauded the voice from the back which shouted, 'That bloke's a nutter.'

Those 1,000 miles north, and in front of the screen, the black manager of the Cresta President Hotel stood up and made a short speech thanking the sponsors. Gabs RC were not impressed. The manager started to tail off. Gabs RC started to heckle. The manager stuttered his gratitude nervously and left, luckily before the toss. They wanted blood in Gabs – anybody's. They watched to see who had won the toss. South Africa.

'Yis!' said the crowd.

'South Africa have already won the toss. They've already won the cup,' shouted Angus.

They played the national anthems and the camera panned from face to face of the two teams lined up in Cape Town, each man showing fear or pride as he sang, or standing silently with silent tears, and in Gaborone the bloody yells of Gabs RC as they shouted the names of the players and encouragement. This was the start of a war.

The noise died down for the action, and the eyes of the audience stuck hard to the screen. Then they shouted support as if they were there. They leaned forward and poured their collective will into the screen.

Three minutes into the match and Australia's captain and kicker, Michael Lynagh, put the Wallabies 3–0 up with a penalty. Three voices in a room of sixty were shouting for Australia.

A few seconds later, South Africa got a penalty for offside. Gabs RC erupted. 'Raaaaaaa. Send him off!' Joel Stransky took it and it went over. 'Raaaaaaa!' It was now 3–3.

But Lynagh came back. He had another kick in front of South Africa's posts. The lined-up Springbok faces looked tired already, maybe even defeated. 'He won't have many easier kicks than this,' said the commentator. But he missed. 'Raaaaaaa!' went the crowd. 'Well, I'd almost put his name down on the scorecard,' commented the commentator.

Lynagh had his chance again. With his third kick, and with 'no concern for the distance', according to the commentator, he did it. 6–3.

'Yes pleeeeeaaase!' said a lone Australian voice.

'Hey, man – the door's over there,' replied Terry.

The crowd went a shade more quiet until Stransky levelled it to 6–6 with a second kick, then it was group singing of 'Shosholoza', an old Zulu song currently favourite to be the new South African national anthem. It sounds like a version of the 'Bread of Heaven' chorus where the singers can only remember the first line. One of the babies at the back of the room started crying, but it could only just be heard over the whistles and shouts.

Play on the screen started to hot up. All the nerves of the first minutes had evaporated and South Africa began to think they might have a chance. So did Gabs RC. The room was thick with tension and beer. The waiter with the painted face was chain-smoking. Eyes glued to the screen, he stubbed out his latest cigarette on the table, missing the ashtray by several inches.

'We're going to score now, I'm telling you,' predicted Angus.

It was so close. Joost van der Westhuizen had the ball, had the gap, heard the whistle for a penalty against Australia.

'*Advantage!*' implored Gabs RC.

'Advantage, for f ... ADVANTAGE!' added Angus. Then, privately, to us: 'He's so slippery, that Joost van der Westhuizen. Always finds the gap.'

But Stransky had no problem with the kick. It was 9–6 to South Africa. This got the Wallabies' collective goat, or whatever marsupial passes for goat in Australia, and the pressure came back on to the Springboks, and hard. Gabs RC went quiet.

The commentary switched to Afrikaans, and the match was now between Orstrarlia and die Bokke. The Afrikaans and English commentators split each half into two to get both the old official languages in. Since the elections and Mandela's rise to presidency, South Africa now had eleven official languages which, we pondered, might make commentary a little too complicated. Later on in the tournament the halves were split into thirds to get Xhosa in as well.

Orstrarlia scored a try through Michael Lynagh – or, in Afrikaans, 'Michael Lynaaaaaagh.' He had 16 tries in 70 internationals, said the screen. Mutter, mutter, mutter, said Gabs RC.

'He's the top points-scorer in the World Cup so far,' observed Terry. Lynagh converted his try. It was 13–9 to Orstrarlia. Mutter, mutter, mutter, mutter. Even the three Wallabies supporters did not say much.

From the restart die Bokke came straight back to Orstrarlia's line. Up went Gabs RC. The ball was kicked away from behind the line.

'I don't believe that,' said Angus.

But Pieter Hendriks had it, and with a triumphant fist gesture brought it sailing down the left to score for the home team. Gabs RC went wild. Stransky did not convert the try, but the score now stood 14–13 to South Africa. Arms went up, blocking the projector; they danced. 'And that's Hendriks, our second-stringer. Hey!' shouted Terry, delighted. The whistle went for the end of the first half.

After a pause in which Gabs RC removed to the bar and reremoved back again, the whistle went for the start of the second half. South

Africa came back to lengthen their lead to 17–13 with a penalty kick
from Stransky. There was a big cheer from Gabs RC, but it happened
so quickly that most people were still at the bar. They swarmed back
to their seats, singing, 'Here we go, here we go, here we go,' and
breaking once more into 'Shosholoza'.

'We're going to win this game,' said Angus with belief.

'There are only four points in it,' said the commentator, back in
English again.

South Africa had found their proper form. The players piled on
the pressure. The ball began a long period of kicks backwards and
forwards along the Newlands Stadium. Gabs RC settled into a sweaty
round of edge-of-seat cheering. And it happened again. We rose an
inch from our seats as the Springboks set it up.

'They're going to score now. Watch,' said Angus. Louder: 'Stransky
with the drop.' He stood up. 'Drop-goal!' It went over. 'I *told you*, I
told you!' He danced. Gabs RC stood around blocking the screens
again. The score was 20–13. As we subsided, Angus claimed a little
glory for Botswana. 'I played with one or two of these guys in the
Under-20s,' he said. 'They've come on. I can't believe it. What
happened to me? Ha, ha.'

'Well, South Africa has really come up trumps with just – er –
twenty minutes left of the match,' said the commentator.

Scrum.

'They're going to score now; there's going to be a try now,'
said Angus.

The scrum turns into a free kick. The Springbok forwards push
it – push it – heads down. They push it over.

'It's a try! It's a try!'

No.

'Get a LIFE, REF!' bawled Terry.

Down behind Australia's dead-ball line – 'Yeeeees' – and a five-yard
scrum on the right.

'They're going to score,' came back Angus's refrain.

It goes to a line-out on the left, and Australia return to the game.
'Line-outs won,' says the screen, 'Australia 13, South Africa 6.' As the
Afrikaans commentary cuts in again, Australia start their big push.
This is Gallipoli, South Africa the Turks, and forget the coach, the

manager, the Old Farts – we are the generals. We cut them down again and again, in support in Gaborone, in action in Cape Town. We push them back to their own lines. And from a five-metre scrum, Stransky scores a try. Gabs RC goes mad.

'SCOOOOOOORE! YEEEEEEEEES!'

'Joel Stransky:' says the screen, '5 tries from 8 internationals.'

And he converts it. South Africa 27, Australia 13. They pogo in Gaborone. Glasses splinter. Beer stains the grey carpet. Rounds of the local vodka cocktail, Sneaky Puff-Adder, come to the table half empty from jubilation.

'BRRRRRRRRRAAAAAAAAAA!' Terry yells. His great-great uncle would have been perplexed.

Ten minutes left.

'Bye bye happiness,' sings a painted face.

At last Australia do score another try, but it is only a battle, not the war. There is some clapping from Gabs RC.

'The game'll be over after this,' says a girlfriend as Lynagh lines up his kick. He misses.

'He's missed! He's missed!' from the painted faces.

South Africa 27, Australia 18. '39th minute in the second half,' says the screen.

'I wouldn't worry, the game's as good as over,' says Angus.

The TV clock starts counting down the seconds. There are shots of the crowd. Gabs RC start chanting. South Africa 27, Australia 18. Minutes remaining: 0.

The whistle goes – 'EEEEEEEEAAAAASY!' – and Gabs RC are everywhere. Someone trips over the projection wire. 'Just plug it in,' says a voice in the dark, but who wants to listen to stuffy post-mortems? They dance to the bar, and they dance to the gents. There is mayhem. Painted faces are peeing in the basins.

'Man, I bet you've got a hard-on now,' says one PF to another.

'Eeeeeeeeaaaaasy,' he replies.

'They were so psyched up,' shouts Séamus. 'Anything that's got orange, you fucking flatten it.'

'Did I have any doubt?' asks Angus rhetorically. 'From five minutes out,' he adds, 'did I have any doubt?'

The painted faces make up a song:

It's so EASY
Against CamPESE.
You can suck my COCK
You'll never be a BOK.

The lights come on, and the children bring everyone back to earth.

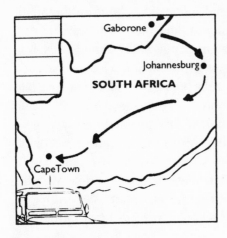

C h a p t e r   19

THE
CRUNCHIES

South Africa. The World Cup.

A few miles away from Gaborone, I finally crossed the border into South Africa, the last of the eighteen African countries whose stamps filled my passport. The sense of euphoria was difficult to describe. It was almost over. The World Cup was within my grasp. The end was in sight. After eight months on the road, I could almost go home.

South Africa is a big country by African standards, and a prosperous one even by European standards. It has deserty scrubland, hot wet forests and even mountains and ski resorts. It has its African poverty, its townships, its mud huts in the country, but it has a truly first-world feel. It is so advanced that even the whites commit crimes. They do not do that in Zimbabwe, beyond the odd innocent murder. There was outrage in Zimbabwe when a white was caught running stolen cars over the border into Zambia. Whites simply did not do that sort of thing.

South Africa is an uneasy mixture of Dutch and English. The Boer War is not over, though it has been superseded by the apartheid war between blacks and whites. The Dutch, or Afrikaners, arrived in Cape Town 400 years ago. The English have pushed them further north since then, as they found more and more riches beneath the South African soil, first gold, then diamonds, and then platinum.

Even though the blacks are now in charge under President Nelson Mandela, rugby is still king. Rugby is the binding element between Dutch and English, and is becoming the binding element between white and black. The Rugby World Cup was to do more good for black–white unity than any single event in South Africa's troubled history.

The first recorded rugby match in Africa was in Cape Town on 23 August 1862. It was the Army versus the Civil Service, and one of the civilian players was John X. Merriman, the future Prime Minister of the Cape. The preview in the *Cape Argus* read: 'We are happy to find that this fine old English school game has been introduced among us.'

Sportingly enough, the game was called off due to high winds. The *Cape Argus* reported: 'At 4.45 the wind changed, setting in right on to the civilians' goal, and their generous antagonists, who only seek a fair victory, deferred the game until a future day.'

The first recorded club, Hamilton Football Club, was founded in 1875. The Hamilton–Sea Point Rugby Football Club still exists. Clubs in those days used to play matches mostly between their own teams: Colonial v Home-Born; Married v Single; even Handsome v Ugly. The first rugby union, the Western Province Rugby Union, was set up in Cape Town in 1883.

The British brought with them a trophy, presented by Donald Currie, a Scotsman who ran a London-to-Cape Town steamship company, the Castle Packet Company. The cup was donated to be kept by the best of the South African sides. The Currie Cup has been the most hotly contested prize among clubs in the country since. The competition is now sponsored by Bankfin.

South African rugby developed throughout this century, especially under the guiding hand of Dr Danie Craven, the father of the game in South Africa. He is dead now, and his shoes have been filled by Morné du Plessis, the Springboks' manager, and the most influential man in South African rugby circles at the time of the World Cup. Despite the sanctions which meant the Springboks could not play international matches, the team claimed to be the best in the world, a boast it proved in 1995. You do not need the suspense. I expect you remember it; if not, I can tell you now: the Springboks won the World Cup. You will find out in the following pages how it happened.

South Africa was also the country where I first saw third-world whites. One of the reasons that the black people in this book may come across as unreliable and stupid and the whites as broadly brave, noble, super etc. is that they are split into first- and third-world people: the whites are first-world, the blacks are third-world. There were exceptions. Gervais Coffie in the Ivory Coast was an example of a first-world black.

In South Africa there are whites who have never seen a lightbulb. They still believe in slavery, and the right to shoot on sight. The first-world whites mock them more mercilessly than they mock the blacks. They call them crunchies, Dutchmen, wingnuts (because they behave like Frankenstein's monster with the wingnuts on his neck) clutchplates, rocks or rock-spiders and rope (because they are thick, coarse and hairy). The worst a first-world white will say and actually mean about a black is, 'Hey, you can take a blick out of the bush, but you can't take the bush out of the blick.' This is a day-to-day observation. Of course, a white in a rich suburb of Johannesburg who has just been burgled and strongly suspects the blacks from a nearby shanty-town will say a lot of worse things about his neighbours.

In one sense, the further south you go in Africa, the more liberal people become. Big Tom in Kenya said he found it amazing that there were whites working in the Wimpy burger bars in Zimbabwe. Auntie Dorothy in Zimbabwe said that some people in South Africa had white domestic staff. At South Africa itself you run out of land, so there is no way of knowing what the Afrikaners suspect of the people who might have lived to their south.

Dowson, the white tea planter in Kenya, was in the Kenya army at the end of the 1960s. He had a bolshy black sergeant under his command, a man chippy about white power in Kenya. This sergeant went on a six-week course in England and came back a changed man – much friendlier to Dowson. 'Sir,' he said to Dowson, 'you never told me that whites drove the buses in England.'

Less liberally, perhaps, Danie Craven once said that if a black wanted to wear a Springbok jersey, he would have to step over his dead body first. But immortality is a great charlady, and that remark has been neatly swept away.

South Africa is a rainbow nation. There are those who speak Afrikaans and those who speak English, those who speak Zulu and those who speak Xhosa, and there are many more languages besides. Because I was white, most South Africans expected me to speak Dutch as my first language. Luckily, most of them spoke English. There are dozens of races in South Africa, but the main four are black, white, Indian and coloured. The first three are easily defined. Coloured is a mixture of white and black, mulatto they call it in Latin America. The big coloured population is in Cape Town in the south. They have strong Afrikans accents and often a curious squawking way of talking.

I hitched a ride from the Bostwana border to a stubbornly Afrikaner town in the north of the country. I wanted to catch up with the Ivory Coast team, who were playing in Rustenburg, an unashamedly crunchie place.

There was an irony here. Rustenburg had been chosen to host the team which won the Africa Group qualifying matches in Casablanca. For the pool matches of the World Cup finals, half the national teams were based in one town and the other half travelled around to play them (England were based in Durban, for example). Of course, the winner of the Africa Group matches should have been either Namibia or Zimbabwe, which were both predominantly white teams. There was even a rumour that someone in Casablanca had been blasé enough to fax Rustenburg to say that Namibia had won. But they had not won. Ivory Coast had. Rustenburg was now hosting the only all black national team in the competition.

Rustenburg sits on a flat brown pan ringed by the limestone cliffs of the Magaliesburg mountain range. It was founded by the *voortrekkers* as a place of rest, safe from attacks by the natives. The first South African President, Paul Kruger, retired there. He is commemorated all over the town. There are even Oom Paul (Uncle Paul) schools in Rustenburg. But there was platinum in them there hills, which, when it was discovered in 1925, led to a new burst of prosperity for the town.

Its isolationist spirit was still going strong. The man who drove me in his *bakkie*, South African for pick-up truck, to the platinum mines singles quarters where I was staying was appalled by the number of blacks lolling around on the pavement. 'Look at the kaffirs,' he said on the way. 'They're everywhere on the streets. You don't see whites walking round like this.'

He was steamed up, so I did not want to venture that that was perhaps because the blacks could not afford cars.

'And what can we do? Hey. Nothing,' he went on. 'We have a kaffir President. Did you know that?'

I told him that the news had filtered out.

I met the Ivory Coast team and the French who ran them in their hotel, just out of town. They were all there – Cassagnet, Davanier, Jean-Michel, and the rest of the Gaulish village in Abidjan. They had the air of racehorse-owners out to see how their beast will run. Even Gervais Coffie was there, looking a little less grand than he did on his own stamping ground in Ivory Coast.

There was gossip to catch up on: Bernard had had a heart attack. Poor Bernard. But his restaurant was fine. Thierry was well. Oh, and Roland? Well – shrug – Roland was, er, still Roland.

The team members themselves were enjoying staying in such a smart hotel. Its manager, Andrew, talked about the ups and downs of having them there. 'They wanted a private block to themselves,' he said. 'They wanted to eat together, and to have a room for team talks and to watch the other matches. We gave them that. Their diet was funny, though. Their doctor and manager worked out a special diet for them, but they didn't like it. They were used to eating rice. The captain, Athanase Dali, came to me and asked whether he have rice. I said, "How much?" He said, "One kilo per player per meal."' Andrew laughed. 'We were getting through nearly three hundredweight of rice a day for them.'

After my experience with the crunchie, I asked the French how they were getting on with the indigenous Rustenburgians. Coffie came up with the official comment. 'We have met only kindness from the people of Rustenburg,' he said.

But Jean-Michel reported some difficulties. He went into a bar one evening with another of his French friends and one of the

Ivorians in the team. The Afrikaners there asked him to get out. 'There were three of us and twenty-five of them so we did not want trouble. We left,' he said. 'I don't understand the apartheid here,' he added. 'We have an economic apartheid in Ivory Coast. You go into a restaurant and there are mostly Europeans in there, but that is because the Ivorians cannot afford it. When they do come, we welcome them. I have many friends among the Ivorians, most of them more intelligent than me.' He put on a stupid face.

The Elephants had only one more match to play in the pool stage when I arrived. They had been crushed by Scotland in their first game. The tartan army beat them 89–0 and Scotland captain Gavin Hastings broke World Cup records with his forty-four-point individual score.

'We took a cold shower with Scotland,' admitted Coffie with a grin. 'We are more confident after playing France.' Ivory Coast had at least scored some points in that match. But things were not looking good. Their last opponents in Pool D were Tonga. At the end of the training session the day before the Tonga game, a prop said wearily, 'That's the last training of this World Cup.'

'No,' responded Davanier, ebullient as ever. 'We can win, and Scotland might fail a dope test and be disqualified. That will put us through.'

The day of the big match dawned. The people of Rustenburg took their seats in the stadium. Every town worth its salt – or its gold, diamonds or platinum – in South Africa has its own rugby stadium. The country is rugby mad. The blacks sat on one side of the stadium and the whites on the other. A few braver or more liberated members of each race were scattered around each other's sides, standing out like blue-clothed Chelsea football supporters in the middle of a Millwall crowd. A private security firm in paramilitary uniforms and armed with machine-guns filed out and took their places around the pitch.

The Ivory Coast team looked gleaming as they came out. Sponsorship of the Elephants' kit – boots, tracksuits, rugby shirts and shorts – cost US$40,000, as much money as most Ivorians would hope to see in a lifetime. The sponsor's representative, Philippe from Paris, said it was worth it just for the television coverage.

First of all there was tragedy to report. Athanase Dali's brother, himself a rugby player, had died of an illness the night before in Abidjan. A staccato Afrikaner voice on the crackly tannoy ordered the crowd to observe a minute's silence. The minute lasted almost fifteen seconds; the whites in charge were keen to get on with the match.

The next announcement was to beg silence for the national anthems. This really did mean a minute's silence, if not two, as the teams stood, right arms across their chests in salute, and the stadium technicians searched vainly for whichever unplugged electrical lead meant that the Ivory Coast anthem could not be heard. We caught the dying seconds of the music before the tape launched directly into the Tongan anthem.

If the Ivory Coast team call themselves Elephants, it was the Tongan team who were the real jumbos in this match. They were big. They gave the Elephants their intimidating *haka*. It looked like it would be bloody; we just did not know quite how bloody.

In South African terms, the Tongans were all coloureds. Coloureds versus blacks: a superb irony for Rustenburg. Danie Craven would be turning in his grave. 'Op die Vrei Stat,' shouted an Afrikaner supporter from the stands, looking at all the dark faces on the field. 'Up the Free State'.

Poor Ivory Coast did not have a chance. The Tongans hammered them. Every five or ten minutes Ivory Coast players were stretchered off. And sadly Max Brito broke his neck, an injury that would leave him paralysed for life. The helicopter took him to hospital in Pretoria. It was a travesty. It was a non-match, like the butchery in a bad bullfight.

After the game Cassagnet was fuming. 'Our problem?' he demanded. 'The physique of the players. Their fitness. It was a scandal. We will start again for the next World Cup and with the juniors.'

Everyone in the hotel was saddened, and there was most despondency about Brito's injury. 'In a group of forty people like the Ivory Coast team, there are always six or seven who stand out,' said Andrew the hotel manager. 'Max was one of them. Everyone is very depressed.' For a moment, rugby kicked out his usual professionalism. 'It was the referee's fault, Max's injury,' he said grimly. 'I saw the referee afterwards in the president's box, and I went up to him and I said, "What nationality are you?" and he said, "American." I said, "Do you believe in free speech?" He said, yes, and I said, "Well, you're a fucking wanker.'"

The result of that weekend's rugby was that the following weekend Ireland would face France, Scotland would be pitted against the All Blacks, and England had to contend with Australia. All in all, it did not look like being a good weekend for the British Isles.

I decided to go to Cape Town to watch the England–Australia match. On the way I went through Johannesburg. Jo'burg is ugly. It ranks somewhere between Nairobi and Lagos for unpleasantness. It was built on gold-rush fever and has the shallow transience of that Klondike-type spirit stamped on its heart. The great yellow slagheaps of spoil from the mines rise round the city like the mounds on graves. The mines of the Jo'burg area, the Witwatersrand, go as deep as two kilometres beneath the surface of the earth. There was gold in these spoilheaps, and new processes to extract it, and they were slowly being razed to the ground. It smacked of grave-robbery.

People carried guns everywhere, both the good guys and the bad guys. You can be robbed in Jo'burg in one of two ways. Either they take your stuff or they kill you and take your stuff. I was lucky. In my first two hours in the town I was robbed twice in the first way.

I was on a bus on a ten-minute journey out of town. Knowing Jo'burg's reputation, I was clutching my bag to my chest. Stupidly, I was clutching it zip outwards. The clever man beside me unzipped it without my noticing, removed my binoculars, and zipped it up again. As I got off the bus, someone whipped the watch off my wrist, the one I bought to replace the previous one, stolen in Nairobi. Again I did not notice, but looking at where it should have been immediately afterwards I saw it was not there. Amid the irritation, I felt a certain regard for the skill of whoever had done it. When I discovered that the binoculars had gone I felt no regard at all.

I went to stay in a suburb of Johannesburg with a couple I had met in Gaborone. Dave and Karin lived in an area of wall-to-wall horse studs, livery stables and farms. Karin was a top horse-trials rider, and in demand all over the country to give lessons. She was one of those fiery blonde horsey ladies who used to terrify me in the Pony Club. I had a few days there before leaving for Cape Town. Karin kindly let me go out to exercise one of her beasts.

She put me on one of her top event horses. I garnered everything I could remember from my Pony Club D-test, which I had passed mainly, I believe, because the person testing me was a friend of my mother's.

There is such a lot of leather involved with horses. I was still convinced that the bridle was upside-down when Karin told me to mount. Perhaps she was being tactful in not telling me. No, she told me I was trying to get on the wrong side of the horse. I must have been lucky with the bridle.

This horse had nous. It also had muscle. I reckoned I would have a few minutes' grace to assert myself with it before it realised I was not a top rider. It must have been used to being given good riders, people with a good seat who do the right things with their hands, and I guessed it would assume I would be one of those. In the event, it worked out how bad I was in only a few seconds.

We went out into the dry grassland country around Karin's house. All the tracks there had horsy names, like Bit Road and Bridle Avenue.

'Trot on,' called out Karin imperiously.

Right. Er. Shorten the reins. Squeeze with the knees. Apply gentle pressure with the heels.

Vrooom. The horse went off like the bolt from a crossbow.

'He used to be a racehorse, you know,' shouted Karin as I roared past her.

'Terrific,' I muttered.

By now, the horse knew that he had me. I was putty. I would agree to anything.

'Hoi. Slow down,' shouted Karin from the distance behind me.

Where are the brakes on this thing? Ah yes, I remembered, pull to stop. I hauled on the reins. He went faster, and broke into a canter. I hauled again. He started galloping.

Karin came galloping up beside me. 'The thing is,' she said between strides, 'being an ex-race horse, if you pull on the reins you move your body forward and he goes faster.'

That is bloody marvellous, I thought. He goes fast when you

squeeze with the legs and even faster when you haul him in. What makes him stop? The whip?

Somehow, perhaps because Karin was alongside me, I talked him into slowing down. I think Karin generously put the incident down to rustiness. I obviously had not been on a horse for months. I should have corrected her. Years, actually. Round 1 to the horse.

Next round, seconds out, ding-ding. He was so revved up by his cavalry charge that he would not simmer down to a walk. He managed to affect a kind of trot-on-the-spot style. This jogging did not allow for a classic rising trot motion from his rider, the one action I remember being praised for in my D-test and being reasonably confident I could carry off again. I sat glued to the saddle as he did his pneumatic drill act.

Karin started to become properly concerned about my ability. 'Charlie, are you sure you are all right on him?' she asked.

'Oh. Yes. Kar. In. Don't. Wor. Ry. Ab. Out. Me.'

'Wouldn't you prefer to swap with me? This mare is a lot quieter.'

'No. No. Ab. So. Lute. Ly. Fine. Kar. In. Thanks. Ve. Ry. Much.'

She gave it a moment's thought.

'I really think you ought to, you know.'

'Well. Ac. Tu. Al. Ly. Per. Haps. You're. Right. He. Does. Seem. A. Lit. Tle. Spright. Ly.'

And to the general relief of both horses and both riders, we swapped. I did not go riding again with Karin.

I took the overnight train from Jo'burg to Cape Town. It crossed the Orange River just before Kimberley, the diamond-mining centre, and went on through Bloemfontein, the capital of the white homeland, the Orange Free State. As the sun rose the next morning, the countryside started to change from dusty scrub to mountain valleys with snow-capped peaks above and vineyards below. We were in Cape Province. We came in at last to beautiful Cape Town, the last city in my long journey from London.

The next day I set off for the England-Australia match at Cape Town's Newlands Stadium. I boarded a big red London bus that someone had hired for a party of England supporters. We were on a beer mission. The bus was stuffed with iceboxes full of cans of lager. I climbed the stairs up to the top deck.

Upstairs, wearing an England rugby shirt and a plastic policeman's helmet, sat George. He had arrived in Cape Town two days before.

'Ah,' we both said.

'Charlie,' said George.

'George,' I said.

If not quite lines to rank with 'Dr Livingstone, I presume?' it was a big moment for us nonetheless. I was pleased to see him. I had been happy to see the back of everyone in Kenya, but I had missed them badly since.

George told me his news. He had been in Durban 800 miles away watching England's success in the pool matches. He had joined up with a gang of England supporters who were also on the bus, and also wearing plastic policemen's helmets. They were already well known to television viewers at home in England as the Bobbies.

Wicky had flown back from Harare, claiming that rugby was dull and fearing that it would bring out the worst in George. Toy helmets, beer cans and a London bus through Cape Town was proof that she was right. The regiment would be devastated. Amazingly, he said, Mistress Quickly had made it too, though extremely slowly. She was in poor shape. We would have to try and sell her. This, though, was the day of the big match. There was time to ponder our Land Rover's future later.

We reached the stadium and disembarked. It was to be the match of a lifetime, we were convinced. This was where Carling's army would wipe the eye of the national team which pipped them to the last World Cup. Heavens, yes: this would be my first sight of Will Carling, the man I had come so far to see.

The stadium was filling up as we took our places in the standing-room section down by the barrier in the middle of the south side. Everyone wearing white felt the same. England were going to win this quarter-final and go on to meet New Zealand next weekend, and then South Africa or France at Ellis Park in Johannesburg. The atmosphere was buzzing.

There were players out on the pitch practising their kicks.

'Rob Andrew,' observed George, thickly from beer by now, from under his helmet.

So it was.

England coach and original Old Fart Jack Rowell stood in front of the photographers in front of us and saluted the 'Do it for the Old Farts' banner that was being waved in the crowd. There were Old Fart baseball caps for sale.

The players came out. The crowd bellowed a roar into the Cape sky. This was blood. This was it. This was England, and they were going to be victorious. They stood for the anthems. 'God save the Queen,' we bawled. This was England – Engerlaaand!

The match. And such a match. The score was needle all the way; the roar never let up. There were chants and singing. We knew we had to do it; we knew we had to keep up the noise level. At half-time we had the same sort of pep-talk about supporting as we knew the players would be having about playing. The players were still amateur for the 1995 World Cup. We were professionals. We had to do it.

The whistle went again. The play blurred backwards and forwards. Great rugby. Magnificent play. Terrifyingly close, all the way. There was nothing in it. Engerlaaand – for God and country's sake, just do it.

And then that last drop-kick in the dying seconds by Rob Andrew. For a moment the Cape went quiet as a mouse. All eyes were on the ball, sailing towards the uprights. All eyes at Newlands went back to Andrew. He knew he had done it before anyone else in the stadium, and his face said it. 'It's good!' came up in silly writing on the big screen at the end of the stadium. His arms shot up and he raced back down the pitch. The world erupted. He had put England into the semi-final.

When the final whistle went, the teams dashed for the tunnel. The crowd spilled on to the pitch. The Bobbies ran round it. George was draped in the flag of the cross of St George. We were famous. We were fantastic. We were English in truly proud English style. We were even on television for those at home to see us.

After security had removed the last hysterical Brit from the stadium, we took the bus back into town. We went to the waterfront to tour the bars and celebrate. We wanted beer and elation.

Full-back Mike Catt, lucky Catt, who had never been on a losing English side, came down the stairs to talk to supporters at one of the bars. That was when we twigged that the England team were having sit-down eats upstairs from us.

Not worthy to go to their table, the crowd gathered below their restaurant balcony. We stood in a haze of fishy smells from the colony of Cape fur seals that lounged their days away as tourist attractions for drinkers behind us, beyond a glass-and-rail fence. 'Warning,' said a sign. 'Do not touch or provoke the seals.'

'We-want-Dean-o-we-want-Dean-o-we-want-Dean-o!' we chanted, and Dean Richards appeared on the balcony to take a cheer. Other people having supper with the team came out to look at us, just like we looked at the seals, or like we looked at them. 'We-want-Vic-tor-we-want-Vic-tor-we-want-Vic-tor!' And out came Victor Ubogu for more applause. 'Who-the-fu-u-u-cking-hell-are-you?' we sang to the tune of the 'Bread of Heaven' chorus whenever someone came out whom we did not recognise. And the whole team came out. And there was Will Carling. 'We-want-Rob! We-want-Rob! We-want-Rob!' and Rob Andrew came to us, and we yahooed him into the night as we remembered that his last-minute dropped goal was our saviour. Will's comment to us was, 'Rob can walk across the harbour,' and we loved it, glasses high, and, 'Swiiing loooow, sweet chaaaariiioooot, comin'-for-to-car-ry-me-hooooome!' we sang back at them all.

We were on a pub crawl now, a crawl to celebrate victory over Australia, to triumph over the bars of Cape Town, and to conquer Africa. The big red London bus lurched out to pubs away from the city centre, down the corkscrew coast road towards Cape Point. I left the others in a pub singing another appalling chorus of 'Shoshaloza'. They still only knew the one word of it, 'Shoshaloza', which they sang over and over again. I walked away from the lights of the bar, and across a football pitch towards the sea, the Atlantic mingling with the Indian Ocean.

Bursts of Africa came into my head: the sky over Spain from the Straits of Gibraltar; George's head down and elbows up, driving through the desert; Red's face intent on coaxing a Land Rover over our makeshift bridges in Zaïre; Emma's face meeting Danny at the airport in Nairobi. I found the gap in the steel fence and trod down to the beach. A foot slipped into the foamy water – it looked like sand – and another on the slippery seaweedy rocks – it did not matter – into the sea. I dipped a hand into the lapping end of the surf, and splashed the water on to my face. Great grandfather HP would have been proud. That's it. That's it. It's done. Let's go on.

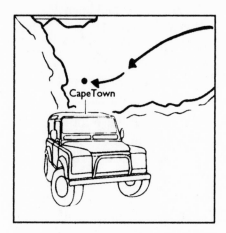

Chapter 20

DAVID

South Africa. The World Cup.

They were heady days following England's victory against Australia. We spent a lot of time watching other matches on the television, competing with the resident South Africans in our vocal support. We felt sure our two countries would clash in the final.

We watched South Africa beat France at King's Park in Durban on the television in a bar. The South Africans sang their new national anthem, 'O-LEEE, olé, olé, olé, O-LEEE, O-LEEE.'

On the England table next door we sang the French version, 'AU-LAIT, au-lait au-lait, au-lait, AU-LAIT, AU-LAIT. WITH-MILK, with-milk, with-milk, with-milk, WITH-MILK, WITH-MILK.'

The King's Park Stadium was flooded in a rainstorm before the match. 'DE-LAY, de-lay, de-lay, de-lay, DE-LAY, DE-LAY.'

Then England lost to New Zealand, though from where we were standing at Newlands Stadium it looked like England lost to Jonah Lomu. Before the match we even felt we had won in one of Newlands' underground bars, crowded and half thick with evaporating beer. We reduced New Zealand supporters there to spitting fury by doing our own *haka*, complete with hand movements. You can do it yourself, in the safety and comfort of your own home. Just look menacing and say, 'HUMP-ty-DUMP-ty-SAT-on-a-WALL. HUMP-ty-DUMP-ty-HAD-a-great-FALL. ALL-the-king's-HORS-es-and-ALL-the-king's-MEN,' etc.

Still, we lost. The Underwoods were tossed aside. The captain Carling and kicker Rob Andrew were fallen angels. Even Catt's luck was up. It was not good. We felt slightly sick. English foreign policy has always been to win. It was inexplicable to lose. There was no Dunkirk spirit about battling on in the future, because there was no future. The 1995 World Cup was over.

But nothing can stop the Englishman abroad from having fun, we decided, even in adversity. We won the pub singing afterwards. 'Win or lose we're at the booze, doodah, doodah, win or lose we're at the booze, all the doodah day. Going to drink all NIIIIGHT! Going to drink all DAAAAY. Win or lose we're at the booze, all the doodah day.'

Oh, but sod it, we had lost, hadn't we? We could not forget it. It was all over for Will Carling and his team. It was a day of sad commiseration in Cape Town.

That night, trying not to be daunted, we toured the bars in our big red bus. There seemed to be as many Union Jacks and St George's crosses on the street as New Zealand flags. You might even have been confused about who had won. The bus's token New Zealander sang his national anthem for us as we covered him with beer, but there was cheering and pats on the head when he finally finished it. We were in a mood to be sporting.

'Op die Bokke!' rang out as we left.

'Yes,' we agreed. 'Punish the All Blacks.'

George went north to Pretoria to watch England lose to France in the play-off. I stayed in Cape Town in order to put Mistress Quickly in a container back to England. We were not able to sell the old girl.

I sat in a pub, the Dunkley Inn in Dunkley Square in Cape Town, with David. David had given up his management consultancy firm in Brighton and left England on a motorbike, a Kawasaki 550, to drive to Cape Town at about the same time as us. He made it to

Cape Town on almost the very day that George and I did. We had seen a bit of him on the way south through the continent. Now the trip was finished, and I found myself reverting, quite comfortably, into the home dynamic – not moving about much, knowing where your friends and food live, that sort of thing; sitting in the Dunkley Inn with David.

We spent two weeks in that quiet pedestrianised Victorian-looking square, in or outside the Dunkley Inn. The landlord could not have been more charming. Richard was English and an old friend of David's. After a few days he gave us the keys to the pub, letting us open up in the morning, and wash up and close up at night.

David and I sat and played cribbage, and talked. We talked and talked, and we sat. Table Mountain stood tall and Gibraltarish above us. The cable car was a short walk away. David and I often thought it might be nice to go up it. Everyone said the view from the top was magnificent. But somehow we never did. We just talked.

When David left England on his motorbike, his plan had been to cross Algeria; even though he knew that the border was closed, he thought he could still get through. But he discovered they were being strict about it. That is the great advantage of the travelling dynamic: knowing where you are going next and where you can stay and find food and fuel. You find out about how closed a border really is from people on the same route, and not from misinformed newspapers and embassies. Once you know about the travelling dynamic, you do not have to worry about how unprepared you are for a trip. He changed direction and went the normal route, via Morocco into Mauritania.

He tried to catch the early-afternoon ferry from Spain to Tangiers in Morocco, but it did not exist. 'My diary starts: "What a day . . ."' he told me. 'Just before leaving was when I first started feeling apprehensive. It was quite a moving experience leaving one continent by boat for another. Even though it was only a few miles, I saw Gibraltar twinkling in the night and I felt it was a kind of surrogate home. I was starting this mission, this trek, all by myself. I felt lonely, but also excited.'

'The country you are going to is coloured by your first experiences at its border, and the two hours clearing Customs into Morocco was a pain in the butt. A guy said he'd help me fill out forms. Then he wanted paying, even though all he had done was to hand me the forms and I had filled them in. I couldn't pay him anyway – I didn't have any Moroccan money and I wasn't going to admit to any other currency I had. He wanted me to go to a bank, but luckily a customs guy told him to get lost. He still hung around a bit.'

David soon grew tired of Tangiers. 'I had problems with endless members of people trying to show me round the town and rip money off me, all that kind of crap, so I headed off to Rabat,' he said. 'After Tangiers I thought Rabat was wonderful, because you weren't hassled every time you set foot out somewhere. I arrived in Rabat – as one always does when one is looking for a visa – on a Friday. It took a week to get a Mauritanian visa in Rabat, mostly because of roadblocks and people wanting to practise their English.'

We were sitting outside the Dunkley Inn in the sun as he told me his story. Dunkley Square is a little way away from the city centre, and is not so noisy. But, like the city centre it is light, airy and old-world, and has the look of a place built for having fun in. The square made you feel slightly foolish whenever you tried to leave it, because all that you could ever want for a stationary way of life could be found within it. It was a square of terraced houses full of small business, a scattering of restaurants, residential properties, and the Dunkley Inn, dominating the middle of the top end.

The square drew you in as if it were a subtly comfortable high-powered magnet. You started to rely on the place. After a while you felt you could not leave it. It was a twenty-minute walk up the hill to where I was staying and, each evening, after a day sitting, drinking and talking to David in the Dunkley Inn, I regretted making that walk. I could happily have stayed and swapped stories with David all day and all night in the inn, occasionally ordering food and more beer from the coloured barman, whose name was Black, or if he was not around, fetching it myself and writing it down on a tab.

David told me how he met two Americans in the Moroccan capital, Rabat. Tim and Geoffrey were to play a big role in the rest of his trip. They had motorbikes. He went up to say hello to them at the campsite. Within a minute, he said, he could tell that there were stresses between Tim and Geoffrey, who were both planning to travel the same route as him. 'Tim started bitching about Geoffrey within a few minutes of Geoffrey not being there, and Geoffrey was always bitching about Tim,' he said.

They went together to the Mauritanian Embassy and after that agreed that, because they were all going the same way, they would travel together. They had a meal with a Moroccan, one Boubka, who used to stand around outside the campsite selling drugs. Geoffrey immediately wanted to make Boubka middle-class. Geoffrey was like that. He had plans to get Boubka over to the United States, where he could earn some money and then go back to Rabat and buy a boat and be middle-class. 'But it was evident that Boubka was already middle-class,' said David. 'That was typical of Geoffrey. He was very naïve. He paid any money for parts for his bike in Morocco on the basis that it was still cheaper than America.'

Geoffrey was scared of losing Tim and David to start with. Geoffrey's starter-motor would not work when they reached Marrakesh on the edge of the desert. Tim and David left him to sort it out. It had to be fixed in case he needed to kick-start the bike in the desert. He was scared of being on his own, and desperately pleased to see them again when he caught up with them in Agadir, further down the Moroccan coast.

'Agadir could be a seaside resort anywhere in the Mediterranean,' said David. 'It was very western, with pizza parlours, car-rental places and moped-hire touts. We did our first oil-change there. Tim fucked it up. He did the classic of forgetting to put the plug in, so he poured it in and it came straight out again. Tim also bought a petrol can in Agadir. This became quite a joke. It broke. He bought another one on the way to Dakhla. This one broke too. The next one broke. He didn't even need it – he had a forty-litre tank anyway.'

On the day the three of them arrived in Dakhla, the peninsula town in southern Morocco from where the army escort you to the Mauritanian border, they went from place to place to place to fill in all the forms, and finally joined the convoy. 'In the convoy there were lots of comments by the French about the unsuitability of my bike. I felt angry about that,' said David. 'One of the French in a Peugeot ended up having a leak in his radiator in the desert, and we had to help him out.'

An army Jeep led the convoy, and made the motorbikes travel at the back. This was so that if anyone broke down, a bike could go forward down the line quickly to tell the Jeep. This annoyed Tim. It meant he was among the last to pitch tent and camp that night. So David asked Tim to go forward at the end of the day and set up the tents. This left David at the back with Geoffrey. 'Geoffrey was delighted about that, to be at the back with me,' he said, 'because by that time Tim and Geoffrey were really at each other's throats. But I got rather pissed off with Geoffrey, and told him to drive on. Then, thinking I had plenty of time, I stopped with some people to admire the scenery for an hour. Around the next corner we found the whole convoy standing waiting for us.

'Next morning, after starting, I fell off, and that was when the French really laid into me. They said that I shouldn't be driving across the desert. We met an overland truck-driver who had done Scottish bike trials. He showed us how to drive in the desert on Tim's bike' – a BMW GS100 that Tim was quite precious about – 'and he took it full-throttle in a big circle over the sand, and came back and jumped the road. Tim's jaw dropped. "Oh my God, my bike," he said. After that we were the fastest bikers in the desert, much faster than the French. But just when I was getting confident, I tramlined it and dropped it.'

David's reminiscences seemed hundreds of years ago to me. I had been so much younger in Morocco. I still felt young in Cape Town – it is a city for the young – but sitting outside a bar, not moving further than into the bar, and that only once an hour, I felt like a younger version of those old and dribbling explorers who spend their twilight years occupying the big leather chairs in proud national geographical societies, recounting their exploits until they fade eventually into dimness and death. It was an old kind of youth.

I was comfortable in Cape Town. I fell squarely on my feet with accommodation there. Two resident friends, Anthony and Andrew, lent me a twenty-roomed house they had just bought. It was on the slopes of Table Mountain in Cape Town's smartest residential area, and came with a swimming pool and a large garden. I was unpaid *askari* while the friends worked on plans to turn it into a hotel.

In front of my room was the wide arc of the city and the foreshore, ending on Green Point. Behind me were the sheer sides of the mountain, covered in a tablecloth of clouds which sometimes dripped rain on to me during my sallies to Dunkley Square, forcing a retreat into the bar itself. This was winter. The weather was normally bright and clear, but it could be cold. I did not use the pool.

The day before the England–New Zealand match (oh, the disastrous England–New Zealand match), Anthony and Andrew came round to the house with three swarthy-looking people in tow, a woman and two men, all in sunglasses. I was there, preparing to wander down the hill to Dunkley Square. Nondescript lot, I thought, ignoring them. Andrew introduced them. 'This is so-and-so, this is Charlie, this is so-and-so, and this is Kiri.'

I did not take much notice. 'Kiri?' I thought vaguely. Stupid name for a woman. Sounds like a soft drink, or a Maori singer, I joked to myself.

A Maori singer.

It *was* a Maori singer.

Kiri te Kanawa was in Cape Town to sing her heart out for the All Blacks, and she was an old friend of Andrew's. Gosh. How do you treat a diva? On your knees? Act natural? Act natural, I decided. Anthony and Andrew showed her around.

'This will be your room when we open it,' said Anthony, showing her my room, which, with the battered remains of nine months of camping detritus scattered across the polished wooden floor, looked like part of the aftermath of the Bishopsgate blast.

'Great,' she enthused – she was tremendously enthusiastic. 'Where's the round jacuzzi?' and joky. She was in a bright mood that day. She had just been given the Order of New Zealand to go with her Dame award from the Queen.

I tried to sell her Mistress Quickly. She said she did not really need a Land Rover. I felt like falling down and worshipping. 'I am not worthy . . .'

Back in Mauritania, David, Tim and Geoffrey had trouble with the same checkpoint guard who had tried to confiscate Emma's camera. The guard had told David that he did not need to declare a ten-dirham note from Morocco. The guard stamped the form, but then he changed his mind. He said it was all right for David to add the ten dirhams to his currency declaration form after it had been stamped. And then he decided that it was not all right after all, and that David had committed a contravention.

They argued about it. David said the note was a souvenir. The guard said that that was not good enough. David screwed the note up and threw it out of the hut into the desert. The guard threatened David with five years in prison and a beating. David told him to fuck off.

Geoffrey came into the hut. David and Tim had warned Geoffrey not to come in, to leave the talking to them, because Geoffrey had changed money on the black market. Geoffrey, of course, was caught, and fined heavily, which took the heat off David. Geoffrey was fined even more heavily for carrying a knife. Tim and David agreed that Geoffrey was a fool.

There were a number of overland trucks in the convoy. They were in trouble with the guard for not having individual insurance policies for each person they carried. They sat down and made tea for several hours, hoping the guard would crack. The guard, unfortunately, was adamant. I remembered him being adamant with Emma. Finally, the truck-drivers lined up all their women passengers and said to the guard, 'Choose whichever one you want.' Being a good Muslim – or despite being a good Muslim – the guard was shocked at this. And his embarrassment turned into good humour in that especially whimsical Mauritanian way, and he let everyone go.

That night in the Mauritanian desert, the convoy found a spring with sweet water. Everyone in the convoy took turns to shower. 'It really struck me, the difference between the Anglo-Saxons and the Mediterraneans in the convoy,' said David. 'The Mediterraneans were showering mixed and naked. The English truckies showered women first, men second, and all wearing their knickers. I wondered how long that would last.'

On the big drive south down the coast to the Mauritanian capital, Nouakchott, Geoffrey and Tim fell out properly. Geoffrey was worried about driving in the desert. He was older than Tim, and had had bad bike accidents in the past. In the sand, if your bike starts fishtailing, you power on to get out of it, but Geoffrey was too nervous to do this, so fell over more often. They fought over this.

The three of them got dehydrated on the bikes, which sapped morale as well. It is not like being in the cab of a lorry or a Land Rover, where you can take a swig of water. David found himself drinking five litres of water whenever he stopped. He started to let other people ride his bike when they wanted to so that he could ride in a truck and drink. As soon as he cottoned on to David's idea, Geoffrey hardly used his bike again. Tim would never let anyone ride his bike. They fought over that, too.

Geoffrey's bike started to have mechanical problems. He was, typically, unprepared for them. He enlisted the help of the Scottish bike-trialling truck-driver to fix it. It caused arguments with Tim.

He had also failed to bring enough petrol, and tried to buy some in the village where we had got the parking ticket. And it was there that he started his old trick of engaging people in conversation. Because he could not speak French, he asked David to translate. David quickly grew fed up with this. 'Eventually I said, "Look, if it's just a casual conversation, learn French. Don't get me involved."'

On their arrival at Nouakchott, Tim, David and Geoffrey obtained their Zaïrean visas and planned to set off after the trucks, which were carrying some of their luggage and had departed two hours before. They had to leave at once to catch up. Geoffrey delayed them all the time. Tim got cross with him. And at that moment Geoffrey struck up one of his crass conversations with a local. It was really not the moment. Tim and David left. Geoffrey got the message, and came after them, but stopped shortly out of town with a puncture. Tim, fuming, went back and helped him. It always seemed to happen to Geoffrey.

While Tim was changing the wheel, Geoffrey said he thought he was holding up Tim and David, and that he would prefer to go back to Nouakchott. Tim came back to tell David. They knew they would not see him again. 'We both breathed a sigh of relief,' said David. 'As far as I know, he went back to America.'

It was so peaceful in Dunkley Square. The events David was telling me about did not seem important any more. It was so relaxing. It was detached from all the arguments and stresses between members of my own team of which normally David's stories would have reminded me. Dunkley Square was a limbo world between the end of England in the World Cup and the restarting of my life in the UK. At one end of the square, builders were putting up new houses. Even the motion of them placing brick on brick was soothing, especially to those who feel they have done their work, and do not need to begin again for a bit.

The landlord, Richard, would potter around or sit at the bar, or make occasional forays to buy, from outside Dunkley Square, the necessary ingredients for his big English breakfasts and toasted cheese sandwiches. Richard was young, as Cape Town demanded, but long-faced and often serious, as a senior figure in Dunkley Square should be. He had not been running the bar for many months, but was already holding dinner parties in his house for other establishment Square people. They would come to his house – a little furtively, because Dunkley Square had a mildly communist atmosphere, and elite parties did not quite fit in with it – and spend evenings being young and serious with each other.

Richard had a dog called Ella, a large black curly-furred Belgian bouvier, who would lie in the sun and fret about the few strangers who walked past, or sit inside the bar, and trip people over to provide spontaneous elements of uncertainty in Square life.

Cape Town is the economic and social powerhouse of South Africa's south coast. It is to South Africa what the Ivory Coast capital, Abidjan, is to West Africa. It was in Abidjan that David and Tim first met us.

'I was extremely pleased to meet people who were just out to enjoy themselves,' said David. 'You seemed to me to be extremely enthusiastic about your trip, but basically you were a whole load of piss-artists.'

His diary of the time reads: 'Redmond – Irish and worked for conference organisers. Charlie Jacoby – journalist and writing rugby articles without any knowledge of the game. George – ex-Blues & Royals short-service commission officer. Emma – photographer from Donegal. And another girl – George's quiet girlfriend. They were on their way to South Africa for the Rugby World Cup. They seemed the intellectual types with higher opinions of themselves than they merit. Bags of ex-public school confidence. I like them because they are enjoying themselves.'

In the next country, Ghana, his diary reads: 'Met Emma in the Land Rover outside the Togo Embassy. Tim seems very interested in travelling with them. I think Tim is after Emma. Back to the campsite and Charlie forges a couple of laisser-passer documents for us. Tim was still keen to chase off after the Land Rover. I didn't want to. We decided to stay another night.'

We were all stuck in Togo, next door, trying to get Nigerian visas. 'The English Land Rover was given the run-around by the Nigerians and they are here another night,' reads the diary. 'Red beats me 4 – 3 at Connect Four. I discussed Christianity and the Roman Catholic Church with Red and Emma. Emma says little, despite her need to go to Mass.'

There were surprises to Dunkley life. One afternoon, Richard made David and me do some work for the Dunkley Inn: proper work. He asked us to go round local offices and deliver leaflets advertising the pub.

This was disastrous. I realised how institutionalised I had become. I was being asked to go on a mission beyond the safety of the Square. David felt the same. We nervously took the leaflets and set forth.

We need not have worried. One of the curious aspects of Dunkley Square is its access. It is surrounded by a knot of little roads. I knew I found my way through them every morning, though on automatic pilot at that hour, and I knew I stumbled out through them after every evening. The square was even signposted from the main road. But making a conscious daytime effort to leave, we found we could not. Every road seemed to dump us back at another corner of the square. There was no logic to it. They wound and wound like loops and coils of snakes and brought you home every time. We felt no sense of panic about this, more a kind of soothed relief. It was now impossible for us to travel.

Six months before this sensation, Tim and David had been travelling hard, driving into Nigeria, home of the dreadful Mr Musa. Unlike me, they had no problem with the borders and paid no bribes, despite one officer asking, 'Have you got any presents for me?' to which they simply gave him a negative answer and drove off.

The traffic was hell in the capital, Lagos, and so was Lagos itself. They found a hotel for the night they stayed there. Tim slept on the floor because there was too much life in his bed. They left the hotel early the next morning, but not early enough to miss the traffic.

They got lost. They saw the human torso on the road that everyone saw. 'Those Nigerian drivers were mad, mad,' said David. 'They were fucking crazy.'

They passed through a drugs check. A Nigerian policeman asked them if they ever felt tired riding their bikes. They said yes, of course they did. He said, 'Do you ever take any pills to keep you going?'

'Oh, give up,' they said.

There were always bad guys in Africa. It is the continent for them. They thrive there, crying havoc at every opportunity and letting slip dogs of war, dogs quite the opposite in nature to Ella.

There was a bad guy in the square. He was fat, foreign and obscene and wore glasses. We called him Herman the German. He ran a small publishing company from one of the buildings in the square. He was working hard to produce a book, *The Story of the World Cup South Africa 1995*, within twenty-four hours of the end of the final between South Africa and New Zealand. It was to be a publicity coup when it happened. He was praying for a South African victory. It would mean victory for his book.

He had a shadow called Louisa. She played the yes-woman to his Lord Copper of the *Daily Beast*. When he came to the Dunkley Inn to be loud and rude and drunk, she smiled wanly at him in paid-for admiration. When he opined that so-and-so was stupid, or mad, or black, she nodded winsomely. Nobody really liked Herman.

'Tim always went ahead in Cameroon,' said David, 'because his was more the off-road bike, and inexplicably, despite the muddy roads, I had road tyres on. I don't know why. Terribly British, I suppose, but also fucking crippling, because for every hour he drove I drove for an hour and a half.'

They crossed Cameroon quickly in order to make it to crime city Bangui, the capital of Central African Republic, in time for Christmas. They were well ahead of us by the time they reached Bangui. We were still in Limbe on the coast of Cameroon.

'There were bits of Bangui I liked,' said David. 'The food was good, but it got extremely boring. You couldn't go out for a long walk. You might not come back.'

They spent Christmas playing cards and Boggle with each other. 'Tim lost,' said David. 'Tim always lost. Tim only started winning towards the very end of Bangassou' – the last town in Central African Republic before Zaïre – 'which was still a long way off, as it turned out, despite the fact that we only had a five-day visa for Central African Republic.'

The tarmac ended outside Bangui on the Bangassou road. But the roads were still good. They had only just been graded. 'We passed roadworks and the road got worse,' said David. 'We had been on worse, but it was shortly after this that I hit some rough ground, and, partly because I was going too fast, I slid and fell to the left.'

'The first thing I noticed when I got up was bleeding from my left hand. There wasn't much left of the glove, so I took it off, and was horrified by what I saw. All the jokes in England about open-wound fractures and needing to do my own amputations came flooding back. Instead of a complete finger, as God had made it, there was just bone sticking out of the middle joint, and a bit of fingernail still holding on on top. Blood was dripping out.'

'My first feelings were of organised panic. The first thing I did was to call out Tim's name. The calls were heard by the local village fifty yards away. I started looking for strong painkillers and antibiotics. One of the villagers helped me off with my jacket, and I tied my finger in a tourniquet with thread. The villager picked up the bike and pushed it and took me to the village, where someone took me to his grandfather's house. They gave me water, which I sterilised with purple potassium permanganate. Quite a large group came in to have a look.'

'Tim came back to look for me and was concerned to see gesticulating villagers, my bike, but no me. They brought him to me, worried. He was not keen to look at the wound. He didn't like that sort of thing. I waved the raw bone around like a tiny wand.'

'A villager recommended that I remove the signet ring from my finger in case it swelled later. I carefully pulled the ring over the bone and loose flap of skin. I whipped it over the end and plunged my hand into the purple water, which I had been putting off. I then swabbed round with antiseptic wipes. I put that experience into the "disturbing" category. It did not hurt as I expected it to, but all the people around me were visibly wincing.'

'Next course of action: I established that there was a hospital five kilometres down the road, and I dispatched Tim. I was issuing a lot of orders at this time; not aggressively, it was just the thing to do. Before Tim left he installed me on to a sleeping mat on the floor with my hand up on a chair. I popped a couple more painkillers.'

'My host insisted I could stay as long as I liked. I smoked heavily for the next few hours, and shared the cigarettes around. Tim came back in a car, having found a surgeon in a town an hour away. We went there. The driver talked all the way about the fee for the journey and whether my injury merited a discount. It was still fucking expensive.'

'At the hospital, a young black doctor beckoned me in and started examining the finger. This was the surgeon. I started to feel nauseous. He said it would be a local anaesthetic. I started to feel sicker. The injection in the base of the finger was agony. I couldn't feel a thing in the finger after that, but hearing the amputation was a different matter. He cut away the flesh and chopped the bone with a pair of secateurs. I tried not to look. He bandaged the finger and I thanked him.'

'He offered me a room, but it was not a very clean hospital, so I camped. I had an uncomfortable night, and woke the next morning, New Year's Eve, to a minor audience. What I was doing and why I was here? There was lots of Bonne Années and Do-you-have-any-cigarettes-I-can-have? I got to bed at 10pm.'

David had to convalesce in that town in Central African Republic until the surgeon took his stitches out. He had lots of visitors. One came and pinched Tim's tentpoles. Tim was furious. A tent without poles is as useless as poles without a tent. Tim could not see the logic.

The commandant of the local gendarmerie visited David. He was excited that David had been to the hospital, because his wife was there at the time expecting her fifth child. Shocked about the loss of the poles, he promised to help Tim find eggs in the local market. He came back a couple of days later with a present of five eggs and the good news that his wife had given birth to a boy.

By now David was up and about, and he went to change some money at a Lebanese man's shop. He met a local man there who was convinced that everyone in America and the UK lived like he had seen them live in *Dallas* on the television, and that they were paid to travel through Africa by their governments. He would not believe anything else.

David met the commandant again at the shop. The commandant was still upset about the poles. He said he would call his new son Robert, which was David's second name, if that was any help; he already had a son called David, he announced proudly.

We drove through the little town at this time, and hearing that there was a white man with no finger staying there we went to search him out. We were delighted to find David and Tim. David was already finding it odd having only nine digits. There are things you do without thinking – scratching behind your ear, for example – for which you suddenly have to find another finger to use. By the time he reached Cape Town, he was quite used to it.

The moment came to take the stitches out. 'It was not fun,' said David. 'Not fun. I was expecting an anaesthetic, but they said it would hurt more. After the event I believe it would have been less painful.'

David still was consciously careful of his missing finger when shuffling cards for cribbage. Heavens, we played a lot of that game. We played solidy all day and every day, with a pause one afternoon to deliver those leaflets. The scores stayed even, in a typically Dunkley way. It is a mind-numbing and purposeless game played with such frequency, but we felt an urgency, as close to any urgency anyone might feel in Dunkley Square, to fill our waking hours with cribbage. It was like marriage: something one can do to fill in time with someone when you have run out of conversation.

After the stitches were removed, David and Tim were free to go. They headed for the Baptist mission in Bangassou. David, being a sick case by now, was a hugely attractive candidate for the full weight of the Baptists' charity. During their stay there, Tim and David ate pancakes and maple syrup, cookies, beans and sausages, and a chocolate pudding topped with a sprinkling of best intentions for Tim's birthday.

'They were very generous people,' said David, 'but stuck in the 1950s. After supper with them on the first night they played a tape of a preacher talking about the Beatitudes and the mercy and righteousness of Jews at the time of Christ. I couldn't help comparing that righteousness with the self-righteousness of the Baptists. They were having problems getting the locals, not to adopt Baptist beliefs, but to relinquish local customs, like having as many wives as they liked.

'As for the main Baptist family being called the Waltons and having five sons – even though none of them were called John – I nearly gagged.'

David and Tim also met Jeff the Peace Corps worker. 'Jeff seemed confused as to why he was there,' said David. 'He was a really mixed-up character. He had to find work to do there. We met the black girl who was being pushy about their relationship, but who was sleeping with a *fonctionnaire*. He couldn't make up his mind why he was there.'

It was time to go into Zaïre. They bought petrol, changed their US dollars into local currency, and went to the police to stamp out of Central African Republic. The police did not notice that they were nearly a month over their five-day visas. You develop a cavalier attitude about niceties like visas in Africa.

They finished packing and went to the border to take the ferry across the River Ubangi. Then two customs officers caught up with them on a moped and made them go back to their office for 'processing'. This processing, it turned out, would cost so much money that it would have left nothing to pay for the ferry. It was a dilemma.

They went back to the Baptists to stay another night there. David changed the dressing on his finger and was appalled by what he found. It was not infected, but it was going black. He decided it would go bad quite quickly in Zaïre. One of the Baptists gave him sulphate powder to put on it date-stamped 1957.

They decided to abandon the Zaïre plan, so they sold their petrol back to the mission and changed their money back into dollars again.

Tim found that the mission was flying a DC3 from Bangassou to the Kenyan capital, Nairobi. The mission kindly arranged for them and their bikes to go on the aeroplane. It was not cheap, but Tim persuaded David that it was worth it. Tim was more keen to fly than David was.

They went to another Baptist service 'n' supper that night, where they made the final arrangements with their hosts, ate hamburgers and listened to another tape. 'This tape was about a woman who had a problem, and then met some Christians who solved her problem,' said David. 'It was about how you should never introduce people to Christianity heavy-handedly. They discussed it afterwards, and talked about how wonderful it was. They really are living in cloud-cuckoo land.'

When the aeroplane arrived, it was not a DC3 but a Beachcraft. It was too small to take the bikes, so they left them for a later flight. Their pilots were Don and Scott, typical American bush pilots in cowboy boots, but they got them to their first stop, Entebbe in Uganda, and then on to Nairobi.

Tim and David waited in Nairobi for a month for the bikes to turn up. 'With the benefit of hindsight, I wish we had gone through Zaïre, especially after hearing that you did it so quickly,' said David ruefully. I told him that Zaïre was still taking its toll on Mistress Quickly. Her handbrake had broken, George had gone, and I did not know how to repair it. Cape Town is a hilly city, and all approaches to junctions uphill had to be timed so that she was still rolling forward as the traffic lights turned green. Parking was also difficult. She had a tendency to jump out of her lower gears, so I could not just leave her in gear on a hill, especially the one outside my smart house, which was steep. I would drive in great circuits around the slopes of Table Mountain at constant but slow speeds trying to find flat areas to park her with a building site nearby from which to appropriate bricks to put under her wheels. And you had to be quick to appropriate them: not in case you were caught, but in case when you turned round, she had trundled off by herself to another part of Cape Town.

She looked a mess by now. South Africans are keen on outward appearance, and Mistress Quickly did not have one. George and I had placed an advertisement in the the local newspaper to try to sell her, but people who came round to look tended to drive straight past when they saw her. They wanted flash appeal. A straight English 'Honest, guv, a lick of paint would see her right' did not wash with them.

'Nairobi was a shit-hole,' said David, continuing his story. 'It was nice to be there initially, because it was civilisation, but after a short while I hated it.'

It was in Nairobi that Tim and David split up, quite unintentionally. One extraordinary theme of Africa is that, despite its size, it is possible to meet the same people again and again in different places. We all followed much the same route, and I met David and Tim again in Nairobi. But the opposite is also true: you can miss each other just as easily, and once you are no longer with someone, it can be extremely difficult to find him or her again.

Tim did not have the right documents to get his motorbike out of Customs in Nairobi. David did. He left to go south to Tanzania, where he arranged to meet Tim again. Tim followed a fortnight later, but inexplicably missed David, and the two never saw each other again. Tim kept heading south to Cape Town, thinking that David was in front of him. David waited in Tanzania thinking that Tim was behind him.

David went to stay with friends in Tanzania and began to get sucked into the marvellously relaxed existence there. This was healthy outdoor relaxation, not the Dunkley Square variety at all. He went to dinner with them and stayed for three weeks. 'People dropped in. My hosts would go away and leave me, and then come back. The big excitements were events, like going shopping,' he said. 'I read a lot. I felt I was imposing at times, but they would say: go on, stay a bit longer. I remember lying on the top of a Land Cruiser going through Arusha National Park thinking, "My God, this is the life."'

He was right, it was the life, but after doing it for a while, so was moving on and finding that Dunkley Square was the life. So, again, would be moving on from Dunkley Square for a life back home in England. I only hoped I was not held in a vortex that might make me miss my flight to London. Or that, like Rip van Winkle, I would not arrive in London a hundred years late.

Even essentials like money were provided from the bosom of the Square. There was a market for the contents of the Mistress Quickly

– even though they were grubby and quite un-South African. A Dunkleian called Roelf and some of his friends, all quite the reverse of the blustering Herman, bought the ripped and rotting army campbeds that had seen us through all the way, the chipped enamelled-metal diesel jerrycans and the big black plastic water containers. They paid money for filthy artefacts (perhaps purely as curios) like the gas camping stove and the huge mosquito net that velcroed to the canvas awning under which Red and George and Emma and I had first slept, nine months earlier in Madrid – and under which, I was glad to say, I had not slept since Nairobi. Actually, no money changed hands, but, as much of a mystery as Roelf wanting these goods, my bar bill at the Dunkley Inn seemed to be paid.

I had stopped camping in Africa to go and stay at the Horrible Tom's idyllic farm upcountry in Kenya. It was while I was there that David was tearing himself away from his own private heaven in Tanzania to drive south to Malawi. He met George and Wicky in Mistress Quickly there. 'They said that you and Red were still in Nairobi,' he told me. 'It stuck in George's mind that you knew where they were in Kenya, but you didn't come and say goodbye.'

'They were right,' I replied. 'I was having far too good a time.'

David stayed with Wicky and George in Malawi, and got back into the travelling dynamic, the campsite way of life. 'Wicky did all the cooking,' continued David. 'We went to see a film in a local town, *Mission Terminate*. It was very popular among the locals. It was packed solid. Being white, we got a seat. The sound was inaudible, but the locals loved it. At every bit of violence there was a cheer, and at every kung fu scene they went hysterical. Wicky thought the innuendo hugely funny.'

They met some whites in Malawi who asked them to come and play rugby at the Blantyre Sports Club. Wicky and David did not play, but George did, and he scored a try. 'Wicky was very excited about the try,' said David.

After travelling with them to Zimbabwe, David grew tired of George and Wicky's indecision. 'They spent hours and hours – really, hours – looking at curios,' he said. 'I was beginning to get bored with George and Wicky insofar as I was just as happy reading a book.'

He left them when they fell out with him over a game of Monopoly. 'I had always played Monopoly with more aggressive players,' David complained. 'I had one card of every set. They had the other two cards of each set. I wanted to stay in the game, even though I knew I was going to lose, by offering to sell them my cards at a high price so they could have the sets; by being a power-broker. I sold a card to Wicky to complete a set for her, and that pissed George off, and George refused to buy any more from me. George was just moody.'

David's diary of the time reads: 'I thought they had gone off me, but I was trying to keep out of their way. I am not surprised that George fell out with Red, and probably Charlie, too.'

They travelled separately to Victoria Falls. Some of David's luggage was still in Mistress Quickly, and he planned to pick it up when they met again. Unfortunately, it was stolen in Bulawayo. George and Wicky were upset about it when they met David again at the Falls. 'I missed my leather trousers and films most,' said David. 'But it really was good to see George and Wicky again. To spend a continual amount of time with them was frustrating, but to see them occasionally was good.'

The renewed friendship did not last long. George complained to David that he had lost some money. Diary note: 'God, I hope he improves.' Both George and Wicky seemed to be unhappy about not seeing enough wildlife in the national parks. Diary note: 'George and Wicky really are impossible.' On the way back from Victoria Falls, Mistress Quickly broke down, and David did not see them again. He headed south once more, this time for South Africa.

'It was freezing on the bike without leather trousers on the way to Cape Town. It got warmer the further I got from the high veldt and the closer to the coast. I arrived in Jeffrey's Bay on the south coast at the time of the opening match between Australia and South Africa. The Australian and the South African surfers there had a punch-up after the match. Then I drove on to Cape Town. I had done it. That was it.'

George and I first met David in Cape Town coming out of a bank. That was the kind of coincidence that Tim had needed in order to see David again. It was also the kind of coincidence that introduced me to Dunkley Square.

I was so overcome with the Dunkleyness of the place that I did not wake up until halfway through the Rugby World Cup final on that last Saturday afternoon in Africa. I knew it would happen eventually, to become so Dunkleyed that you actually missed a day.

I woke up to complete silence in Cape Town. Walking down the hill from my mansion to the Dunkley Inn to watch the remains of the match, I was aware that South Africa had ceased to be. It was life, but not as I knew it. There was nobody on the streets, not even the drunk coloureds who lolled and yelled all day around the parks. There was quiet throughout the city. Yet, every few minutes, a curious groaning came from within every fifth or sixth house. It was as though the fog from James Herbert's nightmarish novel had passed through the city while I had been sleeping, and everyone had gone round to certain friends' houses, all over the city, for group sex.

'Yis!' chorussed a house as I passed. 'Yis! Yis! Yis! YIS! YIS! AAAAAAH, YIIIS! Yis-yis-yis!'

Everyone, but everyone, was indoors watching the match on the television. There was not a car moving anywhere.

I arrived at the Dunkley Inn in time for the last half of the second half. The bar was packed. There were a dozen people crowding below the television. They were all hooting and cheering at the screen high in the corner of the bar.

As well as the noise, there was a sense of intense concentration. Even Black, the coloured barman, was rapt. He would have ignored any orders for drinks, had anyone lapsed for long enough to ask for one. He was watching his idol, Chester Williams, the coloured Capetonian in the Springboks – in fact the only vaguely dusky player in the South African team.

Richard saw me come in. David held up a hand in greeting. Richard went off to fetch me breakfast – David and Richard, being English, were not so caught up by the wave the others were surfing, Roelf, Black, even Herman the German.

'YOU WON'T BEAT CHESTER, YOU WON'T BEAT CHESTER,' shouted Black. Chester had had a shove from a New Zealand player.

He flashed a grin at the crowd to show he was not hurt. 'Look, he's smiling,' said Black.

'Brilliant!' boomed Herman.

'Brilliant,' echoed Louisa beside him.

This was the match of their lives.

The commentary switched to Xhosa: 'Eega fo rasi yebo gogo ee-preshaaah playaaar,' it streamed out. 'No for go la ti do ee-twentee-two-meetaaars so ra mabokoboko ee-dead-ball-line.'

Garry Pagel came on for Balie Swart. 'Ooh,' went the crowd.

'Dess de guy we need now! Dess de guy!' shouted Black.

I had got there just in time to see South Africa at its most excitable. On the television, Morné du Plessis, the South African team manager, walked around looking anxious and chewing his tongue.

'Come on, guys,' roared Herman, banging the bar.

'Come on,' agreed Louisa.

Not many more minutes to go now. The Dunkley biker in leathers at the back of the bar jumped up and down, lit cigarette after cigarette, paced down and up, jogged on the spot. 'GO ON, GO ON, GO ON. DO IT, DO IT,' he exhorted. The score was 9–9. It was nearly the end.

New Zealand kicked for goal from the halfway line. 'Shit,' went the crowd. 'Shit, shit, shit. Aaaaah!' – scream – he'd got it. New Zealand 12, South Africa 9.

New Zealand kick for the tryline again. It bounces. Chester picks it up. 'RUUUUN, RUUUUN.' He passes it. It's a knock-on, and so close to the All Black line. 'That was a fucking try, man!' New Zealand still 12, South Africa still 9.

'I think the crowd are a bit partisan,' said David quietly. 'I haven't heard you shouting for New Zealand,' he added. 'I suppose you could always publish your book posthumously.'

'This is really energy-sapping stuff,' said the TV commentator, back in English again for the final few minutes. Those eyes not glued to the screen above the bar were sunk in their hands. 'It's a cat-and-mouse situation for both teams,' added the commentator.

Then a South African kick at the uprights. 'WOOOOOOOOOOOO!' 12–12. The television shows a shot of Nelson in Bok cap and jersey, singing 'Shoshaloza' in the crowd. 'He's so sweet,' said a girl.

But it was not enough. There had to be more points for a winner. The referee had one eye on the clock, but he looked set to let the match go on until those points were scored. 'Give us TRY,' implored Herman, one eye on the profit margin. 'Give us a TRY. Give us a TRY,' like a rally chant.

There was a scrum.

There was a tiny silence after the scrum. South Africa had possession.

'Stransky drop?' suggested a girl in a tight whisper.

He did.

'YEEEEEEEES, WOOOOOOOO.' The room went berserk. South Africa 15, New Zealand 12. They danced on the floor and on the bar. Black was up there with Roelf and the biker. Chairs and tables rattled and fell over. Herman thumped and thumped away. And they were snogging in the seats that stayed upright. Cape Town's reaction to world events is always oversexed. People were on bar stools, smelling victory. Richard and David beamed.

Just a minute to go. Penalty to South Africa. There is a bit of shoving on the pitch. 'Off! off! off!' – 'Do they know it's over?' – and at long last, at nine-months'-travel-and-very-long-last, the final whistle.

South Africa went up as a man, and national team captain François Pienaar was crying, and even Morné du Plessis permitted himself an anxious smile. Herman had two fist salutes to the air. 'Yes! Yes!' Olé, olé olé olé. Even Ella was excited. 'We are the power,' shouted a drunk coloured, stumbling around outside.

'Stransky, you beauty,' said Pienaar on national television. The crowd at Ellis Park in Johannesburg was on its feet. Nelson's cute face under his Bok baseball cap gave a cute smile. 'Papa, Papa,' the whites in Cape Town called him – high praise. 'Nelson, BAAAABY,' shouted Herman.

'This is the BIST game I've IVER seen in my WHOLE LIFE,' shouted Black.

Cape Town was white noise, bouncing and blasting off Table Mountain. Just as Rio de Janeiro is the party city of the world for southern Europeans, so is Cape Town for northern Europeans. The young came out for carnival in Cape Town. They roller-skated;

motorbikes roared by; cars going up Long Street and Kloof Street hooted. All races drank and sang in the streets. The exuberance of black toytoy demonstration met the dancing hooliganism of whites having fun. Cars and *bakkies* were crammed with flag-wavers and shouters. Tramps white and black shook hands with yuppies black and white. People ran round and round Shortmarket Square with arms raised, screaming hoarsely.

Intelligent analysis of the game took place in the Gents of bars all over town, the only places you could hear yourself think.

'Thit was a disperate mitch,' said a man at a urinal.

'We fucked them good,' said a voice from behind a lav door.

'Close, hey,' said the urinal man.

'We rilly fucked them good,' emphasised the door, warming to his theme.

'Olé, olé olé olé,' added another door.

Outside, Table Mountain rang to the puberty of a new nation. 'SHOOO-SHA-LOOOOSA,' cried out the crowds. 'Shooooo-shoo-ooosa,' echoed back the cliffs. 'Shush,' whispered the trees, silhouetted on the top of Signal Hill. 'Shush, shush.'

Chapter 21

POSTSCRIPT

It all comes down to what it means to be English. It is the pride and the arrogance, the power and the glory, that saw us through the continent. It is, once again, that foolish cross between passion and vanity that made us do it. It is those games of rugby or cricket or empire that are captained by Carlings. There is no room for the self-loathing that can beset national character at home.

I flew home at 35,000 feet, crossing tracts of Africa in minutes that had taken weeks on the ground. I overtook Mistress Quickly in her container ship at several hundred miles per hour. The dotted line marking our course on the screen at the front of the aeroplane zipped callously through Zaïre, ignoring the hardship and temper we had sweated in just a few miles below, just a few months before. Yet in all that I felt a surge of conceit that I had done it and that it was truly, as obsolete as the feeling may be, a brave and super and noble thing to do. And that was its Englishness.

The postscript is this. Red stayed in Nairobi and started working for the Red Cross, escorting convoys of trucks to Rwanda. Both he and the Horrible Tom have had their first doses of malaria. The Horrible Tom had remained immune to it for twenty-five years. Wendy-Woo is thinking of moving to Kenya now to see what living there is like. If only putative British royal family members could do the same.

George is back in the West Country, living with Wicky and managing an outdoor training and activities centre in Dawlish. Emma and Danny are in Dublin – as is Bunbury – and Emma is hard at work at her photography. Michael the German is continuing training to be a doctor near Hanover after making a short trip to Brazil. Urs is going back to Africa on a motorbike.

Nancy was ill and had to go to London, but is now back in Nouakchott running her dairy. Father is planning a diving trip to the Galapagos Islands. Jane Charley is still in London and knows hundreds more people.

Hazel and Neil are in Zimbabwe. Neil has a job flying aid equipment from Harare to Sudan and Angola. He flew back to visit us all in England and who should he bring with him but Lara from the original Swiss Family Robinson, who is now based in Germany, but there is definitely nothing going on between them. Hazel is working with horses upcountry in Zimbabwe at Kwekwe, though she plans to come back to England, and Georgina is also working with horses, but in Hampshire, in England. Beat from the Turbo Twins fell out with Weirdo and is back in Switzerland. Weirdo, last heard, is still in Africa, somewhere in the south.

Paddy from Kenya spent some time in Ireland and now plans a trip to Cape Town. Roberta and Justin had to give up Segera Ranch in the end and now represent an American holiday company in Nairobi as well as running a sandwich business. They are also trying to buy back part of Segera. Bede and Winters are in London, Butch is working in Tokyo and Muppet is on an expedition in Zaïre. David is still, as far as anyone knows, at the Dunkley Inn in Cape Town.

Oh, yes – and I got a letter from Jesper.

Hi Charlie!
It is me the mad Dane!
How's life?
I'm writing this letter very slowly because I know you are not a fast reader.
The weather here in Denmark is normal. Last week it rained two times. First time three days and next time four days.
You are probably surprised how I got your address but I met the German couple in Malawi: the people you had to leave behind going through Zaïre because their Hanomag was too slow.
Did you have a splendid time in South Africa? At that time I

was in Malawi doing some diving courses. My girlfriend came in the end of June and together we did a five-day white-water rafting tour on the Zambezi. It's a long story, but the reason for doing five days was the price: 60 US dollars incl. food and the one-day tour was 80 USD.

I did the bungee and we continued hitching to SA, where we had a great time.

One month ago I flew back, and sitting here thinking about it all I'm amazed and a bit proud that I made all the way – but who cares anyway? The most annoying part is that you can't explain what it was like so therefore I'll come to London one day and tell you for two weeks.

Where is Red now? Does he still look funny? Have you got his address? please. What is Neil and Hazel doing now?

Your friend

Jesper

PS: I wanted to send you 100USD but I closed the envelope already.

Have you got a photo of your girlfriend – nude?

ACKNOWLEDGEMENTS

Jane Charley, for not going; Tim Titheridge of the London Society of Rugby Football Union Referees; Keith Barnes, Martin Fletcher, Jacquie Clare and Gillian Holmes of Simon & Schuster; Rohina Grewal; Liza Helps; Arabella Robb; Clive Graham-Ranger of *Salmon & Trout* magazine; Patrick & Susan Rose and Richard & Rebecca Osborne for looking after Cutsey; Julian Brinton for looking after Trevor; Georgina Beach, Cazzie White, Annabel Nash and Emie Hannay for looking after the London operation; Martin Atkinson of NatWest Bank, Deptford; Chip & Susie Stidolph and David & Venetia Lascelles for expedition equipment; my father Martin Jacoby; Lt–Col Christopher Anderson, military attaché, British Embassy, Rabat; Nicholas McDuff, consul (Commercial), British Consulate, Casablanca; Abderrahim Bougja, president of the Moroccan Rugby Federation; Ben Bowerman of Drovercare in Winchester; Mark Wilson of Land Rover; Neil & Hazel Jackson and Michelle Dunford; Urs Kobelt and Lara Petsch; Mike & Clive Garnham, Jeremy Franklin and Derek Pringle; Jesper Nielsen; Nancy Abeiderrahmane, honorary British consul in Mauritania; Christine Peters, Peace Corps, Mali; Hans Fogh of Kampihl in Sikasso, Mali; Tim Ripley and David Johnson; Jean-Michel Macia, Dr Thierry Barbe, Dominique Davanier and Pierre Cassagnet of Lambert's Rugby Club, Abidjan; Gervais Coffie, president of the Ivory Coast Rugby Federation and Benjamin Dakoury, vice-president; Siobhan & Roisin Walsh; Peter Bills and Gaynor Clarke of *Rugby World* magazine; Lisa Sykes of *Geographical* magazine; Camilla Scott; Jenny Sayer, honorary British consul in Togo; Rennie Thomas Ahiekpor, Lomé; Mike Honvoh, UTC shipping director, Benin; Sammy Rossum; Mary Ajaba of Pension de

Famielles, Cotonou; Steven Allard of Truck Africa; Michael Mansour and Kay Stietenroth; Heinz & Christa Jansen; Rusty Riddick, Buea, Cameroon; Jeff Lawhead, Peace Corps, Central African Republic; Gothard Neumeister and Beat Overhage; Simon Martin, Arua, Uganda; Edward Kitaka Kizito and Peter Dow of the Uganda Rugby Football Union, Kampala; Dominic Symes and Bukulu; Gavin Bell and his father, Gordon Bell, of the Rugby Football Union of East Africa, Nairobi; Danny Buckley; Louise Wood of *Rainbow Runner* magazine, Nairobi; Richard & Anne Wilson, Kilifi; Michael Cheffings of Bateleur Safaris, Nairobi; Bruce Buckland and Adrian Paul of the Malindi Sea Fishing Club; the Hon. Tom Cholmondeley and his parents, the Lord & Lady Delamere; Wendy Anthony-Hoole; Jamie Daniell and David & Adrienne Craddock; Patrick Hughes; Roberta Fonville, Justin Mayhew and Marcus Russell of Segera Ranch; Buffalo Warshow; Bradley Sailes; Patrick Dowson; Paris Foot and his father, Keith Foot; Emanuele Azzaretto; Luigi Melecchi; Danilo Malatesta; John Gregson and Garry Coward-Williams of *Shooting Times* magazine; Deidre Shields of *The Field* magazine; Simon & Tim Bates, Karin Bernardi, Des & Guy Bowden, Luisa Esposito, Sean Garstin, Sarah Knecht, Mark Laurence, Steve McLean, Grace Mwangi, Katrina Paterson, Peter Schewan, Erik van Vliet and Tom Walden-Jones of Team 101, Kenya Safari Rally; Francis Musonda of the Zambia Police Force Public Relations Office; Eleanor Key and Rasna Grewal, Harare; Collin Osborne and Oriel Brown of the Zimbabwe Rugby Union; Marthinus Grobler of the Big Buff, Harare; Farayi Mungazi and Brian Murphy of ZBC, Harare; Peter Winterbottom, Chris Butcher, Bede Bruce-Lockhart and Kevin Muggleton; Wendy Sherrin of Team Talk Promotions in London, and her mother, Memory van Rooyen, Bulawayo; Gary Ludick, Bulawayo; Emma & Lucy Hunter and Ezra Mosha, Gaborone, Botswana; Nigel & Julia Hunter; Dave & Lindy Parry and Mike Murray-Hudson; Séamus & Bridget O'Neill; Karin Duthie of Illustrative Options, Gaborone; Mike Small of Botswana Rugby Union; Lee Gorman, Gaborone; Ollie Olwagen, Rustenburg Rugby Club; Dr Camille Anoma, Ivory Coast press liaison officer; Paul Roodt; Sakkie van der Bank of Impala Platinum, Rustenburg; Philippe Huart, marketing director for Hi Tec, Paris; Piet Goosen, Pretoria; Dave & Karin

Evans, Johannesburg; Kate Everingham, Sue Clarkson, Gail Wildes and Maura Humphries; Toni Allan; John Robbie and Daniel Moyane of 702 Radio, Johannesburg; England supporters Luke Archer, Simon Attwell, Anthony Bagshaw, David Blackstone, Ollie Cadle, Sarah Cook, Nick Demain, Anna McLaughlin, Mark Offer, Sam Rockney, Mike Spurr and Tracey Willis in Cape Town; Anthony Watterson and Andrew Satow of No. 1 Chesterfield, Cape Town; Michael Inglesby and Roelf Mulder; Richard Small of the Dunkley Inn, Cape Town; Trudy Merz and Sue Taylor of South African Airways; to my mother Cicely Jacoby and to Christopher Drewe for being excellent ground crew in Devon, for running the whole show; and to Wicky, Emma, Red and George, sine qua non.

PICTURE CREDITS

The author and Abderrahim Bougja © Emma Tindal

Lara from the Swiss Family Robinson in Mauritania © Emma Tindal

The Dust Busters in Nouakchott © Emma Tindal

Red in a pirogue at Assini Mafia, Ivory Coast © Emma Tindal

The author in Morocco © Emma Tindal

The Dust Busters in Zaire © Emma Tindal

Christmas at Limbe © Emma Tindal

Gaborone Rugby Club celebrates South Africa's win over Australia © Karin Duthie

Red Guides Weirdo over a bridge in Zaire © Emma Tindal

Hazel and the head of a gnu © Emma Tindal

Urs, George and Red © Emma Tindal

The train across Zambia to Lusaka © Emma Tindal

Wicky is carried to her boat in Lake Victoria © Emma Tindal

Red sleeps off Christmas © Emma Tindal

The author and Red admire the crater in Mount Longonot, Kenya © Emma Tindal

Derek Pringle in the Sahara © Emma Tindal

Emma reaches the top of Mount Cameroon © Hazel Jackson

A camel gets a lift in Morocco © Emma Tindal

Ronda in Spain © Emma Tindal

Camping in Mali © Emma Tindal

Wildebeest and hippo © Emma Tindal

A local post office in Mauritania © Emma Tindal

Mistress Quickly crosses a bridge in Zaire © Emma Tindal

The author crosses a bridge in Zaire © Emma Tindal

Red coaxes the Dust Busters across a bridge in Zaire © Emma Tindal

Mistress Quickly advances across bridge in Zaire © Emma Tindal

Camping in Sese Islands © Emma Tindal

Mistress Quickly goes through a bridge outside Buta © Emma Tindal

Red practises rugby in Kenya © Emma Tindal

Giraffe in Zimbabwe © Emma Tindal

George and the author lost in the Sahara Desert © Emma Tindal

A bobby boots a ball off Cape Point © Charles Jacoby

Roberta and Justin at Sergera © Charles Jacoby

Paddy on a cattle truck at Moyale © Charles Jacoby

The Horrible Tom and staff © Charles Jacoby

The author and George at Cape Point © Ollie Cadle

David playing cribbage at the Dunkley Inn, © Charles Jacoby

Mistress Quickly lies on her side in Zaire © Michael Mansour

Red guides the Dust Buster Neil into deep water in Zaire © Michael Mansour

The author revolutionises the fishing industry in the Congo Basin © Michael Mansour

The author and his catch © Michael Mansour

Gettng a parking ticket © Emma Tindal

Dominique Davanier © Emma Tindal

The desert at Dakhlar © Emma Tindal

Outside the Kitale Club in Kenya © Georgina Beach

Peter Winterbottom at a village training session © Kevin Muggleton

Opening stockings on Christmas morning in Cameroon © Hazel Jackson

Having supper with Nancy © Hazel Jackson

Grubby in Zaire © Neil Jackson

On the Sese Islands, Uganda © Hazel Jackson

Steve from Truck Africa © Hazel Jackson

Thomson's Falls, Kenya © Hazel Jackson

Wicky and Emma at Christmas lunch with Sage and Onion © Neil Jackson

Neil on a bridge in Zaire © Hazel Jackson

On a granite coll in Congo Basin, Zaire © Hazel Jackson

MYSELF: Yes.

THE PLAIN PEOPLE OF IRELAND: Very guttural languages the pair of them the Gaelic and the German.

It's not fanciful, behind that, to hear his despair.

Or behind this:

I tried to get it many a time. O many a time.

Well I never could see any harm in it.

I seen it in a shop once on the quays, hadn't any money on me at the time and when I came back to look for it a week later bedamn but it was gone. And I never seen it in a shop since.

Well, I can't see what all the fuss was about.

You read it, did you?

I couldn't see any harm at all in it there was nothing in it.

I tried to get it many a time meself . . .

There's no harm in it at all.

Many's a time I promised meself I'd look that up and get it.

Nothing at all that anybody could object to, not a thing in it from the first page to the last.

It's banned, o' course.

Not a thing in it that anybody could object to, NO HARM AT ALL IN IT, nothing at all anywhere in the whole thing.

O indeed many's a time I tried to get it meself.

Three days a week; five days a week. Often at great length, and often in Irish, which (he savagely knew) half his readers couldn't read. Or he'd torment them by modulating from English cliché into Latin:

How are heights?

Great. (How's yourself?)

How are great heights reached?

Pardon me. ATTAINED. By soaring, of course.

Whom may we expect (with proper coaching) to soar to great heights?

Certain promising youngsters. . . .

What is the unit of measurement applied generally to commodities or articles which are available in gigantic quantities?

The oodle. . . .

Quid dicerent Dublin Transport Company?
Falsus in uno, falsus in omnibus.

Quis custodiet ipsos custodes?
Mulieres eorum.

Which omnibus line is best augured?
Fortuna favet 40 Bus.

—Day after day after day. The column was at its most magisterial in war-time, six years of Irish solipsism during which Myles's schemes for making jam out of used electricity or concocting emergency supplies of midnight oil—in general his knack for rigging up alternate universes—had a kind of derived plausibility.

The one book he published in the forties was *An Béal Bocht* (1941), a send-up of the cult of rural Irish, translated after his death as *The Poor Mouth*. After he'd retired from or been forced out of the civil service he did manage a couple more: *The Hard Life*, *The Dalkey Archive*. The former attempts a *funny* rescription of turn-of-the-century lower-middle-class life, something he and his readers knew chiefly from *Dubliners*. He bitterly dubbed it "this misterpiece," dedicated "to Graham Greene, whose own forms of gloom I admire." In one chapter, a papal audience, he is in his best form. The latter is a tired hodge-podge of recycled stuff with one splendid new sub-theme: James Joyce alive in the fifties and living quietly in Skerries. The two books show how obsessed O'Nolan had become with U.C.D.'s other famous liter-ary graduate, the man everyone used to think he ought to have equalled.

The Joyce of *The Dalkey Archive* wrote a small collection of "Dublin characteristics," also some unsigned pamphlets for the Catholic Truth Soci-ety, notably on matrimony. That is all. The rest consists of spurious attrib-utions. He is especially horrified by mention of *Ulysses*, a vile thing he had nothing to do with: various hangers-out in Paris scribbled sections for the price of a drink, and it was his name, alas, that got put to it. There is no bottom to human wickedness. And now he is experiencing a late vocation. His fond hope is to be admitted into the Jesuit order at last. That proves more than can be managéd, but the Jesuits do accommodate him as far as they can. He is granted the privilege of mending the Reverend Fathers' underclothes. It's impossible to miss the revenge of "Flann O'Brien." How dare U.C.D.'s black sheep have achieved all that fame?

And how dare "Flann O'Brien" have tried to suppress his own great book? Neither Joyce nor he ever surpassed the nested ingenuity of its contrivances, the insidious taut language to make anything at all seem plausible, or the unforced beauty of such episodes as our man's dialogue with his soul, when, not knowing he's already dead, he supposes he's about to be hanged:

You know, of course, that I will be leaving you soon?
That is the usual arrangement.
. . . You have no idea where you are going . . . when all this is over?
No, none.
Nor have I. I do not know, or do not remember, what happens to the like of me in these circumstances. Sometimes I think that I might become part of . . . the world, if you understand me?
I know.
I mean—the wind, you know. Part of that. Or the spirit of the scenery in some beautiful place like the Lakes of Killarney, the inside meaning of it if you understand me.
I do.
Or perhaps something to do with the sea. "The light that never was on sea or land, the peasant's hope and the poet's dream." A big wave in mid-ocean, for instance, it is a very lonely and spiritual thing. Part of that.
I understand you.
Or the smell of a flower, even.

"A very lonely and spiritual thing"—that phrase has been minted by the Irish aspective, it has on it the signature of Myles, the same who on the first page of his first book had achieved so idiosyncratic a construction as "The Pooka MacPhellimey, a member of the devil class . . . ," and it lets us glimpse lyric emotions he never disclosed again. There was much, after 1940, that he never did do again, save enact furtive details of *The Third Policeman*. Toward the end Dublin gossip even has him suffering an amputated leg, like the nameless man in the book (though he merely broke it). He died, aged fifty-four, on April Fool's Day, 1966.

THE TERMINATOR

I suppose this—might seem strange—
this—what shall I say—this what I
have said—yes—were it not ... that
all seems strange. (*Pause.*) Most strange.
(*Pause.*) Never any change. (*Pause.*) And
more and more strange.

Happy Days

Not bottled for export, Myles during the war years was a bitter antic conscience, exclusively Dublin's. In the post-war decades Sam Beckett became the world's. Irish claustrophobia spread itself round a planet on which there was no longer any place to hide. More than one counterculture infant of the sixties was awaited nine months and then christened "Godot." Such as have survived to the eighties are ambulant footnotes.

The name "Godot" haunts. In a play written in French, it contains as though by accident the English word "God," the way "sor" ("Good mornin', sor") sounds the Irish for "louse." In the English version of the play it preserves the French accentuation, not heavy on the first syllable but light, from a language you accent evenly like Irish. Godot is part of the name of a Paris street; spelled Godeau, it is the name of a French bicycle racer; spelled I do not know how, the name of an Air France pilot in whose care Beckett once had the misfortune to cross the Channel. "Le capitaine Godot vous accorde des bienvenues," came the voice on the intercom. At Heathrow an ashen Beckett required an immediate drink.

Such is by common consent the authenticity of his bleak vision, he has been translated into every language that comes to mind. Himself, is he part of French literature, or part of English? Not part of Irish, certainly. Like his master Joyce, he belongs to International Modernism, though the word "Modernism" in his case retains too strident a sound of willful daring. He is "modern" in this precise sense, that everywhere he is recognized as a contemporary. There are said to have been few performances of *Godot* to equal one staged by the prisoners in San Quentin, where Sartre's *No Exit* would have seemed like, well, playacting. "Nothing to be done. . . ." "Rien à faire." "Nichts zu tun." Like the "Who's there?" that opens *Hamlet*, that opening line is indifferent to idiom. So, unlike the rest of *Hamlet*, are its successors.

This universality, though, has local roots, in the Ireland of the running-down of the Revival. Beckett's good fortune was to come in late, when the shaping enthusiasms seemed quaint and remote and how Mayo peasants should behave on stage was no longer an urgent issue. By 1926, to a lad of twenty, it was not *The Plough and the Stars* that was abnormal but the archaic passions he saw mobilized against it.

He was a baby in Foxrock, near Dublin, in 1906, when W. B. Yeats was in his forty-first year. So around Easter 1916 he turned ten, and at the height of the Civil War he was sixteen. Far from tempting him, like boys just slightly older, O'Connor or O'Faolain, with a romantic choice of sides, that whole frenzied story was little more than a turbulence in the background of his adolescent years. Between his eleventh and his twenty-first years, a walk up O'Connell Street took him past the untended wreckage of the post office. If you cast a cold eye on that, what it emblematized was demolition, not glory.

Being Protestant also immunized him from those passions; they had become Sinn Fein, IRA, hence *Catholic* passions. He belonged to what was left of the old Ascendancy, which, as you choose to put it, was left out, or stayed aloof.

The family's middle-class comfort, in a house where bells summoned servants, had exceptional features too. Unlike the Yeatses and the Joyces, the Becketts did not belong to the obsolescent landowner class, condemned to watch their fortunes dwindle. Nor, like the Synges and Gogartys, were they prosperous from public role-playing: doctor, lawyer, Protestant bishop. Sam's attendance at the best schools—Portora Royal, Trinity—was underwritten by the immutable powers of arithmetic, used by his father in an arcane unspectacular skill, quantity surveying, i.e. preparing estimates of

materials on which contractors could base their bids. Many Beckett characters share a passion for calculation.

Also, he came in late on the story of public entertainment. Joyce grew up
on decadent opera, a passion in his time. Yeats helped found the Abbey,
another passion and a hotbed of passions. But when Beckett was at Trinity
in the twenties the Abbey had competition from the cinemas: from Chaplin,
the tramp; from Keaton, for whom, long after, he wrote a screenplay; from
Laurel and Hardy, in whose queer universe is rooted Didi and Gogo's
inexplicable friendship, bluster protecting bemused incompetence. They
also provided emblematic bowler hats.

He attended the Abbey too, no longer a cause but one alternative to the
cinema: a shabby place north of the river: a declining Abbey, something
O'Casey kept solvent. Correspondingly, Beckett's plays assume a small theatre, and work best when the audience is sparse. The old Abbey that was
burned in 1951 had eccentric sight-lines and could seat some five hundred.
The Théâtre Babylone where Godot first failed to appear was less preten-
tious even than that.

It was at the old Abbey that Beckett saw all of Synge, the tenement plays
of O'Casey, some pseudo-*Noh* of Yeats. His homages to these abound.
O'Casey's dramaturgy of disintegration we've already heard him commend.
When Winnie in *Happy Days* says "I call to the eye of the mind . . . ," she is
repeating the first line of *At the Hawk's Well*. The minimal set of *Godot*—
one pathetic tree—recalls the *Noh* set Yeats had players create by doing no
more than unfold and fold a cloth.

And Yeats had anticipated a discovery Beckett greatly exploits, how little,
in an intimate place, actors need to *do*, and how powerful can be that little.
Ito, Yeats wrote, had been able "as he rose from the floor, where he had
been sitting cross-legged, or as he threw out an arm, to recede from us into
some more powerful life." So Winnie, immobilized, can invoke some less
powerless life by no more than her ceremony of opening a parasol, and when
her parasol bursts into flames, to the anguish of fire marshals in every city
where the play is performed, a higher life has plainly intervened. As for
Hamm in *Endgame*, the ritual for disclosing him seems derived from the
Yeatsian cloth. He seems kept on stage on his chair perpetually, under a
sheet lest he grow dusty. Before each new performance Clov uncovers him,
at the end covers him again; and Hamm's own first act, once uncovered, is
to remove in turn the handkerchief that covers his blind face.

More fundamental things could be learned from Synge. "Who else but
John Millington Synge?" was Beckett's response in 1972 to a question
about playwrights he'd learned from. Undistracted by the questions that

absorbed Synge's first viewers and colleagues— idiom, verisimilitude—he learned to be Synge's successor, the only one.

Synge died when Beckett was three, not yet having attained the age (forty-two) at which Beckett would write *En Attendant Godot*, and had possibly not come to isolate his own principal innovations. *The Shadow of the Glen* had introduced to the stage and to the Irish imagination the eloquent tramp who became Beckett's specialty. (That play got jeered at as "French.") In *The Well of the Saints* he showed how two actors, old and battered and blind, could hold an audience by scarcely moving from where they sit. That was a special gratification for Yeats, who had been so exasperated by actors' restlessness he longed, he said, to imprison them in barrels. "The barrels, I thought, might be on castors, so that I could shove them about with a pole when the action required it." That's in the October 1902 *Samhain*, a sixpenny review of the Irish Dramatic Movement. Had Beckett heard of it, when he put Nagg and Nell in *Endgame* into barrels? Or devised the pole, increasingly long and eventually fitted with wheels, that comes in from the wings in *Act Without Words #2* to wake up players who sleep? If he hadn't, the coincidence is wonderful.

The claustrophobic set of *Riders to the Sea* was another innovation, unremarked in the early days amid fuss about getting authentic Aran Island pampooties to put on the actresses' feet. In that play all we see is confined to a little bare room that shuts out the great violent world of the sea and the horses. Everything of importance to the play has happened previously or happens elsewhere, to be brought into this room by the vivid words. Greek drama has been adduced in precedent, but the Greeks with their music and spectacle and choric dancing never entrusted so much dramatic leverage to so little visible movement, so little variety. This principle leads from Synge's world straight into Beckett's: to *Embers* for instance, a play for radio that confines the whole of a novelistic plot and subplot within the head of a man who sits talking, talking, to drown out the sound of the sea and the sound of the remembered voices of the dead. All that confronts us, in this tour de force of expressive monotony, is the wreckage of a story, a wrecked life, wrecked words:

> Stories, stories, years and years of stories, till the need came on me, for someone, to be with me, anyone, a stranger, to talk to, imagine he hears me, years of that, and then, now for someone who . . . knew me, in the old days, anyone, to be with me, imagine he hears me, what I am, now.

And we know, of course, that that is Beckett, not Synge.

For where he differs markedly from Synge is in his concern for the stony resonances of utterly simple words. Here Synge was a prisoner of history, like so many who have aspired to renovate the drama in English and suppose that the way to resume its glories is through verse or some usage equally patterned. He aspired to a rhetoric of formal rhythm and exotic diction like Shakespeare's. It was to that end, and not for "realism," that he devised a stage language with the help of Irish idioms, in that unique cultural moment when literate men, as though first looking into Chapman's Homer, were discovering a national treasure in the speech of the Irish West. It takes skillful voices indeed to render his tunes. Badly spoken, they will cross the footlights as "Synge-song," and it's easy to speak them badly. Willie Fay remembers how Synge, though he knew how he meant them to sound, could never say them properly himself. He simply coached and corrected skilled professionals. Blank verse gives similar trouble, whether Shake-speare's or that of *The Countess Cathleen*. Yeats was decades achieving a verse you need not intone or declaim but can simply *speak*.

Beckett trusts his actors less than Synge did, his repetitive patterns more. "Finished, it's finished, nearly finished, it must be nearly finished"—Clov's first words in *Endgame* exert their power if spoken, as they should be, in a monotone. Let no thespian saw the air with his hand, thus, nor even speak the speech trippingly on the tongue.

He has parts for thespians, though: the Pozzo who sprays his throat with an atomizer before reciting his encomium to the sunset; the prince of play-ers, Hamm, whose opening words are "Me to play," whose closing ones include "Our revels now are ended," and who reminded the British drama critic Harold Hobson of "a toppled Prospero." It should not be forgotten that in his Trinity years the greatest actor in Ireland was available for study, the man who had been all his life perfecting for the ages an orotund nobility: William Butler Yeats. He still made his ceremonious appearances at the Abbey, to count the house, to confer the touch of the poet.

Those were still the years of Yeatsian dominion, when O'Casey could be denied production of *The Silver Tassie* with a wave of the tyrannic hand. The Hamm who asks "Can there be misery . . . loftier than mine?" the inescapable presence who will allow no escape from his domain, seems studied from him; is not "lofty" a Yeatsian word? In Beckett's last Irish years the Great Founder was in the Senate and in the Tower, pacing upon the battlements, preoccupied with horoscopes and historical geometries, arranging lives and events into lunar patterns that bespoke an inevitability of rude decline, spinning his stories of beautiful lofty things which were artfully cadenced stories of his own past. He seems incapable of an uninteresting sentence.

But they are solipsistic stories. Nowhere in the *Autobiography* he worked on in the twenties does W. B. Yeats for instance *name* his brother Jack, though he mentions "my brother" a few times. We need information extraneous to the book we're reading to know that "my brother" refers to Ireland's greatest painter.

Jack Yeats too was by way of being a playwright, and when W. B. was entoiled in *The Shadowy Waters*, with its Formorians and its Pirates and its harp that takes fire like Winnie's umbrella, J. B. was issuing seagoing plays of his own that resemble a sardonic critique of all that. In 1901 Elkin Mathews, whose list would later include Joyce's *Chamber Music* and the first books of Ezra Pound, published Jack B. Yeats's *James Flaunty, or, The Terror of the Western Seas*, and in 1903 *The Treasure of the Garden*, also *The Scourge of the Gulph, or, Fierce Revenge*. As you'd guess from the titles, there are aesthetic claims these don't make, and staging them never depended on Frank and Willie Fay. You were to cut out the paper actors and mount them on cardboard, the paper scenery likewise, and in a little box, by lamplight, push the colored figures around while you mouthed such lines as "Turn your eyes to the stern windows, James Flaunty. Do you see his body swinging there?" Is that a theatre for children, or for the mind? It's less high-falutin' anyhow than

> ... love is made
> Imperishable fire under the boughs
> Of chrysoberyl and beryl and chrysolite
> And chrysoprase and ruby and sardonyx.

The Yeats whose path would cross Beckett's several times was not W. B. but Jack, a painting by whom he owned and cherished. Their vision is not altogether dissimilar. Nothing, said Sam's dying Malone, is more real than nothing; and Jack ended *The Scourge of the Gulf* with a hollow enigma: "An empty skull, a black box, a dead skipper! Have I done anything or nothing?"

In Paris in 1928 he promptly commenced frequenting James Joyce, another man who worked all his life with what he had taken out of Ireland. Having left earlier (October 1904), Joyce was unimpressed with the theatre. The Abbey was not to open until December, and what preceded it bespoke chiefly ignominious ignobility. The Lower Camden Street hall where Joyce saw *In the Shadow of the Glen* rehearsed on 10 June had (Willie Fay recalled) a leaking roof, "a stage so small you couldn't swing a kitten," and an entrance hall crowded with the overflow stocks of a grocer on the left and a butcher on the right. You got in by slithering between crates of eggs and carcasses of beef. "Ye told me Mr. Yeats was queer," said one old lady, "but this is the queerest theatre that ever I saw." In those days "a race of clodhoppers" was a judgment that came readily to Joyce, and a National Theatre might have been ensconced in such quarters for the express purpose of confirming him. One indication that he saw *The Shadowy Waters* in January 1904 is that the "Brideship and Gulls" sequence of *Finnegans Wake* seems conceived in mockery of it. Joyce could cast a very cold eye.

He cherished more miscellaneous Dublin bric-à-brac: street sounds, toilet bowls in a plumber's window, a man who always walked on the outside of lampposts, the pedestrian obstacle (a manhole cover) that still rises above pavement level on the south side of Eccles Street.

Odder things linked in his mind. Day by day in 1895, a white-bearded man in a top hat could be glimpsed at the Westland Row end of College Park behind Trinity, attempting to get off the ground on batlike wings amid which he was fitted in a harness, upright. This was George Francis Fitzgerald, FRS, Professor of Physics, discoverer of the Fitzgerald Contraction that shortens you in the direction you are travelling, an effect not appreciable till you can measure your velocity in substantial fractions of that of light. Thanks to this piece of space-time headiness, Professor Fitzgerald is part of the history of relativity. He is not, however, part of the history of flight, since the greatest elevation he attained was six inches. But if (as seems probable when you think how word of queer sights gets round Dublin) one of the faces one day at the College Park railings was that of thirteen-year-old Jim Joyce, then the imprint of tophatted George Francis Fitzgerald, fabulous artificer, would-be hawklike man, may be just discernible on the margins of literature. It was the next year, in Latin class, that Joyce read the story of Daedalus in Ovid, to recognize, as he later would on a vast scale, a Dubliner reenacting a classical myth.

Another thing he seems to have remembered is how his first fiction, "The Sisters," had looked in AE's paper, machine-set paragraphs fitted above a half-page ad for Effektiv milk pumps and Alfalaval cream separators. At Dundrum the Cuala Press was preparing elegant little hand-set volumes in 14-point Caslon, and within a few years W. B. Yeats had brought into the Cuala series every Irish writer he thought worth notice: himself, AE, Lionel Johnson (Irish by courtesy), John Eglinton, Lady Gregory, Katharine Tynan,

Synge, even Lord Dunsany. The conspicuous omission was *Chamber Music*, by James A. Joyce, eventually issued in London by Elkin Mathews with "an open pianner" on the frontispiece.

On the last page of *Finnegans Wake* ("O bitter ending!") Joyce recapitulates his previous beginnings and endings: the "Yes" of *Ulysses* is conspicuous, the "old father" of *A Portrait*, the terminal cold of *Dubliners*. Near the top of the page the date 1904 is encoded—"my cold mad feary father," MCM*vier*. Further down "my leaves have drifted from me. All. But one clings still. I'll bear it one me. To remind me of." These are printed leaves as well as treeleaves on the river, and adjacent to them is "Avelaval": the *Ave atque vale* of Catullus (and Moore) entangled with the cream separator's name that *Irish Homestead* page of 1904 had displayed so prominently. In such style had dear dirty Dublin launched a master, much as it launched its glorious dramatic movement in a hall guarded by hanging sides of beef for W. B. Yeats of the pince-nez to push his way past.

> The years like great black oxen tread the world,
> And God the herdsman goads them on behind,
> And I am broken by their passing feet.

"Every syllable can be explained," Beckett recalls Joyce claiming. The way of the explainer must be to disengage Dublin trivia (advertisements, a cuckolded Jew, a tophatted professor) from classical entanglements (*Ave atque vale*, Homeric exploits, Daedalus). So it is with all dreams of nobility; they are entangled. The splendid lines of *The Countess* are not separable from Maud Gonne's shrill fanaticisms, nor the bizarre alert beauty of *The Third Policeman* from quarry lorries rumbling out of Tallaght.

Nor can the great Revival be disentangled from the simple fact that its originators—Yeats, Hyde, Lady Gregory, Synge—were Ascendancy Protestants, a minority inside a minor land, merely (Shaw said) "John Bull's Other Island." Their node of loyalty should have been John Bull. But, Romantics all, they cherished the Romantic dream, Shelley's dream, liberty: in their land, as it proved, an Irish Bull, not John. Yet none of them could disengage from the entanglements of origin.

Minds cannot dream away into disengagement. Beckett has said nothing would bring him back to Dublin; it is also told of Beckett that when others count sheep, he brings on dreams by playing over in his mind the nine holes of the golf course at Carrickmines, near Foxrock. Whether or not this commends the course is not certain. The one thing certain of Beckett is that he is not Irish as Irishness is defined today by the Free State. He is willing to be the last Anglo-Irishman, of the austere tradition of Protestant professional culture: "the people of Burke and Grattan," free to refuse. Unlike Joyce's his very agnosticism is Protestant; Nothing, like the Quark, comes in distinct flavors.

When Beckett fled the island of "formless spawning fury," he took his language away with him to *save* it: partly, to save it from the aftermath of the Revival. His fancy was that this could be achieved if he kept it aloof from Irish and crossed it with something as tough as French. *Watt*, which he wrote in English, simulates a translation from the French; its Dublin tram makes a "facultative" stop (*un arrêt facultatif*). No Irish movement has ever won Beckett's allegiance: certainly, though he is a lifelong athlete, nothing sponsored by the Gaelic Athletic Association. At Trinity he played the English game, to such effect he is likely the only Nobel laureate to be listed in the cricketer's Bible, Wisden's.

If the Literary Movement was started by the Anglo-Irishman Yeats, then the Anglo-Irishman Beckett terminates it, not least in his self-condemnation to works minimal and more minimal. What goes on now in Ireland is a different story.

In sight of Ben Bulben, Yeats from the grave addresses horsemen exclusively: no tourists in chartered buses, no Paddys afoot. Horsemen are neither to ponder their mortality nor to involve themselves in the busyness of this world. Perhaps because mounted visitors to Drumcliffe are scarce, the injunction goes unheeded.

As so often in his life, Yeats in death contrives to obliterate a tradition in the act of subsuming it. Who now remembers the past voices that are summoned and rejected by his gravestone's imperious words?

There was a collective voice the Christian dead used to assume, Church Latin on a stone to bid travellers pause, in countless epitaphs that commenced, *Siste, viator*. "Siste": stay, linger, ponder: ponder on the fact of death. I have died, so shall you; be admonished. Thus, on many thousand stones, the voice of Christian death; and in 1745 Jonathan Swift's single voice presumed to defy that voice. *Abi, viator*, Swift says from his plaque in St. Patrick's, *et imitare si poteris*: . . . get moving, traveller, and imitate if you can. . . . Let the late Dean's savage indignation infect you, and like him perform public acts on behalf of fuller human life.

Yeats follows Swift's example of imperiousness. The lines in "Under Ben Bulben" that lead up to the epitaph make that much explicit.

> . . . On limestone quarried near the spot
> By his command these words are cut . . .

"By his command" is the voice of a man who expects to be obeyed, being dead. The way that voice envisions advantages in death is worldly, not Christian. It says, "I am no longer the diffident poseur who came to Coole Park, the 'one that ruffled in a manly pose / For all his timid heart'; no, in death, having wholly assumed my imperious anti-self, I shall effect it that these words shall be cut in the world where the living are."

But if he will not have our meditations swoon into death the Christian way, neither are we to esteem like Swift the involvements of living. Elsewhere his book has told us that "Death and life were not / Till man made up the whole." Therefore:

> Cast a cold eye
> On life, on death.
> Horseman, pass by.

That is his hard-won minimalism, his epitome of many hundred wonderful pages: his last lordly rebuff of all the Irish rebuffs his work on behalf of Ireland underwent. He had aspired, with the aid of the Abbey, to win his countrymen into what he called Unity of Being, but they got (and get) bitterer pleasure out of division, the courtroom still the theatre of their pleasure, the ambush the recourse of their plot construction, a fine explosion their ecstasy of climax. "Shattered glass and toppling masonry," wrote Joyce; improved explosives now permit local rains of blood and severed limbs. As in the Western World of Synge's imagination, a murderer can still get idolized.

Meanwhile official Ireland has commemorated W. B. Yeats the best way bankers know how, by putting his engraved likeness on the Republic's £20 notes. Foreknowledge of that would have gratified the Pollexfens, those tough Sligo shipowners who thought their Susan might have made a luckier match than J.B.Y., failed barrister, failed painter. There's a Yeats Summer School in Sligo, and in Dublin the Tourist Board (Board of the Welcomes, *Bord Fáilte*) has discovered a good thing in Joyce.

From Stephen's Green, Marjorie Fitzgibbon's fine bronze head of the fabulous artificer broods toward a door across the street, the door that closed behind Stephen Dedalus when he entered the old University to hear the Dean of Studies say *home*, *Christ*, *ale*, *master* in a tongue that would be alien always. A plaque by the door claims distinction for the place, citing three names, one of them Irish: John Henry Newman, first Rector; Gerard Manley Hopkins, Professor of Greek; James Augustine Joyce, Student. American Express paid for the bronze head. Reciprocally, Joyce pilgrims buy Travellers' Cheques.

Some years ago a Joyce pilgrim from Berkeley, California located and identified the birthplace of Leopold Bloom. It is at 52 Clanbrassil St. Upper, where a few Jewish names are still discernible on shops nearby. Thereafter a scripture in *Ulysses* cried out for fulfillment: "That the house in which he was born be ornamented with a commemorative tablet." The argument against commemorating a fictional character was countered with the post office statue of Cuchulain, who is surely less well documented than Bloom, and in June 1982, at the height of the Joyce Centennial doings, a blue Bord Fáilte tablet was unveiled. The ceremony drew a small crowd and stirred the tongues of neighbors, who were instantly telling a delighted press that the scholars had as usual got the wrong house. "The Blooms didn't live there at all," said one old lady; "they lived down that way." So Irish Facts multiply still, and it's fair to say that Dublin remains obsessed with the writers it doesn't read. One Trinity undergraduate told a pressman the inside truth, that it was all an American cod, the books being unreadable. Not even of *A Portrait* could she make head or tail. She didn't say what she was doing at Trinity.

One way or another they're obsessed too with the North, and they've lost the battle for Irish. Nameplates blossom with the words of multinational commerce: "UNILOKomotive (European Division) (Local Office)." Whatever that is, it's on O'Connell Street, near the post office with its bronze Cuchulain. At an adjacent McDonald's the counter-girl wears her name-tag: Emer: Cuchulain's queen. If you recover an heroic past, then face the fact that you'll have it splattered all around you. Recover Irish: it will be mispronounced, mocked, co-opted for slogans, forgotten. Recover the mystique of the lost land and the Four Green Fields: your fanatics will make a routine of blowing up babies in their efforts to reclaim the lost fraction of the fourth. That nightmare has not begun to be awakened from.

Impart literacy; people may read. Worry about what may get read; hire censors to block it. And the lot of the censor is to stall between fools.

Forty years ago prominent Irish writers tended to be defined by their banned books. Beckett turned the tables; enraged by bans, he banned his plays in Ireland. There is logic, yes, logic, behind every public proposition in the unfortunate country, behind every action however perverse it looks. The famous "smile and tear" are camouflage, thin as the publicized green on the chill North Atlantic rock maps now call Eire. The weather on that rock breeds a race of dissident logicians, Mylesians. Myles is their unacknowledged legislator. From premises chosen at whim ("Do you know what it is? Do you know what I'm going to tell you?") the Plain People of Ireland will argue you off the face of the Erse.

Though logic, Yeats knew, is a machine, and machines seize up.

Perverse likewise meanwhile, defying their nation's perversity which deems the written word (when you come down to it) unnatural, Yeats, Synge, Joyce and Beckett somehow defined themselves: four of the foremost bookmen of their century in a language that less than a hundred years ago there seemed strong reasons to extirpate from Ireland.

NOTES

The following editions are cited throughout:

YEATS

Autobiography: W. B. Yeats, *Autobiography*, Collier paperback, 1965.
Memoirs: W. B. Yeats, *Memoirs*, ed. Donoghue, 1972.
Variorum Plays: Alspach, ed., *The Variorum Edition of the Plays of W. B. Yeats*, 1966. (I used the third printing. The main text in all printings is dismayingly corrupt.)
Variorum Poems: Allt and Alspach, eds., *The Variorum Edition of the Poems of W. B. Yeats*, 1957.
Letters: A. Wade, ed., *The Letters of W. B. Yeats*, 1955.
Other Yeats references are to standard Macmillan editions except where specified.

JOYCE

Ulysses: James Joyce, *Ulysses*, Random House, 1961; Vintage paperback has identical pagination.
All other Joyce page references are to Penguin editions.
All references to the Ellmann biography of Joyce are to the first (1959) printing. A revised edition was announced for the centenary year; I had not seen it when this book went to press.

SYNGE

All references are by volume and page to the four-volume Oxford edition of Synge's *Works*, ed. Robin Skelton, Alan Price, and Ann Saddlemyer, 1962–1968. This was out of print as *A Colder Eye* went to press, but a reprint had been promised by Colin Smythe.

WARNING

4 "a different church": the Chapel of Ease, Roundtown. Vivien Igoe, "A Cab at the Door," in *Ireland of the Welcomes*, May–June 1982, 8, and private communication. His given names appear as "Jacobus Augustinus."

5 "proving he is alive": See Swift's pamphlets against the astrologer Partridge.

5 "Mr. Hunter": see Joyce, *Selected Letters*, 286 for Clonliffe Road, 112 for the first intimation of the story.

6 "Boylan with impatience," "That's the bucko," "Tipping her": *Ulysses*, 267, 319, 274.

6 "a cuckold": Richard Ellmann, *James Joyce*, 1959, 238.

7 Gogarty's broadcast on Joyce. See the transcript in W. R. Rodgers, *Irish Literary Portraits*, 1972, 24–25.

7 "remembered to the pound": J. F. Byrne, *The Silent Years*, 1953, 157.

8 "How, demands Byrne": Byrne, 158.

8 "insinuating, upflowing," "carved out of a turnip": *Autobiography*, 283, 271.

8 "pants": *Autobiography*, 271.

10 "Interview": Maria Jolas, ed., *A James Joyce Yearbook*, Paris, 1949. Mme. Jolas has assured me it was among J.J.'s papers, and Prof. John V. Kelleher is convinced (on "O'Brien"'s authority and others') that "O'Brien" wrote it; and how these allegations are to be combined is unclear. The man Prof. Kelleher suggested might have taken the ms. to Paris denies having done so. Though I quoted it myself in 1956 (*Dublin's Joyce*) I now judge it too vivid to be true: what a miraculously accurate transcriber, for those days before tape! Prof. Ellmann alludes (759) to questions J.J. had his friends put to J.S.J. during the 1920's, but such notes on these as I've seen are bare fact-lists.

10 "The unfacts": Joyce, *Finnegans Wake*, 57.

10 "clear solution," "Dublin toper": *A Tale of a Tub*, of course, and *Ulysses*, 341.

THE THREE PROVINCES

16 "moralist with a corncob": chapter heading in Wyndham Lewis, *Men Without Art*, 1936.

16 "a roof for Thoor Ballylee": Frank Tuohy, *Yeats*, 1976, 172.

17 "shorthand for sociologies": for a lucid exposition, see Conor Cruise O'Brien, *States of Ireland*, 1972 (rev. ed. 1974).

17 "public opinion defined": thank you, Joe Sobran.

A BAG OF CATS

James Kilroy, *The "Playboy" Riots*, 1971, a hundred pages of contemporary reports, is the one indispensable source-book. My notes nowhere cite it, only because I'd not know where citations should begin and end.

19 "Tin trumpets": Lady Gregory, *Our Irish Theatre*, 1913, 112–13.

19 "greatcoats": shown in contemporary cartoons of the event.

20 "bad language": Gregory, 133.

20 "Don't strike me": Synge, *Works*, IV, 73.

20 "cut in rehearsal": Gregory, 133–34.

20 "making mighty kisses": Synge, *Works*, IV, 149.

21 "What good'd be my life-time": Synge, *Works*, IV, 165.

21 "Pegeen I'm seeking only": Synge, *Works*, IV, 167.

21 "Holloway": Robert Hogan and Michael J. O'Neill, eds., *Joseph Holloway's Abbey Theatre: A Selection from His Unpublished Journal*, 1967, 81. See also David H. Greene and Edward M. Stephens, *J. M. Synge, 1871–1909*, 1959, 237–38.

23 "Yeats had pointed out": in *Samhain*, December 1904, 7.

23   Note: "Fay's account": W. G. Fay and Catherine Carswell, *The Fays of the Abbey Theatre*, 1935, 214–15.

27   "large umbrella": George Moore, *Hail and Farewell*, repr. 1976, 188.

27   "He was alone": Joyce, *A Portrait of the Artist as a Young Man*, 226.

28   "from his head only": *Autobiography*, 356.

28   "Constrained, arraigned": "The Double Vision of Michael Robartes," *Variorum Poems*, 382.

28   "leave the theatre": Denis Johnston, *Dramatic Works*, 1977, I, 8.

30   "Joyce records": *Ulysses*, 542.

30   "Bend down": *Variorum Plays*, 163. These are lines Joyce has Stephen remember in *A Portrait*.

30   "Have I not seen": "A Prayer for My Daughter," *Variorum Poems*, 405.

31   "Yeats phrased": *Autobiography*, 278–79.

31   "In using what I considered": *Autobiography*, 279.

32   "Lady Gregory had given them": Gregory, 113.

34   "Some blasted little theatre": see "Song of a Shift," in *Drums Under the Windows*, vol. 3 of O'Casey's autobiography.

35   "Lady Gregory had made the mistake": Gregory, 114.

37   "thick as blackberries": Holloway, quoted by Greene and Stephens, 246.

39   "bag of cats": Joyce, *Dubliners*, 132–33.

40   "the height of a table": Gregory, 171.

40   "drive the vile thing": Gregory, 180.

40   "hell-inspired ingenuity": Gregory, 190.

40   "threw a good many potatoes": Gregory, 204.

41   "Nothing was thrown": Gregory, 219.

41   "demoralize a monastery": Gregory, 227.

41   "Not while the curtain was up": Gregory, 229.

41   "shot off a shovel": *Ulysses*, 345.

A   TALE   OF   A   POT

43   "no mastery of speech" and other Yeats citations: from the Notes to his *Plays in Prose and Verse*, 1922, reprinted in *Variorum Plays*, 254.

43   "stony silence": Willie Fay's account is in W. G. Fay and Catherine Carswell, *The Fays of the Abbey Theatre*, 1935, 127–29. Students of the Irish Fact will want to compare Yeats's brief version, *Variorum Plays*, 254.

44   "notorious Irishman": Oscar Wilde, of course. See "The Decay of Lying," antepenultimate paragraph.

44   "I sigh over the pig": for his contribution to the Coinage Committee's report (1928) see Donald R. Pearce, ed., *The Senate Speeches of W. B. Yeats*, 1960, or Brian Cleeve, ed., *W. B. Yeats and the Designing of Ireland's Coinage*, 1972. Cleeve reproduces the lost pig on p. 14.

45   "pragmatical pig": "Blood and the Moon," *Variorum Poems*, 480; first printed in Ezra Pound's *The Exile* (Spring 1928), the same year the Dublin Stationery Office published *Coinage of Saorstát Éireann*. This poem records the suspicion that every modern nation is "half dead at the top," to which Pound responded from the Pisan stockade, "My dear William B.Y. your 1/2 was too moderate" (*The Cantos of Ezra Pound*, 1970, LXXIX, 487). The presence of coinage in both poets' minds, Pound's programmatically, Yeats's accidentally, makes a pleasant historical rhyme.

45   "laughing *Ceres*": Pope's Epistle IV (to Burlington), ll. 173–76.

46   "nettles wave": "Coole Park, 1929," *Variorum Poems*, 489.

47   "roofless ruin": "Meditations in Time of Civil War," *Variorum Poems*, 423.

47   "violent bitter man": "Ancestral Houses," *Variorum Poems*, 418.

48   "leaves whirling on the road": Yeats's note to "The Hosting of the Sidhe," *Variorum Poems*, 800.

48   "And if any gaze": "The Hosting of the Sidhe," *Variorum Poems*, 141.

48   "likeness of a newspaper": "The Devil," in Yeats, *The Celtic Twilight*, repr. 1962, 59.

THE CONQUEST OF ENGLISH

49   "the language": Joyce, *A Portrait of the Artist as a Young Man*, 189.

50   "used to complain": recorded in Ford Madox Ford, *Joseph Conrad: A Personal Remembrance*, 1924, 229.

50   "sentimental and self-pitying": Anthony Burgess, *Joysprick*, 1973, 27.

50   "He feels the inferiority": *Joysprick*, 28.

51   "barrel-staves": J. C. Beckett, *The Making of Modern Ireland*, 1966, 28–29. There was military clearance indeed, but it's only part of the story.

52   "my own music": *Autobiography*, 103.

52   "instantly admired": details from the Hone biography of Yeats, 1943, ch. iii, 7; xiii, 5; xviii, 4.

52   Note: "reading Thoreau": *Autobiography*, 47

53   "infarm the audience": many sources, e.g. R. F. Rattray, "A Day with Yeats," in E. H. Mikhail, ed., *W. B. Yeats: Interviews and Recollections*, 1977, I, 157.

53   "bulgar in your bowels": Joyce, *Finnegans Wake*, 563.

54   "it darkles": Joyce, *Finnegans Wake*, 244.

54   "I don't envy yeh": O'Casey, "Dublin's Gods and Half-Gods," in *Inishfallen, Fare Thee Well*, 1949.

54   "wind in the chimney": *The Cantos of Ezra Pound*, 1970, LXXXIII, 533–34.

54   "What's riches": Yeats, "The Peacock," *Variorum Poems*, 310.

55   "nearly all Wordsworth": Canto LXXXIII, 534, where we learn that W.B.Y. preferred "Ennemosor on witches."

55   "*animosity*": Introduction to Marianne Moore's *Selected Poems*, 1936.

56   "Irishman's house": *Ulysses*, 110.

56   "Hohohohohome": *Ulysses*, 607.

57   "fish, flesh and fowl": "Sailing to Byzantium," *Variorum Poems*, 407.

57   "Calvary's turbulence": "The Magi," *Variorum Poems*, 318.

57   "tingling stars": in "Morte d'Arthur."

57   "witty Aristotle": see "The Holy Office." in Richard Ellman, *James Joyce*, 172.

58   "fight," "logic": "An Irish Airman Foresees his Death" and "Sixteen Dead Men," *Variorum Poems*, 328, 395.

58   "passionate intensity" *et seq.*: in order, "The Second Coming," "Prayer for My Daughter" (twice), "Byzantium," "In Memory of Major Robert Gregory," *Variorum Poems*, 402, 403–4, 498, 325.

60   "Clean," "Tully": *Ulysses*, 55, 394.

61   "So Thursday": *Ulysses*, 396.

THE LORE OF IRISH

62   "Hyde was reporting": in "The Necessity for De-Anglicising Ireland," contained in *The Revival of Irish Literature*, London, 1894, 117–61; see the long footnote on 137–38.

63   "census-takers": figures from F.S.L. Lyons, *Ireland Since the Famine*, rev. ed. 1973, 88.

63   "nobody did anything in Irish": Moore, *Hail and Farewell*, repr. 1976, 55.

64   "Synge's text": the following paragraphs draw on Declan Kiberd, *Synge and the Irish Language*, 1979, 19–23, and letters from John V. Kelleher.

65 "at bottom abominable": W. B. Stanford and R. B. McDowell, *Mahaffy: A Biography of an Anglo-Irishman*, 108.

65 "silly or indecent": *Mahaffy*, 104.

65 "great-bladdered Emer": "Crazy Jane on the Mountain," *Variorum Poems*, 628.

65 "two thousand octavo pages": cited by Lady Gregory, *Cuchulain of Muirthemne*, 267. "five hundred to a thousand printed volumes": Aodh de Blácam, *Gaelic Literature Surveyed*, 1929, xi.

66 "Kinsella version": in Thomas Kinsella, *The Tain*, 1969, 8–20. Lady Gregory's is in *Cuchulain of Muirthemne*.

66 Note: "real Gaelic ballads": see Derick S. Thomson, *The Gaelic Sources of Macpherson's "Ossian,"* Aberdeen University Studies, No. 130, 1952.

67 "Ferguson": quoted from Padraic Colum's little selection, *The Poems of Samuel Ferguson*, 1963, 85, 70, 64.

67 "Yeats twice rewrote": *Variorum Poems*, 550. The main versions are 1922 (for a revision of *The Pot of Broth*) and 1935 (in *A Full Moon in March*).

68 "Brown tells us": Malcolm Brown, *The Politics of Irish Literature*, 1972, 316. Brown exaggerates little when he numbers "The Fairy Thorn" among "the immortal lyrics of the English language" (60).

68 *"Irish Fireside"*: Yeats, *Uncollected Prose*, I, 82–83.

68 "their best music": Brown, *Politics of Irish Literature*, 316, 407, citing Austin Clarke, *Poetry in Modern Ireland*, 1951, 15.

69 "Max Beerbohm caricature": often reproduced, e.g. in Mac Liammóir and Boland, *W. B. Yeats and His World*, 1971, 65.

69 "Then all at once": Standish O'Grady, *The Coming of Cuculain*, 1894, ch. 1.

69 "AE recalled": in his "Introduction" to an undated Dublin reprint of O'Grady's *The Coming of Cuculain*, x. The "Introduction" can be dated pretty closely: after O'Grady's death in May 1928 but before the book came to Johns Hopkins late in 1930. So AE was about sixty-two when he fanned up this old glow.

70 "Paradise of pretenders": *Ulysses*, 45.

70 "Wisha, faith": opening sentence of "Biddy the Matchmaker," in *Some Strange Experiences of Kitty the Hare*, circulated with a straight face, God help them, by the normally responsible Mercier Press, Dublin and Cork, 1981.

71 "Moore describes": *Hail and Farewell*, 238.

71 "Mala Néfin": Hyde, *Love Songs of Connacht*, 9.

71 "'Tis the cause of this song": *Love Songs of Connacht*, 75–77.

72 "mountain stream," "coming of a new power": Yeats, *Uncollected Prose*, I, 293; Yeats, *Explorations*, 93.

72 "I shall not die": *Love Songs of Connacht*, 138–39.

73 "O woman": see, e.g., John Montague, ed., *The Book of Irish Verse*, 1974, 107.

73 "Muses' blade": see "Coole Park, 1929," *Variorum Poems*, 489.

74 "valuable exposition": Maire Cruise O'Brien, "The Two Languages," in *Conor Cruise O'Brien Introduces Ireland*, 1969, 43–60: an otherwise touristy book, not without lore.

75 "Sean O'Casey": both examples from Act II of *The Plough and the Stars*, in *Collected Plays*, 1949, I, 200, 201.

75 Note: "Pepys and Jane Austen": Thomas MacDonagh cited them in *Literature in Ireland*, 1916, 11. George Moore has similar observations in *Hail and Farewell*, 551.

76 "Synge's": all from *In the Shadow of the Glen*, but the mannerism is everywhere in Synge.

77 "Moore thought": *Hail and Farewell*, 549–51. "It consists of no more than a dozen turns of speech, dropped into pages of English so ordinary, that redeemed from these phrases it might appear in any newspaper without attracting attention."

77   "a Falcon": Gerard Manley Hopkins, "The Windhover."

78   "on verbs": D. D. Paige, ed., *The Letters of Ezra Pound*, #95, dated June 1916. For more on Fenollosa see my *The Pound Era*, 1971, 223–29 and 289–91.

78   "Pound divulged": in *Confucius to Cummings*, 1964, 327.

79   "sentence of Tennyson's": from *The Holy Grail*.

79   "THE FISH": *Variorum Poems*, 146.

81   "All that was sung": "Parnell's Funeral," *Variorum Poems*, 542.

IRISH WORDS

82   "Hamlet": Brendan O Hehir, *A Gaelic Lexicon for Finnegans Wake*, 1967, 387.

83   "Hill of the Lark": example from Mr. Séan Golden.

83   "Latin *devotus*": Aodh de Blácam, *Gaelic Literature Surveyed*, repr. 1973, 4.

83   "*fadó*": pointed out by Conor Johnston.

84   "Dolphin's Barn": lore from Séan Golden.

84   "the bannocks": Joyce, *Finnegans Wake*, 53.

84   "mhuith peisth": Joyce, *Finnegans Wake*, 91, unriddled by O Hehir, *A Gaelic Lexicon*, 62.

84   "Boildoyle": Joyce, *Finnegans Wake*, 17.

85   "At the Abbey Theatre": *Variorum Poems*, 264.

85   "I copied": note to his 1895 *Poems; Variorum Poems*, 840–41.

85   "Lady Gregory's spelling": note to his 1933 *Collected Poems; Variorum Poems*, 840.

85   "Clooth-na-Bare": in "The Hosting of the Sidhe," *Variorum Poems*, 140. The poem dates from 1893.

86   "Is it not brave": *Tamburlaine*, what else?

87   "Baile and Aillinn": *Variorum Poems*, 189.

87   "names of the demons": *Variorum Poems*, 52.

YOUNG YEATS

90   "He has come": George Moore, *Hail and Farewell*, repr. 1976, 244.

90   "Carpets muffled": Frank Tuohy, *Yeats*, 1976, 138.

90   "malicious account": *Hail and Farewell*, 187.

91   "tomb of Shakespeare": Frank Tuohy, *Yeats*, 1976, 136. In *Hail and Farewell*, 209–10, Moore has himself reflecting on a Yeats "no longer able to appreciate anything but literary values." "The heart of Yeats seemed to me to have died ten years ago [i.e. about 1891]; the last of it probably went into the composition of *The Countess Cathleen*."

91   "Yeats had told": *Uncollected Prose*, I, 267 ff.

93   "Shelley could write": example from Eric Havelock, *The Literate Revolution in Greece*, 1982, 20.

93   "Yeats tells it": *Variorum Poems*, 410.

93   "Hyde's translation": in Douglas Hyde, *Songs Ascribed to Raftery*, 1903, 331–35. My transcription ignores the typographic system by which Hyde mapped the assonances of the Irish.

93   "A girl arose": "The Sorrow of Love," *Variorum Poems*, 120.

94   "Professor Havelock": *The Literate Revolution in Greece*, 58.

95   "dishevelled": "Who Goes With Fergus?," *Variorum Poems*, 125; originally a song in *The Countess Kathleen* (1892).

95   "Bloom left": according to Joyce's chronological notes (reproduced by John Henry Raleigh in *The Chronicle of Leopold and Molly Bloom*, 1977, 3), Bloom left school in 1880. Whether Joyce knew he'd arranged this near-miss is uncertain. The details of Yeats's biography were not in print at the time, but then Dublin knowledge is independent of print.

95   "held his own": William M. Murphy, *Prodigal Father: The Life of John Butler Yeats*, 129.

96   "duel of song (I.1, 1–100)": *Variorum Poems*, 645–48.
96   Patmore on Crashaw, quoted in *The Verse in English of Richard Crashaw*, 1949, 16.
96   "lily, chilly": *Variorum Poems*, 647.
97   "Romantic Ireland": the refrain of "September 1913," *Variorum Poems*, 289.
97   "Roman coin," "Beautiful Lofty Things": *Memoirs*, 42; *Variorum Poems*, 577. For a clarifying account of Yeats and O'Leary see Murphy, *Prodigal Father*, 140–46.
97   "genius": John Malcolm Brown, *The Politics of Irish Literature*, 1972, 314.
97   "first published prose": Yeats, *Uncollected Prose*, I, 81–87.
97   "last essay": Allan Wade, *A Bibliography of the Writings of W. B. Yeats*, 3rd ed., 1968, 23.
97   "Thomas Davis": quotations from *The Poems of Thomas Davis*, a New York printing (1854) to raise expatriate consciousness. "The West's Asleep," 37–38; "Tipperary," 31–33; "Celts and Saxons," 53–56.
98   "ten thousand copies": Frank Tuohy, *Yeats*.
99   "planet Neptune": *Uncollected Prose*, I, 333.
99   Note: "The Erne": Colin Meir, *The Ballads and Songs of W. B. Yeats*, 1974, 35, says this is quoted by Yeats but does not say where.
100   "stands on the highest pavement": see T. S. Eliot, "La Figlia che Piange," written 1910.
100   "came to call": Murphy, *Prodigal Father*, 160, and Yeats, *Memoirs*, 40–43. His version in *Autobiography*, 82, is much condensed to fit that book's perspectives.
100   "elaborate paragraph": *Memoirs*, 40.
101   "Mona Lisa": e.g. in Walter Pater, *The Renaissance*, ed. Donald L. Hill, 1980, 98–99.
101   "akin to lines Swinburne wrote": Samuel Chew's suggestion, adduced in Hill's notes to *The Renaissance*, 380. The Swinburne is in *Rosamond*, scene 1.
101   "touch of the artist,""first spoken words,": *Ulysses*, 235, 65.
101   "five feet ten": Nancy Cardozo, *Lucky Eyes and a High Heart: The Life of Maud Gonne*, 1978, 27.
102   "Pet monkey": Yeats, *Letters*, 1955, 108, reporting to John O'Leary.
102   "hating the Shepherdess": Yeats, *Letters*, 106.
102   "Did that play": "The Man and the Echo" (1939), *Variorum Poems*, 632.
102   "Who dreamed": "The Rose of the World," *Variorum Poems*, 111.
102   Note: "She recorded": Murphy, *Prodigal Father*, 172.
103   "old bellows": "A Prayer for My Daughter," *Variorum Poems*, 405.
103   "walked the cliff paths," "Yes," "nannygoat": *Memoirs*, 46; the scene is wonderfully evoked in Benedict Kiely's story, "A Ball of Malt and Madame Butterfly"; *Ulysses*, 783, 176.
103   "white birds": *Variorum Poems*, 121.
103   "drunken, vainglorious": "Easter 1916," *Variorum Poems*, 393.
104   "There is a thicket": *Letters*, 106 (31 Jan. 1889, to Katharine Tynan).
104   "Lay of Oisin": Russell K. Alspach identified this and other sources in *PMLA*, LVIII: 849–66. The trouble to which he was put reflects something Yeats did all his life: mentioning peripheral sources and being evasive about a primary one. He was unhappy to think that people might collate his words with those in the books he'd had open.
105   "three incompatible things": *Letters*, 111.
105   "Vain gaiety": "The Circus Animals' Desertion," *Variorum Poems*, 629.
105   "Antaeus-like": "The Municipal Gallery Revisited" (1937), *Variorum Poems*, 603.
105   "I hear my soul": *Variorum Poems*, 45.
106   "holding down": *Ulysses*, 9.
106   "Fergus": *Variorum Plays*, 52–54, the 1892 text, the only one that contains the song. Thereafter readers had to seek it among Yeats's Poems, as in *Variorum Poems*, 125.
107   "William Empson": see his *Seven Types of Ambiguity*, rev. ed., 1947, 187–90.
107   "God and God's mother": the first (1892) text: *Variorum Plays*, 16.

108   "Bow down": "The Rose of the World," *Variorum Poems*, 112.

108   "O Colleens": "The Lover Speaks to the Hearers of His Song in Coming Days," *Variorum Poems*, 173; I cite the earliest version of 1896. Later he had the decency to change the "Colleens" to "women," and "Maurya [Mary] of the wounded heart" to the brisker "Attorney of Lost Souls."

109   "Impetuous heart": *Variorum Plays*, 129, where, incredibly, "lonely" is misprinted "lovely."

109   "At the grey round": in "The Dreaming of the Bones," *Variorum Plays*, 776.

109   "the poet's exact time-sense": *Variorum Plays*, 1008.

109   "I said": "Adam's Curse," *Variorum Poems*, 204.

110   "burst into Moore's bedroom": *Hail and Farewell*, 248.

110   "French draft": *Hail and Farewell*, 250–54.

110   "literary lunatics": *Hail and Farewell*, 254.

111   "Matheson Lang": in his autobiography, *Mr. Wu Looks Back*, 1940, 48. I've made typographic corrections in quoting. And my thanks to Richard J. Finneran for providing the item.

111   "surviving typescript": printed in *Variorum Plays*, 1168–1222.

111   "We have reformed": quoted by the editor in *Hail and Farewell*, 1976, 752.

112   "Bloom told 'Thank you'": *Ulysses*, 650.

112   "Stephen Dedalus": in the disquisition on aesthetics, *A Portrait of the Artist as a Young Man*, ch. v.

112   "our national epic": *Ulysses*, 192, where Stephen overhears someone (AE or John Eglinton?) say "Moore is the man for it." Moore certainly conceived *Hail and Farewell*, with its title from Catullus, on a (mock) epic scale.

THE LIVING WORLD FOR TEXT

113   "The only truth": Synge, *Works*, III, 168

113   "highest figure": Synge, *Works*, III, 223.

114   "On a given census day": Nancy Scheper-Hughes, *Saints, Scholars, and Schizophrenics*, 1979, 65.

114   "She did what was right": Synge, *Works*, III, 165.

115   "Where nobody": *Variorum Plays*, 184.

116   "Thus do the spirits": *Variorum Plays*, 210.

116   "experiments": George Mills Harper, *Yeats's Golden Dawn*, 1974, 7.

117   "Denis Johnston": in his *Synge*, 1965, 14.

117   "the grouse, and the owls": Synge, *Works*, III, 57.

117   "It's a queer thing": Synge, *Works*, III, 51–3.

118   "detail Synge struck out": Synge, *Works*, III, 56.

118   "not be sitting": Synge, *Works*, III, 57.

118   "Adieu, sweet Angus": Synge, *Works*, I, 38.

118   "Under the Moon": *Variorum Poems*, 209.

118   "a quiet man": Synge, *Works*, III, 59.

118   "The man I had a love for:" Synge, *Works*, I, 80.

119   "I have met an old vagrant": Synge, *Works*, II, 195.

119   "naturally a nomad": Synge, *Works*, II, 195.

119   "waiting these days": Synge, *Works*, IV, 59.

120   "The stars are out": Synge, *Works*, IV, 211.

121   "ungodly ruck": writing to Stephen MacKenna; D. H. Greene and Edward M. Stephens, *J. M. Synge, 1871–1909*, 1959, 264.

121   "his attempts": "In Memory of Major Robert Gregory," "Coole Park, 1929," "The Municipal Gallery Revisited," *Variorum Poems*, 324, 489, 603.

121 "I knew the stars": Synge, *Works*, I, 32.

121 "My arms are round you": Synge, *Works*, I, 47.

122 "The ordinary student of drama": Yeats, *Essays and Introductions*, 304.

122 "but the more hated": Yeats, *Essays and Introductions*, 310.

123 "Practical movements": *Memoirs*, 247.

124 "John Synge, I and Augusta Gregory": "The Municipal Gallery Revisited," *Variorum Poems*, 603.

124 "shamrock," "wolfhound": Jeanne Sheehy, *The Rediscovery of Ireland's Past*, 1980, 10–13.

125 "J. M. Synge and the Ireland of His Time," Yeats, *Essays and Introductions*, 311–42; first published by the Cuala Press, 1911, 350 copies.

125 "One evening in 1912": *Memoirs*, 263.

125 "And that enquiring man": "In Memory of Major Robert Gregory," *Variorum Poems*, 324.

126 "Give up Paris": Yeats, *Essays and Introductions*, 299.

126 "where men must reap": Synge, *Works*, III, 64.

126 "have a peace": Synge, *Works*, II, 162.

126 "total of four and a half months": Greene and Stephens, 76.

126 "I have been sitting": Synge, *Works*, II, 48.

126 "Frenchmen and Danes and Germans": Synge, *Works*, II, 60.

126 "Walking about with two sticks": Synge, *Works*, II, 57.

127 "a curious dreaminess": Greene and Stephens, 121.

127 "Willie Fay would ask": W. G. Fay and Catherine Carswell, *The Fays of the Abbey Theatre*, 1935, 139.

128 "each keystroke": information on the Blickensderfer's foibles from typewriter expert Donald Sutherland, relayed by Mr. Barry Ahearn.

128 "good day's work": Greene and Stephens, 266.

128 "too full": Thomas MacDonagh, *Literature in Ireland*, 1916, 48.

128 "I work always with a typewriter": Synge, *Works*, IV, xxxii–xxxiii.

128 "notebook draft": this reconstruction follows that of David H. Greene, in Thomas R. Whitaker, ed., *Twentieth Century Interpretations of "The Playboy of the Western World,"* 1969, 100–1, with further details gleaned from Synge, *Works*, IV.

128 "flourish from a letter": Greene and Stephens, 103.

129 "Six yards of stuff": Synge, *Works*, IV, 57.

129 "stripped itself": Synge, *Works*, IV, 166.

129 "the old story": Declan Kiberd, *Synge and the Irish Language*, 1979, 118.

129 "It's a power": Synge, *Works*, III, 111.

130 "poor fellow would get drunk": Synge, *Works*, IV, 123.

130 "you'd see him": Synge, *Works*, IV, 123.

130 "a walking terror": Synge, *Works*, IV, 101.

130 "Weren't you off racing": Synge, *Works*, IV, 161.

131 "his journal recalls": Greene and Stephens, 168.

131 "old boatman's lament": Synge, *Works*, II, 305.

131 "But we'll come round him": Synge, *Works*, I, 57.

132 "Yeats was told": Yeats, *Essays and Introductions*, 338.

132 "about a Connaught man": Synge, *Works*, II, 95.

132 "Synge reflected": Synge, *Works*, II, 95.

132 "in Act I we should see": outline in Synge, *Works*, IV, 295.

133 "Yeats explained": *Uncollected Prose*, II, 400.

133 "With that the sun came out": Synge, *Works*, IV, 103.

134 "Prof. Henn": in the Notes to his 1963 edition of the Plays.

135 "The blessing of God": Synge, *Works*, IV, 151.

135   "What's that": Synge, *Works*, IV, 141.

136   "It's a fright": Synge, *Works*, IV, 137.

136   "as metaphysical as he pleased": *Autobiography*, 218.

136   "Did you ever hear tell": Synge, *Works*, IV, 133.

137   "With what rare gold": Synge, *Works*, I, 117.

137   "Yeats noted": Yeats, *Essays and Introductions*, 300.

137   "Ten thousand blessings": Synge, *Works*, IV, 173.

139   "The ruck of muck": Hogan and O'Neill, eds., *Joseph Holloway's Abbey Theatre*, 1967, 133.

140   "Draw a little back": Synge, *Works*, IV, 267.

141   "rich in implications": William Empson, *Seven Types of Ambiguity*, 1930, 2nd ed., 1947, 5; see also 38–42 for further response to Synge's language. Writing fifty years before Declan Kiberd, Empson was especially acute in guessing at notions "not fully translated out of Irish" beneath Synge's most magical effects.

142   "Do not raise": Synge, *Works*, IV, 265.

142   "nervous breakdown": *Memoirs*, 140.

142   "lankylooking galoot": *Ulysses*, 109. For a photo of the 1902 Joyce in a macintosh in Paris see Richard Ellmann, *James Joyce*, 1959, facing page 81.

143   "more original": Ellmann, 276.

143   "list of Lord Mayors": Joyce, *Finnegans Wake*, 549, line 3; see Roland McHugh, *Annotations to Finnegans Wake*, 1980, 549.

BERLITZ DAYS

145   "in a Book": "Le Livre, Instrument Spirituel"; see Anthony Hartley, ed., *Mallarmé*, 1965, 189.

145   "his inkwell": quoted in Hartley's Introduction, xxii; I've retouched the translation to point up an echo of Genesis I.3, "Que la lumière soit."

145   "sea is summed up": This was Georges Rodenbach, quoted by Hartley, xv.

145   *"The Tables of the Law"*: reprinted in Yeats, *Mythologies*, 1959; it had first appeared in book form in June 1904.

146   "Why are these strange souls": *Autobiography*, 210.

146   "most beautiful book": *Ulysses*, 216.

147   *"Mrs Mooney"*: opening of Joyce, "The Boarding House," *Dubliners*, 61.

147   "English dictionary": *Autobiography*, 229.

147   "by the hour": Joyce, *Stephen Hero*, 26.

147   "still in Dublin": the first version appeared in the 13 August 1904 *Irish Homestead*. Don Gifford reproduces its text in *Joyce Annotated*, 1982, 289–93.

148   "Dublin joke": remembered by Leopold Bloom; *Ulysses*, 105.

148   "on record": in Holloway's journal for 10 June 1904: Hogan and O'Neill, eds., *Joseph Holloway's Abbey Theatre*, 1967, 40.

148   "I am writing": Joyce, *Selected Letters*, 22.

152   "thought of a story": *Selected Letters*, 112.

153   "whole book chiasmic": As Hans Walter Gabler discovered. See his "The Seven Lost Years" in Staley and Benstock, eds., *Approaches to Joyce's Portrait*, 1976, 25–60.

154   "chiasmic pattern": *Finnegans Wake*, 13–14.

A DWINDLING GYRE

159   "To keep these notes": *Memoirs*, 139.

159   "To oppose": *Memoirs*, 142.

159   "So much of the world": *Memoirs*, 142.

159   "Logic a machine": *Memoirs*, 139.
160   "ill-breeding of the mind": *Memoirs*, 140.
160   "In our age it is impossible": *Memoirs*, 185.
160   "never really understands": *Memoirs*, 141.
160   "a clown": her "kisses to a clown" spurred an epigram he never published, *Memoirs*, 145.
160   "Sweetheart, do not love": *Variorum Poems*, 211.
161   "brawling of a sparrow": "The Sorrow of Love," *Variorum Poems*, 119–20.
161   "Dun Emer," "Cuala": for the story see W. M. Murphy, *Prodigal Father*, 1978, 240–42 and
        334.
162   "city of tedious and silly derision": quoted in W. M. Murphy, *Prodigal Father*, 244.
162   Note: "Blake of Irish birth": I've not seen this Encyclopaedia article, for word of which I'm
        indebted to J. E. and M. L. Grant of the University of Iowa.
163   "sleepers wake": *Variorum Poems*, 639.
163   "Men think they can Copy": G. Keynes, ed., *Poetry and Prose of William Blake*, 1941, 623.
163   "fourfold vision": Blake, *Poetry and Prose*, 861–62.
164   "worst books": all Holloway details from the prefatory matter to Robert Hogan and Michael
        J. O'Neill, eds., *Joseph Holloway's Abbey Theatre*, 1967—an exquisitely culled selection.
164   "preserves for us": *Joseph Holloway's Abbey Theatre*, 5, 27, 28, 87, 94–95.
165   "this unmannerly town": *Variorum Poems*, 351.
165   "those beautiful productions": Joseph Hone, *W. B. Yeats*, 1971, 270.
166   "making his peace": Joseph Hone, *W. B. Yeats*, 221.
166   "I might have lived": "The People," *Variorum Poems*, 352.
166   "Three types": "Poetry and Tradition," in Yeats, *Essays and Introductions*, 251. It is dated
        "August 1907."
167   "you gave": "To a Wealthy Man . . . ," *Variorum Poems*, 287.
167   "Since 1906": *Letters*, 478; 21 Sept. 1906, "I am deep in Ben Jonson."
168   "Would'st thou heare": Ben Jonson, "Epitaph on Elizabeth, L.H."
168   "And since": Ben Jonson, "An Ode. To Himselfe."
168   "Come leave": Ben Jonson, "Ode to Himselfe."
168   "My curse": "The Fascination of What's Difficult," *Variorum Poems*, 260.
169   "five poems": "To a Wealthy Man . . . ," "September 1913," "To a Friend Whose Work Has
        Come to Nothing," "Paudeen," "To a Shade," *Variorum Poems*, 287–92.
169   "What need you": "September 1913," *Variorum Poems*, 289.
169   "counted all her cards," "knew that she would have": Joyce, *Dubliners*, 65, 64.
169   "Base-born": "Under Ben Bulben," *Variorum Poems*, 639.
169   "lidless eye": "Upon a House Shaken by the Land Agitation," *Variorum Poems*, 264. Date,
        1910.
170   "A man": "To a Shade," *Variorum Poems*, 292.

A R R A Y !   S U R R E C T I O N !

172   "a little play": *Letters*, 607.
172   "remains at a distance": "Certain Noble Plays of Japan" (April 1916), in Yeats, *Essays and
        Introductions*, 224.
172   "English versions": published in Pound's *Noh, or Accomplishment*, 1917; but Yeats in effect
        had preempted them for Irishry the previous year, when the Cuala Press published selections
        with his introduction: *Certain Noble Plays of Japan*, September 16, 1916, 350 copies. And
        "Noble" is of course his adjective.
173   "archaic Greek statue," "drowning kitten": *Letters*, 610, 609.
173   "no studied lighting": Yeats, *Essays and Introductions*, 224.
173   "Pound has preserved": in *The Cantos*, 1970, CI, 725.

173   "Among School Children": *Variorum Poems*, 443,

173   "An aged man": "Sailing to Byzantium," *Variorum Poems*, 407.

174   "I call to the eye": *Variorum Plays*, 399.

175   "imperfect": *Letters*, 611. "We shall not do it again until June, in order to get rid of Ainley and the musicians. The music Beecham says is good, but one cannot discuss anything with a feud between Dulac and a stupid musician at every rehearsal."

175   "O'Connor has noted": *My Father's Son*, 1968, last sentence of ch. 18.

175   "sacredness of *place*": Yeats, *Essays and Introductions*, 232, 236.

175   "happier than Sophocles," "hoarse": *Letters*, 610; Hone, 302.

175   "blew up": for a detailed analytic account of the Rising that confronts most questions of fact and principle, see F.S.L. Lyons, *Ireland Since the Famine*, rev. 1973, Part III, ch. 1–3. Roger McHugh's *Dublin 1916*, 1966, repr. with illustrations 1976, is a collection of firsthand testimonies. Ulick O'Connor's *A Terrible Beauty*, 1975, embeds the story, with details you'll find nowhere else, in a short narrative running from Parnell to "Bloody Sunday," 1920.

175   "the epicentre": *Ulysses*, 344.

176   "on its east side": F. O. Dwyer, *Lost Dublin*, 1981, 16.

176   "Bernard Shaw thought": quoted in McHugh, *Dublin 1916*, 360.

176   "Joyce's famous hope": Frank Budgen, *James Joyce and the Making of Ulysses*, 1972, 69.

176   "*Freeman's Journal*": McHugh, *Dublin 1916*, 59.

176   "prompt to urinate": O'Connor, *A Terrible Beauty*, 76.

176   "Bloom made to unroll": *Ulysses*, 487.

176   "summoned Cuchulain": "The Statues," *Variorum Poems*, 611.

176   "voice out of heaven": *Ulysses*, 345.

177   "episode of *Murphy*": Samuel Beckett, *Murphy*, 42.

177   "From confusion": Lyons, *Ireland Since the Famine*, 350–52; "wireless expert," 356.

177   Note: "John P. Roche tells it": *National Review*, 11 June 1982, 717.

178   "Connolly recounted": O'Connor, *A Terrible Beauty*, 89.

178   "Ireland would have pitied": W. M. Murphy, *Prodigal Father*, 1978, 453.

178   "2.5 million": Lyons, *Ireland Since the Famine*, 802, note 12.

178   "1909 journal": Yeats, *Memoirs*, 177–78.

179   "he counseled": Thomas MacDonagh, *Literature in Ireland*, 1916, 69. For the poem see John Montague, *The Book of Irish Verse*, 1974, 245.

179   "mother's rosary": McHugh, *Dublin 1916*, 263.

179   "to Lady Gregory": *Letters*, 613.

180   "A young girl": "On Being Asked for a War Poem," *Variorum Poems*, 359.

180   "world swept away": *Letters*, 614.

180   "Easter 1916": *Variorum Poems*, 391.

180   "lugubrious exercise": "Mourn—and Then Onward!"; he never collected it but its ghost mocks his in *Variorum Poems*, 737.

180   "beauty like a tightened bow": "No Second Troy," *Variorum Poems*, 256.

180   "*Kuthera deina*": Pound, *The Cantos*, 1970, 511; a classical sentiment if not a classical phrase.

181   "devil era": Joyce, *Finnegans Wake*, 473.

181   "beauty is Borneo": O'Casey, *Inishfallen, Fare Thee Well*, chapter heading.

182   "pruning": Richard Ellmann, *James Joyce*, 1959, 416–17.

182   "dropped out": Ellmann, *James Joyce*, 62.

182   "ten better ones": Joyce, *Finnegans Wake*, 3, 23, 44, 90, 113, 257, 314, 332, 414, 424. They've 1001 letters among them.

182   "fumble and stumble": Sean O'Faolain, *Vive Moi!*, 1964, 130.

183   "horror": Frank O'Connor, *An Only Child*, 1961, 154.

183   "sheltering in doors": O'Faolain, *Vive Moi!*, 169.

183   "storm in a chalice": Frank O'Connor, *My Father's Son*, 1968, ch. 2.

183   "dipped the tip": O'Faolain, *Vive Moi!*, 135.

183   "Shepherd and Goatherd": *Variorum Poems*, 338.

185   "Some burn": "In Memory of Major Robert Gregory," *Variorum Poems*, 323–28.

185   "He who can read": *Variorum Poems*, 429.

THE *ULYSSES* YEARS

187   "Occam's Razor": W. M. Murphy, *Prodigal Father*, 1978, 247, and Richard Ellmann, 1959, *James Joyce*, 179.

187   "That bloody Joyce": quoted in J. B. Lyons, *James Joyce and Medicine*, 1973, 68.

188   "stripped," "met": *Ulysses*, 16, 17. Peter's bitter weeping is in Matthew xxvi. 75.

188   "Yeats's tonsils": Joseph Hone, *W. B. Yeats*, 1971, 332.

188   "George Moore wrote": *Hail and Farewell*, repr. 1976, 354.

189   "young man from St. John's": Richard Cave supplies this version in his edition of Moore's *Hail and Farewell*, 725. There are also laundered rescriptions.

189   "one of the great lyric poets": W.B.Y.'s Introduction to *The Oxford Book of Modern Verse*, 1936.

189   "majesty of the occasion": Miss Anne Yeats in conversation, May 1975.

189   "Ringsend": *The Collected Poems of Oliver St. John Gogarty*, 1954, 102.

190   "Polyfizzyboisterous": Joyce, *Finnegans Wake*, 547.

190   "Wipe your glosses": Joyce, *Finnegans Wake*, 304, note 3.

190   "imperial British state": *Ulysses*, 20.

191   "Gogarty's fat back": quoted by J. B. Lyons, *James Joyce and Medicine*, 67.

192   "guess about 'blind' ": Eric Partridge's, in *Origins*.

193   "jeered at George Moore": *Letters*, II, 71.

194   "He watched the bristles": *Ulysses*, 56.

194   "Jews and Irish": credit for discovering this particular base for the conception of *Ulysses* belongs to Herbert Howarth; see his *The Irish Writers*, 1958, 24–25, 259–60.

194   "such regulations": Douglas Hyde, *A Literary History of Ireland*, 1899, 609.

195   "measurement": *Ulysses*, 668, where Bloom climbing over a railing "lowered his body gradually by its length of five feet nine inches and a half."

195   "coming over here": *Ulysses*, 323.

198   Yeats, Moore: Richard Ellmann, 545, 543.

198   "blackguardism": Sylvia Beach, *Shakespeare and Company*, 1959, 52.

200   "You have a filthy mind": quoted from Lady Gregory's *Journals* by David Krause, *Sean O'Casey: The Man and His Work*, 1975, 339.

200   "the colonel's daughter" and other phrases hereabouts: Sean O'Casey, *Inishfallen Fare Thee Well*, 1949, chapter called "The Temple Entered."

200   "To ride abroad": Tennyson, *Guinivere*.

200   "hurled the little streets": "No Second Troy," *Variorum Poems*, 256.

200   "Born John Casey": biographical details from Krause, ch. 1.

201   "Who's gettin' excited?": O'Casey, *Collected Plays*, I, 1949, 208–9.

201   "darlin' motto": O'Casey, *Collected Plays*, I, 88.

201   "Why d'ye take notice": O'Casey, *Collected Plays*, I, 174–75.

202   "Sean O'Faolain would note": in *The Bell* in 1953; quoted at length by Krause, 44–45.

202   Note: "Robert Lowery": I take this information from a review (*James Joyce Quarterly*, XIX.2: 201) of *Sean O'Casey Centenary Essays*, which I've not seen.

203   "They think": delivered in 1915; quoted in Roger McHugh, *Dublin 1916*, 1966, 397. O'Casey's version (*The Plough and the Stars*, II) is virtually identical. Another source for the

words of the Man in the Window was Pearse's 1913 essay "The Coming Revolution"; see F.S.L. Lyons, *Ireland Since the Famine*, rev. 1973, 336–37.

203   "Jammed as I was": O'Casey, *Collected Plays*, I, 195.

203   ". . . a gorgeous dhress": O'Casey, *Collected Plays*, I, 199.

203   "One critic": Andrew Malone, in the *Dublin Magazine*, March 1925, quoted by Krause, 81.

204   "Sam Beckett": in a review of O'Casey's *Windfalls* in *Bookman*, December 1934.

204   *"The End of the Beginning"*: O'Casey, *Collected Plays*, I, 263–92.

205   "Dope, dope": O'Casey, *Collected Plays*, 203.

205   "I am sad and discouraged": for the correspondence see Krause, 101–5 and 348–49.

205   "infringement of the canons": responses cited from Krause, 129.

206   "The trees": "The Wild Swans at Coole," *Variorum Poems*, 322.

207   "all that I have handled least": "Ego Dominus Tuus," *Variorum Poems*, 367.

207   "men improve with the years": *Variorum Poems*, 329.

209   "What are the hopes of men?": Byron, *Don Juan*, I, ccxix.

209   "first use of it": I'm not sure of this. "Ancestral Houses" and the opening of "Nineteen Hundred and Nineteen," where we find *ottava rima* again, belong to long poems that shared time on his worktable. But I'd guess that "Ancestral Houses" occupied him first.

209   "What if the glory": "Ancestral Houses," *Variorum Poems*, 418.

210   "An ancient bridge": "My House," *Variorum Poems*, 419.

210   "desolation of reality": from "Meru," *Variorum Poems*, 563.

210   "two provisos": Lyons, 311.

211   "We must recognize": Quoted in Lyons, 397. Though published by Béaslaí in his *An t Oglách*, it was written by Ernest Blythe, later Minister of Finance in Cosgrave's 1923 cabinet.

211   "thirty-four of its sixty-nine": Lyons, 400.

211   "Weasels": *Variorum Poems*, 429.

212   "traffic in mockery": *Variorum Poems*, 432.

212   "some four thousand": Lyons, 468.

212   "poem that records": "Meditations in Time of Civil War, v," *Variorum Poems*, 423–24.

212   "best book I have written": *Letters*, 742.

212   "time that I wrote my will": *Variorum Poems*, 414.

213   "scholarship": T. L. Dume, "Yeats' Golden Tree and Birds in the Byzantine Poems," *Modern Language Notes*, LXVII: 404–7.

213   "Such thought": *Variorum Poems*, 474.

214   "Death and life were not": *Variorum Poems*, 415.

214   "Another emblem," "What's water": *Variorum Poems*, 490.

THE WAKE OF WAKES

215   "Rory O'Connor": see F.S.L. Lyons, *Ireland Since the Famine*, rev. 1973, 467.

215   "20 March 1923": date from Richard Ellmann, *James Joyce*, 1959, 801.

216   "one to do": Joyce, *Finnegans Wake*, 382, rearranged on the page to guide newcomers. Here as elsewhere I quote the final versions, not the drafts. What Joyce drafted in 1923 is lost, but for something pretty close to it see David Hayman, *A First-Draft Version of Finnegans Wake*, 1963, 203–4.

216   "You can't impose": *Finnegans Wake*, 378.

217   "secular colleges": J. C. Beckett, *The Making of Modern Ireland*, 1966, 329–31.

217   "Guns": Joyce, *Finnegans Wake*, 368.

217   "the boomomouths": Joyce, *Finnegans Wake*, 367.

217   "seven times": page and line numbers of Joyce, *Finnegans Wake*: 358.30, 369.24, 386.20, 390.29, 482.20, 528.33, 619.19. For more on "document number two" see Lyons 448–49.

217   "obsessive preoccupation": Lyons, 442.

218 "huge James Laughlin": he told me this story in 1980.

218 *"blue, blown"*: this etymology for "blue" was suggested in Charles Richardson's 1839 *Dictionary of the English Language.*

219 "stuck to his guns": *Ulysses*, 654.

219 "inadvertent pun": the next few pages plagiarize freely from my article "The Jokes at the Wake," *Massachusetts Review*, XXII.4 (1981): 722–33.

220 "Illiterate writers": Johnson, Preface to the *Dictionary.*

220 "scribblers for provincial newspapers": such as the *Kilkenny People* Bloom consults in the National Library (*Ulysses*, 200). This suggestion, which I've not had the resources to verify, came from Mr. Anthony Cronin.

220 "plebeian, degenerate": see Brendan O Hehir, *A Gaelic Lexicon for Finnegans Wake*, 1967, 419–22.

221 "wan warning": Joyce, *Finnegans Wake*, 6.

222 "Now be aisy": Joyce, *Finnegans Wake*, 24.

222 "A rogue": Seán Ó Súilleabháin, *Irish Wake Amusements*, 67. The Joyce people seem not to have happened on this book, the author's translation from his 1961 Irish original: Mercier Press, Dublin and Cork, 1967.

222 "unusual use of words": Ó Súilleabháin, 32.

223 "young Boasthard's fear": *Ulysses*, 395.

223 *"Silentium!"*: *Ulysses*, 424–25.

224 "Welter focussed": *Finnegans Wake*, 324.

225 "We are now diffusing": *Finnegans Wake*, 359–60.

226 "Elmar Ternes": paper published in *The Canadian Journal of Irish Studies*, VI (1980): 50–73. The parts of interest here are excerpted in Robert O'Driscoll, ed., *The Celtic Consciousness*, 1982, 69–78.

226 "early books": Stuart Gilbert, *James Joyce's Ulysses*, 1930, and Frank Budgen, *James Joyce and the Making of Ulysses*, 1934.

226 "Mr. Pope's *Iliad*": I have lifted much of this paragraph from my own book *Ulysses*, 1980, 3.

227 "Jacques Mercanton": Richard Ellmann, 723.

227 "lying in death": Richard Ellmann, 559.

227 "story of this Chapelizod family": Eugene Jolas, "My Friend James Joyce," in S. Givens, ed., *James Joyce: Two Decades of Criticism*, 1948, 11.

228 "Fritz Senn": in *James Joyce Quarterly*, XIX.2 (1982): 177–78.

228 "Chapelizod houses": reported by Fritz Senn in *A Wake Newslitter*, VIII.1: 88–89.

229 "insane British officer": Lyons, 373, a good summary. For a much more detailed narrative by Skeffington's widow, see Roger McHugh, *Dublin 1916*, 1976, 276–88. It was she, by the way, who ten years later led the attack on *The Plough and the Stars.*

230 "mirror on mirror": "The Statues," *Variorum Poems*, 610: by no means a "source" for *Finnegans Wake*, since it wasn't published until March 1939.

231 "a spectator": that was Stephen MacKenna; see Nancy Cardozo, *Lucky Eyes and a High Heart: The Life of Maud Gonne*, 1978, 220.

231 "Shakespeare pervades": see Adaline Glasheen, *Third Census of Finnegans Wake*, 1977, 260: "To my mind, Shakespeare (man, works) is the matrix of FW . . . ."

TWO ECCENTRICS

232 "Mucker" and "the holes" from Kavanagh's *The Green Fool*, 1938, ch. 1; "1791 cabin" from Darcy O'Brien, *Patrick Kavanagh*, 1975, 30. Anyone who reads O'Brien's little book will perceive my indebtedness to it.

232   "great roots of hands" and other quoted phrases from O'Brien, 16; the custom shoes specified by Anthony Cronin, *Dead as Doornails*, 1976, 125.

232   "destructive power": Cronin, 171.

232   "I turn the lea-green down": "Ploughman," in Kavanagh, *Collected Poems*, 1972, 3. For "the origin of my ploughman ecstasy," see *The Green Fool*, ch. 28.

233   "dreams and visions": *Ulysses*, 186–87.

233   "Primal Language": see Herbert Howarth, *The Irish Writers*, 1958, 178. Like his whole book, Howarth's chapter on AE can be recommended without reservation.

234   "Ireland's imminent Messiah": Howarth, 174.

234   "the wastrel Joyce": Richard Ellmann, *James Joyce*, 1959; for the money, 184; for the *Homestead* commission, 169.

234   "knocked at AE's door": *The Green Fool*, ch. 29.

235   "down to one mistress": O'Brien, 29.

235   "Jewish antique dealer": J. B. Lyons, *Oliver St. John Gogarty*, 1980, 182–94.

235   "lawsuit about a book review": Howarth, 167. It was a book of Gaelic songs.

235   "one evening in 1941": O'Brien, 21–22.

235   "O he loved his mother": Kavanagh, *Collected Poems*, 37.

237   "John Synge, I": "The Municipal Gallery Revisited," *Variorum Poems*, 603.

237   "English-bred lie": O'Brien, 23.

237   "found what I wanted": Yeats, *Letters*, 922.

238   "desolation of reality": "Meru," *Variorum Poems*, 563.

238   "Every discoloration": *Variorum Poems*, 567.

239   "*Hamlet*": I.v.149 ff.

240   "Czar, I bless thee": John Mitchel, *Jail Journal*, Dublin, n.d., 358.

241   "kinetic vulgarity": Kavanagh, *Collected Poems*, xiv.

241   "unnecessarily harsh": Joyce, *Selected Letters*, 109–10. The date is 25 September 1906. He had written all of *Dubliners* save "The Dead."

241   "dreadful stage-Irish": Kavanagh's comments on *The Green Fool* are from his 1963 "Self Portrait," *Collected Pruse*, 1973, 13. No, "Pruse" is not a misprint.

241   "seacoastless, bearless": see *The Winter's Tale*, III.iii, which opens on "the seacoast" of Bohemia (with "deserts" specified) and ends "(*Exit, pursued by a bear.*)"

241   "Dublin is the administrative capital": Cronin, 95.

242   "Mr. T. O'Deirg": *Kavanagh's Weekly*, 12 April 1952, 6.

242   "Heaven's high manna": "Bank Holiday," Kavanagh, *Collected Poems,* 100.

243   "The important thing": "Is," Kavanagh, *Collected Poems*, 154.

244   "O commemorate me": "Lines Written on a Seat on the Grand Canal, Dublin, 'Erected to the Memory of Mrs Dermot O'Brien,'" Kavanagh, *Collected Poems*, 150.

243   "A backhanded catch": O'Brien, 62.

244   "Heaney acknowledges": O'Brien, 67.

244   "generally considered": Thomas Kinsella, in Robert Hogan, ed., *Dictionary of Irish Literature*, 1979, 157. And Kinsella's opinion carries weight.

244   "Pot Poet": Samuel Beckett, *Murphy*, 1938, 84.

244   "bulging with minor beauties": *Murphy*, 89.

244   "Gogarty urged Clarke to sue": Lyons, *Gogarty*, 1980, 232.

244   "Paddy of the Celtic Mist": Kavanagh, *Collected Poems*, 90. For the identification, O'Brien, 45–46.

244   "Founder Member," "Should I?": *Letters*, 801, 795.

245   "I load myself with chains": quoted in Thomas Kinsella, Introduction to Clarke's *Selected Poems*, 1976, xi.

245   "the clapper from the bell": Clarke's note in a 1928 collection, see Clarke, *Selected Poems*, 190.

245   "Summer delights the scholar": Clarke, *Selected Poems*, 5.

245   "Before the day": Clarke, *Selected Poems*, 18.

246   "Unpitied, wasting": Clarke, *Selected Poems*, 59.

246   "manifold illusion": "Meru," *Variorum Poems*, 563.

247   "Such thought": "All Souls' Night," *Variorum Poems*, 474.

249   "Life returned": *Variorum Poems*, 831.

250   "now none living": *Variorum Poems*, 571.

250   "Soul must learn": *Variorum Poems*, 573.

250   "From pleasure of the bed": *Variorum Poems*, 575.

250   "But a coarse old man": *Variorum Poems*, 590.

251   "Crazy Jane on the Mountain": *Variorum Poems*, 628.

251   "Down the mountain walls": "News for the Delphic Oracle," *Variorum Poems*, 612.

252   " Becfola quickly undressed": Clarke, *Collected Poems*, 1976, 543.

THE MOCKER

253   "haul Kavanagh": Anthony Cronin, *Dead as Doornails*, 1976, 124–25.

254   "Did you never study atomics?": Flann O'Brien, *The Third Policeman*, 1967, 84–85.

254–55   "de Selby": cited phrases from *The Third Policeman*, 166, 146, 144.

255   "Like many alcoholics": Cronin, 116.

255   "A northerner": for the drab facts of his life, see Anne Clissmann, *Flann O'Brien: A Critical Introduction to his Writing*, 1975, 1–37.

256   "The next witness": Flann O'Brien, *At Swim-Two-Birds*, 1960, 294.

257   "Brian became fixed": Cronin, 111.

258   "a much milder book": *The Dalkey Archive*, 1964.

258   "I notice these days": *The Best of Myles*, 1968, 104.

259   "I tried": *The Best of Myles*, 99.

259   "How are heights?": conflated from *The Best of Myles*, 213 and 217.

261   *"You know, of course"*: *The Third Policeman*, 161.

THE TERMINATOR

262   "Le capitaine Godot": anecdote from Mr. John Calder.

264   "as he rose": Yeats, *Mythologies*, 224.

264   "Who else": from Mr. James Knowlson, *viva voce*. See Mr. Knowlson's "Beckett and John Millington Synge" in James Knowlson and John Pilling, *Frescoes of the Skull: the Later Prose and Drama of Samuel Beckett*, 1979, 259–74, which I came upon after this chapter had been drafted. It has pointed me to additional details.

265   "special gratification": Knowlson quotes Yeats, "An Introduction for My Plays," 1937: "It was certainly a day of triumph when the first act of *The Well of the Saints* held its audience, though the two chief persons sat side by side under a stone cross from start to finish."

266   "Willie Fay remembers": W. G. Fay and Catherine Carswell, *The Fays of the Abbey Theatre*, 1935, 138.

267   "Turn your eyes": Robin Skelton, ed., *The Collected Plays of Jack B. Yeats*, 1971, 45.

267   "Imperishable fire": *The Shadowy Waters*, 1900 version, *Variorum Poems*, 765.

268   "Joyce saw": his presence is recorded in *Joseph Holloway's Abbey Theatre*, 1967, 40.

268   "Willie Fay recalled": Fay and Carswell, 125–26.

268   "man in a top hat": Liam Byrne, *History of Aviation in Ireland*, 1980, 28–9.

268   "the next year": Bruce Bradley, S.J., *James Joyce's Schooldays*, 1982, 129.

269 "open pianner": Richard Ellmann, *James Joyce*, 1959, 241.

269 "The years": ending of *The Countess Cathleen*, Yeats, *Variorum Plays*, 169. Joyce quoted these lines in the *Portrait*.

269 "told of Beckett": by Michael Beausang, in "L'Exil du Samuel Beckett," *Critique*, #421–22, (1982): 563.

270 "formless spawning fury": Yeats, "The Statues," *Variorum Poems*, 611.

271 "one that ruffled": "Coole Park, 1929," *Variorum Poems*, 488.

271 "Death and life": "The Tower," *Variorum Poems*, 415.

272 "a Joyce pilgrim": Prof. John Henry Raleigh. See *James Joyce Quarterly*, VIII.2: 131.

272 "That the house": *Ulysses*, 479.

INDEX

A Note About the Author

Hugh Kenner is Professor of English Literature at The Johns Hopkins University. He has written many distinguished books on modern literature, including two on Ezra Pound, three on Joyce, two on Beckett, and one on T. S. Eliot. Among his other books is a study of Buckminster Fuller's mathematical equations.

A Note on the Type

This book was set in a film version of Monticello. The face, based on the original Roman No. 1 cut by Archibald Binny and cast in 1796 by the Philadelphia type foundry Binny & Ronaldson, was named Monticello in honor of its use in the monumental fifty-volume *Papers of Thomas Jefferson*, published by Princeton University Press. Monticello is a transitional type design, embodying certain features of Bulmer and Baskerville, but it is a distinguished face in its own right.

Composition by Centennial Graphics, Inc.,
Ephrata, Pennsylvania

Printing and binding by The Haddon Craftsmen, Inc.,
Scranton, Pennsylvania

Typography and binding design
by Dorothy Schmiderer

Spiders on Sese Islands © Hazel Jackson
Jesper with spiders in Uganda © Neil Jackson
Zairean lie detector © Neil Jackson
Emma not keen on lunch © Neil Jackson
Peter Winterbottom © Kevin Muggleton
Chris Butcher falls in love with a local © Kevin Muggleton
Training sessions in Zimbabwe © Kevin Muggleton
Peter Winterbottom meets a local scrum machine © Kevin Muggleton